**Identities, Ethnicities and Gender in Antiquity**

# Trends in Classics – Supplementary Volumes

Edited by
Franco Montanari and Antonios Rengakos

Associate Editors
Stavros Frangoulidis · Fausto Montana · Lara Pagani
Serena Perrone · Evina Sistakou · Christos Tsagalis

Scientific Committee
Alberto Bernabé · Margarethe Billerbeck
Claude Calame · Jonas Grethlein · Philip R. Hardie
Stephen J. Harrison · Stephen Hinds · Richard Hunter
Christina Kraus · Giuseppe Mastromarco
Gregory Nagy · Theodore D. Papanghelis
Giusto Picone · Alessandro Schiesaro
Tim Whitmarsh · Bernhard Zimmermann

# Volume 109

# Identities, Ethnicities and Gender in Antiquity

Edited by
Jacqueline Fabre-Serris, Alison Keith
and Florence Klein

DE GRUYTER

ISBN 978-3-11-111590-0
e-ISBN (PDF) 978-3-11-071994-9
e-ISBN (EPUB) 978-3-11-071997-0
ISSN 1868-4785

**Library of Congress Control Number: 2021931445**

**Bibliographic information published by the Deutsche Nationalbibliothek**
The Deutsche Nationalbibliothek lists this publication in the Deutsche Nationalbibliografie;
detailed bibliographic data are available on the Internet at http://dnb.dnb.de.

© 2022 Walter de Gruyter GmbH, Berlin/Boston
This volume is text- and page-identical with the hardback published in 2021.
Editorial Office: Alessia Ferreccio and Katerina Zianna
Logo: Christopher Schneider, Laufen
Printing and binding: CPI books GmbH, Leck

www.degruyter.com

# Contents

List of Figures —— VII

Jacqueline Fabre-Serris, Alison Keith, Florence Klein
Introduction —— 1

## Part I: Masculinity, Dress and Body

François Lissarrague
**Ionians, Egyptians, Thracians: Ethnicity and Gender in Attic Vase-Painting** —— 17

Florence Gherchanoc
**Dress, Ethnic Identity, and Gender in the Achaemenid Empire: Greek Views on the Persians, and Political Ideology in the Classical Time** —— 27

## Part II: Gender, Political Leaders and Ethnic Identity

Giulia Sissa
**What Artemisia Knew: The Political Intelligence of Artemisia of Halicarnassus** —— 49

Alison Keith
**Cicero's Verres, Verres' Women** —— 69

Jacqueline Fabre-Serris
**Identities and Ethnicities in the Punic Wars: Livy's Portrait of the Carthaginian Sophonisba** —— 93

## Part III: Cleopatra's Survival and Metamorphosis in Roman Poetry

Florence Klein
**Gendered Intertextuality: Feminizing the Alexandrian Models in Propertius' Actian Poetry** —— 115

Andrew Feldherr
**Caesar or Cleopatra? Lucan's Tragic Queen** —— 135

## Part IV: Love, Oriental Ethnicity and Gender in Roman Literature

Federica Bessone
**The Indiscreet Charm of the Exotic: *Amores Peregrini* as Explorations of Identity in Roman Poetry** —— 155

Judith P. Hallett
**Latin Literary Lenses on Phoenician Female Speech** —— 175

Alison Sharrock
**Babylonians in Thebes: Some Ovidian Stories of Barbarians and Foreigners** —— 195

## Part V: Constructing or Deconstructing Female Ethnicity in Late Antiquity

Therese Fuhrer
**Thessalian Witches: An Ethnic Construct in Apuleius' *Metamorphoses*** —— 219

Charles Delattre
**Exemplary Gallic Wives in the *Erotikos* and *Mulierum Virtutes* of Plutarch: Stereotypes and Comparisons** —— 235

Henriette Harich-Schwarzbauer
***Africa, Famula Romae*: Constructions of Ethnic Identity in Claudian's Panegyrics** —— 251

List of Contributors —— 265
General Index —— 267
Index Locorum —— 279

# List of Figures

**Fig. 1:** Boston 13.199, red-figure lekythos. —— **18**
**Fig. 2:** Paris, Louvre G4bis, red-figure cup. —— **19**
**Fig. 3:** Syracuse 26967, red-figure lekythos. —— **19**
**Fig. 4:** Athens NM 9683, red-figure pelike. —— **21**
**Fig. 5:** Munich 2428, red-figure hydria. —— **21**
**Fig. 6:** Berlin 3172, red-figure column crater. —— **22**
**Fig. 7:** St Petersburg St1685, red-figure amphora. —— **23**
**Fig. 8:** New York 96.9.37, red-figure cup (detail). —— **24**
**Fig. 9:** Paris, Louvre G285, red-figure cup. —— **25**
**Fig. 10:** Ferrara inv. 609, red-figure cup. —— **25**
**Fig. 11:** New York 96.9.37, red-figure cup. —— **25**
**Fig. 12:** Detail of the Darios Vase, circa 340–320 BC; Napoli, MAN, n° 81947 [3253] (necropolis of Canosa in 1851). —— **30**
**Fig. 13:** Map of Thessaly. —— **225**

Jacqueline Fabre-Serris, Alison Keith, Florence Klein
# Introduction

The issue of 'identity' in all its forms — personal, social and cultural — arises for any individual or ethnic group when they come into contact with a foreigner or another ethnic group, whether in a peaceful or in a hostile environment. It results in the construction of ways of life, customs, traditions, and forms of society, some of which are presented as specific cultural features and others considered as characteristic of peoples of more or less distant lands, described as very 'different'. These views of the 'Other' resulting from contact and comparison are often reductive and contradictory. They usually take the form of stereotypes in which the beliefs about what constitutes the characteristic features of a foreign group reveal more about the peoples which produce them than about the groups they are presumed to describe. As any process to define an object aims to shape but also to freeze it in an understandable format, defining another as Other is a way of trying to ensure a dominant position: since otherness is commonly evaluated by opposition and negativity, attempting to define it also leads to the reinforcement of a sense of one's own community.

The concept of alterity is used in a number of academic disciplines, such as philosophy, anthropology, geography, and sociology, and has been especially well theorised in postcolonial discussions of Western 'Orientalising' readings of Eastern cultures.[1] It is less usual to include gender as a third parameter when discussing identity and ethnicity. However, insofar as any society is structured by the division between the sexes in all the fields of public and private activities, the modern concept of gender can be used as a discriminating factor not only to highlight the explicit and implicit rules governing the relations between the sexes in society, but also as a key comparator to be taken into account in order to understand how the notions of identity and ethnicity are articulated when the norms, values, ways of life and behaviours of other cultures are evaluated.

This volume collects papers presented at a symposium which took place 29– 30 November and 1 December 2018 at the University of Lille, under the auspices of the European Network on Gender Studies in Antiquity, EuGeStA. The symposium investigated how gender has been integrated as a secondary but highly significant factor in Greek and Roman discussions of how to better understand both who they themselves were, culturally speaking, and who these others with whom

---

1  Said 1978.

https://doi.org/10.1515/9783110719949-001

they had come into contact were. The object of this book is thus to provide insights into the varying ways the Ancients defined their identity, both cultural and gendered, by reference to their neighbours (bordering cities and peoples) and foreign nations at different times of their history.

In Greece, and more precisely in Athens, in classical times, the cultural identity of citizens was built both on the exclusion of women from political life and on their own differentiation from foreign peoples, called 'barbarian'. As has been well documented, the Greeks invented the concept of the 'barbarian', by portraying him as the opposite of the ideal male citizen.[2] The Greek term invented to denote the foreigner was formed by duplicative onomatopoeia with oriental resonance that was supposed to mimic the sound produced by a foreigner's incomprehensible speech.[3] Although the criterion of Greekness seems to be linguistic, the opposition between Hellene and Barbarian emerged in a specific political context, which resulted from the military conflict between Greeks and Persians. During the early years of the fifth century BCE, the image of the enemy outside the boundaries of Greece, identified with the Persians, was deployed by the Athenians to foster a sense of community among the allied states grouped together under the Delian League. The most important differentiation between the Greeks and the Barbarians was political.[4] As Edith Hall has emphasized, the Greeks, and more specifically the Athenians, described themselves as democratic and egalitarians, while they considered foreigners tyrannical and hierarchical. The other main features, also derogatory, associated with Barbarians were immoderate luxuriousness and unrestrained emotionalism. A gendered perspective was also clearly included in the cultural antinomies by which the Greeks sought to distinguish themselves from the Barbarians. The Greeks were monogamous, they restricted socio-political ascendancy to males and excluded women from public life. By contrast, the Barbarians took a number of both wives and concubines, and some female political and military leaders could be seen to control important regions such as Halicarnassus. The archetype of the Other was projected onto the mythical plane with the Amazons, who themselves were often considered 'historical', with the result that these female societies, located in Cappadocia or in Africa, were described as enjoying by inversion the political rights and military roles Hellenic men exercised in Greece. Gender relations were also a focal element, although in a less drastic way, when the Athenians compared their

---

2 Hall 1989.
3 Hall 1989, 5.
4 Hall 1989, 2

social practices with those of geographically (and ethnically) closer peoples such as the Spartans. After the conquest of most of the barbarian world, the polarization between Greek and non-Greek remained but became more complex as Greek leaders presided over very cosmopolitan societies. Ptolemaic Alexandria, for example, was home to Egyptians, Jews, Africans and Greeks from all over the Mediterranean world. However, while showing an eager interest in the culture and the land of Egypt, the Greek-speaking élite did not engage with the languages of their subjects, at least initially, with the result that cultural interactions between Greeks and Egyptians were relatively limited, and conducted only through Egyptian scribes and administrators who were bilingual.[5]

Conversely, the Romans initiated an unpreceded cultural project when they began to translate Greek literature into the vernacular in order to create the conditions of emergence of a national literature. Unlike the Greeks, who were particularly concerned with preserving their cultural specificity, Rome endeavored indeed to be an open and inclusive city from the start, as symbolized by the *asylum* established by its founder, Romulus. This myth of a safe place for any person (free men or slaves according to Livy, 1.8; freeborn political refugees according to Dionysus Halicarnassus, 2.15.5), who wanted to come and participate in the establishment of the new town, as Emma Dench shows,[6] brings to light a specific feature of Roman culture, conceived as the result of the interaction between groups of various ethnic origins. The complement of the *asylum*, which remedied the young city's lack of men, was the rape of the Sabines, which resolved the problem of the lack of women more violently but again through the inclusion of foreign elements, by incorporating a neighboring people into the new polity.

This cultural project was reinforced by Rome's expansionist aims. The Romans integrated, in the space that they controlled, first the Italian peoples, then all those who lived around the Mediterranean, and they also came into contact with those of Northern Europe. Romulus' creation of the *asylum* can be read alongside the story of Aeneas,[7] but also in relation to the Arcadian myth. As stressed by Evander in *Aeneid* 8, successive emigrations punctuated the history of Italy and Latium and left various legacies, some of them ambivalent. Negative aspects of the Romans' Trojan ancestry (such as luxury and immoral behavior)[8] could be offset by the virtues embodied in the Arcadians (*paupertas*, *pietas* and

---

5 Feeney 2016, 19–22.
6 Dench 2005.
7 Dench 2005, 102.
8 Horace, *Odes* 3.3.

military courage). Being formed and reformed by cultural fusions, Roman heritage was considered to result from choices based on a two-way process of incorporation and transformation of foreign elements. According to Livy (1.8.3), for example, the Romans borrowed the institution of lictors, the curule seat (*sella curulis*), and the *toga*, the formal dress of Roman citizens, from the Etruscans.

This global policy of openness and integration, the strongest sign of which was to be the grant of citizenship to a growing number of inhabitants in the Empire, led to a political and cultural crisis that forced the Romans repeatedly to reexamine their identity and question the evolution of their city from its origins. This process had already begun by the end of the third century BCE when the Romans completed their conquest of the Italian peninsula and engaged with Greek culture, and it was intensified with the conquest of all the empires and monarchies from Africa to Greece and Asia, achieved a hundred years later. As Erich Gruen has argued,[9] "the pivotal time came when circumstances called forth a form of collective introspection, when the Roman elite felt compelled to articulate national values and to shape a distinctive character for their own corporate persona". In fact, interaction with Greek culture was ancient, since Hellenism was originally mediated to the Romans through non-Greeks: as Denis Feeney has underlined,[10] there was no period when the Romans were not interacting with Greek culture, in art, religion, and social practice. Timothy P. Wiseman has convincingly argued, for example, that Greek myths were in circulation during the archaic period.[11] However, when the lure of Hellenism became stronger, upperclass Romans positioned themselves as guardians of the *mos maiorum* and defenders of military and moral virtues promoted as specific to their culture. As "a fierce critic of Greek culture and denouncer of Greeks, but at the same time widely read in Greek literature and profoundly influenced by Hellenic intellectual traditions",[12] the elder Cato was a good example of this ambivalent position.

The increasing crisis of the Roman culture in the first century BCE, across all aspects of social life (politics, beliefs, morals), did not inhibit movement towards inclusion, initiated at the foundation of the city, from continuing in the form of cultural transfers in all fields of knowledge and ways of thinking from Greece to Rome, and especially from the Hellenistic kingdoms. These transfers were made through adaptations and changes in relation to the cultural, intellectual, moral and political practices identified and promoted as specifically Roman. Several

---

**9** Gruen 1994, 1.
**10** Feeney 2016, 9.
**11** Wiseman 1994, 1–36.
**12** Gruen 1994, 3.

texts written in this period are particularly interesting as they try to describe and analyze this complex process, often through the mythic perspective. As it has been well studied by Alessandro Barchiesi,[13] for example, in the *Aeneid*, Vergil portrays the Roman people as arising from a series of contacts and fusions between Mediterranean peoples while highlighting the catalytic role played by their Trojan ancestors. In his reconstruction of the Roman past, Italic peoples, such as the Volsci, the Sabines, and the Marsi, have a twofold function. They are portrayed as "the Nordic and occidental barbarians", who will not only be transformed in the future through the civilizing dynamic of the Roman Empire, but also as constituent peoples contributing in an insightful way to the melting pot of the Roman culture to come.[14] In this respect the gender dimension is also a parameter to be taken into account. As noted by Alison Sharrock,[15] the Volscian political female leader, Camilla, is represented "both positively as a beautiful and admirable thing, and negatively as something that does not quite fit with the grand march of Roman progress". However, by giving to the three female soldiers surrounding Camilla (*Aen.* 11.655–8) significant names: Larina, Tulla and Tarpeia[16] that "place them in Italian and pre-Roman geographical and genealogical history", Vergil stresses "the native Italianness" of these women "as characters who, like so many others in this story, will be not wholly rejected but transformed into Romans, at least in their genealogical line if not in their individual persons".

Although identity, ethnicity and gender are particularly fruitful vectors of analysis when applied to classical Mediterranean societies because the Ancients themselves deployed these three parameters more or less explicitly, in major crisis situations, to reflect upon cultural identities and differences, it appears that the articulation between them has been reflected on only sporadically. Compared to the previous studies on ethnicity and alterity in Antiquity, the special feature of our book is to include the parameter gender in a more precise and systematic way. We focus on how gender has played a major role as very useful reading grid when the Ancients have sought to define themselves. Our aim is thus to consider how the intersection of ethnicity and gender can illuminate the way the Ancients

---

[13] Barchiesi 2008.
[14] Barchiesi 2008, 248. As also underlined by Barchiesi (2008, 255), the conflicts between these peoples and the Trojans and their allies, the Etruscans and the Arcadians, might remind the reader not only of the recent civil wars but also of the *Bellum sociale*.
[15] Sharrock 2016, 165.
[16] The name Larina derives from the Samnian town, Larinum. Tulla is the feminine form of a Roman *praenomen* held by the King of Rome Tullus Hostilius, Tarpeia alludes to the young woman who betrayed Rome to the Sabines.

spoke of identity. This issue is examined, deepened and/or questioned, in the thirteen papers collected in this volume, and organized into five thematic sections, mostly in chronological order.

# 1 Masculinity, dress and body

The first chapter, by François Lissarrague, shows how a critical approach using the categories of ethnicity and gender sheds a new light on three series of images in Attic vase paintings — comasts commonly called 'anacreontics'; Burisis and Herakles; and Orpheus — which he had previously studied through the grid of alterity and otherness. Scrutinized with the new analytical tools used in current research trends, and particularly with an eye on the gender issue, his re-examination sheds an interesting light on the categories at stake in these three groups of images: the clothes and bodies represented on the vases are not delivering the same message he found earlier. For example, the long chitons and the earrings sometimes worn by Egyptians priests in images can be taken as feminine markers. Yet, when they are combined with some elements of clearly exhibited masculine anatomy, such as genitals, beard and moustache, the images do not sustain this first reading. As a result, by crossing elements supposed to discriminate gender, this visual logic appears to be rather more complex than it could have seemed: foreign peoples like the Egyptians are represented as both male and female, as is also the case with the Thracian women, who dress like warriors but can be identified as female by their tattoos.

Dress is recognized as an obvious marker both of ethnicity and gender. As a visual element, immediately perceived, it allows us to identify not only ethnic origin and gender, but also social, political and religious status. The next chapter compares clothing but also bodily practices supposed to characterize, and differentiate, the Barbarians of the Achaemenid Empire and the Greeks (i.e., more precisely, the Persians and the Athenians). It is often assumed that Asian clothing practices were interpreted by the Greeks in such a way as to construct a discourse on ethnic identity that integrated gender as a discriminant parameter. Thus, because of their luxury, Oriental costumes, with their abundance of gold and purple, could be considered as having a feminine connotation. In fact, however, the connotations are more complicated: for similarly rich and colorful costumes were not unknown to the Greeks since the Archaic period and yet then they only rarely had a gendered connotation. Florence Gherchanoc shows that more than the clothes, the physical aspect of bodies, when they are naked, functioned as a feature of gender. Compared to strong and vigorous Greek bodies, trained in the gymnasium, Barbarian bodies, because of their white and fatty complexion, their oily and soft flesh, could be assimilated to those of women. What was supposed to explain the two different types of bodies? According to Florence Gherchanoc, it was the respective political regimes of the Greeks and the Barbarian. The former were free citizens, the latter subjected to kings. Therefore, the Greeks can dress in Persian clothes: such clothes would never effeminize them because their bodies corresponded to the Greek ideal of masculinity.

## 2 Gender, political leaders and ethnic identity

The second section focuses on how the Greeks and the Romans have portrayed female and male political leaders, in time of war or when performing their official duties, by using gender and ethnicity as a way of shedding a negative or (more rarely) positive light on the acts, behaviors and speeches attributed to them. In a chapter focused on female political intelligence, Giulia Sissa examines the role that, according to Herodotus, Artemisia, Queen of Halicarnassus, played as a commander-in-chief of her own navy and counsellor of the Persian King, before and after the battle of Salamis. Before the battle, Artemisia offers prudent advice to the Great King, telling him that it is unwise to engage in a maritime conflict with the Athenians: for at sea they will be invincible because they excel over Persian sailors, as men excel over women. After Salamis, Artemisia provides the Great King with another wise and effective piece of advice, in her suggestion that he give up and sail home. The second time Xerxes complies. The strategic competence attributed to Artemisia contradicts the Athenians' point of view about the respective roles of men and women, which institutes men's superiority to women and restricts the role of women to childbearing. As a private counsellor, Artemisia leads the Great King to judge the respective military behaviour of the Greeks and the Persians from a gendered perspective: the Persians became like women. If the Greeks won, it was because of their form of government: the Athenians have more ἀνδρεία ('manliness') as an effect of their political system, democracy, which increases their θυμός ('ardour'). It is no surprise that Herodotus credits a woman, half Greek and half Carian, with political intelligence: as a woman and a foreigner of mixed origin, Artemisia has an insightful knowledge of ethnic and political specificities that distinguish the Greeks and the Persians, but also of their shared convictions about gendered social roles and male supremacy.

In the next chapter, Alison Keith examines how gender and ethnicity function rhetorically in Cicero's various strategic charges to discredit Verres' provincial governance in Cilicia and in Sicily. Cicero's violent attacks on Verres denounce him as a bad representative of Roman authority and a new example of the lecherous Greek tyrant, using violence to satisfy his inveterate debauchery and immoderate cupidity. The detailed description of Verres' criminal behavior in many sexual and financial affairs involves the portraits of foreign and Roman women represented as his victims or depicted as his active partners. In the first group we find a Greek young girl, daughter of the leading citizen of Lampsacus, and some respectable Roman women such as Annius' daughter and wife, Malleolus' mother and grandmother. The second group includes an upmarket prostitute like his mistress Chelidon, and three elite Sicilian women: Aeschrio's wife Pipa, Cleomenes' wife Nike, and the mime Isidorus' daughter Tertia, all wealthy women portrayed as belonging to Verres' 'royal harem'. In this way, Cicero indirectly offers valuable testimony and instructive evidence for women's financial, legal, sexual and social standing in this period — despite, indeed even because of, their frequent rhetorical stylization according to stereotypes of ethnicity and gender.

The Punic Wars were the longest and most dangerous military conflict Rome ever experienced. The third chapter of this section focuses on the narrative of the Hannibalic war in which Livy treats the events from the Numidian leader Masinissa's hasty marriage to Sophonisba (resulting from his sudden sexual arousal to his captive) to her death by suicide. Livy, convinced that the superiority of the Roman cultural model rests on the practice of virtues such as loyalty (*fides*), restraint (*temperantia*) and self-control (*continentia*), employs these concepts as elements of identity to explain and assess the differences in behavior between the Roman general, Scipio, and the Numidian leaders, Syphax and Masinissa. Both Numidians are described as subject to their sexual impulses,[17] whereas the *temperantia* ('self-control') and *fides* embodied by Scipio are represented as peculiarly Roman. According to David Levene,[18] Livy also makes a clear distinction between the two Numidian leaders: Syphax is "the unreliable 'barbarian', Masinissa 'the quintessentially loyal ally'." Scipio tries to ensure that Masinissa will not follow the same path as Syphax by suggesting to him that he imitate his own virtues, in particular his sexual continence. In this chapter, Jacqueline Fabre-Serris argues that the comparison made by Livy in this episode between different behaviors supposedly resulting from membership in a particular ethnic group also aligns the Carthaginians with Sophonisba, described as an intractable

---

**17** Levene 2010, 258–9.
**18** Levene 2010, 247–8.

enemy of Rome, who prefers to die rather than become a prisoner. Gender complicates the ethnic perspective adopted by Livy, especially as the historian interprets Sophonisba in the light of Rome's recent history and, more precisely, of the threat posed by Cleopatra. Livy characterizes Sophonisba's manner of death with the adverb *ferocius*, which alludes to Horace's verses on Cleopatra's suicide in *Odes* 1.37. In doing so, he also highlights how, though courage and impassivity in the face of death are both values shared with their victors, the conduct of Cleopatra and Sophonisba differs from the practice of these virtues by the Romans because of their (female) ferocity, implicitly interpreted as a manifestation of the 'wild' nature of all women.

## 3 Cleopatra's survival and metamorphosis in Roman Poetry

Whereas Jacqueline Fabre-Serris has highlighted the presence of Cleopatra in Livy's portrait of Sophonisba, the third section focuses on the Egyptian Queen, from the perspective of her reception in Augustan and Neronian poetry.

As brilliantly shown by Denis Feeney, the creation of an original literature in Rome has taken the form of 'translations' into the vernacular, with changes and adaptations, of Greek tragic, comic and epic texts.[19] This systematic process can be recognized as an intrinsic part of Roman conquest and inherent in Rome's geopolitical ambitions. After the conquest of the Ptolemaic kingdom, when some Augustan poets are echoing Alexandrian literary models, their intertextual appropriation can be also viewed as a form of triumphant imperialism, parallel to military conquest. In the first chapter of this section, Florence Klein considers how intertextuality intersects with gender and ethnicity. How can the gender parameter illuminate our intertextual reading of some famous Roman texts in relation to Hellenistic poems taken as models and rewritten from the perspective of the victors — both as an act of homage and, simultaneously, a display of imperial domination? In other words, how do the categories of ethnicity and gender map into each other, in order to assess, by literary means, the Roman domination over an hegemonized foreign culture? Studying Propertius 3.1 and 4.6 — two elegies picturing Cleopatra as a threat to Roman masculine and Western values and celebrating Augustus' victory over the Egyptian queen —, Florence Klein shows that both poems duplicate the gendered vision of the military encounter on the poetic

---

**19** Feeney 2016.

and intertextual level, precisely by emphasizing the femininity of their literary models. Through a close reading of some corrections and tendentious contrastive allusions to Posidippean and Callimachean texts, she suggests that the representation of the appropriated culture as female enhances the Roman (literary) domination. Thus, the whole literary culture of Hellenistic Alexandria, being the male Roman poet's spoil and captive (as Cleopatra is for Augustus), gets included in Propertius' strongly gendered and orientalist rhetoric.

In the second chapter of this section, Andrew Feldherr examines the particular techniques Lucan employs to confuse the foreign past with the Roman present. He shows that this confusion operates in two directions: Nero is already immanent in Cleopatra, but Cleopatra can be re-visualized as Nero. The two essential attributes of Neronian culture with which they may be connected and which play a crucial role in characterizing the epoch, are luxury and theatricality. At the same time, the general condemnation of the Neronian regime as foreign, effeminate, and incestuous draws on the very rhetorical strategies used to castigate Cleopatra. As a result, Cleopatra will be defeated by the Romans but she will rule at Rome in the person of Nero. Instead of being used for difference the axes of gender, ethnicity and temporality are in fact aligned in Lucan's imaginary, allegorical Roman world.

## 4 Love, oriental ethnicity and Gender in Roman literature

As a symbol of the seduction of oriental luxury, Cleopatra belongs to the long series of female characters that embody in Roman poetry the charm and otherness of the 'exotic' through the motif of foreign love. In her paper Federica Bessone investigates the forms in which Roman poets describe these *peregrini amores* and their way of threatening Roman culture 'from within'. The excess of refinement (*luxuria*), imported into Rome from oriental peoples, is stigmatized as a corrupting force dangerous to both women and men. It can confuse a *puella*, or even a *matrona*, with a *meretrix*; and, through erotic enticement, it can reduce a *uir* to a half-man (*semiuir*). The elegists describe love as a powerful agent of an exchange of gender roles. Combined with oriental luxury, the slavery induced by love results, as demonstrated in the story of Hercules and Omphale, in the loss of identity and infamous confusion of gendered clothes and behaviors that supposedly differentiate men and women.

A similar topic is examined by Judith Hallett who focuses on Phoenician ethnicity and love in the portrayal of two fictional women whose foreign origin is highlighted in relation to their modes of self-expression in love. The first is a young brothel slave, characterized as Phoenician quite literally by her name, *Phoenicium*, in Plautus' *Pseudolus* (191 BCE). The second is the Carthaginian queen Dido, presented by Vergil as an exile from Phoenicia in the *Aeneid*, written over 150 years later. All Phoenicians, male and female, were stereotyped as masters of verbal artifice, and often practitioners of verbal deception. Judith Hallett shows how both women are represented as similarly preoccupied with, and skilled at voicing, erotic desires and demands that their lovers value their erotic investments. Plautus and Vergil thereby exemplify negative stereotypes applied to Phoenician men: by attributing emotionally manipulative words to these women, they characterize them as exemplary of a foreign people, untrustworthy in speech and action. Their modes of speaking and acting distinguish these fictional Phoenician women from the Latin poet Sulpicia, who makes erotic appeals and demands that exude a self-confident air, in accordance with her social standing as an elite Roman woman.

However, if the construction of Other as Eastern is dominant in Augustan Rome, there can be more similarity and less difference in some representations of others than we might expect. Alison Sharrock examines from this perspective the stories told by the daughters of Minyas in *Metamorphoses* 4, when they are weaving while the rest of the Theban women celebrate the rites of the new god Bacchus. Despite the explicit untimeliness of their work and its disruption of the festival, these women who weave resemble Roman 'good women'. In the same vein, Alison Sharrock observes that Ovid has chosen to move the first story from Cilicia further East to Babylon, but that his way of presenting Pyramus and Thisbe as "remarkably ordinary" lovers who want to "marry in the normal bourgeois way," in spite of their parents' opposition as in the middle class-world of the New Comedy, makes this story no more foreign than is the Theban setting in which it is told. She suggests that Ovid is playing with the interaction of the universal and the particular. The universal trumps the particular, with love stories being the same the world over, or perhaps this point subsists in the characterisation of the secondary narrator herself, who may like to choose a sexual partner, irrespective of her geographical and cultural origins. Alison Sharrock concludes her analysis of the stories told by the three sisters by observing more generally that, despite a small number of examples of ethnographic stereotyping, in the *Metamorphoses* much more extensive are the "stories" of exotic provenance, which are naturalised and domesticated in such a way as to neutralise ethnic difference.

## 5 Constructing or deconstructing female ethnicity in late Antiquity

This fourth and final section gathers three examples of constructing and/or deconstructing female ethnicity in the literature of late Antiquity. In the first chapter, after exploring the reasons why Thessaly came to be regarded as a center of magic and witches since the classical period (5th century BCE), Therese Fuhrer focuses on how Apuleius makes use of geographical and ethnic stereotypes in the *Metamorphoses* when he represents the town of Hypata in the Roman province of Thessaly as a 'witches' town'. She argues that Apuleius deconstructs the notion of 'Thessalian witches' in the *Metamorphoses*, since the cliché of the corpse-robbing and ugly old witch is invoked only in embedded tales. In the 'real life' of the main narrator, Lucius, the only sorceress he meets is the 'All-Loving' Pamphile whom Apuleius then makes into a new type of Thessalian witch, rejuvenating and re-defining her existence as a marginal figure who lives on the edge of town, disregards bourgeois conventions and is excluded by urban society. She remains however a female fantasy figure, created by male narrators and protagonists. Once turned into an ass, Lucius is kidnapped by true robbers and finds out about the world of magic and witches only from tales told by others.

In his treatise *Mulierum Virtutes*, Plutarch draws up a series of striking portraits, which repeatedly highlight the courage of women, individually or in groups. Charles Delattre examines the example of a Galatian woman, Camma. After her spouse Sinatos has been murdered by the tetrarch Sinoris, who wanted to marry her, she shares with him a cup of poisoned mead, causing the almost immediate death of Sinoris, whom she soon follows into the grave while claiming the rightness of her act. Plutarch tells the same story a little differently in another treatise, his *Erotikos*. Camma's characterisation as a Galatian introduces a regional identity in addition to her gender identity. However, in both narratives, this story illustrates Plutarch's conviction that conjugal *eros* is conditioned by a sentimental alliance (φιλία) independent of ethnicity, and based on the moral excellence (ἀρετή) that it also guarantees. Conjugality is thus both the source and the consequence of moral excellence. As highlighted by Charles Delattre, Greek women, Persian women and Gallic women act in a similar way, with any linguistic or ethnic distinction being erased. They even take the place of defaulting men when a situation requires it. The decisive factor is conjugal status: these women are considered exemplary only because they have confined themselves to their role as wives.

In the classical rhetorical tradition, Rome and her various imperial provinces are represented as female characters, while rivers are characterized as masculine. Henriette Harich explores Claudian's descriptions of the female personifications of Rome and Africa, mediated by the rhetorical tradition of *prosopopoeiae*, and asks what criteria of femininity he activates in relation to ethnicity. In the *De bello Gildonico,* Roma, who fears her end and seeks help from Jupiter, is described as an old woman, with feeble voice, slow steps and downcast eyes. Her appearance, emphasized in relation to her infertility, symbolizes her loss of power. Yet, when she tries to convince the gods and especially Cybele to intercede with Jupiter, her performance is convincing: she is rejuvenated by the supreme god. Moreover, as a young woman she stands in need of the male protection symbolized by the Roman general Stilicho, who is described as a strong man with white hair, radiating far and wide. Africa too appears on Olympus and begs for help. She is described as a woman who has been physically abused, with torn clothes and wounded head. She wants to become a desert in order to escape the tyrant Gildo, who will be obstructed by enlarged drought zones. Later Africa dissociates herself from ethnic groups like the Ethiopians, Moors and Nasamones, whom she accuses of crimes against women, brute violence, and lawlessness. If, Henriette Harich observes, femininity is associated with mental and physical weakness in both *prosopopoeiae*, then ethnicity may not in fact be relevant to the characterization of Claudian's Rome, since she symbolises the 'body' of the Roman Empire. This is likewise true in the case of the epiphany of the river Tiber in another of Claudian's panegyric, whose power is emphasised only as *pater familias* and for his dignified age, i.e. from gendered perspective.

To conclude, as Classicists, one of our main aims is to try to enrich the contemporary debate by showing that we have yet to learn from the Ancients' discussions of social and cultural issues that are still relevant today. In an international context in which the cultural confrontation is marked by the exacerbation of the issues of Identity and Otherness, we hope that studying and analyzing various examples of the way Greek and Roman authors, at the beginning of the Western Culture, have reflected on these issues can be useful: indeed, by articulating them with a strong focus both on ethnicity and gender, they show how different and complex answers can be provided, according to the circumstances, times and societies.

## Works Cited

Barchiesi, A. (2008), "*Bellum Italicum*. L'unificazione dell'Italia nell'*Eneide*", in: G. Urso (ed), *Patria diuersis gentibus una*, Pisa, 423–60.

Dench, E. (2005), *Romulus' Asylum. Roman Identities from the Age of Alexander to the Age of Hadrian*, Oxford.

Feeney, D. (2016), *Beyond Greek. The Beginnings of Latin Literature*, Cambridge MA/London.

Gruen, E. (1994), *Culture and National Identity in Republican Rome*, Ithaca/New York.

Hall, E. (1989), *Inventing the Barbarian. Greek Self-Definition through Tragedy*, Oxford.

Saïd, E.W. (1978), *Orientalism*, London.

Sharrock, A. (2016), "Warrior Women in Roman Epic", in: J. Fabre-Serris/A. Keith (eds.), *Women and War in Antiquity*, Baltimore, 157–78.

Wiseman, P. (1994), *Historiography and Imagination: Eight Essays on Roman Culture*, Exeter.

Part I: **Masculinity, Dress and Body**

François Lissarrague
# Ionians, Egyptians, Thracians: Ethnicity and Gender in Attic Vase-Painting

More than 40 years ago, around 1977, I began a dissertation project dealing with 'the representation of Barbarians' in Attic vase-painting. The topic was suggested to me by Pierre Vidal Naquet, to whom I had submitted a paper on the fight between Pygmies and cranes. He was at that time interested in 'marginals', forms of alterity and 'otherness' (without any Lacanian perspective). No one spoke of 'ethnicity'. As to 'gender', that was still to come. The great novelty of the time was, some years later, the development of the history of women.[1]

During that research on 'Barbarians' I was using an 'emic' concept, βάρβαροι ('barbarians'), and dwelled on a saying attributed to Thales, who was happy "to be a human being, not an animal; to be a man, not a woman; to be a Greek, not a Barbarian".[2] This Hellenocentric scheme fit perfectly with Athenian vase-painting, and I only had to collect the evidence and organize it to produce a relatively complete catalogue of such documents. I never wrote that dissertation, because a German colleague published his own dissertation under the title *Zum Barbarenbild in der Kunst Athens*.[3] So I shifted my project, limiting it to Thracians and Scythian warriors.[4] However, I used some of that evidence in separate articles, written in collaboration.

The first one deals with images of comasts commonly called 'anacreontics', in the scholarly tradition; it was written in collaboration with Françoise Frontisi and published in 1983.[5] The second, written with Jean-Louis Durand, analyzes the story of Herakles and Busiris.[6] A third group of images was discussed at length with Marcel Detienne, when he was working on Orpheus; it was not published as a joint article, but I dedicated a later paper, published in 1994, to him: "Orphée mis à mort."[7]

The reason for turning back to these articles is not just selfish nostalgia; it seems that they can be usefully combined in terms of articulation around the notions of identity, ethnicity, and gender. This last notion, in particular, which was

---

1 See Schmitt Pantel 1990.
2 Thales, DK 11A1 = Laks Most 5 P17b = Diogenes Laertius 1.33.
3 Raeck 1980.
4 Lissarrague 1990.
5 Frontisi and Lissarrague 1983.
6 Durand and Lissarrague 1983.
7 Lissarrague 1994.

not used in these early papers, sheds an interesting light on the categories at stake in these three groups of images.

In this short paper I will briefly summarize the main aspects of each of these three series of pictures, using a sample of characteristic examples, in order to underline the relationship they suggest between identity, ethnicity, and gender, and to show how gender, as an analytical tool, helps to better understand the contrasts involved in these groups of representations, and also to better understand the way images build a network of discriminating signs structuring the Athenian imagination.

# 1 'Anacreontics'

Let us begin with the so called 'anacreontics'.[8] It is a group of vases showing a bearded figure in a long chiton, wearing a σάκκος ('headgear'), sometimes earrings, these last two signs being a visual mark of female dress (fig. 1).[9]

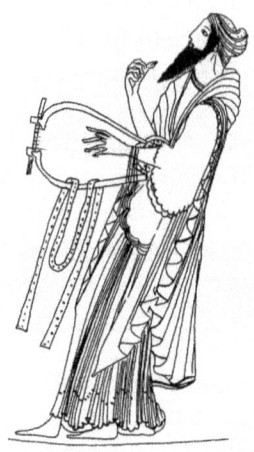

**Fig. 1:** Boston 13.199, red-figure lekythos.

---

**8** Since our article, several studies have focused on that topic; among others, note Price 1990 and Miller 2013.
**9** Boston 13.199, red-figure lekythos; early Mannerist, ARV2 588/73; BA 206804.

When such figures wear an open dress, the male sex is visible, which demonstrates that these figures are not bearded women dressed as men, but the opposite: men dressed as women, playing the Other (fig. 2).¹⁰

**Fig. 2:** Paris, Louvre G4bis, red-figure cup.

The beard is a graphic way of showing the maleness of these figures. Some of these images are labelled with the name of Anacreon and some authors think they are portraits of the poet himself (fig. 3).¹¹

**Fig. 3:** Syracuse 26967, red-figure lekythos.

---

10  Paris, Louvre G4bis, red-figure cup; Nicosthenes painter, ARV2 125/16; BA 201044.
11  Syracuse 26967, red-figure lekythos; Gales painter, ARV2 36/2; BA 200207.

We have demonstrated that this is not the case; the word 'anakreon' appearing on some vases is not a label naming the poet, but a reference to a poetic genre, and to a kind of κῶμος ('dancing group'), popular in Athens when Anakreon paid a visit to that city.

This series of images plays with the reference to the Ionian world, without really marking a specific ethnicity, as the Athenians do not need to distinguish themselves form the Ionians. In this series, it is the experimentation of feminine alterity which is displayed, in the frame of the Dionysiac practice. Gender is temporarily put into question as a category, which can elucidate the shift from anatomical maleness to social experimentation of the other sex.

## 2 'Busiris'

The Heracles and Busiris series has much to do with ethnicity. Heracles reaches Egypt at the time of a drought; Busiris, the Pharaoh, in order to obey an oracle, sacrifices every oncoming foreigner; so Heracles is to be sacrificed. We see him taken to an altar, and suddenly realizing he is the victim; he fights against the priests and destroys the entire order of the ritual. We were interested, Jean-Louis Durand and myself, in this story because these images show a kind of human sacrifice in which the sacrificial ritual is inverted, and all the elements of the standard sarifice are displaced; the sacrificial basket is falling down, and the μάχαιρα ('sacrificial knife'), the sacrificial knife, which is almost never shown in standard sacrifices, is here clearly visible. By this displacement, these images reveal what is usually hidden, or at least not shown, in the standard sacrifice. Clearly these images have nothing to do with ethnographic documents; they do not describe the Egyptian way of sacrificing. They show how the Greek vase-painters imagine the Egyptian episode in the Heracles saga. All the instruments reproduced in these pictures are perfectly Greek (altar, basket, knives, spits, etc.).

More interesting, in terms of ethnicity and gender, is the way the Egyptians are conceived and depicted. On a pelike by the Pan painter (fig. 4),[12] the Egyptians are bald, pug-nosed, and their chitons are systematically lifted to show their genitals, and that they are all circumcised. A different masculinity is exhibited by the painter, clearly a non-Greek masculinity. On other images in that series, the Egyptian priests wear long dress and earrings, which are feminine markers (fig. 5).[13]

---

12 Athens NM 9683, red-figure pelike; Pan painter, ARV2 554/82 ; BA 206325.
13 Munich 2428, red-figure hydria; early Mannerist, ARV2 297/13 ; BA 203080.

Ionians, Egyptians, Thracians: Ethnicity and Gender in Attic Vase-Painting — 21

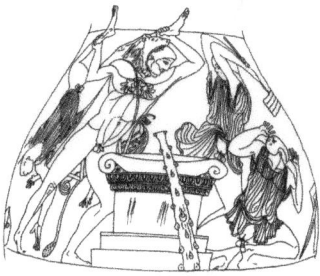

**Fig. 4:** Athens NM 9683, red-figure pelike.

**Fig. 5:** Munich 2428, red-figure hydria.

The alterity of the Egyptians involves a feminine dimension; their gender is ambivalent and their image mixes male features (genitals, beard, and moustache) and female features (dress, jewelry), thus blurring the social marks that normally distinguish the one from the other. Looking at these pictures one wonders which gender is involved; as a tool, gender helps us to differentiate between the anatomical sex and the social status, of these Egyptian priests.

## 3 Orpheus

This series depicting Orpheus is more complex, because Orpheus' picture and identity change with time; the narrative strategies of the painters underline different aspects according to different periods. Archaic and classical Orpheus are not the same.

In the archaic period, Orpheus, the Thracian musician, is shown as perfectly Greek in appearance (fig. 6).[14]

**Fig. 6:** Berlin 3172, red-figure column crater.

Pausanias, writing in the 2nd century AD, notes in surprise when he describes the Cnidian Lesche in Delphi and the Nekyia painted by Polygnotos.[15] This is because Orpheus, from the end of the 5th century on, is always seen as a Thracian, not as a Greek. In early classical vase painting, among vases attributed to the Villa Giulia painter, what distinguishes Apollo, Mousaios, or Orpheus is not their ap-

---

14 Berlin 3172, red-figure column crater; Orpheus painter, ARV2 1103/1 ; BA 216168.
15 Pausanias X, 30, 2.

pearance, but their audience. Orpheus is surrounded by Thracian warriors listening to his song, characterised by their dress: fur cap ἀλωπεκίς and heavy cloak ζειρά. The ethnic contrast between Orpheus and the warriors is clear.

At that period of time, around 450 BC, Orpheus is also differentiated from another Thracian musician, Thamyras, by his audience – Muses for Thamyras, Thracian warriors for Orpheus –, as well as through his dress: Orpheus wears Greek dress, Thamyras, Thracian (fig. 7).[16]

**Fig. 7:** St Petersburg St1685, red-figure amphora.

Greek vs Thracian: the opposition is clear. The Thracian warriors are mesmerized by the charm of the music and the song of Orpheus. In the oral tradition Orpheus is entirely devoted to Apollo, and despises Dionysos. He is also, in the mythological tradition, the inventor of homosexuality. This aspect is not developed in the pictures, but it explains the violence of the Thracian women against Orpheus. They attack Orpheus to stop the effects of his music; the earliest pictures of Orpheus, in Attic vase painting, depict this moment, when these violent avengers kill Orpheus. What the images do not show is their motivations, that is whether to fight homosexuality or to restore the role of Dionysos. These women are violent but have no maenadic pictorial characterisation.

What the images do show about these women are Thracian elements, like dress and tattoos (fig. 8).[17]

---

16  St Petersburg St1685, red-figure amphora; later Mannerist, ARV2 1123/6; BA 214848.
17  New York 96.9.37, red-figure cup; Brygos painter, ARV2 379/156; BA 204053.

**Fig. 8:** New York 96.9.37, red-figure cup (detail).

Their dress recalls what men wear: they have heavy coats like the ζειρά, which they use as shields. Tattoos on the other hand are exclusively found on women. Thracian warriors are not tattooed; only women can be identified as Thracian through their tattoos. From the Greek viewpoint, tattoos are an infamy, a branding reserved for slaves. Plutarch recalls that the Thracians tattooed their women to punish them after they had killed Orpheus (the narrative chronology is in that version different from what we see in vase-painting). In terms of ethnicity, the opposition Greek/Barbarian is neat in that story. This opposition is doubled, on the Thracian side, by another, gender-based one, using tattoos as a discriminating mark. Later in time, Orpheus becomes a visually Thracian figure, his image no longer in competition with that of Thamyras. The painter's choices move towards a different iconography, where Orpheus is not charming the Thracian warriors, but all the animals, including the wild ones. The articulation at stake is no longer Greek/Barbarian, but Human/Animal; and this is another story.

# 4 Conclusion

In this network of images, when we confront these three groups of representations, which are almost contemporaries, we see the interplay of graphic signs producing ethnic or gender determinations : Greek/non Greek ; Male/Female. This visual logic is not just binary; it gets more complex, within every category, by crossing discriminating elements. Egyptians are both male and female, whereas

Thracian women become male warriors when men stop being so. In the 'anacreontic' series, the dionysiac κῶμος allows for male experimentation with the feminine. The image maintains the male-female tension by preserving the beard of the comast when he/she wears the dress of a dancing woman.

**Fig. 9:** Paris, Louvre G285, red-figure cup.   **Fig. 10:** Ferrara inv. 609, red-figure cup.   **Fig. 11:** New York 96.9.37, red-figure cup.

Thus we can see how the visual corpus of images cannot be considered as merely a simple lexical system. It is a combinatory system, which develops a network of contextualised signs; image after image, series after series, it elaborates a global vision of the Athenian culture, an ethnical and gendered imaginary in which these categories are problematised through images as much as through mythical and historical narratives.

## Works Cited

Durand, J.-L./Lissarrague, F. (1983), 'Héros cru ou hôte cuit : histoire quasi cannibale d'Héraklès chez Busiris,' in: F. Lissarrague/F. Thelamon (eds.), *Image et céramique grecque*, Rouen, 153–67.

Frontisi, F./Lissarrague, F. (1983), 'De l'ambiguïté à l'ambivalence : un parcours dionysiaque', *AION Arch St*, 5, 11–32; English version in: D. Halperin/J. Winckler/F. Zeitlin (eds.), *Before Sexuality*, 1990, Princeton, 211–56.

Lissarrague, F. (1990), *L'Autre guerrier. Archers, peltastes, cavaliers dans l'imagerie attique*, Paris/Rome.

Lissarrague, F. (1994), 'Orphée mis à mort', *Musica e Storia* 2, 269–307.

Price, S. (1990), 'Anacreontic vases reconsidered', *GRBS* 31 2, 133–75.

Miller, M. (2013), 'Clothes and Identity : the case of the Greeks in Ionia c. 400 BC', *Antichthon* 47, 18–38.

Raeck, W. (1980), *Zum Barbarenbild in der Kunst Athens im 6. und 5. Jahrhundert v. Chr.*, Bonn.

Schmitt-Pantel, P. (ed.) (1990), *L'Antiquité*, vol. 1, in: G. Duby/M. Perrot (eds.), *Histoire des femmes en Occident*, Paris.

Florence Gherchanoc
# Dress, Ethnic Identity, and Gender in the Achaemenid Empire: Greek Views on the Persians, and Political Ideology in the Classical Time

In the 5th century BC, Herodotus (8.144) stated that the Greeks were united against the Barbarians by the sharing of the same blood and language, by a community of gods and religious practices, and finally by the same behaviour. In this way, a common identity was affirmed in the confrontation with the Other on the occasion of the Greco-Median Wars that led the Greeks to think of themselves as a united people and 'invent' the Barbarians.[1]

However, at the end of the 5th century BC, the old Oligarch emphasised the singularity of the Athenians among the Greeks, a singularity based on language, diet or lifestyle, δίαιτα and σχῆμα ('look and character'): 'the Greeks individually tend to use their own dialect, way of life, and type of dress [costume], but the Athenians use a mixture from all the Greeks and non-Greeks.'[2]

By way of focusing on clothing and body practices, I propose to consider the question of Greek unity, and in addition of Athenian singularity, in juxtaposition to the Barbarians of the Achaemenid Empire (and more specifically of the Persians) in the classical period. This is in fact precisely what the ps.-Xenophon text invites us to do. Indeed, among the particular features he cites, the σχῆμα designates a distinctive costume, recognizable by all; it defines both the shape of the garment and its perception beyond the shape. It characterizes the visual representation that allows the viewer to accurately identify the wearer: his or her ethnic origin, gender, social, political, or religious status — and, finally, the type of behaviour that can be expected from one wearing this costume. The σχῆμα is in principle a display of identity.[3] However, the Greeks in the archaic period and the Athenians in particular, still in the 5th century adopted/wore certain oriental clothing (the χιτών 'tunic' with pleated sleeves; κάνδυς 'Median cloak with

---

[1] See *Grecs et Barbares*, 1962; Hartog 1980; Hall 1989; Cartledge 1993; Bichler 2001; Perrin/Nourisson 2005; Gruen 2011; Borello/Pollini 2015.
[2] [Xenophon], *Constitution of the Athenians* 2.8 (transl. by E.C. Marchant, G.W. Bowersock, 'Loeb Classical Library', London, 1925): καὶ οἱ μὲν Ἕλληνες ἰδίᾳ μᾶλλον καὶ φωνῇ καὶ διαίτῃ καὶ σχήματι χρῶνται, Ἀθηναῖοι δὲ κεκραμένῃ ἐξ ἁπάντων τῶν Ἑλλήνων καὶ βαρβάρων.
[3] On the word σχῆμα, see Casevitz 2004 and Papadopoulou 2013.

sleeves'; ἐπενδύτης 'upper garment').⁴ They also depicted themselves dressed in foreign/barbaric costume (Scythian, Thracian, etc.)⁵ — which is an aspect of the mixture (κρᾶμα) mentioned by the old oligarch.

Therefore, without focusing on this last point, I would like to explore two aspects of how the Greeks instrumentalized the clothing practices of Asians, and then how they proposed a discourse on ethnic identities sometimes combined with a discourse on gender. The aim will be to see how clothing and bodies construct cultural and symbolic boundaries, articulate otherness, and prioritize individuals; how discourses about these markers of identity underlie or accompany a social and political ideology among Greeks, especially Athenians and Lacedaemonians; and whether and in what way this ideology changes, especially during the classical period.

In other words, without entering into historiographical debates about the notion of ethnicity,⁶ I will investigate how the Greeks perceived Persian clothing practices (in the broad sense) as defining common qualities or traits, and how gender interferes in these constructions of ethnic identity.

Initially, I had assumed equivalence between oriental costumes and femininity and wanted to understand how it was structured. Things are, however, more complicated. I will therefore first discuss this equivalence, which may be related to a fantasized Orient, in particular the links between barbaric clothing/beauty/luxury/ἁβροσύνη/χλιδή (which can be translated as opulence, softness, delicacy) and feminine seduction. Indeed, this equation, even if it is contested, for example, by Christopher Tuplin, is recurrent in many studies. Then, secondly, I will attempt to show that gender becomes more of an operator of 'ethnic' distinction if we consider nudity or naked bodies.

---

4 On 'perserie' and adoption by the Athenians of these clothes with a foreign accent, see Miller 1997, 153–87 and 192–209. Regarding the fascination concerning Persian clothes and other cultural imports, see also Wiesehöfer 2004 and 2009; Gunter 2009.
5 On this Greek (in fact Athenian) way of experiencing the Other or taming it, see Frontisi-Ducroux/Lissarrague 1990; Lissarrague 1990; Kurke 1992; Sparke 1997; Miller 1997; Cohen 2001; Lenfant 2001; Lissarrague 2002.
6 See Barth 1969; Hall 1997 and 2002; Malkin 2001; Luce 2007; Malkin/Müller 2012; McInerney 2014 et Müller 2014.

## 1 Clothes, markers of luxury, therefore emollient, characteristic of women?

Ornaments are ethnic markers. They shape a visual and ideological distinction.[7] Thus, Aeschylus, in *The Persians*, a tragedy performed in 472 BC, evokes the fact that there are visible differences between Greek and Persian clothing. Queen Atossa points this out as she recounts her dream to the coryphaeus:

'There seemed to come into my sight two finely dressed women, one arrayed in Persian, the other in Doric robes (ἡ μὲν πέπλοισι Περσικοῖς ἠσκημένη, ἡ δ' αὖτε Δωρικοῖσιν), outstandingly superior in stature to the women of real life, of flawless beauty.'[8] Each woman embodies an 'ethnic' clothing stereotype, the first one magnificence, the second, simplicity.

On the side of men's clothing, still in *Persians*, the glory and majesty of Xerxes and his father are also displayed in the splendour of clothing. Xerxes is dressed in variegated πέπλοι ('robe') (468; 836), that is, in a beautiful κόσμος ('ornament') (849). As for the Great Darios, whose ghost is invoked by the chorus that invites him to manifest himself, he is distinguished by his saffron-coloured sandal (κροκόβαπτον εὔμαριν) and the boss of his royal tiara (βασιλείου τιήρας).[9]

The two elements, shoes and tiara,[10] as well as long πέπλοι are characteristic of Barbarians and their high dignitaries: their shape, craftsmanship and colour simultaneously express oriental luxury and the magnificence of their power or that of their army.[11]

---

[7] Hall 1989; Georges 1994; Eicher 1995.
[8] Aeschylus, *Persians* 181–85 (transl. by A.H. Sommerstein, 'Loeb Classical Library', London, 2008; Cf. Euripides, *Ion*, 1369, about distinctive 'barbaric fabrics (βαρβάρων ὑφάσματα)'.
[9] Aeschylus, *Persians* 658–64.
[10] About the shoes, cf. Euripides, *Orestes* 1370; about the tiara, cf. Herodotus 7.61.
[11] The figurative image of Darius on the Apulian crater known as the Darius Vase, dated around 340–320 BC (Fig. 12) gives an idea of the splendour of such ornaments for a Greek of the 4th century BC.

**Fig. 12:** Detail of the Darios Vase, circa 340–320 BC; Napoli, MAN, n° 81947 [3253] (necropolis of Canosa in 1851).

According to a description by Herodotus, the Persian costume includes, in addition to the military panoply, 'loose caps called tiaras (τιάρας καλεομένους πίλους ἀπαγέας)', colourful sleeved tunics (κιθῶνας χειριδωτοὺς ποικίλους) and pants (ἀναξυρίδας). The costume 'is Median, not Persian'.[12] Indeed as the historian points out 'of all men the Persians most welcome foreign customs. They wear the Median dress (τὴν Μηδικὴν ἐσθῆτα), deeming it more beautiful (καλλίω) than their own'.[13] The historian of the Persians Wars thus emphasizes their sumptuous costumes' beauty.

In Xenophon's *Anabasis*, elites in the Achaemenid Empire are described wearing medo-persian clothing, bracelets and gold scimitars. These are elements of distinction 'adorned by the best of Persians'[14] and honorary gifts.[15]

Thus, among the Barbarians, status and power are expressed by the richness and brilliance of their worn finery.[16]

Returning to the *Persians* of Aeschylus, although the lexical field around ἁβρο- ('delicat-') and χλιδή dominates the descriptions of the Asians, the costume or κόσμος of the Great King and the high Persian dignitaries is not considered distinctively feminine. On the other hand, following the military defeat, the Persians' behaviour, specifically the 'harsh and barbaric' lamentations suppressed by Solon in 594 BC, are, in the view of the Athenians, characteristics of women.[17] And in fact, among the Greek cities, only Lacedaemon honoured its deceased kings in this way:

> The Lacedaemonians have the same custom at the deaths of their kings as have the foreign people of Asia; for the most of the foreigners use the same custom at their kings' deaths. [...] These then and the helots and the Spartans themselves being assembled in one place to the number of many thousands, together with the women, they zealously smite their foreheads and make long and loud lamentation, calling that king that is lateliest dead, whoever he be, the best of all their kings.[18]

So, in the *Persians*, there seems to be a gap between the virility of the Persians displayed in battle[19] and the lamentation and torn clothes that projects feminine excess upon the Great King and all Asia.

---

12  Herodotus 7.61.1 and 7.62.1 (transl. by A.D. Godley, 'Loeb Classical Library', London, 1922).
13  Herodotus 1.135.
14  Xenophon, *Anabasis* 1.8.28–29; cf. also 1.2.27.
15  Cf. also Xenophon, *Anabasis* 1.5.8, on the 'Persian lords' dressed in the porphyry-coloured κάνδυς, and *Cyropedia* 8.3.13; also Herodotus 3.84. See Briant 1996, 282 and 451–55.
16  On the Persian or Iranian concept of dress as empowerment, see Llewellyn-Jones 2015, 235–39.
17  Cf. Plutarch, *Solon* 12.8 and 21.6–7.
18  Herodotus 6.58.
19  Cf. for example, lines 1025–26 where the people of Ionia are described as brave (ἄρειος). In the same way, in Herodotus' account (8.86), before the debacle, the προθυμία ('ardour') characterizes the Persian fighters because they are afraid of the Great King.

Faced with defeat, the only attested abundance is, in fact, that of tears.[20] First, those of Xerxes, as the messenger tells Queen Atossa:

> Xerxes wailed aloud when he saw this depth of disaster; he was seated in plain sight of the whole army, on a high cliff close to the sea. He tore his robes (πέπλοι), uttered a piercing cry of grief, and immediately gave an order to the land army, sending them off in helter-skelter (without adornment: ἀκόσμῳ ξὺν φυγῇ) flight. Such, I tell you, is the disaster you have to mourn, in addition to the previous one.[21]

His complaints are echoed by the long tears of widows characterized by softness and opulence, especially those of laments.[22]

On the other hand, on the clothing side, we are shifting from opulence to deprivation:[23] Xerxes, dressed in a torn κόσμος, has lost his brilliance and therefore his τιμή ('honour'), a sign of the destruction of the splendour and strength of the Persian Empire defeated by the Greeks:[24] 'all the threads of his richly decorated garments are torn and in rags around his body, πάντα γὰρ / κακῶν ὑπ' ἄλγους λακίδες ἀμφὶ σώματι / στημορραγοῦσι ποικίλων ἐσθημάτων.'[25] And, as Atossa states, 'the misfortune that stings [...] most of all is to hear of the dishonourable state (ἀτιμίαν) of the garments that clothe [her] son's body'. For this reason, she leaves to 'take proper attire from the palace', a finery (κόσμον) valuable, in accordance with its status.[26]

---

20 Saïd 1988, 336.
21 Aeschylus, *Persians* 465–71.
22 ἁβροπενθεῖς ('who abandon themselves to a soft /refined/ pain') in lines 135, and ἁβρόγοοι ('softly plaintive') in lines 541 and 532–47. For all of the passage, cf. Aeschylus, Persians 532–47: 'O Zeus the King, now, now by destroying the army of the boastful and populous Persian nation you have covered the city of Susa and Agbatana with a dark cloud of mourning. Many <mothers in a piteous plight> are rending their veils with their delicate hands (ἁπαλαῖς χερσὶ) and wetting the folds of their garments till they are soaked through with tears, as they take their share in the sorrow; and the soft, wailing Persian women who yearn to see the men they lately wedded, abandoning the soft-coverleted (ἁβροχίτωνας) beds they had slept in, the delight of their pampered youth (χλιδανῆς ἥβης), grieve with wailing that is utterly insatiable. And I too shoulder the burden of the death of the departed, truly a theme for mourning far and wide. For now all, yes all, the emptied land of Asia groans'.
23 See Saïd 1988, 336 and 339.
24 See Thalmann 1980; Saïd 1988, 341; Villacèque 2008, 445, n. 8.
25 Aeschylus, *Persians* 834–36.
26 Ibid., 845–50.

Indeed, as noted by Suzanne Saïd, 'the army becomes Xerxes' adornment, its destruction being materialized by the destruction of the royal costume'.[27] Similarly, the elders who compose the chorus on stage cover themselves with rags. Thus Xerxes' gesture tearing his clothes after his defeat (1030: πέπλον δ' ἐπέρρηξ' ἔπι συμφορᾷ κακοῦ) echoes that of the chorus reproduced on the stage at the king's behest in line 1060: 'Tear the folds of your robe with your hands, πέπλον δ' ἔρεικε κολπίαν ἄκμα χερῶν.'[28]

In summary, the distinctiveness of the Medo-Persian relates to excessive luxury, to the abundance of gold and purple, to the χλιδή or τρυφή ('excessive luxury'), the ἁβροσύνη above all oriental; these are all signs of the ὕβρις of its king, therefore of a despotic power and a political model contrary to that of city life.[29] In addition, the people of Asia are described as brave (ἄρειος); they did not flee, unlike Xerxes. In fact, as demonstrated by the lamenting and tearing of clothes in Aeschylus' *Persians*, and by fleeing during battle, a sign of cowardice, at least in Herodotus' *Histories*,[30] it is behaviour, rather than clothing, that feminizes.[31]

The variegated and rich clothing is therefore a characteristic feature of Asian men and women. These are status markers.[32] In addition, these ornaments, because of their brilliance, sometimes turn the head and bewitch. But do they exercise a 'feminine seduction'? Two cases will be considered.

The first, in the tragedies, concerns Helen's fascination with Paris because of the richness of his costume. Thus, in *Trojan Women*, performed in 415 BC, Hecuba

---

27 Saïd 1988, 340.
28 Cf. also Herodotus 8.99.
29 Cf. also Xenophon, *Anabasis* 3.2.25. On the criticism of luxury, see Villacèque 2013, 140–41.
30 Cf. Herodotus 8.88; 8.97 and 8.100. See Giulia Sissa's analysis in this volume.
31 The only notable exception on the Asian side and in the tragic corpus is the one embodied by Dionysus. But he is an Asian god, he is described as a 'foreigner with the appearance of a woman' or as a stranger with a 'multiple beauty' in the *Bacchae* of Euripides (θηλύμορφος ξένος: 53–4; cf. lines 4 and 353; μυριόμορφος). This foreigner from Lydia has, indeed, 'his blond locks reeking of scent, with a face wine-colored and the charm of Aphrodite in his eyes' (*Bacchae* 235–36, transl. by D. Kovacs, 'Loeb Classical Library', London, 2002). On its ambivalence, see also Aeschylus' *Edonoi*, where he is said to be γύννις ('womanish man'), θηλύμορφος, θηλύτης ('effeminacy'), therefore feminine or with effeminate beauty / nature, χλούνης (effeminate; eunuchoid) or δίμορφος, to have a double nature (*TGF*, vol. 3, frs. 61 and 62 Radt; Philochorus of Athens, *FGrH* 328 F7; Lucian, *Dialogues of the gods*, 22(18). 1). See Gherchanoc 2003, 743–44. On Dionysos and 'Anacreontic' vases, see Frontisi-Ducroux/Lissarrague 1983 and 1990.
32 On using the archaeological evidence from the Achaemenid reliefs in order to compare the Persian view with the Greek imagination, see for instance on clothes Rehm 2006, and on royal robe Llewellyn-Jones 2015.

reproached Helen for her behaviour: 'You saw him resplendent in the golden raiment of the East, and your mind became utterly wanton', ὃν εἰσιδοῦσα βαρβάροις ἐσθήμασιν χρυσῷ τε λαμπρὸν ἐξεμαργώθης φρένας.[33] These colourful fabrics arouse desire. Seductive, they exercise an evil power.

The second concerns the fascination shown by Cyrus, if we think of the ceremony and the royal Medo-Persian pomp, which were well studied by Vincent Azoulay:[34]

> We think, furthermore, that we have observed in Cyrus that he held the opinion that a ruler ought to excel his subjects not only in point of being actually better than they, but that he ought also to cast a sort of spell upon them (καταγοητεύειν). At any rate, he chose to wear the Median dress himself and persuaded his associates also to adopt it; for he thought that if anyone had any personal defect, that dress would help to conceal it, and that it made the wearer look very tall and very handsome. For they have shoes of such a form that without being detected the wearer can easily put something into the soles so as to make him look taller than he is. He encouraged also the fashion of pencilling the eyes, that they might seem more lustrous than they are, and of using cosmetics to make the complexion look better than nature made it. He trained his associates also not to spit or to wipe the nose in public, and not to turn round to look at anything, as being men who wondered at nothing. All this he thought contributed, in some measure, to their appearing to their subjects men who could not lightly be despised (δυσκαταφρονητοτέρους). Those, therefore, who he thought ought to be in authority he thus prepared in his own school by careful training as well as by the respect which he commanded as their leader (οὓς μὲν δὴ ἄρχειν ᾤετο χρῆναι, δι' ἑαυτοῦ οὕτω κατεσκεύασε καὶ μελέτῃ καὶ τῷ σεμνῶς προεστάναι αὐτῶν).[35]

Cyrus, as king 'actor', uses artifices (the clothing (στολή) of the Medes, the soles (ὑπόδημα) and the make-up) to hide the possible imperfections of his body in order to make himself stand out in beauty, stature, and majesty — although these artifices are ultimately unnecessary, his body in fact being very beautiful by nature.

---

33 Euripides, *Trojan Women* 991–93 (transl. by D. Kovacs, 'Loeb Classical Library', 1999). Cf. also Euripides, *Cyclops* 182–86: 'She saw the parti-colored breeches (τοὺς θυλάκους τοὺς ποικίλους) on the man's legs and the gold necklace around his neck (τὸν χρύσεον / κλῳὸν) and went all aflutter after them, leaving behind that fine little man Menelaus' (transl. by D. Kovacs, 'Loeb Classical Library', London, 1994); *id.*, *Iphigenia at Aulis*, 73–4: 'The man who judged the goddesses [...] came from Phrygia to Lacedaemon dressed in gaily colored clothing and gleaming with gold jewelry, the luxury of the barbarians', ἀνθηρὸς μὲν εἱμάτων στολῇ χρυσῷ δὲ λαμπρός, βαρβάρῳ χλιδήματι (transl. by D. Kovacs, 'Loeb Classical Library', London, 2002). On the dangers of multi-coloured finery, see Grand-Clément 2011a, 470–73.
34 Azoulay 2004a, 421, and 2004b.
35 Xenophon, *Cyropedia* 8.1.40–43 (transl. by W. Miller, 'Loeb Classical Library', London, 1914).

This embellishment of the king's body 'finalizes a process already initiated by the mere fact of holding power'.[36] In addition, through these artifices, the king bewitches (καταγοητεύειν). We have a concrete application of this transformation a little further on in Xenophon's account of the πομπή ('solemn procession') organized after the capture of Babylon to thank the gods. Indeed, following after the animals and men carrying fire on the high altar, '[...] Cyrus himself upon a chariot attracted attention wearing his tiara upright, a purple tunic shot with white [χιτῶνα πορφυροῦν μεσόλευκον] (no one but the king may wear such a one), trousers of scarlet dye about his legs, and a mantle/κάνδυς all of purple (ἀναξυρίδας ὑσγινοβαφεῖς, καὶ κάνδυν ὁλοπόρφυρον). He had also a fillet about his tiara'. His attire is splendid. In addition, he placed a large but less tall charioteer at his side to look taller and more majestic. So, '[...] when they saw him, they all prostrated themselves before him, either because some had been instructed to begin this act of homage, or because they were stunned by the splendour of his presence, or because Cyrus appeared so great and so goodly to look upon', ἰδόντες δὲ πάντες προσεκύνησαν, εἴτε καὶ ἄρξαι τινὲς κεκελευσμένοι εἴτε καὶ ἐκπλαγέντες τῇ παρασκευῇ καὶ τῷ δόξαι μέγαν τε καὶ καλὸν φανῆναι τὸν Κῦρον. Πρόσθεν δὲ Περσῶν οὐδεὶς Κῦρον προσεκύνει.[37]

He devised this procedure to give himself a more imposing authority (*Cyropedia* 8.3.1) and 'to arrange the procession in a manner that should prove most splendid in the eyes of his loyal friends and most intimidating to those who were disaffected (πῶς ἂν τοῖς μὲν εὔνοις κάλλιστα ἰδεῖν ποιοῖτο τὴν ἐξέλασιν, τοῖς δὲ δυσμενέσι φοβερώτατα)'.[38]

This political ceremony thus theatricalizes the king's great and beautiful presence, and his ability to fascinate by his stature and by the brilliance of his royal clothes. The leader is both an object of desire[39] and dread. However, if the wearing of the Mede costume does not make Cyrus an 'effeminate and luxurious king'[40] — because, in addition, labor (πόνος) and self-control (ἐγκράτεια) characterize his body, according to Xenophon[41] — can we nevertheless affirm that the protocol leads Cyrus to 'incorporate feminine grace without falling into the dangers of the feminine inversion'?[42]

---

36 Azoulay 2004a, 421.
37 Xenophon, *Cyropedia* 8.3.13–14 (Miller's translation slightly modified).
38 *Ibid*., 8.3.5.
39 Azoulay 2004a, 421–23 and 430.
40 *Ibid*., 426; 422.
41 Cf. Xenophon, *Cyropedia* 8.1.36–38; also Ctesias, *Persica*, F8d (3)–(6), on Cyrus' temperance (σωφροσύνη) and virility (ἀνδρεία).
42 Azoulay 2004a, 427.

The attractiveness of the ornaments is certainly harmful and seductive but in no way feminine! At worst, it denotes excessive power, almost corrupted as the Medes are in the eyes of the Persians. This is also the significance of Thucydides' account of King Pausanias of Sparta and his Asian trip, circa 478–477 BC:

> [He] could no longer bring himself to live in the usual manner of his people, but clad himself in Persian apparel (σκευάς τε Μηδικὰς ἐνδυόμενος) whenever he went forth from Byzantium, and when he travelled through Thrace a body-guard of Medes and Egyptians attended him; he had his table served in Persian style (τράπεζάν τε Περσικὴν παρετίθετο), and indeed could not conceal his real purpose, but by such trifling acts showed plainly what greater designs he purposed in his heart to accomplish thereafter. And so he made himself difficult of access, and indulged in such a violent temper towards everybody that no one could come near him; and this was one of the chief reasons why the allies went over to the Athenians.[43]

The adoption of Medo-Persian clothing does not change his gender; it is evidence of his misconduct against the laws of Sparta. This garment, among other things, becomes the symptom of his ὕβρις (excessiveness). He is thus accused of medism and of excessive luxury (τρυφή), which Thucydides associates with his desire to become a tyrant.

Moreover, even the end of the *Cyropedia* of Xenophon, in Book 8.8, about Persian decadence after the death of Cyrus, does not allow us to conclude, categorically, a massive effeminization of the Persians:

> 8. In the next place, as I will now show, they do not care for their physical strength as they used to. [...] [N]ow the custom of refraining from spitting or blowing the nose still continues, but they never give themselves the trouble to work off the moisture in some other direction. [...] 15. Furthermore, they are much more flabby (θρυπτικώτεροι) now than they were in Cyrus's day. For at that time they still adhered to the old education and the old self-control (παιδείᾳ καὶ ἐγκρατείᾳ) that they received from the Persians, but adopted the Median garb and Median luxury (τῇ δὲ Μήδων στολῇ καὶ ἁβρότητι); now, on the contrary, they are allowing the rigour of the Persians (τὴν μὲν ἐκ Περσῶν καρτερίαν) to die out, while they keep up the flabbiness of the Medes (τὴν δὲ τῶν Μήδων μαλακίαν). 16. I should like to explain their slackness (τὴν θρύψιν) more in detail. [...] 27. I think now that I have accomplished the task that I set before myself. For I maintain that I have proved that the Persians of the present day and those living in their dependencies are less reverent toward the gods, less dutiful to their relatives, less upright in their dealings with all men, and less brave in

---

**43** Thucydides 1.130 (transl. by C.F. Smith, 'Loeb Classical Library', London, 1919). Cf. also Diodorus Siculus 11.44.5: 'For Pausanias emulated the luxurious life of the Persians and dealt with his subordinates in the manner of a tyrant', ζηλώσαντος αὐτοῦ τὴν Περσικὴν τρυφὴν καὶ τυραννικῶς προσφερομένου τοῖς ὑποτεταγμένοις (transl. by C.H. Oldfather, 'Loeb Classical Library', London, 1933).

war than they were of old (ἀνανδροτέρους τὰ εἰς τὸν πόλεμον νῦν ἢ πρόσθεν). But if any one should entertain an opinion contrary to my own, let him examine their deeds and he will find that these testify to the truth of my statements.[44]

From this ideological reconstruction of the Achaemenid Empire by Xenophon, it can only be said that the Persians and the peoples under their dependence are less firm, less strong and probably less powerful enemies, which is one way to make them less terrifying. As for the Median garment, if it is emollient, it does not especially feminize. Moreover, this famous Median garment (στολή), invented by Semiramis, is said to be rather unisex and of a neutral gender:

> First of all, then, since she was about to set out upon a journey of many days, she devised a garb which made it impossible to distinguish whether the wearer of it was a man or a woman. This dress was well adapted to her needs, as regards both her travelling in the heat, for protecting the colour of her skin, and her convenience in doing whatever she might wish to do, since it was quite pliable and suitable to a young person, and, in a word, was so attractive that in later times the Medes, who were then dominant in Asia, always wore the garb of Semiramis, as did the Persians after them.[45]

Useful, this garment hides and protects the whiteness of the skin; it is adapted to difficult travels and therefore to the work of war. Finally, it produces *charis* and symbolizes youth. And it 'erases the gender'.[46]

With few exceptions, the luxury of oriental clothing as known by the Greeks since the archaic times has only rarely, if ever, had a gendered connotation. Both

---

44 Xenophon, *Cyropedia* 8.8.8–27 (Miller's translation, modified).
45 Ctesias, *Persica*, FGrHist 688 F1bn 184–189 (according to Diodorus Siculus, 2.6.6): Πρῶτον μὲν οὖν πολλῶν ἡμερῶν ὁδὸν μέλλουσα διαπορεύεσθαι στολὴν ἐπραγματεύσατο δι' ἧς οὐκ ἦν διαγνῶναι τὸν περιβεβλημένον πότερον ἀνήρ ἐστιν ἢ γυνή. Αὕτη δ' ἦν εὔχρηστος αὐτῇ πρός τε τὰς ἐν τοῖς καύμασιν ὁδοιπορίας εἰς τὸ διατηρῆσαι τὸν τοῦ σώματος χρῶτα καὶ πρὸς τὰς ἐν τῷ πράττειν ὃ βούλοιτο χρείας, εὐκίνητος οὖσα καὶ νεανική, καὶ τὸ σύνολον τοσαύτη τις ἐπῆν αὐτῇ χάρις ὥσθ' ὕστερον Μήδους ἡγησαμένους τῆς Ἀσίας φορεῖν τὴν Σεμιράμιδος στολήν, καὶ μετὰ ταῦθ' ὁμοίως Πέρσας.
46 Azoulay/Sebillotte 2011, 117–18. Strabo (1st BC–1st AD) reports a comparable etiology. The Median garment was said to have been introduced into these regions by Medea (hence its name). Designed to hide the face (her gender), it allowed her to appear in public in place of the king Jason with whom she reigned jointly (Strabo, *Geography* 11.13.10). This costume is nevertheless qualified as feminine by the geographer. Until then, Persians had worn light / bare and simple clothes. This feminine garment is presented as the opposite of nudity conceived as a costume (ὥστ' ἀντὶ γυμνητῶν καὶ ψιλῶν θηλυστόλε). Finally, as an impressive garment (σεμνά), it is appropriate for the august and majestic character of a monarchy (τοῦ βασιλικοῦ προσχήματος οἰκεῖα) (*Geography*, 11.13.9).

the look of the old Athenians of the aristocratic elite at the end of the archaic period⁴⁷ and the appearance of the men who won at Marathon with a brilliant (λαμπρός) σχῆμα, who are described wearing long clothes, sea-purple coats, multi-colored/embroidered tunics, headbands, and golden cicadas in their long hair, typical of their taste for τρυφή and ἁβροσύνη, and praised for their bravery, *andreia*, constitute an interesting parallel for this purpose, even if these men characterize another form of otherness for their 'cadets'.⁴⁸

Their costume designates and distinguishes the best men; it is a sign of excellence: 'And it was men like these who won the battle at Marathon and single-handedly defeated the entire Persian army!'⁴⁹ However, it gradually became an ethnic marker during the 5th century BC, a sign of the wealth of the Achaemenid ruler and elite, characteristic of a despotic regime full of ὕβρις. Nevertheless, can we affirm that this ostentation of wealth is artifice — 'debauchery of colours, by make-up, jewellery or fine clothing — so many artifices that incline towards the feminine'?⁵⁰

## 2 The question of the body, and athletic nudity: Barbarians (Asians) with female flesh

In fact, more than these bright and colourful clothes, the nakedness of the bodies seems more like a gender operator. Indeed, the naked body of the Barbarians, unlike their dressed body, lacks radiance. It is unpleasant and laughable, devoid of seduction and eroticism. In this way, a discourse develops aimed at disqualifying an opponent, making him less terrible once he is described/shown naked. In addition, it is remarkable that these stories concern military leaders from

---

**47** Cf. Thucydides' conclusion (1.6.6): 'And one could show that the early Hellenes had many other customs similar to those of the Barbarians of the present day'. Also for Brulé 2007, § 30–2 (= Brulé 2006, 264–65), it is 'almost feminine manners' as opposed to the simple or measured Laconian costume [*metrios*] (264–65) that underlies an idea of equality (see below).
**48** Cf. Aristophanes, *Knights* 1329–34 (on Demos' σχῆμα); *Clouds* 984–6; *Wasps* 1450–55; Heracleides of Pontus *apud* Athenaeus 12.512a–c. See Bowra 1957, 399–400; Kurke 1992, 102; also Darbo-Peschanski 1989 on temporality among ancient historians and the association between the old Athenians and the Persians in the classical period.
**49** Heracleides of Pontus *apud* Athenaeus 12.512c (transl. by S.D. Olson, 'Loeb Classical Library', London, 2010).
**50** Grand-Clément 2011b, 260.

Sparta, the first city to adopt a 'simple outfit (μέτριος)' and where men practice naked, according to Thucydides.[51]

Thus Agesilaus, in his Asian campaign between 396 and 394 BC, to encourage his soldiers during the war he waged against the satrap of Lydia, Tissaphernes, compared the Barbarians to women:

> Moreover, believing that contempt for the enemy would kindle the fighting spirit, he gave instructions to his heralds that the barbarians captured in the raids should be exposed for sale naked. So when his soldiers saw them white (λευκοὺς) because they never stripped, and fat and lazy (πίονας δὲ καὶ ἀπόνους) through constant riding in carriages, they believed that the war would be exactly like fighting with women (εἰ γυναιξὶ δέοι μάχεσθαι).[52]

The white complexion, as well as oily and soft flesh, expresses the otherness of the Barbarians. The colour of their skin as well as their weight and lack of vigour and strength — and therefore, softness — are explained by the fact that Barbarians never disrobe; unlike the Greeks, they do not exercise naked. They do not go to the gymnasium; they do not know the πόνος of training. So this difference is presented as a specifically distinctive feature of the Greeks and Barbarians.[53] The latter therefore constitute counter-models to the virile 'athletic' beauty of trained, naked, and Greek bodies. Their beauty and their related characteristics are therefore artificial and fragile. Once naked, only barbarian male bodies remain ἄπονοι ('lazy'), ἀγύμναστοι ('unexercised') and ἄνανδροι ('without virility') similar to those of women.[54]

Around 346 BC, Isocrates used similar arguments to support a military alliance between Philip II of Macedonia and the Greeks against the Persians. He says about the battle of Cunaxa (401 BC):

> I, however, am not going to urge you on such grounds, but by the example of men who were looked upon as failures: I mean those who took the field with Cyrus and Clearchus. Every one agrees that these won as complete a victory in battle over all the forces of the King as if they had come to blows with their womenfolk (ὅσονπερ ἂν εἰ ταῖς γυναιξὶν αὐτῶν συνέβαλον), but that at the very moment when they seemed to be masters of the field they failed of

---

51 Thucydides 1.6.4–5.
52 Xenophon, *Agesilaus* 1.28 (transl. by E.C. Marchant, G.W. Bowersock, 'Loeb Classical Library', London, 1925); cf. *Hellenica*, 3.4.19.
53 Cf. Plato, *Republic* 5.452a–e.
54 Cf. Hippocrates, *Diseases of Women* 1, 1.13, about women with more flaccid (ἀραιοσαρκοτέρη) and softer (ἀπαλωτέρη) flesh than men. On πολυσαρκία ('extreme fatness') and εὐσαρκία ('well-fleshed flesh'), see Karila-Cohen 2012. On the whiteness of the skin, see Grand-Clément 2007.

success, owing to the impetuosity of Cyrus. For he in his exultation rushed in pursuit far in advance of the others; and, being caught in the midst of the enemy, was killed.[55]

This *topos* about the barbarian body is used in both military and political contexts. In this respect, an episode in the story of Naucleides of Sparta that can be dated back to the end of the 5th century BC is of interest:

> The same author reports in Book XXVII that in Sparta it was regarded as an extraordinary disgrace, if a person seemed to have a relatively unmanly build or a large potbelly (εἴ τις ἢ τὸ σχῆμα ἀνανδρότερον ἔχων ἢ τὸν ὄγκον τοῦ σώματος προπετῆ ἐφαίνετο), and that the ephors inspected the young men in the nude every ten days [...]. So too in Book XXVII Agatharchides (2nd BC) reported that because Naucleides the son of Polybiades became extremely corpulent and fat, as a result of his addiction to luxury (ὑπερσαρκοῦντα τῷ σώματι καὶ παχὺν διὰ τρυφὴν γενόμενον), the Spartans made him stand in the middle of the Assembly; and after Lysander criticized him at length in public for his [excessive] behaviour (ὡς τρυφῶντι), they all but kicked him out of the city, and threatened to actually do so, unless he straightened out his life. Because Lysander said that when Agesilaus was spending time in the Hellespont fighting the barbarians, he saw that the Asiatics were wearing expensive clothing (ὁρῶν τοὺς Ἀσιαγενεῖς ταῖς μὲν στολαῖς πολυτελῶς ἠσκημένους), but had correspondingly unimpressive physiques (τοῖς σώμασιν δ' οὕτως ἀχρείους ὄντας). He accordingly ordered his men to strip all their prisoners-of-war and take them to the auction block, but to sell their clothing separately, so that the allies would recognize that they were struggling for great prizes, but that the contest was against unimpressive men (εὐτελεῖς), and would feel more eager (προθυμότερον) to attack their enemies.[56]

Dressed barbarians remain impressive by the splendour of their clothes; naked, quite the opposite. In addition, there is an explicit relationship between the body, τιμή and citizenship. At the end of the 5th century BC, an excessive corpulence, out of the ordinary, is a sign of τρυφή, a lifestyle that is appropriate to (qualifies) a barbarian more than a Greek, especially when the latter is Lacedaemonian. During the 2nd–3rd centuries AD, Aelian, reporting the laws and customs of the Lacedaemonians establishes the parallel: 'They threatened [Naucleides] with the additional punishment of exile if he did not for the future change his habits, which were the subject of criticism and Ionian rather than Spartan. They claimed his appearance and physical condition brought disgrace on Sparta and its laws.'[57]

The citizen's ability to represent the ideals of the city can be read on his body; he must be 'well conformed and robust' and not large and flaccid; citizenship is

---

55 Isocrates 5. *To Philip* 90 (transl. by G. Norlin, 'Loeb Classical Library', London, 1928).
56 Athenaeus 12.550c–f.
57 Aelian, *Historical Miscellany* 14.7 (transl. by N.G. Wilson, 'Loeb Classical Library', London, 1997).

incorporated. A non-virile skin colour, therefore a pale complexion, associated with excessive weight and a wrong diet stigmatize and designate the ἄπονοι, those who do not exercise properly in the gymnasium or feed themselves in moderation.[58] However, when one belongs to the group of those who call themselves the 'Similar', one cannot distinguish oneself by one's body.[59] For, in particular, such a body contradicts the virility and ardour expected in combat.

This *topos* has a long life. It was taken up again in the 2nd century AD by Lucian in a fictional dialogue which take place in the 6th century BC between the Athenian archon, Solon, and the Scythian philosopher king Anacharsis, about the comparative values of the Greeks and the Barbarians: unlike women and the Barbarians, among the Greeks, young people 'show no white and ineffective corpulence (οὐ πολυσαρκίαν ἀργὸν καὶ λευκὴν) or pallid leanness (ἀσαρκίαν μετὰ ὠχρότητος), as if they were women's bodies bleached out in the shade'.[60]

Finally, if social practices justify these bodily differences, geography and climate are additional factors that may explain them. This environmental theory, opposing Asia and Europe through the physical aspect/beauty (μορφή) of peoples, is present in Hippocratic discourses:

> So much for the changes of the seasons. Now I intend to compare Asia and Europe, and to show how they differ in every respect, and how the nations of the one differ entirely in physique (περὶ τῶν ἐθνέων τῆς μορφῆς) from those of the other. It would take too long to describe them all, so I will set forth my views about the most important and the greatest differences. I hold that Asia differs very widely from Europe in the nature of all its inhabitants and of all its vegetation. 2. For everything in Asia grows to far greater beauty and size; the one region is less wild than the other, the character of the inhabitants is milder and more gentle (πολὺ γὰρ καλλίονα καὶ μείζονα πάντα γίγνεται ἐν τῇ Ἀσίῃ· ἥ τε χώρη τῆς χώρης ἡμερωτέρη, καὶ τὰ ἤθεα τῶν ἀνθρώπων ἠπιώτερα καὶ εὐοργητότερα). The cause of this is the temperate climate, because it lies towards the east midway between the risings of the sun, and farther away than is Europe from the cold.

So the men have very handsome bodies there; they are well nourished, of very fine physique and very tall. [...] But '6. Courage, endurance, industry and high spirit could not arise in such conditions (Τὸ δὲ ἀνδρεῖον καὶ τὸ ταλαίπωρον καὶ τὸ ἔμπονον καὶ τὸ θυμοειδὲς οὐκ ἂν δύναιτο ἐν τοιαύτῃ φύσει ἐγγίγνεσθαι)'.[61]

---

58 See Gherchanoc 2020, forthcoming.
59 See Powell 2009, 75.
60 Lucian, *Anacharsis, or Athletics* 25 (transl. by A.M. Harmon, 'Loeb Classical Library', London, 1925).
61 Hippocrates, *Airs, Waters, Places* 12.1–6 (transl. by W.H.S. Jones, 'Loeb Classical Library', London, 1923).

Thus, the praise of the middle part of Asia is tempered by a reservation about the character of these so-called 'war unfit' peoples. Indeed, softness (12.2: ἠπιώτερα) is not compatible with courage, endurance, a taste for effort and ardour. These are the qualities of Europeans. And this lack of fighting is further explained by a bad political regime: Asians are subjected to kings.[62]

A similar idea can be found in the conclusion of Herodotus' account: "Soft lands breed soft men; wondrous fruits of the earth and valiant warriors grow not from the same soil (φιλέειν γὰρ ἐκ τῶν μαλακῶν χώρων μαλακοὺς γίνεσθαι· οὐ γάρ τι τῆς αὐτῆς γῆς εἶναι καρπόν τε θωμαστὸν φύειν καὶ ἄνδρας ἀγαθοὺς τὰ πολέμια)'. Thereat the Persians saw that Cyrus reasoned better than they, and they departed from before him, choosing rather to be rulers on a barren mountain side than slaves dwelling in tilled valleys.'[63] Thus ends the *Persias Wars*: on the bravery of the Persians.

If the garment is indeed an identity marker, it is also more than a 'simple' ethnic marker. For the Persians, virile and athletic nudity is inconceivable. Clothes, their wealth and beauty, are markers of a high social and political status, of their belonging to the elite. The sumptuous costumes do not take away courage and virility from those who wear them. Moreover, a naked body is not exposed. Those who are naked are the slaves.

On the other hand, for the Greeks, athletic nudity means virility and beauty; the Barbarians, since they do not exercise in the gymnasium, have white skin and fatty and soft bodies, without strength, which makes them beings similar to women.

These two types of bodily and clothing practices refer to two political models: the city, on the one hand, and barbaric despotism, on the other. Nevertheless, the Greeks, and in particular the Athenians, can play with the Other or tame him by dressing in Persian clothes and appreciating the 'perseries' because these exotic fabrics did not especially feminize or effeminize them, particularly because their bodies, in theory, responded to Greek ideals of masculinity.

Lastly, if Persian clothing builds an artificial beauty, possibly fascinating and seductive, ancient authors do not directly or necessarily associate it with female beauty.

---

[62] Jouanna 1981; cf. *Airs, Waters, Places* 16.1, on the lack of ardour and courage among Asians (Περὶ δὲ τῆς ἀθυμίης τῶν ἀνθρώπων καὶ τῆς ἀνανδρείης) that make them unfit for war (ἀπολεμώτεροι) compared to Europeans. 'For these reasons, I think, Asiatics are feeble. Their institutions are a contributory cause, the greater part of Asia being governed by kings (διὰ ταύτας ἐμοὶ δοκέει τὰς προφάσιας ἄναλκες εἶναι τὸ γένος τὸ Ἀσιηνόν· καὶ προσέτι διὰ τοὺς νόμους. Τῆς γὰρ Ἀσίης τὰ πολλὰ βασιλεύεται)'. See also Aristotle, *Politics* 7.7.1–3.
[63] Herodotus 9.122.

# Works Cited

Azoulay, V. (2004a), *Xénophon et les grâces du pouvoir. De la* charis *au charisme*, Paris.
Azoulay, V. (2004b), 'The Medo-Persian Ceremonial: Xenophon, Cyrus and the King's Body', in: Chr. J. Tuplin (ed.), *Xenophon and his World*, Stuttgart, 147–73.
Azoulay, V./Sébillotte, V. (2011), 'Sexe, genre et politique: le vêtement comme opérateur dans les *Persica* de Ctésias', in: L. Bodiou/F. Gherchanoc/V. Huet/V. Mehl (eds.), *Parures et artifices: le corps exposé dans l'Antiquité*, Paris, 113–28.
Barth, Fr. (1969 [2008²]), 'Introduction à l'ouvrage *Ethnic Groups and Boundaries*', in: Ph. Poutignat/J. Streiff-Fenart (eds.), *Théories de l'ethnicité*, Paris, 203–49.
Bichler, R. (2001), *Herodots Welt. Der Aufbau der Historie am Bild der fremden Länder und Völker, ihrer Zivilisation und ihrer Geschichte*, Berlin.
Borello, C./Pollini, A. (eds.) (2015), *Questions d'appartenance. Les identités de l'Antiquité à nos jours*, Paris.
Bowra, C.M. (1957), 'Asius and the old-fashioned Samians', *Hermes* 85/4, 391–401.
Briant, P. (1996), *Histoire de l'Empire perse. De Cyrus à Alexandre*, Paris.
Brulé, P. (2006), 'Les codes du genre et les maladies de l'*andreia* : rencontres entre structure et histoire dans l'Athènes classique', in: J.-M. Bertrand (dir.), *La violence dans les mondes grec et romain*, Paris, 247–57.
Brulé, P. (2007), 'Les codes du genre et les maladies de l'*andreia* : rencontres entre structure et histoire dans l'Athènes classique', in: *La Grèce d'à côté: Réel et imaginaire en miroir en Grèce antique*, Rennes, 103–20 (https://books.openedition.org/pur/6223?lang=fr#bodyftn1).
Cartledge, P. (1993), *The Greek, A portrait of Self and Other*, Oxford/New York.
Casevitz M. (2004), 'Étude lexicologique: du *schêma* au schématisme', in: M.S. Celentano/ P. Chiron/M.-P. Noël (eds.), Skhema. Figura. *Formes et figures chez les anciens. Rhétorique, philosophie, littérature*, Paris, 15–30.
Cohen, B. (2001), 'Ethnic Identity in Democratic Athens and the Visual Vocabulary of Male Costume', in: I. Malkin (ed.), *Ancient Perceptions of Greek Ethnicity*, Washington DC, 235–74.
Courrént, M. (2007), 'De l'humidité au soleil: le corps des peuples dans la littérature gréco-latine', in: P. Carmignani/M. Courrént/Th. Éloi/J. Thomas (eds.), *Le corps dans les cultures méditerranéennes*, Perpignan, 43–57.
Eicher, J.B. (1995), *Dress and Ethnicity. Change accross Space and Time*, Oxford.
Frontisi-Ducroux, Fr. (2003), 'La beauté en question', *Uranie* 10, 33–53.
Frontisi-Ducroux, Fr./Lissarrague, Fr. (1983), 'De l'ambiguïté à l'ambivalence : un parcours dionysiaque', *AION Arch St* V, 11–32.
Frontisi-Ducroux, Fr./Lissarrague, Fr. (1990), 'From ambiguity to ambivalence: a Dionysiac excursion through the "Anakreontic" vases', in: D.M. Halperin/J.J. Winkler/F.I. Zeitlin (dir.), *Before Sexuality: the Construction of Erotic Experience in the Ancient Greek World*, Princeton, 211–56.
Georges, P. (1994), *Barbarian Asia and Greek Experience. From Archaic Period to the Age of Xenophon*, Baltimore/London.
Gherchanoc, F., 'Les atours féminins des hommes: quelques représentations du masculin/féminin dans le monde grec antique. Entre initiation, ruse, séduction et grotesque, surpuissance et déchéance', *Revue historique* CCCV/4, 739–91.

Gherchanoc, F. (2008), 'Nudités athlétiques et identités en Grèce ancienne', in: F. Gherchanoc/ V. Huet (eds.), *S'habiller, se déshabiller dans les mondes anciens*, Mètis N. S. 6, 75–101.

Gherchanoc, F. (2020), 'De beaux corps, "ni trop maigres, ni trop gras", en Grèce ancienne', in: E. Galbois/S. Rougier-Blanc (eds.), *Maigreur et minceur dans les sociétés anciennes. Grèce, Orient, Rome*, Bordeaux, 2020, 113–24.

Grand-Clément, A. (2007), 'Blancheur et altérité : le corps des femmes et des vieillards en Grèce ancienne', *Corps* 3, 32–9.

Grand-Clément, A. (2011a), *La fabrique des couleurs. Histoire du paysage sensible des Grecs anciens (VIIIe s.– début du Ve s. av. n. è.)*, Paris.

Grand-Clément, A. (2011b), 'Du bon usage du vêtement bariolé en Grèce ancienne', in: L. Bodiou/F. Gherchanoc/V. Huet/V. Mehl (dir.), *Parures et artifices: le corps exposé dans l'Antiquité*, Paris, 255–73.

*Grecs et Barbares* (1962), 'Entretiens sur l'antiquité classique' (Fondation Hardt), Genève/Vandoeuvres.

Gruen, E.S. (2011), *Rethinking the Other in Antiquity*, Princeton/Oxford.

Gunter, A.C. (2009), *Greek Art and the Orient*, Cambridge.

Hall, E. (1989), *Inventing the Barbarian. Greek Self-Definition Through Tragedy*, Oxford.

Hall, J.M. (1997), *Ethnic identity in greek Antiquity*, Cambridge.

Hall, J.M. (2002), *Hellenicity: between ethnicity and culture*, Chicago.

Hartog, Fr. (1980), *Le miroir d'Hérodote. Essai sur la représentation de l'autre*, Paris.

Iriarte, A. (2007), 'Le genre des habits et le tissage de la nudité', in: V. Sébillotte Cuchet/N. Ernoult (eds.), *Problèmes du genre en Grèce ancienne*, Paris, 299–300.

Jacob, Chr. (2017 [1991]), *Géographie et ethnographie en Grèce ancienne*, Paris.

Jouanna, J. (1981), 'Les causes de la défaite des Barbares chez Eschyle, Hérodote et Hippocrate', *Ktéma* 6, 3–15.

Karila-Cohen, K. (2012), 'Les gourmands grecs sont-ils bien en chair?', in: K. Karila-Cohen/ F. Quellier (dir.), *Le corps gourmand d'Héraclès à Alexandre le Bienheureux*, Rennes/ Tours, 121–27.

Kurke, L. (1992), 'The Politics of ἁβροσύνη in Archaic Greece', *Classical Antiquity* 11/1, 91–120.

Lenfant, D. (2001), 'Mélange ethnique et emprunts culturels : leur perception et leur valeur dans l'Athènes classique', in: V. Fromentin/S. Gotteland (eds.), *Origines gentium*, Bordeaux, 59–78.

Lissarrague, Fr. (1990), *L'autre guerrier*, Paris/Rome.

Lissarrague, Fr. (2002), 'The Athenian Image of the Foreigner', in: Th. Harrison, *Greeks and Barbarians*, Edinburgh, 101–24.

Llewellyn-Jones, L. (2015), 'That My Body is Strong': the physique and appearance of the Achaemenid Monarch', in: F. Wascheck/H.A. Shapiro (eds.), *Fluide Körper — Bodies in Transition*, Köln, 211–48.

Luce, J.-M. (ed.) (2007), *Identités ethniques dans le monde grec antique*, Pallas 73.

Malkin, I. (ed.) (2001), *Ancient Perceptions of Greek Ethnicity*, Washington DC/Cambridge.

Malkin, I./Müller, Chr. (2012), 'Vingt ans d'ethnicité: bilan historiographique et application du concept aux études anciennes', in: L. Capdetrey/J. Zurbach (eds.), *Mobilités grecques. Mouvements, réseaux, contacts en Méditerranée de l'époque archaïque à l'époque hellénistique*, Bordeaux, 23–35.

McInerney, J. (2014), *A Companion to Ethnicity in the Ancient Mediterranean*, Oxford.

Miller, M.C. (1997), *Athens and Persia. A Study in Cultural Receptivity*, Cambridge.

Müller, Chr. (2014), 'Introduction: *La fin de l'ethnicité ?*', in: Chr. Müller/A.E. Veïsse (eds.), *Identité ethnique et culture matérielle*, *Dialogues d'Histoire Ancienne*, Supplément 10, 15–33.

Papadopoulou, M. (2013), 'The terme "Schema" as Garb; Two Incompatible Notions', *Verbal and Nonverbal Representation in Terminology. Proceedings of the TOTh Workshop on Terminology and Ontology: Theories and Applications*, Copenhagen 8 November 2013, 133–46.

Perrin, Y./Nourisson, D. (eds.) (2005), *Le barbare, l'étrange : images de l'autre*, Saint-Etienne.

Powell, A. (2009), 'Sparte : comment déchiffrer ses idéaux ?', in: L. Bodiou/V. Mehl/J. Oulhen/Fr. Prost/J. Wilgaux (dir.), *Chemin faisant : mythes, cultes et société en Grèce ancienne. Mélanges en l'honneur de Pierre Brulé*, Rennes, 71–86.

Rehm, E. (2006), 'Purpur und Gold, die persische Tracht', in: A. Koch/E. Rehm (eds.), *Das persische Weltreich. Pracht und Prunk der Großkönige*, Stuttgart, 202–9.

Saïd, S. (1988), 'Tragédie et renversement. L'exemple des *Perses*', *Mètis* 3, 321–41 (doi : https://doi.org/10.3406/metis.1988.919).

Sparkes, B. (1997), 'Some Greek images of Others', in: B.L. Molyneaux (ed.), *The Cultural Life of Images: Visual Representation in Archaeology*, London, 130–58.

Thalmann, C.W. (1980), 'Xerxes' Rags. Some Problems in Aeschylus' *Persians*', *American Journal of Philology* 101, 260–82.

Tuplin, Chr. (1996), *Achaemenid Studies*, Stuttgart [= *Historia Einzelschriften* 99].

Villacèque, N. (2008), 'Histoire de la ποικιλία, un mode de reconnaissance sociale dans la démocratie athénienne', *Revue des Études Anciennes* 110, 443–59.

Villacèque, N. (2013), 'Des palais éclaboussés d'or. La dramatisation du luxe dans l'Athènes classique', in: M.P. Castiglioni/M.-C. Ferriès/Fr. Létoublon (eds.), *Forgerons, élites et voyageurs d'Homère à nos jours, Hommages en mémoire d'Isabelle Ratinaud-Lachkar*, Grenoble, 127–45.

Wiesehöfer, J. (2004), 'Persien, der faszinierende Feind der Griechen', in: R. Rollinger/C. Ulf (eds.), *Commerce and Monetary system in the Ancient World. Means of Transmission and cultural Interaction*, Stuttgart, 295–310.

Wiesehöfer, J. (2009), 'Greeks and Persians', in: K.A. Raaflaub/H. van Wees (eds.), *Companion to Archaic Greece*, Oxford, 162–85.

## Part II: Gender, Political Leaders and Ethnic Identity

Giulia Sissa
# What Artemisia Knew: The Political Intelligence of Artemisia of Halicarnassus

> A king sate on the rocky brow
> Which looks o'er sea-born Salamis;
> And ships, by thousands, lay below,
> And men in nations; — all were his!
> He counted them at break of day —
> And when the sun set, where were they?
>
> Lord Byron, *The Isles of Greece*, 19–23.

Artemisia of Halicarnassus in Herodotus' *Histories* has attracted increasing scholarly interest.[1] In one way or another, this rich scholarship focuses on the strangeness of a female military command and on Xerxes' surprise at Artemisia's tactical intelligence. At the battle of Salamis, caught between her allied ships sailing ahead of her, and an Athenian trireme commanded by Aminias of Pallene on her tail, Artemisia gives the order to sink one of her allies' ships. Aminias reckons that the attacking boat must be on the same side as his own. As a result, he stops chasing Artemisia. On the Persian side, when the king and his advisors see the queen and recognize her vessel, Xerxes delights in her feat. She has brilliantly managed to lose her pursuers. 'My women have become men!' he claims. 'My men have become women!' (Οἱ μὲν ἄνδρες γεγόνασί μοι γυναῖκες, αἱ δὲ γυναῖκες ἄνδρες).[2] It's the world upside down. It's a woman who leads the game, who commands and wins. You wouldn't expect it because, of course, women are not cut out for it. Xerxes himself provokes his readers to marvel at these permutations, which certainly deserve our full attention.

---

**1** Weil 1976, 215–31; Rossellini/Saïd 1978, 949–1005; Hornblower 1982; Jouanna 1984, 15–26; Munson 1988, 91–106; Tourraix 1990, 377–86; Lateiner 1990, 230–46; Martyn 1998, 15–26; Blok 2002, 225–42; Harrell 2003, 77–94; Payen 2015, 214–27; Sebillotte Cuchet 2008, 15–33; Penrose 2016; Gera 1997; Hoffmann 2010, 1–31; Visconti 2002, 63–75; Iriarte 2013, 95–116; Lockwood forthcoming. I am grateful to Malika Bastin-Hammou, Michel Briand, Rose Cherubin, Charles Delattre, Therese Fuhrer, Irene Han, Ana Iriarte, Bryant Kirkland, Adrienne Mayor, Jordi Redondo, Livio Rossetti, and to the anonymous reviewers for their helpful input.
**2** Hdt. 8.87–8. Herodotus will be quoted from *The Persian Wars*, Loeb Classical Library, my translation.

If we place ourselves in the position of the Athenians – these warrior citizens, exclusively and rigorously male, who govern themselves, in what is called a democracy – we can affirm, with Violaine Sebillotte Cuchet, that Artemisia's 'appearance at Salamis contradicts the Athenian gender order which institutes that men are always superior to women by confining (or claiming to confine) women to the world of childbirth.'[3] It is from an Athenian point of view that the feat of Artemisia is a θῶμα, whereas the 'Persian perspective' is compatible with the audacity of a woman in power.[4]

Herodotus of Halicarnassus highlights the complexity of a situation that stems, first of all, from the fact that the Persian Empire is fighting a coalition of Greek cities, some of which are composed of mixed populations and are allied with the Great King. Located on the Ionian coast, Halicarnassus (now Bodrum) is, according to Herodotus, a border city, more precisely a colony of Trezene and Epidauros, subject to the Persian Empire, and which participates in the war as an ally of the Persians. Secondly, Artemisia herself is the daughter of a Carian father and a Cretan mother.[5] Carian and Cretan, half Greek in consequence, but faithful to the Great King, woman of political and military power, queen, and admiral, Artemisia is a multicultural, social, and gendered mosaic. All this, I said at the outset, has been the subject of careful study.

I wish to build on the existing scholarship, and to offer an additional insight. Since Herodotus places Artemisia first in the decision-making drama that precedes the Battle of Salamis, and then in the urgency of determining a course of action after the debacle, we must question his narrative montage. And this is not only a principled appeal to the text, but the attempt to understand the construction of Artemisia's character and the logic of her deliberate action. The attribution of multiple qualities to Artemisia, in what we would now describe as the intersection of gender and ethnicity, is achieved verbatim in the staging of a strong character, able to speak and act, which presupposes a marked ability to think in a reasonable and practical way. Herodotus has no problem assigning a fully-functional deliberative faculty – what Aristotle will call τὸ βουλευτικόν – to a woman; this is especially striking as the author of the *Politics* will, a century later, insist that the βουλευτικόν is 'without authority' (ἄκυρον) in women.[6] This

---

[3] Sebillotte Cuchet 2008, 29. See also Harrell 2003, 77–94.
[4] Penrose 2016, 159–61. I too have proposed a polyphonic reading of the *Histories*, especially about the constitutional debate in Book 3, in Sissa 2012, 227–61.
[5] Hdt. 7.99.
[6] Arist. *Pol.*, 1.1260a.13–14. Aristotle is quoted from *Politics*, Loeb Classical Library, my translation; see Sissa 2018, 141–76.

woman is perfectly equipped, better than her Great King who, in turn, is certainly not feminized by his Persian identity, and even better than her Athenian chaser, Aminias. She is in the same league as Themistocles. The intersections are much more subtle.[7] Thus, beyond the tactical prodigy in the waters of Salamis, we need to understand better the role played by the Queen of Halicarnassus, when she sets foot on the ground and takes her rightful place in the design of the story.

# 1 What Artemisia knew

The Battle of Salamis of September 480 BCE is not merely a military episode among others; it is the catastrophe that makes Xerxes understand that he has lost not only a battle, but the war. He now must retreat — to the Ionian coasts, and finally to the Hellespont. The conquest of the West, the great dream of his father, Darius, which had become his own, has proved to be impossible. The Greek campaign has ended in complete failure. He will never try to conquer the Greek cities again. Salamis is the point of no return. All that remains is to limit the damage. Now, in the narrative montage, Artemisia intervenes with her advice before and after this turning point, thus framing a battle that is the most momentous of all. The event around which Herodotus organizes the entire storyline of the *Histories*, is set between two demonstrations of this woman's intelligence.

Before the battle, Artemisia explains to the king how she thinks the enemy might ultimately defeat him. If Xerxes does not rush into a sea battle, but instead attacks the Peloponnese, he will easily achieve his objectives. For the Greeks, she predicts, will disperse their forces and flee, city by city. According to her information, she goes on to say, they do not have any supplies on the island of Salamis, nor do they consider it their territory. Were the king to send his troops against the Peloponnese, it would be unlikely that a Peloponnesian army would be prepared to defend Athens. If, on the contrary, Xerxes were to launch a naval

---

[7] On Herodotus' representation of gender in non-Greek societies, I generally agree with Boedeker 2011, 211–35. Boedeker pays due attention to complexity, surprise and irony in Herodotus' thought about women. I also share the conclusions of Dewald, in her systematic and path-breaking article, Dewald (1981, 93–127 now in Munson 2013, 151–79), especially on the acknowledgement of women's wisdom. Tamyris and Artemisia, 'like other women we have noted, take pains to articulate the moral and political basis for their actions. Both see, as their Persian and male counterparts do not, that human power has its limitations; both predict defeat for the Persian if he oversteps these bounds,' (Dewald 1981, 111). The argument of this paper starts precisely from this superiority.

battle now, his fleet would be destroyed, followed by his infantry. 'Why take the risk of naval action?', Artemisia asks the King. 'Do you not hold Athens, which is the particular objective of your campaign, and do you not control the rest of Greece?'[8] And she warns him that, at sea: 'Those men are stronger than your men, as much as men are stronger than women' (οἱ γὰρ ἄνδρες τῶν σῶν ἀνδρῶν κρέσσονες τοσοῦτο εἰσὶ κατὰ θάλασσαν ὅσον ἄνδρες γυναικῶν).[9] Xerxes refuses to listen to her. The battle takes place and ends exactly as she had predicted, with the destruction of the Persian fleet in the straits of Salamis. After the battle, Artemisia once again advises the Great King: the Persian army should now retreat. This time, Xerxes agrees.[10]

Herodotus gives Artemisia a role as decisive as the battle itself. He casts her as the only person who might have prevented the battle from being fought in the first place. Before and after the defeat, it is she, and only she, who knows what to do.

The dialogues between Xerxes and Artemisia are part of a series of typical scenes of moments of uncertainty, deliberation and counsel.[11] There are many advisors, according to Herodotus, in the entourage of the Persian kings. Remember the debate between Xerxes, Mardonios and Artabanus before the expedition.[12] Consider Xerxes' questioning of his guest, the self-exiled Spartan king, Demaratus,[13] in which Xerxes asks him for information about the Greeks and finally bursts out laughing at his warnings about how dangerous they are. Even before Darius came to power, the famous "Constitutional Debate" among the Persian nobles over the best political regime for the empire had been an exchange of opinions (without follow-up).[14] Herodotus' narrative construction proceeds from one crossroads to another, from one uncertainty to another — from one path not taken to another, from one underestimated exhortation to another. Rarely listened to, advisors open counterfactual perspectives. Artemisia, for sure, is in good company.

But although she is not the only councillor to a king, she is unique. No other advisor intervenes twice, and in this way: first intelligently but in vain, then wisely again and, at last, successfully. The focus on what Artemisia *knew* should guide our reading. To understand the character's place in the narrative means to

---

8 Hdt. 8.68–9.
9 Hdt. 8.68.
10 Hdt. 8.101–3.
11 Lattimore 1939, 24–35.
12 Hdt. 7.8–16.
13 Hdt. 7.101–7.
14 Hdt. 3.80–3.

understand the impact of her superlative knowledge — quick-wittedness, empirical information, and clairvoyance in Herodotus' overall vision of the war. Let us look at this specificity.

First of all, in the melee, as commander of her ship and in the heat of the moment, Artemisia acts as a fine tactician. Her success demonstrates a tremendous ability to seize an opportunity and devise expedients in a moment of danger. Is it by chance that a Calyndian ship cut her off, forcing her to ram it? Did she callously calculate the strategic benefits of a treacherous attack, being ready to sacrifice one of her own allies? Did she take advantage of the confusion to settle her score with the commander of the ship, the Calyndian king, Damasithymos, with whom a conflict might have arisen?[15] Herodotus asks these questions only to leave them open. Accident, machination or revenge? Each implies a clever, resourceful and cunning handling of the situation, on the spot. Alexandre Tourraix rightly associates this sharp wit with the kind of intelligence called μῆτις.[16]

This trick does not change the course of the war. With or without Artemisia, the Athenians prevailed, thanks to their good order of battle, as we shall see in a moment. If the Athenian commander who chased Artemisia's ship had captured the Queen of Halicarnassus, he would have added only an extra trophy to the glory of the Athenians. But Herodotus amplifies the importance of this striking episode. It is Artemisia's ingenuity that matters in the event. And her cleverness also reveals, by contrast, the mistakes of all the other characters involved. On the one hand, Aminias of Pallene rightly surmises that the ship which has been sunk must belong to a Persian ally but takes for granted that the boat of the attacker, which he is unable to recognize, must belong to his own side, or to a 'deserter from the Barbarians fighting for the Greeks'.[17] On the other hand, the Persians who watch the battle from Mount Elaios identify Artemisia's flag, but obviously not the Calyndians', therefore supposing that she must have destroyed an enemy, not a friend.[18] On both sides, these men only see one boat at a time. In haste, they all make bad inferences.

In addition, they apply their gender biases. The Athenians, as ever dogmatic in their expectations about women, had offered a prize of ten thousand drachmas to the one who would take this female warrior alive. Aminias of Pallene would

---

**15** Hdt. 8.87.
**16** Tourraix 1990, 377–86. The use of cunning does not create a 'contradiction' between the courage of Artemisia and her tactical cleverness, as Tank (2019, 74–88) argues. The simple fact that Artemisia takes up the challenge of war shows her ἀνδρεία. Sinking a boat does so as well.
**17** Hdt. 8.87.
**18** Hdt. 8.88.

certainly not have let Artemisia's ship escape, Herodotus explains, if only he had known that she was in command.[19] But the Athenian fails to ask himself who might be in charge of the mysterious trireme he is chasing as if the admiral of an unknown galley had to be a man by default. He fails to doubt. He misses the opportunity. As for the Persians, they rejoice in Artemisia's manly bravery. She has sunk an enemy vessel, they believe, and she has also eluded her pursuers. She cannot possibly be a woman any longer. 'My men have become women', the Great King says, 'and my women men'.[20] The narrator seems to be savouring this double misunderstanding, while his queen is cruising ahead.

This singular achievement illustrates Artemisia's practical intelligence, and yet represents only one aspect of her talents. It's a stroke of genius. The King is happy. The Athenian admiral can't see a thing. Both men are fooled. But it is not this instantaneous prowess, in which luck, and not merely virtue, plays a crucial role, that prompts Herodotus to express his admiration.[21] For it is in the unfolding of the narrative over the long term that Artemisia demonstrates the supreme acumen and remarkable bravery that the narrator values so much. 'I consider her an object of admiration because she was a woman who fought in the war against Greece' (Ἀρτεμισίης δέ, τῆς μάλιστα θῶμα ποιεῦμαι ἐπὶ τὴν Ἑλλάδα στρατευσαμένης γυναικός), he claims in order to justify the exceptional place he gives her in the story.[22] Her role 'in the *war* against Greece', therefore, goes far beyond the battle of Salamis. In Herodotus' eyes, in short, it is all her interventions throughout the campaign that make her a θῶμα. 'She went to war thanks to her resolve and courage, though she did not need to go (ὑπὸ λήματός τε ἀνδρηίης ἐστρατεύετο, οὐδεμιῆς οἱ ἐούσης ἀναγκαίης)'.[23] Her courage and determination are revealed on the ship's deck, to be sure, but even more strikingly in her warnings to the Great King. Unlike the other commanders who flatter him, she does not hesitate to warn him about the mistakes he may commit. Insubordinate, honest, direct, she takes risks. And the King, paradoxically, appreciates her audacity. Thus, since she intervenes from beginning to end as the Prince's best advisor, it is above all her epistemic authority that arouses wonder. This is how the Queen of Halicarnassus truly proves herself. The narrator brings to the fore this aspect of her agency. As readers, we should be paying close attention to what she thinks and

---

19 Hdt. 8.93.1–2.
20 Hdt. 8.88.
21 Hdt. 8.87. On Artemisia's trick, see Lateiner 1990, 232; Payen 2015, 214–27 rather emphasizes the narrator's 'sarcastic' tone vis-à-vis the Athenians who found 'terrible' the fact that a woman should wage war against Athens.
22 Hdt. 7.99.
23 Hdt. 7.99.

what she argues. Then we can understand the interplay of gender and cultures in the life of this amazing widow and mother.

## 2 A Sibyl's knowledge

She is amazing, but why and how, exactly?

Artemisia is very well informed. Herodotus highlights her mastery of the geopolitical situation of the Greek cities and her knowledge of their military power, which allows her to predict their vulnerability on land rather than at sea. She is able to assess not only the quality of enemy troops, but also their probable reactions. The infantry, she claims, is likely to disperse. The fleet, on the other hand, is going to resist.[24] At the outset, the narrator praises her judgments, which he tells us are the best of all (πάντων τε τῶν συμμάχων γνώμας ἀρίστας βασιλέι ἀπεδέξατο).[25]

Artemisia deploys a strategist's foresight. She has previously acquired an excellent reputation for her fleet.[26] She knows what to avoid – a naval battle. She knows when to stop the fight – right after the defeat. She knows the terrain – the sea, the islands and the Peloponnese. She knows the enemy – his strengths and weaknesses. She seems to have gathered proper military intelligence. She seems to have mastered Greek history and geography. It is therefore she who is able to advise the Great King who, at the head of the largest army of land and sea, suddenly finds himself at a loss as to the strategy he should adopt. At Salamis, the shock of being defeated by the Greeks, those little people he underestimated to the point of laughing at them, overtakes him and leaves him stunned. After trying to prevent it, Artemisia forces Xerxes to understand his miscalculations, to review his geopolitical vision, to measure the damage of his ethnocentrism and, I might add, of his egocentrism. She introduces him to who the Greeks are – and who women are.

This focus on knowledge is macroscopic in a text that is constantly concerned with the forms of knowledge it reports or implements.[27] Herodotus, takes his place

---

**24** Hdt. 8.68.
**25** Hdt. 7.99; Payen 2004, 24; See also Payen 2015, 214–27. On Artemisia's political competence, see also Ducrey 2015, 185–6. On the comparison of women and men, already in Homeric poetry, see Foley 1978, 7–26.
**26** Hdt. 7.99.
**27** See Demont 2009, 179–205; Luraghi 2001, 138–60. For a converging approach to Artemisia, see Lockwood forthcoming.

in the story next to his queen. Speaking in his own name, he insists that Artemisia's judgments are excellent. We are therefore invited to believe it. We are invited to endorse — with him — the wisdom of the queen's point of view. Her opinions are the best among all. That is why they are made the keystone, in the construction of the storyline.

Once we have taken stock of Herodotus' focalization on how much Artemisia knew, we still should ask ourselves what kind of knowledge she deploys. Three qualities stand out.

First, Artemisia knows how to take advantage of chance. In this she is the equal of the great Athenian general Themistocles who immediately understood how best to use the silver suddenly discovered in the Laurion mine, how to interpret the enigmatic oracle of the 'wooden wall' pronounced by the Pythia in Delphi, and how to exploit the physical configuration of the Straits of Salamis.[28] Both do not hesitate to cheat in order to achieve their ends: the queen of Halicarnassus sends a friendly ship to the bottom of the sea, the Athenian general uses misinformation in order to attract the Persians into the waters of Salamis.[29] Like Themistocles, Artemisia is quick-witted, quick to seize an opportunity, to design a project and to act accordingly. Faced with unforeseen events, she immediately finds a way out and turns a disadvantage to her favour. Moreover, she shares the clever and cunning character of the Athenians in general. We owe to Rosaria Munson the full picture of this resemblance.[30]

Then, as we have seen, she predicts what will happen in the future.

Finally, Artemisia explains to Xerxes what happened to him in the past. Artemisia reminds the King of what he has already done and of how he has brought his project to fruition. His mission was to punish the Athenians. By ravaging Athens and burning the temples on the acropolis, he has now accomplished that mission. That was the goal. That's enough. Now he can go home. It is as if the Great King knew neither how to wage war nor how to assess his own actions. She is the one who takes stock of the situation in its temporal development. It is she who helps the Great King to understand in retrospect the design of his own history. Gabriella Bodei Giglioni has claimed that by reminding him of his true success, Artemisia is trying to comfort Xerxes.[31] Out of context, her words may well sound that way. If we pay attention to the narrative development, however, we realize

---

28 Hdt. 7.140–4.
29 Hdt. 8.75.
30 Munson 1988, 99–102; Sebillotte Cuchet 2008, 15–33.
31 Bodei Giglioni 2002, 22.

that Artemisia offers Xerxes much more than a meagre consolation: she hands him an oracular mirror.

Artemisia therefore knows the present (what to do on the spot, right now, immediately); the future (what to decide and what to avoid); the past (what has already been achieved). Her mastery of events over time is only comparable to the panoramic vision that Herodotus himself attributes to oracles. The Pythia in Delphi is able to see through time and space, as the long subplot of Croesus' consultation of the oracle shows.[32] The priestess, Herodotus claims, utters γνῶμαι ('judgments, advices') to the Lydian king, which are veridical although the addressee misinterprets them, on account of his self-assurance.[33] This parallels Artemisia's own optimal γνῶμαι to the Persian ruler, who also thinks that he knows better. More generally, the Muses have, since Hesiod, been given the power of telling 'what has been, what is and what will be' (τά τ' ἐόντα τά τ' ἐσσόμενα πρό τ' ἐόντα).[34]

Not surprisingly, the suspicion that Herodotus attributes to Artemisia a kind of all-embracing insight whose source is usually divine was already part of the ancient reception of the *Histories*. In *The Malice of Herodotus*, Plutarch offers precisely this interpretation. By showing Themistocles in an unfavourable light, Herodotus mocks the Greeks. But about the battle of Salamis, his mockery goes even further, writes Plutarch. It was not enough for him to say that Themistocles — although nicknamed 'Odysseus' for his intelligence — never understood what had to be done, Herodotus went as far as to attribute a superior knowledge to his own compatriot, Artemisia, who, without prior knowledge, and 'by devising alone by herself' (αὐτὴν ἀφ' ἑαυτῆς), could see what the King needed to be told. According to Herodotus, Plutarch laments sarcastically, Artemisia knew better than Themistocles and Xerxes: the historian only needed to use versification to 'present Artemisia as Sybil, accurately prophesying the future' (ἀκριβῶς ἀποφῆναι τὴν μέλλοντα οὕτως τὰ προθεσπίζουσαν Σίβυλλαν).[35] Although making fun of Herodotus, Plutarch is right; Artemisia does indeed share the omniscience of the Pythia and of the Muses in Hesiod's poetry.

---

32 Hdt. 1.50ff.
33 Hdt. 1.53.
34 Hes. *Theog.*, 32–8, at 38. Hesiod is quoted from *Theogony, Works and Days, Testimonia*, Loeb Classical Library, my translation.
35 Plut. The Malice of Herodotus, 38.869–70. Plutarch here is quoted from *Moralia*, Volume XI: *On the Malice of Herodotus, Causes of Natural Phenomena*, Loeb Classical Library, my translation.

# 3 What Xerxes didn't know

And, above all, Artemisia knows the gender of Persians and Greeks. The Greeks are to Xerxes' soldiers, she says, what men are to women.[36] This is the focal point of Artemisia's story.

We could simply say, with Jennifer Roberts, that Artemisia is identified so closely with men, that she adopts male stereotypes.[37] This is obviously true. War is the male activity par excellence in ancient Greece, therefore any normative thinking about war must be filled with male stereotypes. Artemisia knows well that war demands courage, more precisely 'manliness' (ἀνδρεία), which usually characterizes men. But does she really do no more than mimic male-centred, self-serving banalities? We could agree that in saying that the Greeks are to Xerxes' soldiers what men are to women she is repeating a culturally-codified, binary opposition, but the mere fact that it is she who utters the sentence changes the meaning of the enunciation. Herodotus puts this potential platitude in the mouth of a queen who reigns at least as effectively as a king, a warrior full of tactical resources, a counsellor with superlative strategic wisdom, an awesome commander who is herself courageous and determined. She is infinitely more successful than most male leaders — more than Aminias, and far more than the Great King. Although her own excellence is atypical in the context of ancient cultures, she cannot possibly be treated as a parrot. She rather embodies a singular possibility, I would argue, namely the possibility that a universal quantifier such as "men are courageous" might be disavowed — firstly because some men, and even an entire large population of males, can actually become as uncourageous as (stereotypical) women, and secondly because Artemisia herself proves that one can be a woman *as well as* a manly warrior.[38] Moreover, by saying that Greek men can be more manly — more properly men — than Persian men, she is problematizing, not merely exemplifying, the interplay of gender and ethnicity. Far from being just a multi-faceted character to be understood in terms of female/male; Persian/Greek, Artemisia herself reflects on these categories — as an internal theorist, so to speak. Herodotus' women "take pains to articulate the moral and political basis for their actions".[39] Artemisia, I would add, does so in many ways, including by voicing her awareness of gender and cultural difference.

---

**36** Hdt. 8.68.
**37** Roberts 2011, 72.
**38** Iriarte (2013, 95–116) has made this crucial point.
**39** Dewald 1981, 111.

Artemisia speaks ironically to a Great King who is excessively proud of his might, first and foremost his innumerable troops, his men. Faithful to her daring and subtlety, she goes so far as to play with language. She tries to tell him that gender is a transferable attribute. Ἀνδρεία can shift. Warriors who were perfectly male may find themselves in a position of "femininity", compared to others whose virility has increased over time. But the Great King cannot doubt the valour of his ἄνδρες and, consequently, does not take her seriously. Artemisia seems to be the only one who knows where the real ἀνδρεία is — "real", of course, from Herodotus' point of view. At sea, it is Xerxes' enemies who have now become real men. Under the banal essentialist comments, this is a history lesson.

Artemisia knows exactly what Herodotus knows. Both are aware that the Athenians have been trying to take the lead of the Pan-Hellenic forces and that, in a naval battle at Salamis, they would use all their recently acquired maritime power, with the help of Aeginetan ships. Herodotus and Artemisia also know that the Athenians have transformed themselves through their form of government: they have become the best warriors because, at home, everyone is now fighting for himself. This is what Herodotus, speaking in his own name, tells us of the Athenians:

> The Athenians became more powerful. It is clear that equality of speech (ἡ ἰσηγορίη) is an excellent thing (χρῆμα σπουδαῖον), and not from a single point of view, but in every sense. For the Athenians, as long as they were under the domination of tyrants (τυραννευόμενοι), were not better than their neighbours in war, but as soon as they got rid of the tyrants, they became the first, and by far (ἀπαλλαχθέντες δὲ δὲ τυράννων μακρῷ πρῶτοι ἐγένοντο). This shows that when they were oppressed (κατεχόμενοι), they were cowards because they worked for a master (ἐθελοκάκεον ὡς δεσπότῃ ἐργαζόμενοι), but when they became free (ἐλευθερωθέντων), everyone was ready to rush enthusiastically to work for themselves (αὐτὸς ἕκαστος ἑωυτῷ προεθυμέετο κατεργάζεσθαι).[40]

The importance of this passage in the architecture of the *Histories* cannot be overestimated. In their conciseness, these words reveal Herodotus' point of view on the reasons for an improbable defeat and an even more unexpected success. How is it possible that the Persians, despite their resources and manpower, mass and equipment, ended up failing to conquer Greece? How is it that the Greeks managed to resist, despite their numerical disadvantage? This is what makes the Herodotean narrative so thrilling. And the answer is distributed throughout the *Histories*, one battle after another, but also in the multiple episodes that show the Persian elite's systematic misunderstanding of their enemies.

---

**40** Hdt. 5.78.

Among the aspects of Greek history that are especially relevant in the current circumstances are the military effects of the form of government chosen by the Athenians. Democracy, which Herodotus characterizes here as 'the equal right to public speech' (ἡ ἰσηγορίη) has gradually strengthened Athenian military power. While acting with eagerness, "every man for himself", democratic warriors fight more valiantly than if they were "working hard" to obey a tyrant. This is what contributes to the general interest of the city. Everyone is willing to fight, with 'pro-active enthusiasm'. It is by this expression that I would like to gloss the verb προ-θυμέομαι, trying to capture both the intensity of the ardour (θυμός) and the temporal orientation of this ardour (προ-). Thus, the sentence quoted above would sound: 'Everyone was eagerly proactive to work for himself' (αὐτὸς ἕκαστος ἑωυτῷ προεθυμέετο κατεργάζεσθαι).

Herodotus underlines the commitment of everyone to act 'for himself' (αὐτὸς ἕκαστος ἑωυτῷ) and not, as one might expect, for the people or for the city. Προ-θυμέομαι refers to a manner of contributing to the common good, which appears both in Attic inscriptions, particularly decrees that confer honours on a deserving citizen, and in public eloquence. In these contexts, the recipient of the eagerness is usually the city or the people.[41] Herodotus, by contrast, understands the dynamics of Greek democracy as an effective cooperation among individuals concerned about their own interests. Everyone for himself, for the good of all. For it is obvious that an army of fighters so fierce that they surpass all their neighbours is what gives power to the whole city. But to obtain this collective success, individual spiritedness is needed. Democracy intensifies θυμός, namely the psychosomatic energy that mobilizes every single warrior, while directing such energy towards (προ-) a goal. This is the paradoxical selfishness that leads each citizen to defend the freedom of all, because it matters to him.

It is this political and military transformation that the Persians fail to see. As Emily Greenwood notes about Xerxes' reaction to Artabanus' advice, 'Xerxes wilfully ignores and rejects the insights to be gleaned from history'.[42] He is not interested in innovation, which is particularly unfortunate in the situation in which he find himself while he, needing to make an urgent strategic decision, consults his allies. It is precisely these increasingly valiant and personally motivated Greek men that the Persian soldiers are going to be confronted with. The Athenians enter the battle of Salamis with 180 triremes. It is the trireme of Aminias of

---

**41** Whitehead (1993, 37–75) includes προθυμία among the virtues mentioned in Attic inscriptions. See Cook 2009, 44. Both scholars show the circulation of these words in public eloquence and epigraphic documents.
**42** Greenwood 2018, 171.

Pallene, an ἀνὴρ Ἀθηναῖος, who launches the attack, followed by his fellow citizens.[43] It is the Athenians, under the command of Themistocles who, with the Aeginetans, will sink the largest number of ships. The majority of the ἄνδρες who, according to Artemisia, risk putting the Persians in the position of 'women' are therefore Athenian hoplites, ready to fight face-to-face while boarding the enemy ships. The ships' commanders are also responsible for the order of battle, a *taxis* that, as we will see in a moment, is responsible for the success of the Hellenic forces.

The king should have known these facts; he should have learned what Artemisia knew.

## 4 Προθυμία

The king himself, the commander-in-chief of the Persian army, seems to be unaware of the history of the process of democratization in the Greek cities. Above all, he does not seem to be concerned about the effects of democracy on warfare, namely the remarkable improvement in the level of the hoplites, thanks to the individual motivation that freedom brings. Darius already despised democracy as the government of an indistinct mass, as he asserts in the "Constitutional Debate." As for Xerxes, he makes fun of the Greeks on the battlefield in general. Everything points to the fact that Xerxes does not know what the narrator knows, above all that the Athenian soldiers, thanks to their recently acquired form of government, have become 'the first, and by far' (μακρῷ πρῶτοι).[44] It is the fact of fighting in a certain state of mind, putting all their hearts to work (προ-θυμέομαι), that makes the difference. Προθυμία reveals, amplifies and intensifies ἀνδρεία. To redouble their efforts (προθυμέομαι) on the battlefield, the Athenians must be courageous. They even know how to show themselves προθυμότατοι.[45]

However, the emphasis on the energetic attitude of προθυμία does not place the Persians in a binary opposition — Greeks, courageous; Persians, cowards. Quite the contrary. The Greeks are not immune to pusillanimity, far from it. In the Herodotean narrative, the Athenians have become excellent over time. It is a historical process: whereas before they were used to behaving like cowards, and deliberately so, now, thanks to the overthrow of the tyrants, they are better than all

---

43 Hdt. 8.84.
44 Hdt. 5.78.
45 Hdt. 9.60.

the others. To be eager to fight (προθυμέομαι) and to be voluntarily a coward (ἐθελοκακέω) are two extreme attitudes in the experience of war. More generally, in the particular context of this war, the many Greek cities that are united by a more or less forced agreement with the Persian Empire are sometimes divided between conflicting allegiances. This creates a dilemma for commanders and soldiers, between dragging their feet and redoubling their efforts. Thus in Plataea, while Mardonios' Greek allies refuse to fight against other Greeks, the Thebans take the opportunity to settle their scores with the Athenians. They 'had not little ardor for combat, and did not behave like cowards at all (οὗτοι εἶχον προθυμίην οὐκ ὀλίγην οὐκ μαχόμενοί τε καὶ οὐκ ἐθελοκακέοντες)'.[46] In short, the warriors from Thebes had to choose between two extreme dispositions in the face of danger, hyper-courageous momentum and intentional fleeing.

The same choice presents itself among the Persians. The Persian elite is distinguished by its bellicose enthusiasm. Cyrus was a champion of προθυμία, as his determination to wage war on the Massagetae shows.[47] King Cambyses, says Xenophon in the *Cyropaedia*, had instructed his son, Cyrus, to consider προθυμία as an essential component of the art of war. Among the most useful military skills, he said, the most precious of all was the ability to inspire προθυμία in his soldiers because 'ardour or lack of it makes all the difference' (τὸ πᾶν διαφέρει ἐν παντὶ ἔργῳ προθυμία).[48] This is the best way to ensure obedience on the part of an army. Later, Plutarch tells that another member of the Achaemenid dynasty, Artaxerxes, thought that cowardice and softness were not always due to luxury and extravagance, but to a vile and despicable nature under the influence of bad ideas. For in the case of the Persian king, neither gold, nor a precious tunic, nor the twelve thousand talents of adornment that always covered his body prevented him from tackling the works and trials of war like anyone else. With his quiver slung over his shoulder and his shield on his arm, Artaxerxes used to abandon his horse to walk at the head of his troops on steep mountain roads, so that, 'when they saw his ardour and vigour' (τὴν ἐκείνου προθυμίαν καὶ ῥώμην ὁρῶντας), the rest of the army thought they had wings and felt that their burdens had become lighter.[49]

---

**46** Hdt. 9.67.
**47** Hdt. 1.204.1; 1.206.2.
**48** Xen. *Cyr.*, 1.6.13. Xenophon is quoted from *Cyropaedia, Volume I: Books 1–4*, Loeb Classical Library, my translation.
**49** Plut. *Life of Artax.*, 24.11. Plutarch is quoted here from *Lives, Volume XI: Aratus. Artaxerxes. Galba. Otho*, Loeb Classical Library, my translation.

As for the warriors of Xerxes struggling with the Greeks in the waters of Salamis, they show προθυμία. 'Devoting himself with ardour and fearing Xerxes, everyone thought that the king was observing him' (πᾶς τις προθυμεόμενος καὶ δειμαίνων Ξέρξην ἐδόκεέ τε ἕκαστος ἑωυτὸν θεήσασθαι βασιλέα).[50] Xerxes was right, therefore, to expect that his mere presence, sitting on a clearly visible throne above the battlefield, would awaken the ardour of his troops. The soldiers had deliberately shown cowardice (ἐθελοκακέειν) because of his absence, he thought, but it was up to him to change their attitude.[51] The Great King thus relied on his charismatic power, which led him to trust his men. In doing so, he followed in his father's footsteps, Darius, who had ordered the Ionians to protect the bridge built on the Hellespont by putting all their efforts into it (πᾶσαν προθυμίην), which, he said, would give him 'great pleasure' (ταῦτα δὲ ποιεῦντες ἐμοὶ μεγάλως χαριεῖσθε).[52] There is a synergy between the king and his troops: Darius is personally delighted with their προθυμία. In the same spirit, Xerxes derives his authority from the influence he exercises over his men, whom he anticipates will be afraid of him, if only he looks over them — and this fear, the narrator confirms, has the effect of encouraging them to fight boldly. All it takes is for him to show himself, in short, for his ἄνδρες to give the best of themselves.

However, the theme of προθυμία is particularly relevant to our purpose. Because, as Herodotus points out, the προθυμία of the Persians is not identical to those of the Athenians. It is associated with the fear they feel in front of the king when he supervises the progress of operations. It is a valour that depends entirely on the King, and not on the character of individuals who have discovered autonomy and attachment to their own freedom. It is the ruler who arouses their ardour, it is dread that causes their momentum in battle. The soldiers need Xerxes: he himself knows this well and has no problem with it. That is why he casually rejects Artemisia's advice. Among the Greeks, Artemisia tells him, 'those men are as much stronger than *your men* at sea, as much as men are stronger than women' (οἱ γὰρ ἄνδρες τῶν σῶν ἀνδρῶν κρέσσονες τοσοῦτό κατὰ θάλασσαν ὅσον ἄνδρες γυναικῶν).[53] Confronted with the ἄνδρες opposite, the King's men will find themselves in the position of "women". The use of the possessive is revealing in this passage. The King replies that he knows how to deal with his own men. It is his gaze that will make them real ἄνδρες. But this is the blind spot in Xerxes' vision, because the προθυμία of his own soldiers alone could not possibly be enough. He

---

50  Hdt. 8.86.1.
51  Hdt. 8.69.2.
52  Hdt. 4.98.3.
53  Hdt. 8.68.

should consider the superiority of the opponent, namely the Athenians' exceptional προθυμία; he should listen to Artemisia's words as real military information, not as a joke. He should try to find out more, ask why exactly these ἄνδρες would be more manly. He should worry.

Xerxes would be right, we should say, to think that his presence alone would mobilize his men, if there were not, in front of them, enemies so powerful, so determined to win and so passionate — that they could "feminize" them.

## 5 Τάξις

In the tumultuous waters of the Straits of Salamis, the obstacle that proved insurmountable for the Persians was the enemy's tactical ability. As their ships scatter in chaos, colliding with each other, the Greeks under Themistocles' orders hold their positions in the melee. Their advantage lies in this essential detail: they fight in order and in formation (σὺν κόσμῳ ναυμαχεόντων καὶ κατὰ τάξιν). The Persian navy, on the other hand, does not manoeuvre in orderly battle (τάσσω) and nothing seems to have been thought out intelligently (σὺν νόῳ).[54] Hence the tragic fate of the Persian soldiers, despite all their ardour under the gaze of the Great King.[55]

Maintaining order, discipline and focus is a matter of dexterity, of course, but it cannot be reduced to a simple technique. To control the situation, you must not give in to the temptation to abandon your post by fleeing. That is the very definition of courage. A moral disposition to brave danger and resist, courage is the essential springboard for the art of directing battalions and ships in combat. But courage belongs to a political culture. Because of democracy, the narrator has explained to his audience, Athenian warriors have become 'the first, and by far'.[56] They are now much more capable of προθυμία and, consequently, of bravery, compared to soldiers trained under other regimes. It is therefore logical that their superlative enthusiasm should allow them to prevail over the Persians, whose προθυμία proves relatively insufficient.

Moreover, courage is the gendered virtue par excellence. Ἀνδρεία is manliness. And manliness has a history. To show its intensification in the context of democracy, is to draw attention to a transformation that affects men and — by

---

54 Hdt. 8.86.1; Podlecki 1976, 396–413.
55 Hdt. 8.86.
56 Hdt. 5.78.

contrast, or by analogy — women. The relevance of gender runs through the entire plot. We began by highlighting the unique mission that Herodotus entrusts to the Queen of Halicarnassus, before and after the battle of Salamis. She is an intelligent and well-informed, determined and courageous woman. In her gendered singularity, she is herself a wonder. She also theorizes, so to speak, gender difference since it is in these terms that she describes the forces at play. She does so in a witty, sophisticated fashion, by redistributing female and male capabilities, in a novel proportion: in strength, the Greeks are to the King's men as men are to women (ἄνδρες τῶν σῶν ἀνδρῶν κρέσσονες τοσοῦτο εἰσὶ κατὰ θάλασσαν ὅσον ἄνδρες γυναικῶν).[57] This occurs not in general, she specifies, but at sea. Once again, the attribution of gender qualities is a matter of variable circumstances. Artemisia is not an essentialist. She is a historian.

This is her competitive advantage. Artemisia is the only one who knows the threat posed by the enemies who are waiting for the Persians around the rocks of Salamis. She knows, it seems, what they have become: more ἄνδρες than the Persian men. In the naval battle, one of these ἄνδρες, the same Athenian captain who has launched the attack against the Persian fleet, Aminias of Pallene, is now chasing her. The king's forces, on the other hand, are 'in great disarray' (ἐς θόρυβον πολλόν).[58] Between an Athenian who pursues her and her messy allies, she finds a way of making a double profit. And there is here a double irony. Aminias, the women's hunter, lets Artemisia escape. The Great King, who was supposed to oversee the combat in person, fails to grasp what really happens between Artemisia and the Calyndians. Worse, he is wrong about what he calls 'his' women. When he comments on Artemisia's exploit with the glib: 'my women have become men, and my men have become women', Xerxes echoes her wit, but still cannot see that it is not Artemisia who has become a man, but that the true men (ἄνδρες) in this conflict are in fact the Greeks, as Artemisia had predicted they would be. He does not realize yet that he is losing the battle. By trying to outsmart her, he misses the point.[59]

Finally, Salamis is a test of manliness, as we can see in the decision-making drama that precedes the attack. Herodotus highlights the competition between the Spartan general, Eurybiades, and Themistocles for the command of the operations and the choice of a strategy: the former would like to engage in combat with the Persian infantry in order to protect the land that matters to Sparta, the

---

57 Hdt. 8.68.
58 Hdt. 8.87.
59 Xerxes does not indict "himself", as Munson (1988, 102) claims. At this point, the Persians are not defeated yet.

Peloponnese, while Themistocles insists on a naval battle.⁶⁰ In agreement with Ryan Balot, we should take seriously the novelty of the Athenian redefinition of courage, as the boldness of going ahead and moving the theatre of operations from a territory to be defended and surrounded with walls, to the open sea.⁶¹ In this debate, Themistocles challenges Eurybiades to behave like a proper ἀνήρ, a good male, and therefore to launch himself with enthusiasm on the triremes, for the sake of all the Greeks. 'If you remain here you will be a good man' (ἀνὴρ ἀγαθός), he says. Otherwise, the whole of Hellas would be ruined.⁶² Exactly like Artemisia, Themistocles thinks that, on land, the diverse Greeks who participate in the war would disperse, fleeing to their respective cities.⁶³ On the contrary, again like Artemisia, he sees the Greeks prepared to fight at his command at sea, as invincible ἄνδρες.

The battle confirms the subtlety of the interplay between gender and ethnicity. It is a gradation, not a polarity; it is a proportionality, not a simple binary opposition. The Greeks attached to their lands can very well run off like cowards. The Persians are capable of valour, but not as much as their enemies. Compared to the Athenians, they may become less ἄνδρες. Gender is a relative and transferable predicate.

This is what Artemisia knew.

## Works Cited

Aristotle, *Politics*, transl. H. Rackham, Cambridge, 1932.
Balot, R. (2014), *Courage in the Democratic Polis: Ideology and Critique in Classical Athens*, New York.
Blok, J. (2002), 'Women in Herodotus' Histories', in: E. Bakker/I. de Jong/H. van Wees (eds.), *Brill's Companion to Herodotus*, Leiden, 225–42.
Bodei Giglioni, G. (2002), *Erodoto e i Sogni di Serse: L'invasione Persiana dell'Europa*, Rome.
Boedeker, D. (2011), 'Persian Gender Relations as Historical Motives in Herodotus', in: R. Rollinger/B. Truschnegg/R. Bichler (eds.), *Herodot und das Perserreich*, Wiesbaden, 211–35.
Cook, B. (2009), 'Athenian Terms of Civic Praise in the 330s: Aeschines vs. Demosthenes', *Greek, Roman, and Byzantine Studies* 49, 31–52.
Demont, P. (2009), 'Figures of Inquiry in Herodotus's Inquiries', *Mnemosyne* 62, 179–205.

---

60 Hdt. 8.58–62.
61 Balot 2014, 90–97.
62 Hdt. 8.57–62. This is the view of an Athenian, called Mnesipilus, which Themistocles likes and approves of.
63 Hdt. 8.68.

Dewald, C. (1981), 'Women and Culture in Herodotus' *Histories*', *Women's Studies: An Interdisciplinary Journal* 8, 93–127.
Ducrey, P. (2015), 'War in the Feminine in Ancient Greece', in: J. Fabre-Serris/A. Keith (eds.), *Women and War in Antiquity*, Baltimore, 181–99.
Foley, H. (1978), '"Reverse Similes" and sex Roles in the *Odyssey*', *Arethusa* 11, 7–26.
Gera, D. (1997), *Warrior Women: The Anonymous Tractatus De Mulieribus*, Leiden/New York/Köln.
Greenwood, E. (2018), 'Surveying Greatness and Magnitude in Herodotus', in: Th. Harrison/E. Irwin (eds.), *Interpreting Herodotus*, Oxford, 163–86.
Harrell, S. (2003), 'Marvelous *Andreia*: Politics, Geography, and Ethnicity in Herodotus' *Histories*', in: R. Rosen/I. Sluiter (eds.), *Andreia. Studies in Manliness and Courage in Classical Antiquity*, Leiden/Boston, 77–94.
Herodotus, *The Persian Wars, Volume I: Books 1–2,* transl. A.D. Godley, Cambridge, 1920.
Herodotus, *The Persian Wars, Volume II: Books 3–4,* transl. A.D. Godley, Cambridge, 1921.
Herodotus, *The Persian Wars, Volume III: Books 5–7,* transl. A.D. Godley, Cambridge, 1922.
Herodotus, *The Persian Wars, Volume IV: Books 8–9,* transl. A.D. Godley, Cambridge, 1925.
Hesiod, *Theogony. Works and Days. Testimonia*, transl. G. Most, Cambridge, 2018.
Hoffmann, G. (2010), 'Artémise d'Halicarnasse ou la valeur d'une femme dans la bataille de Salamine', in: M. Trévisi/Ph. Nivet (eds.), *Les Femmes et la guerre de l'antiquité à 1918*. Actes du Colloque d'Amiens, 15–16 novembre 2007, Paris, 1–31.
Hornblower, S. (1982), *Mausolos*, Oxford.
Iriarte, A. (2013), 'Despotisme et modes de communication: de l'enquête tragique au drame hérodotéen', in: J. Alaux (ed.), *Hérodote: Formes de pensée, figures du récit*, Rennes, 95–116.
Jouanna, J. (1984), 'Collaboration ou résistance au barbare: Artémise d'Halicarnasse et Cadmos de Cos chez Hérodote et Hippocrate', *Ktema* 9, 15–26.
Lateiner, D. (1990), 'Deceptions and Delusions in Herodotus', *Classical Antiquity* 9, 230–46.
Lattimore, R. (1939), 'The Wise Adviser in Herodotus', *Classical Philology* 34, 24–35.
Lockwood, T. (forthcoming), 'Artemisia of Halicarnassus: Virile woman or intellectual?'
Luraghi, N. (2001), 'Local Knowledge in Herodotus' *Histories*', in: N. Luraghi (ed.), *The Historian's Craft in the Age of Herodotus*, Oxford, 138–60.
Martyn, J. (1998), 'Artemisia and Xerxes: A new Look at Herodotus' Account of Salamis', *Ancient History* 28, 15–26.
Munson, R. (ed.) (2013), *Herodotus: Volume 2*, Oxford.
Munson, R. (1988), 'Artemisia in Herodotus', *Classical Antiquity* 7, 91–106.
Payen, P. (2004), "Femmes, armées civiques et fonction combattante en Grèce ancienne (VIIe-IV[e] siècle avant J.-C.)', *Clio: Histoire, Femmes et Sociétés* 20, 15–41.
Payen, P. (2015), 'Women's Wars: Censored Wars?', in: J. Fabre-Serris/A. Keith (eds.), *Women and War in Antiquity*, Baltimore, 214–27.
Penrose, W. (2016), *Postcolonial Amazons: Female Masculinity and Courage in Ancient Greek and Sanskrit Literature*, Oxford.
Plutarch, *Lives, Volume XI: Aratus. Artaxerxes. Galba. Otho,* transl. B. Perrin, Cambridge, 1926.
Plutarch, *Moralia, Volume XI: On the Malice of Herodotus. Causes of Natural Phenomena*, transl. L. Pearson/F.H. Sandbach, Cambridge, 1965.
Podlecki, A. (1976), 'Athens and Aegina', *Historia: Zeitschrift für Alte Geschichte* 25, 396–413.
Roberts, J. (2011), *Herodotus: A Very Short Introduction*, Oxford.

Rossellini, M./Saïd, S. (1978), 'Usage de femmes et autres *nomoi* chez les sauvages d'Hérodote: Essai de lecture structurale', *Annali della Scuola Normale Superiore di Pisa* 8, 949–1005.

Sebillotte Cuchet, V. (2008), 'Hérodote et Artémisia d'Halicarnasse: Deux métis face à l'ordre des genres athénien', *Clio: Histoire, Femmes et Sociétés* 27, 15–33.

Sissa, G. (2012), 'Democracy: A Persian Invention?', *METIS* 10, 227–61.

Sissa, G. (2018), 'Bulls and Deer, Women and Warriors', in: M. Formisano/Chr. Shuttleworth Kraus (eds.), *Marginality, Canonicity, Passion*, Oxford, 141–76.

Tank, H. (2019), 'Powerful Women and Gender Ideology in Herodotus' *Histories*', in: T. Tsakiropoulou-Summers/K. Kitsi-Mitakou (eds.), *Women and the Ideology of Political Exclusion: From Classical Antiquity to the Modern Era*, London/New York, 74–88.

Tourraix, A. (1990), 'Artémise d'Halicamasse chez Hérodote, ou la figure de l'ambivalence', in: M.-M. Mactoux/E. Geny (eds.), *Mélanges Pierre Lévêque Tome 5: Anthropologie et société*, Besançon, 377–86.

Visconti, A. (2002), 'Artemisia di Alicarnasso Ovvero il Potere Visibile', in: S. Marino/Cl. Montepaone/M. Tortorelli Ghidini (eds.), *Il potere invisibile: Figure del femminile tra mito e storia: Studi in memoria di Maria Luisa Silvestre*, Napoli, 63–75.

Weil, R. (1976), 'Artémise ou le Monde à L'envers', in: A. Plassart (ed.), *Recueil Plassart: Études sur l'antiquité grecque offertes à André Plassart par ses collègues de la Sorbonne*, Paris, 215–24.

Whitehead, D. (1993), 'Cardinal Virtues: The Language of Public Approbation in Democratic Athens', *Classica et Mediaevalia* 44, 37–75.

Xenophon, *Cyropaedia, Volume I: Books 1–4*, transl. W. Miller, Cambridge, 1914.

Alison Keith
# Cicero's Verres, Verres' Women

Cicero's oratorical portrait of Verres has been well analyzed by generations of scholars.[1] Their acute investigations have shown how thoroughly our access to the historical Verres is shaped by the generic conventions of rhetorical theory and forensic performance.[2] Thomas Frazel, in particular, has explored Cicero's debts to the progymnastic exercises that not only shaped his rhetorical training but also structured his practice of oratory in the *Verrines*, from the opening skirmish over his right to prosecute Verres in *Diuinatio in Caecilium* to the monumental *Actio Secunda*, never delivered but put into circulation in the aftermath of Verres' flight into exile late in the summer of 70 BCE.[3] Frazel has thoroughly documented the role of specific progymnastic topoi and their order in the construction of Cicero's argument, in which he characterizes Verres as a 'temple robber' (ἱερόσυλος) and 'Greek rhetorical tyrant' (τύραννος), whose plunder of Sicilian artworks and extortion of taxes led to the agricultural devastation (*agri deserti*) of the province.[4]

This study aims to supplement our understanding of the rhetorical contours of Cicero's characterization of Verres.[5] I here focus on the evidence for his use of another conventional weapon in the forensic arsenal, *viz.* his appeal to ethnic and gender stereotypes in his portrait of Verres as an inveterate adulterer and sexual debauchee, whose carnal excesses expose his incapacity for, and criminal discharge of, provincial governance.[6] By far the most frequent motive for Cicero's

---

[1] Alexander 1976; Craig 1985; Citroni Marchetti 1986, 113–23; Innocenti 1994; Butler 2002; Frazel 2004 and 2009. I quote Cicero's *Verrines* from Peterson 1917; translations are adapted from Greenwood 1928 unless otherwise indicated.
[2] Cf. the conclusions of the archaeologists and epigraphers who approach the *Verrines* looking for evidence to supplement the material record of Sicilian history in, e.g., Dubouloz and Pittia 2007. On the contribution of the *Verrines* to our understanding of Roman political history, see Brunt 1980; Vasaly 2009; Morrell 2017, 22–56.
[3] Frazel 2004.
[4] Frazel 2009; cf. Citroni Marchetti 1986, 113–23.
[5] I am grateful to Jacqueline Fabre-Serris and Florence Klein for the invitation to the Eugesta conference on identities, ethnicities and gender; to Stephen Rupp and the Press' two referees for their generous and helpful commentary on my paper; and to Georgia Ferentinou for editorial assistance. All remaining errors are my own.
[6] See Gunderson 2000, 202 on Cicero's 'routine' sexualization of Verres. On sexual stereotypes in Roman, especially Ciceronian, oratory, see Citroni Marchetti 1986, 114; Edwards 1993, 63–97; Corbeill 1996, 128–73; Richlin 1997; Connolly 2007.

strategic introduction of historical women into the *Verrines* is the addition of sexual innuendo to discredit Verres' provincial career.[7] Yet despite the inevitable rhetorical manipulation entailed in Cicero's representation of women in his speeches, many of his orations offer valuable testimony concerning the historical lives of ancient women, both Roman and provincial, during the late Republic. The *Verrines* too are an instructive source of evidence for women's financial, legal, sexual and social standing in this period – despite, indeed even because of, their frequent rhetorical stylization according to stereotypes of ethnicity and gender.

## 1 Verres' criminal lechery

Early in the first action of the *Verrines*, Cicero sketches Verres' character in the broad strokes of the progymnastic temple robber and Greek tyrant, whose criminal lusts (*nefarias eius libidines*, 1.5.14) endanger every Sicilian woman with whom he comes into contact. He repeatedly revisits the leitmotif in the second action as well, describing Verres as 'no common adulterer, but the ravager of all chastity' (*non adulterum sed expugnatorem pudicitiae*, 2.1.3.9),[8] and developing the theme in connection with Verres' youthful history of sexual excess, which took the form of 'nocturnal revels and vigils' (*nocturnis eius bacchationibus ac uigiliis*) and unceasing traffic with 'pimps, gamblers, and panderers' (*lenonum, aleatorum, perductorum*, 2.1.12.33). Far from ending with his youth, Cicero claims, Verres' sexual debauchery only grew more vicious in the course of his political career, beginning with his appointment as a legate in Asia in 80 BCE (2.1.24.62):

> How many women of free birth, how many respectable women (*matribus familias*) do you think he sexually assaulted (*uim attulisse*) during his foul and depraved (*taetra atque impura*) tenure as a legate? In what town did he set foot where the imprints (*uestigia*) left by his shameful lecheries (*stuprorum flagitiorumque suorum*) did not outnumber the physical imprints of his arrival?

Verres' 'crime of lust and wanton passion' (*crimen ... libidinis atque improbissimae cupiditatis*, 2.1.34.86) at Lampsacus offers an early instance of Cicero's strategic representation of provincial women in the *Verrines*.

---

7 Hillard 1989, 167–8.
8 All translations of *Verrines* 2.1 are from Mitchell 1986.

To his review of Verres' plunder of Asian art, during his appointment in 80–79 BCE as legate to the proconsul Cn. Cornelius Dolabella in the province of Cilicia, Cicero appends an illustrative example of his vile lusts, typical of the rhetorical portrait of a tyrant (2.1.24.62): 'I shall select one particular instance of his abominable behaviour (*de nefariis istius factis*), that I may more easily come at last to Sicily'. Although Verres had plundered works of art in every city on his journey from Rome to Cilicia (*Verr.* 2.1.19.49–23.61), far worse, according to Cicero, was his criminal lechery on arrival in Lampsacus, through which he travelled on an embassy to King Nicomedes IV Philopater of Bithynia. For the affair resulted not only in the death of his own lictor, Cornelius, but also in the summary conviction and execution of two leading provincial citizens, Philodamus and his son, with whom Verres' legate Rubrius was billeted (2.1.24.62–34.86).

Cicero depicts Verres instructing his aides, 'men of the most depraved and loathsome character', to be on the lookout for desirable women, whether 'unmarried or married' (*ecqua uirgo sit aut mulier*), to enliven his stay in Lampsacus (2.1.24.63). The orator singles out a certain Rubrius as the 'ideal instrument of Verres' lusts' (*homo factus ad istius libidines*), who reports to him his discovery of

> 'a man named Philodamus, who was easily the foremost of the people of Lampsacus in birth, standing, wealth, and reputation, and ... [his] daughter (*filiam*) who lived with her father because she had no husband (*quod uirum non haberet*), a woman of outstanding beauty (*mulierem eximia pulchritudine*), but with a reputation for the highest integrity and chastity (*sed eam summa integritate pudicitiaque existimari*, 2.1.25.64)'.

Interestingly, Cicero specifically identifies Philodamus' daughter as *mulier* (2.1.25.64), which implies that 'she may previously have been married'.[9] Cicero will have much more to say about Verres' sexual depredations of provincial wives in Sicily. Here, his emphasis on the exemplary modesty of Philodamus' daughter echoes literary and epigraphic descriptions of the classical Roman ideal of womanhood, especially of the Roman *materfamilias*.[10] In treating Verres' violent assault on the provincial Greek woman and her family, Cicero punctiliously observes the Greek social convention necessitating that respectable women remain unnamed in public discourse.[11]

Cicero emphasizes the subaltern provincial character of Lampsacus, its leading citizen Philodamus and, by extension, his daughter. The orator characterizes

---

**9** Treggiari 2007, 175 n. 25.
**10** Riess 2012, 492–3; cf. Treggiari 2007, 16–18.
**11** Schaps 1977.

Lampsacus as a jewel of the Hellespont (2.1.24.63), whose citizens were 'especially conscious of their duty to all Roman citizens'; indeed, he describes the Lampsacenes as 'by legal agreement allies of the Roman state, by fortune its subjects, by inclination its suppliants' (2.1.32.81). The subaltern status of town and townsfolk is exemplified by Philodamus himself who, 'amongst the wealthiest of his community', scrupulously observed 'his graciousness and normal mode of behaviour' — despite having Rubrius thrust upon his household — in the preparation of 'a magnificent and elegant banquet' to honour the Roman delegation (2.1.26.65). Philodamus reluctantly welcomes Verres and his retinue into his home (2.1.26.65): 'He asked Rubrius to invite whom he pleased and to reserve a place, if he so wished, only for him (*sibi soli*); even his son, a most exceptional young man (*lectissimum adulescentem*), he sent away to have dinner with one of his relatives'. He also keeps his daughter well away from the men's party; when pressed by Rubrius to summon her to the party, he 'denied that it was a practice of the Greeks to have women recline at table at a men's drinking party' (*negauit moris esse Graecorum ut in conuiuio uirorum accumberent mulieres*, 2.1.26.66). Philodamus thus observes a threefold, intersecting set of exclusions from the party he hosts for his houseguest Rubrius and the other members of Verres' entourage: no Lampsacenes, no youths, and no women.

By contrast with Philodamus' studied hospitality, Cicero details Verres' outrageous breaches of etiquette as a quasi-military campaign to assault his host's daughter. Following Frazel's lead, we may interpret Cicero's employment of a military lexicon in this episode as an early example in the second action of Cicero's rebuttal of Hortensius' planned defense of Verres as a *bonus imperator*.[12] Verres instructs his troops on the night's campaign and they arrive early to take their places (2.1.26.66). When Philodamus declines Rubrius' request to produce his daughter, Verres' lieutenant takes command, issuing orders to his slaves to close the door and take their stations by the entrance (2.1.25.66). Recognizing the Romans' intent to assault his daughter (2.1.26.67, *ut filiae suae uis adferetur*), Philodamus summons his own slaves to protect her (*ut se ipsum neglegant, filiam defendant*) and sends for his son, who immediately rushes home 'to help defend his father's life and his sister's modesty' (*ut et uitae patris et pudicitiae sororis succurreret*), accompanied by the Lampsacene citizenry (2.1.26.67). At this juncture, Verres' lictor Cornelius 'who had been posted with his slaves by Rubrius in a protected position, as it were (*quasi in praesidio*, lit. 'garrison'), for the abduction of the woman (*ad auferendam mulierem*, 2.1.26.67), was killed'. Several others were

---

12 Frazel 2009, 125–85.

also injured during the engagement: Philodamus drenched by Rubrius with boiling water, Rubrius himself hurt, and some slaves wounded (2.1.26.67). The author of the crime, however, seizes the opportunity to escape unharmed from the mêlée (2.1.26.67).

Philodamus' daughter was apparently unharmed, though we cannot know for certain since she makes no further appearance in Cicero's narrative, which shifts to the repercussions for Philodamus and his son from the ill-fated party — their prosecution, conviction and summary execution (2.1.27.70–30.77). The morning after the fracas, the Lampsacenes meet to deliberate their civic response to Verres' outrage. They determine that they must act 'to safeguard their children's chastity against the Romans' lust' (*pudicitiam liberorum seruare tutam ab eorum libidine*, 2.1.27.68), even if they should thereby attract reprisals. Throughout this part of his narrative, Cicero emphasizes the Lampsacenes' shared social values with their imperial overlords, including their common respect for women's sexual honour and Roman political authority. Indeed, Cicero's characterization of the Lampsacenes' motives assimilates the local citizenry to their imperial masters, as Treggiari (2007, 17) comments: 'the Senate and Roman People could have no objection to provincials defending the *pudicitia* of their children'. The orator draws the rhetorical moral of the episode in lurid colours (2.1.31.78), emphasizing the danger posed to Roman authority in the provinces by Verres' depraved passions and criminal appetites (*tantaene tuae libidines ... libidini tuae cupiditatique ... scelus ac libidinem*).

Cicero's rhetoric elides ethnic differences between Romans and Greeks to underline their shared social and political values. His emphasis on Verres' lust and passion thereby serves to distinguish him from both responsible governors and dependable provincials, enmeshing him in the rhetorical portrait of the Greek tyrant, as Cicero makes explicit in a final narrative flourish (2.1.32.82): 'you behaved in the towns and states of our friends not as a legate of the Roman people but as a lecherous and savage tyrant' (*tyrannum libidinosum crudelemque*). Verres' inglorious stay in Lampsacus bears all the hallmarks of Greek tyranny over a vassal state, where he first plots criminal sexual assault and then, baulked of his prey, demands that the full force of Roman law punish the alleged provincial infraction.

The story that Cicero reports has become justly famous as an example of his command of the rhetorical technique of *narratio*,[13] and it is important to recognize that he shapes his narrative in such a way as to anticipate Verres' crimes of lechery in Sicily. For the theme of Verres' criminal lusts recurs throughout the second

---

13  See, e.g., Quintilian *Inst. Or.* 11.3.162, citing *Verr.* 1.30.76; Mitchell 1986, 188–90 *ad loc.*

action. Cicero reprises the motif at the opening of the third pamphlet (2.3.2.5, 2.3.3.6) and in the fourth pamphlet too, he repeatedly denounces Verres' lecheries, insisting that they must inevitably undermine his claim of Sicilian support (2.4.9.20). The orator's lurid references to his sexual crimes during his Sicilian governorship continue the theme of Verres as 'the ravager of all chastity' (2.1.3.9, quoted above), for *uis* was a standard rhetorical charge against the Greek tyrant (2.4.52.116):[14] 'I say nothing of his sexual assaults (*uim*) committed against freeborn women (*ingenuis*), about married women sexually forced (*matres familias uiolatas*)'. Cicero even suggests that, as befits a lecherous Greek tyrant rather than a good Roman general, Verres chose Cupid and Venus to preside over his praetorship in Sicily, in place of *Honos* and *Virtus*, to whom the conqueror of Syracuse, M. Claudius Marcellus, vowed a temple after his defeat of the Gauls at Clastidium (2.4.55.123);[15] and it is these same libidinous divinities, who oversee the full depravity of Verres' gubernatorial conduct (2.5.10.27–11.28, quoted below).

Cicero pulls out all the rhetorical stops in his narrative of Verres' stay in Lampsacus, which furnishes a historical analogue to the Sicilian mythical exemplum of Greek tyranny, Dis' rape of Proserpina, famously recounted in *Verrines* 2.4 (48.107):[16] 'one feels that the landscape [of Henna] itself confirms the story, familiar to us from childhood, of how the maiden was carried off (*raptum illum uirginis*)... father Dis suddenly issued in his chariot; he seized the maiden (*abreptamque uirginem*)'. Like Dis at Henna, Verres arrives suddenly in Lampsacus; again like Dis, who knows where and when to strike, Verres (or rather Rubrius, on Verres' behalf) has done his homework and knew precisely where and when to attack his prey; unlike the god, however, Verres is cheated of his quarry. In his account of the myth, Cicero brings together the three rhetorical topoi – temple robbery, devastation of agriculture, and Greek tyranny (a political role especially prominent in Sicilian history) – that he applies to Verres throughout his prosecution. Especially illustrative of the tyrant Verres' 'savage lust' (*importunes istius libidines*) is his plunder of the ancient statues of Ceres and Nike from the temple of Ceres and Proserpina/Libera at Henna, which Cicero couches in the discourse of rape (2.4.50.111): 'So extreme was their distress that one might fancy that a second Pluto had come to Henna, and not abducted Proserpina but carried Ceres

---

14 Cf. Frazel 2009, 177 n. 131.
15 Flower 2003.
16 On this famous passage in *Verrines* 2.4, see Baldo 1999 and *id.* 2004, 475–502 *ad* 2.4.105–15; Frazel 2009, 83–6, 215–8.

herself away.'[17] The Lampsacene affair, narrated to lurid effect in *Verrines* 2.1, foreshadows Cicero's strategic use of Sicilian myth in 2.4, providing a decisive point of comparison from Verres' early career to confirm the criminal lechery with which he discharged his governorship in Sicily.

## 2 Verres' criminal avarice

Early in the *Diuinatio in Caecilium*, Cicero 'quotes' Sicily's complaints of Verres' spoliation of her treasures and provincial prerogatives (5.19). Throughout the first action too, Cicero repeatedly sounds the theme of Verres' avarice, which he often links to his potential bribery of the jurors in his extortion trial (1.2.4–5, 1.13.40).[18] According to Cicero, avarice, like lechery, marked Verres' career from its very outset (1.4.12): 'His city praetorship was occupied in a plundering onslaught (*depopulatio*) upon sanctuaries and public buildings, and in awarding, or failing to award, in the civil courts, personal and real property in violation of all legal precedents'. Indeed, Cicero asserts, Verres' avarice in Cilicia was merely the prelude to his full dress rapacity in Sicily.[19]

We have already seen that Cicero precedes his treatment of Verres' attempted rape of Philodamus' daughter in *Verrines* 2.1 with a summary of his spoliation of the treasures of Asia's cities and temples, and he offers a similarly detailed account of Verres' legal chicaneries both within and beyond the inheritance courts after the Lampsacene narrative. Of particular interest is Cicero's insistence on Verres' violation of legal precedents in the award of (or failure to award) personal and real property in the civil courts (cf. 1.4.12, quoted above). For in building the case against Verres on the basis of his long history of criminal avarice and abuse of financial legislation, Cicero introduces evidence for Roman women's routine transaction of financial affairs, and especially their right to inherit (*de mulierum hereditatibus*, 2.1.46.118).

Cicero begins his review of Verres' thefts of legacies with the proquaestorship to which the Roman governor of Cilicia, Cn. Dolabella, appointed him on the

---

**17** I have adapted Greenwood's translation here following Dickison 1992, 188 *ad loc*.
**18** On the passage, see Citroni Marchetti 1986, 115. On the history of the extortion court at Rome, and the role of the jurors at such trials, see Balsdon 1938; Henderson 1951; Gruen 1968; Lintott 1981; Alexander 1990. On the Verrine jury, see McDermott 1977.
**19** On rhetorical approaches to *auaritia*, see Citroni Marchetti 1986, 101–2 and, on Cicero's use of them in the *Verrines*, 119. Frazel 2009 treats *auaritia* fully, especially in connection with *Verrines* 2.5 (138–40).

death of his friend, Dolabella's quaestor, C. Malleolus. To begin with, 'when Verres assumed the position of guardian of the young Malleolus he launched an attack against his property' (2.1.36.90). He seized for his own use the dead Malleolus' silver, many of his slaves and skilled craftsmen ('many handsome fellows among them'), his wine and other Asian products, but 'sold off the rest of his estate and made sure to secure payment' (2.1.36.91). Cicero alleges that Verres 'realized up to two and a half million sesterces' from the sale, but (2.1.36.92) 'sent no record of it on his return to Rome to his ward or to his ward's mother or guardians' (*nullam litteram pupillo, nullam matri eius, nullam tutoribus reddidit*). Since, under Roman law, women could not serve as their children's financial trustees, and indeed at this period required financial oversight for their whole lives, it is instructive to see Cicero's casual expectation that Verres, as the young Malleolus' guardian, should report to his mother concerning the estate.[20] Terentia's management of Cicero's financial affairs and concern for her children's inheritances offer a noteworthy contemporary parallel for the interest Cicero represents Malleolus' mother taking in her son's financial affairs.[21] Indeed, he claims that it was Malleolus' mother and grandmother who pressed the young Malleolus' case with Verres (2.1.36.92):

> When the boy's mother and grandmother repeatedly demanded (*cum saepius mater et auia pueri postularent*) that he should at least tell how much of Malleolus' money he had brought back with him, even if he was not going to return it or give an accounting of it, he finally stated, under pressure from many sources, a figure of one million.

Cicero makes rhetorical capital out of the appearance of the young Malleolus and his modest womenfolk as witnesses at Verres' trial (37.93): 'It is Malleolus I have brought before the court, and his mother and grandmother (*mater eius atque auia*), who in sorrow and in tears (*quae miserae flentes*) testified that the boy has been deprived by you of the property of his father'. He presses his rhetorical advantage home, asking why Verres would compel his deceased friend's wife (*sodalis uxorem*) and mother-in-law (*sodalis socrum*), 'these exceptional and exceedingly modest women' (*pudentissimas lectissimasque feminas*), to appear in court 'before so large a gathering of men' (*in tantum uirorum conuentum*) to give evidence 'against their wishes and their practice' (*insolitas inuitasque*, 2.1.37.94). Cicero underlines the women's unfamiliarity with the masculine forensic context,

---

**20** Gardner 2008[1986], 4–22, 127–9. I thank one of the referees for reminding me that by the late republic, such financial guardians 'seem for the most part to have presented women with little more than a minor annoyance'.
**21** Treggiari 2007, 33, 60, 64–5, 102, 128–9, 159; see also Brennan 2012.

in accordance with their exemplary modesty and womanly 'excellence'. As Mitchell (1986, 201) comments,

> Cicero exploits the piteous consequences of Verres' betrayal of trust as seen in the helplessness of a minor deprived of his father and his father's possessions, and in the vulnerability of his distraught mother and grandmother, forced to put aside their innate modesty and defend their rights in the unfamiliar world of men.

We should resist the temptation to accept Cicero's gendered rhetoric at face value, however, as it is the orator himself who brings Malleolus' mother and grandmother before the tribunal to submit evidence (37.94): 'Read the evidence of all these witnesses beginning "THE EVIDENCE OF MOTHER AND GRANDMOTHER"' (*TESTIMONIVM MATRIS ET AVIAE*). For despite Cicero's emphasis on the masculine context of the trial and on the women's exemplary modesty and unfamiliarity with forensic procedure, the conventional phrasing of the instruction to call their testimony before the tribunal confirms the routine nature of women's appearances as witnesses in Roman republican trials, such as we glimpse elsewhere (e.g., *Pro Caecina, Pro Caelio*).[22] Here it is Cicero himself who magnifies the gender divide in the Roman forensic context, by entering domestic evidence before a political tribunal.

From Verres' outrages as Dolabella's legate and proquaestor, Cicero passes to his abuse of judicial powers as *praetor urbanus* in 74 BCE (2.1.40.103–48.127). At that time too, he alleges, Verres' avarice led to his interference in inheritance cases, some of which involved female heirs and testators. In this regard, Cicero's *Verrines* open a window on the complicated legal landscape of women's financial and testamentary rights in republican Rome. The first case he cites (2.1.41.104) concerned the will of a certain P. Annius Asellus, who died the year before Verres' praetorship, leaving an only daughter (*unicam filiam*). Since 'he was not on the census rolls' and there was no legal bar (*lex nulla prohibebat*), 'he made his daughter heir to his property' (*fecit ut filiam bonis suis heredem institueret*), and she duly became the heir (*heres erat filia*). Cicero implies that Annius drafted his will with an eye to evading the *lex Voconia* of 169 BCE, which forbade testators registered in the highest census class to name a woman as heir and 'prescribed

---

[22] On women in the Roman civil law-courts, see Marshall 1989; on women in the Roman Forum, where trials were held, during the republic, see Boatwright 2011, 105–22. On the rhetoric of gender in Roman oratory, see Connolly 2007, who notes (88) that 'Valerius Maximus counts three Roman women who pleaded cases before magistrates (8.3; cf. Quint. *Inst. Or.* 1.1.6) but elsewhere asks the rhetorical question *quid feminae cum contione*? ('what do women have to do with public meetings?', Val. Max. 3.8.6)'.

that no legacy from such a testator should exceed the amount left to the heir or heirs'.[23] Someone who, like Annius, had failed to register in the census, whether on purpose or because of continuing civil unrest, was not subject to the *lex Voconia*.[24] Cicero asserts that 'everything worked in favour of the young girl' (*faciebant omnia cum pupilla*): 'the fairness of the law, the wishes of her father, the edicts of praetors, the legal usage prevailing at the time of Asellus' death'. He expressly affirms the legality and justice of the will (2.1.42.107). 'On grounds of justice, the law, the opinions of all who were consulted, P. Annius made a will that was lacking neither in moral integrity, nor in duty to family, nor in humanity'. As Mitchell (1986, 207 *ad* 2.1.42.107) puts it, 'Cicero's basic contention in relation to this incident is that Annius' action, at the time it was taken, violated neither law nor justice'.

But Verres, Cicero implies, scented an opportunity for further enrichment and so he approached the reversionary heir (2.1.41.105), L. Annius, about including in his upcoming promulgation of the praetor's edict an unprecedented application of the Voconian law to past as well as future wills. At the same time, however, Verres 'made secret overtures to the girl's mother' (*ad pupillae matrem*, 2.1.41.105). Yet, according to Cicero, the young girl's guardians (2.1.41.106) 'did not see, if they gave the praetor the money in the girl's name (*pupillae nomine*), especially a large sum, how they could record it in the accounts or how they could pay it without risk to themselves ... and so they continued to refuse his repeated demands'. Verres' approach to Annia's mother seems designed to circumvent the legitimate financial authority of the girl's guardians. Cicero's treatment of Verres' maneuvering, however, suggests that her mother and financial trustees worked together to secure the girl's inheritance, without any diminution of her fortune. Unable to come to an understanding with the guardians of Annius' daughter, Verres made the unprecedented amendment to his praetor's edict of the retrospective application of the *lex Voconia* (2.1.41–42.107). As Cicero points out, the praetor's edict was technically valid only for the year of his magistracy, so Verres' edict 'encompassed a greater span of time than would a regular statute' (2.1.42.109).[25] It was thus clear to everyone, Cicero asserts, that 'it was written not in the interest of the public but of the reversionary heirs of P. Annius' (2.1.43.110). Verres himself removed the clause from his Sicilian edict (*ibid.*).

---

**23** Mitchell 1986, 206 *ad* 2.1.41.104. On the *lex Voconia*, see Gardner 2008[1986], 130–5; McClintock 2013; cf. Hallett 2014 [1984], 90–6.
**24** Hallett 2014 [1984], 93–6; Gardner 2008 [1986], 134.
**25** On Verres' unprecedented legal rulings during his praetorship, cf. 2.1.52.137: *noua iura, noua decreta, noua iudicia petebantur*.

The purpose and scope of the *lex Voconia* has been much debated by modern scholars and Cicero's report of the legal skirmishes attending the execution of Annius' will sheds valuable light on the emotional life of the Roman family as well as on the financial and legal issues involved.[26] The orator also adduces comparative evidence to show that Annius was by no means alone in his testamentary practice, including 'a wealthy woman (*pecuniosa mulier*) named Annaea, who recently, because she was not on the census rolls (*quod censa non erat*), made her daughter her heir in her will (*testamento fecit heredem filiam*) with the approval of many of her relatives' (*de multorum propinquorum sententia*, 2.1.43.111).[27] This comparative evidence confirms the requirement that a woman's tutor(s) should approve her testamentary arrangements.[28] But Cicero also attests to the flexibility of Roman law in accommodating the wishes of the testator, whether male or female. His lengthy discussion and abundant citation of written evidence[29] well document the determination of Roman parents, Cicero among them, to leave their daughters fully provided for from their estates.[30] And he here indulges in deeply emotional reflection on paternal love for a daughter (2.1.44.112):[31]

> I have no doubt that, just as this affair seems cruel and shameful to me (*mihi*), as I have a daughter especially dear to my heart (*cui mea filia maxime cordi est*), it seems the same to each of you, who are stirred by similar feelings of tenderness for your daughters' (*simili sensu atque indulgentia filiarum*).

Cicero assumes, and exploits, the fellow feeling of the senatorial Roman judges adjudicating Verres' extortion trial (2.1.44.113):[32] 'Will you then strip the young girl (*eripies igitur pupillae*) of the *toga praetexta* and remove the insignia, not only of her prosperity (*fortunae*), but of her free birth (*ingenuitatis*)? Do we wonder that the people of Lampsacus resorted to arms against this man?' Mitchell (1986, 209) notes that 'the implication of Cicero's question is that Verres might as well remove even the symbols of the girl's free-born status, since he has deprived her of

---

26 Dixon 1985; Crook 1986, 65–7; Gardner 2008[1986], 130–5; McClintock 2013.
27 On the relevance of the *lex Voconia*, see Gardner 2008[1986], 135.
28 Gardner 2008[1986], 127–9.
29 Cf. Butler 2002.
30 On Cicero's testamentary arrangements, see Treggiari 2007, 118–64; on Terentia's *ibid.*, 3, 15, 98.
31 On the passage, see Treggiari 2007, 38–9; on Roman fathers and daughters, see Hallett 2014 [1984]. On fathers and daughters in Menander's comedy (often sampled as a means to understand their relationship in Hellenistic Greek communities), see Cox 2012, 283–6. On Cicero's presentation of distinguished provincials in the *Verrines*, see Rizzo 1980.
32 On the *toga praetexta*, see Olson 2008, 15–20.

her basic rights and all her possessions'. In these reflections, Cicero also draws a direct connection between Verres' avaricious assault in Rome on the young Annia's inheritance and his lecherous assault in Lampsacus on Philodamus' daughter who, though no wearer of the *toga praetexta* as a Greek provincial rather than a Roman citizen, was likewise wealthy and freeborn. The reminiscence confirms the shared social values of upper class Romans and provincial elites at the same time that it contributes to the strong narrative architecture of *Verrines* 2.1, cogently uniting the charges of lechery and avarice in Cicero's rhetorical portrait of Verres.

## 3 Verres' school of mistresses

At the opening of *Verrines* 2.3, Cicero summarizes the reasons for his opprobrium of Verres' public and private vices in a passage that brings together the three charges of avarice, lechery, and impiety that animate his characterization of the Sicilian governor as a textbook tyrant and temple robber, consummate pillager of agriculture, chastity and religion. Of particular note is Cicero's emphasis on 'that man's daily adulteries (*istius cotidiana adulteria*), his school of mistresses (*meretriciam disciplinam*) and his household of panders' (*domesticum lenocinium*, 2.3.3.6). The expression *meretricia disciplina* (also at 2.4.4.7) challenges straightforward translation into English, though Greenwood's rendering, 'school of mistresses', has the merit of bringing to the fore the metonymic sense of *disciplina* as 'learning, knowledge, science, discipline'.[33] This is the sense the word bears in Cicero's reconstruction of the upbringing of Verres' son during his tenure of the governorship of Sicily, where 'even if his natural bent tended to wean him from his father's vices and make him unlike his family, habit (*consuetudo*) and training (*disciplina*) might nevertheless keep him true to type', since 'he never set eyes on one decent or sober dinner-party', 'living amid his father's debaucheries' (*in patris luxurie sic uixerit*) and feasting with unchaste women (*inter impudicas mulieres*) and intoxicated men' (2.3.68.159–60). Both passages implicitly contrast Verres' debauched lifestyle with the disciplined life of statesmanship or philosophy, both better suited to elite Roman men than indulgence in the sexual affairs

---

**33** Lewis/Short s.v. *disciplina* II A, 'Meton. (*causa pro effectu*), all that is taught in the way of instruction, whether with reference to single circumstances of life, or to science, art, morals, politics, etc.', often in Cicero with particular reference to statesmanship (Cic. *De or.* 1.34.159; *Rep.* 1.33, 2.38, 3.3); philosophy (Cic. *Ac.* 2.3; *Fin.* 1.4; *Nat. D.* 1.7, 5.32, 90; *Brut.* 25; *Off.* 3.4.20).

typical of the new comic *adulescens*.³⁴ Yet, Cicero charges, Verres' early history of avarice and debauchery, 'when he lived with prostitutes and pimps' (*cum meretricibus lenonibusque uixisset*, 2.1.39.101), indelibly marked the subsequent course of his political career. In his account of Verres' scandalous praetorship of 74 BCE, Cicero offers abundant evidence of Verres' financial, legal and sexual exploitation of Sicily's provincials, with a particular focus on prostitutes and subaltern wives.³⁵

It is to Cicero that we owe the earliest portrait of a historical courtesan in Latin literature, in his account of Verres' mistress Chelidon ('Swallow'), whose speaking Greek name betrays her unspeakable profession.³⁶ I have elsewhere explored Cicero's representation of Chelidon as a Greek courtesan.³⁷ Here, it will be sufficient to review Cicero's recurrent emphasis on her interference in Verres' administration of justice during his tenure of the praetorship at Rome in 74 BCE, a rhetorical strategy he employs throughout the second action in order to prejudice the extortion court against Verres' Sicilian governorship. He describes Verres' entrance into the office of *praetor urbanus* in the most damaging terms (*Verr.* 2.1.40.104):

> 'Well then, when he became praetor, and when he had risen with favourable omens from the arms of Chelidon (*qui auspicato a Chelidone surrexisset*), he obtained by lot the office of urban praetor, which pleased him and Chelidon more than it did the Roman people (*magis ex sua Chelidonisque, quam ex populi Romani uoluntate*)'.

Mitchell (1986, 205) explains: 'Cicero is suggesting Verres looked for and found his good omens in the embraces of a prostitute, and went on to secure the urban praetorship, a most inauspicious development as far as the Roman people were concerned'. Rather than proceeding to the temple as praetor-elect, to take the auspices before the lots were drawn, Cicero implies that Verres either compelled the augur to attend him in his bedroom with his mistress, or that he may even

---

**34** On the conventional character of the new comic *adulescens*, see Hunter 1985, 95–108; Dinter 2019.
**35** On the law concerning prostitution in the Roman world, see McGinn 1998; on the economy of Roman prostitution, McGinn 2004.
**36** LSJ s.v. 5, citing Aristoph. *Lys.* 770, on which see Henderson (2018[1987], 168 *ad loc.*), who cites in addition Poll. 2.174, Suda χ 185, and Juv. *Sat.* 6.O.6.
**37** Keith 2018, 77–81. Cicero himself testifies to her testamentary disposition of her property after her death (*Verr.* 2.2.116 and 2.4.71), which implies that Chelidon was, in fact, Verres' freedwoman and a Roman citizen, even if still subject to legal *infamia* as a prostitute: see *infra*.

have taken no auspices at all, substituting Chelidon's embraces instead.[38] In this way, Cicero characterizes Verres' house as a brothel (cf. *meretricis domum*, 2.1.52.137, 2.5.15.38),[39] and his praetorship as illegitimate from its inception. Thomas McGinn (2004, 85) has shown that 'brothels were extremely inauspicious' in Roman thought, and his findings illuminate Cicero's rhetorical strategy at this point in the *Verrines*, informed as they are by a long-standing Roman tradition distinguishing elite male political culture from low female company and designed to deter magistrates from mixing, to their own disgrace and the discredit of their office, with their social inferiors.[40]

Cicero presents the legislation enacted during Verres' praetorship as scandalously tainted by female interference, representing his very first piece of legislation (the praetor's edict) as composed to suit Chelidon (*totum edictum ad Chelidonis arbitrium scriptum uideretur*, 2.1.41.106). Cicero focuses his invective energies on the socially marginal Chelidon, Verres' upmarket prostitute, to whom he elsewhere applies the derogatory diminutive *meretricula*, 'a contemptible little whore' (2.3.12.30). Like pimps and other practitioners of disreputable professions at Rome, *meretrices* suffered civic disabilities under Roman law which made all the more disgraceful Verres' revision of the praetor's edict according to the wishes of such a one.[41] Cicero's portrait of Chelidon and her actions during Verres' praetorship at Rome, by emphasizing the courtesan's illegitimate assumption of male power, strategically documents Verres' abuse of his political authority as *praetor urbanus* in order to prefigure his abuse of gubernatorial authority.

For in Sicily too, Cicero maintains, Verres' house was the domain of prostitutes, a brothel (*meretriciam domum*, 2.4.55.123; cf. 2.4.4.7). Indeed, he repeatedly links Chelidon to Verres' Sicilian governorship as a kind of shorthand to discredit his administration of the province. Just as Verres entered his praetorship directly 'from Chelidon's arms' (2.1.40.104), according to Cicero, so he set out for Sicily fresh 'from Chelidon's embrace' (*qui e Chelidonis sinu in prouinciam profectus esset*, 2.2.9.24). Cicero implies that Verres' corrupt administration of Sicily was simply an extension of his criminal dereliction of duty as Chelidon's instrument during his praetorship in Rome (2.2.16.39). As he reminds his readers, 'so far from forbidding Chelidon your house during your year of office, you transferred your office bodily to the house of Chelidon' (*itaque non modo a domo tua Chelidonem*

---

**38** On the passage, and its difficulties of interpretation, see Greenwood 1928, 1.232, with n. a; and Mitchell 1986, 205.
**39** McGinn 2004, 85.
**40** On the Roman horror of class-mixing, see McGinn 2004, 84–93.
**41** On *infamia* in relation to prostitution, see Edwards 1997; McGinn 1998, 21–69.

*in praetura excludere noluisti sed in Chelidonis domum praeturam totam detulisti*, 2.5.15.38).[42] Chelidon's recurrent association with Verres' Sicilian governorship is an especially striking feature of Cicero's rhetorical strategy in the second action, since she neither accompanied him to Sicily nor visited him there; indeed, the orator himself refers to her death during the first year of Verres' governorship (2.2.47.116). Yet he repeatedly conjures the memory 'of that contemptible courtesan Chelidon', and her illegitimate sway over the Verres' administration of the urban praetorship (*iura omnia praetoris urbani nutu atque arbitrio Chelidonis meretriculae*, 2.5.13.34), to reinforce his portrait of Verres in Sicily as a brothel-keeper. In his strategic representation of Verres' relations with Chelidon, Cicero figures the perversion of Verres' political and social bonds with the Roman elite and prefigures his financial and administrative abuses in Sicily.

As in Lampsacus, where his legate Rubrius pimped for him; as in Rome, where leading Roman citizens attended his mistress' house to plead their cases; so in Sicily, Cicero argues, Verres established his household as a brothel in which to enmesh provincials and their womenfolk. Thus, he asserts, Verres would 'briefly' administer the law 'in his bedroom (*in cubiculo*) for an hour or two on principles more profitable than equitable' before retiring 'to devote the rest of the day to the service of Venus and Bacchus' (2.5.10.27). Cicero underlines his scandalous disregard for Roman military standards of travel ('no one ever saw him on horseback', 2.5.10.27) in ironic reference to 'our illustrious commander' (*imperator*, 2.5.11.28), who found 'in all the towns of Sicily … some woman belonging to some respectable family … selected for the gratification of his lust' (*delecta ad libidinem mulier*). The passage resonates suggestively not only with Cicero's treatment of Verres' urban praetorship, headquartered in Chelidon's brothel, but also with his account of Verres' criminal lechery in Lampsacus.

In *Verrines* 2.3, Cicero enlivens his account of Verres' abuse of the Sicilian grain tithe, a topic that he feared might not hold the attention of his audience (2.3.5.10–11), by portraying the Sicilian governor, enslaved to 'license and lust' (*licentiam libidinemque*), as not merely a Greek tyrant (*rex Siculorum*) but an Eastern potentate, like 'the native kings in Persia and Syria' (*reges barbaros Persarum ac Syrorum*), with 'numerous wives' (*plures uxores*) across the province (2.3.33.76–7). Among the members of Verres' royal harem, Cicero presents a trio of wealthy Sicilian women, including two whom he scandalously names as tax collectors in their own right, Pipa and Tertia. Casting Pipa as one of Verres' royal wives, Cicero transforms a provincial Sicilian's wife into a prostituted member of

---

[42] On Cicero's habit of accusing his opponents of turning their homes into brothels, see McGinn 2004, 163 n. 155.

Verres' harem and the provincial himself into a cuckold, a 'counterfeit husband' (*uir adumbrates*, 2.3.33.77). The cuckolded husband is also a counterfeit tax-collector, in Cicero's picture of the people of Herbita at the mercy of his wife's capricious demands (*ad arbitrium libidinosissimae mulieris*). On Cicero's telling, it is Pipa who is the true 'tithe-collector' (*decumana mulier*), in a grotesque inversion of the gendered protocols of Roman financial administration. As a woman who traffics in coin, moreover, Pipa is implicitly cast as a prostitute (*meretrix*, 'a woman who earns money'). Her memorialization in public verse further contributes to the characterization as a woman whose name circulates in public: 'couplets referring to this woman (*de qua muliere uersus plurimi*) were constantly being scribbled over the dais and above the praetor's head'. Pompeii provides a rich stock of evidence for the circulation of the kind of sexual graffiti to which Cicero here alludes (the charge is repeated verbatim at 2.5.31.81).[43]

In conjunction with the tithe-collecting couple Pipa and Aeschrio, Cicero introduces the barley-collecting couple Tertia and Docimus, the latter another counterfeit husband, 'the man whom Verres had assigned as 'husband' to Tertia, the daughter of Isidorus the mime (*Isidori mimi filiam*), after he had carried her off from her Rhodian flute-player' (2.3.34.78). By naming Tertia the daughter of a mime actor, Cicero asserts her low status as not just another provincial Greek woman (like Pipa) but one subject to *infamia* (like Chelidon), though both her name and her husband's profession imply her membership in the wealthy Sicilian elite if not their Roman citizenship.[44] Cicero demeans her social standing not only by the repeated insinuation that her father was a Greek mime actor and her first husband a professional musician, but also by his recourse to comic tropes in his account of Verres' 'theft' of her (*ui abductam*) and 'assignment' to the tithe-collector Docimus (*ad quem iste deduxerat Tertiam*) — by implication for his own use.[45] We may compare the comic competition over sexual access to a subaltern

---

**43** On sex in the Pompeian graffiti, see McGinn 2004, index s.v. 'graffiti'; Milnor 2014.
**44** The familiar Roman process of tax collection, conducted by *publicani*, did not obtain in the case of the grain tax in Sicily, where the Romans continued the practice, instituted by Hiero II of Syracuse, of collecting the grain tax in kind. The Roman governor held annual auctions of the island's tithes in Sicily, with the result that Sicilians rather than Roman citizens constituted the majority of the tithe collectors, who were basically 'commodity speculators', 'small businessmen' who made up their bids by contracting with the farmers in their districts to contribute a fixed amount (one tenth of their projected harvest) to his bid. See Frazel 2009, 196–8, synthesizing Carcopino 1919; Pritchard 1970; Brunt 1980; Rickman 1980; Badian 1983.
**45** On Cicero's use of comic tropes in his speeches, see Corbeill 1996; on Cicero's wit, see Beard 2014, 99–127. On comic tropes in the *Pro Caelio*, see Austin 1964; Geffcken 1973; Leigh 2004.

female in Plautus' *Casina*, in which a father and son compete for sexual possession of the family slave Casina through slave proxies, who draw lots to 'marry' her and make her sexually available to their master. Yet it is really Tertia, according to Cicero, who calls the shots: 'she had more influence (*auctoritas*) over him than any of his other women, more even than Pipa; as much, I would almost venture to say, while he was praetor in Sicily as Chelidon had while he was praetor in Rome'.

Having set the scene for comic contestation, Cicero continues with a description of Verres' tax collection arrangements as bedroom farce (2.3.34.78). Aeschrio and Docimus he casts as Verres' 'rivals in love' (*aemuli*), 'the rascally agents of worthless disreputable wives' (*muliercularum deterrimarum improbissimi cognitores*). His rivals make no difficulty (*non molesti*) for Verres because they have been brought to heel by his generous arrangements for their wives' profit. Against their fellow-provincials at Herbita, however, 'they brought all manner of false charges', requiring them to appear in court and hand over to Aeschrio, 'in other words, to Pipa' (*hoc est Pipae*), the kickback that Cicero insinuates Verres had accepted for knocking down the total sale-price of their grain. As unofficial tax-collector (*mulierculae publicanae*), Pipa is the true recipient of the Herbitenses' payment — in Cicero's untranslatable pun, both a 'publicly earning contemptible woman' (i.e., a prostitute) and a 'contemptibly prostituting publican'. The play underlies Cicero's attribution to Verres of an interest, both avaricious and lecherous, in 'the profits of her own nocturnal profession' (*ab nocturno suo quaestu*).

Just when the Herbitenses imagined they were fully paid up, however, Cicero adds Verres' scandalous interference in their arrangements for paying the barley-tax (2.3.34.79):[46] 'Well now, what are you thinking of doing about the barley and my dear friend Docimus?' Cicero draws the jury members' attention to Verres' transaction of state business on this occasion in his bedroom (*in cubiculo*), indeed in his very bed (*atque in lecto suo*), information which confirms the governor's household as a brothel and the governor himself a pimp. Like the Eastern potentates, moreover, to whom Cicero compares him at the opening of the scene, Verres visibly enjoys the 'conjugal' visits of his 'wives', in this case Tertia, whose imprint is still fresh in his bed (*in lecto decumanae mulieris uestigia recentia*). In Cicero's prejudicial account, she herself appears, like Pipa, as a female 'tax collector' (*decumana mulier*) and avaricious prostitute, her greed rivaling that of Verres, whom she 'stimulates' (Cicero's Latin encodes a different sexual pun, on 'inflaming' Verres) in his determination to fleece the Herbitenses (2.3.34.79): 'Thus, this

---

46 Carcopino 1919, 255–77.

allied and friendly community became tributary to two worthless working women (*duabus deterrimis mulierculis*), when Verres was governor of Sicily'.

Cicero expostulates with Verres that he was even emboldened to reduce the total sale-price of the Sicilian grain tax to pay off his whore (*mulieri deterrimae*, 2.3.35.82), implying that after auction 'Verres would change a sale price, have the new price entered into the public record, and then force the town to hand over the difference to the winning bidder, namely one of his henchmen'.[47] Cicero hints that the fortunate *decumanus* would then share a portion of those profits with Verres. Still worse, the orator here insinuates that Verres has made over the payment to his mistress Tertia, Docimus' prostituted wife. After knocking down the price of the Acestans' tithes to Docimus, 'in effect to Tertia' (*hoc est Tertiae*), instead of pocketing the cash himself 'he made a present of it to Tertia the actress' (*Tertiae mimae condonauit*, 2.3.36.83). Cicero asks his audience: 'Which is worst — the shameless robbery of our allies, the disgraceful present to a whore (*turpius meretrici dedit*), the unscrupulous theft from the people of Rome, or the impudent forgery of official records?' Through his strategic recourse to the rhetoric of gender, Cicero vividly documents Verres' brazen abuse of Roman financial and political protocols in the administration of their wealthiest province. He impugns Tertia's social standing not only by her receipt of the Sicilians' payments but also by calling her a 'mime actress' (*mima*), like her father the 'mime actor' Isidorus (cf. 2.3.34.78, quoted above). Both charges figure her as a prostitute, trafficking in provincial coin for personal profit.

Verres' lust for provincial women imperiled not only Rome's grain supply from Sicily (*Verr.* 2.3) but also Rome's naval control of the province (*Verr.* 2.5). For, Cicero alleges, out of a lecherous desire for the Syracusan Cleomenes' wife Nike, Verres appointed a provincial to the command of the Roman fleet based in Syracuse, in violation of the tradition that the Roman governor should appoint one of his staff to the position (2.5.31.82–32.83). In this way, Nike joined Verres' 'royal harem' of Sicilian 'wives', with whom he routinely spent his summers in 'a fixed camp' with 'a number of pavilions, made of linen canvas stretched on poles' pitched 'in the loveliest part of Syracuse', 'at the very entrance to the harbour' (2.5.12.29–30). This famous set-piece has long been admired for its vivid imagery but it is rarely considered as a textbook case of ethnic and gendered rhetoric.

Cicero describes the governor's summer residence in the most scandalous terms (2.5.12.30): 'To this place came all the women with whom he had associated — and the number of these at Syracuse is beyond belief...'. Especially entertaining is Cicero's imputation of a catfight amongst Verres' women over access to

---

47 Frazel 2009, 198.

his sexual attentions: 'The bringing there of that woman Tertia, after the crafty trick of her abduction from her Rhodian flute-player, is said to have caused a serious upheaval in Verres' camp, as the wife of Cleomenes of Syracuse [Nike], being a lady of rank, and also the wife of Aeschrio [Pipa], who came of a good family, resented the addition to their society of a daughter of Isidorus the mime actor'. Cicero supports his argument that Verres was no *bonus imperator* but a Greek tyrant and Eastern potentate in the scurrilous report of his dress ('in a purple Greek cloak and a long-skirted tunic') and lechery ('reveling with his women'). His expensive Greek dress, lavish summer camp, and royal harem assimilate him to an effete foreign princeling, who might mistake Hannibal himself, Rome's foremost historical enemy, for a Roman model of imperial governance (2.5.13.31).

By publicly naming all three of the Greek women, Cicero figures Verres' sordid traffic in provincial women as a metaphor for his illegitimate administration of the province of Sicily. On the occasion of the Sicilian slave rebellion, for example, a deputation arrived from Valentia to request assistance from Verres at his sea-side retreat, where he had taken 'that woman of yours, Tertia (*Tertia illa tua*), in full view of everyone' (2.5.16.40). Cicero underlines Verres' public display of Tertia before a delegation of respectable provincials, just as he highlights the outlines of her prostituted body in Verres' bed before the Herbitenses' commission (quoted above, 2.3.34.79). The description of Verres at the meeting with the Valentians, scandalously clad in 'a dark tunic and a Greek cloak' (*tunica pulla et pallio*), likewise confirms his abdication from administrative responsibility, for the tunic was a workman's attire and the cloak the distinctive attire not of a Roman general but of a Greek tyrant.[48] Like his inappropriate clothing, the illegitimate circulation of his provincial women documents Verres' abuse of provincial authority. In his strategic representation of Verres' relations with these 'prostituted' provincial women, Cicero figures the perversion of Verres' political and social bonds with the Roman elite.

Cicero's ubiquitous employment of the rhetorics of gender and ethnicity in the *Verrines* arguably tells us more about Roman misogyny and xenophobia than about the lived experience of women and provincials, two intersecting classes of subaltern populations, at the end of the Roman republic — except insofar as both misogyny and xenophobia structured the lives of women and provincials in this period. Nonetheless, it is possible to draw some significant conclusions from this exploration of Cicero's portrait of Verres' lechery, avarice, and tyranny. Every

---

48 Greenwood 1928, 2.348 n. a. On the social conventions of Roman dress, see Edmondson and Keith 2008.

woman in the *Verrines* is portrayed in such a way as to serve Cicero's forensic purpose, his aim to secure Verres' conviction in the extortion court.[49] They are distinguished not according to ethnic identity but sexual availability. Thus, respectable women (i.e., sexually unavailable women) of both Roman citizen and Greek provincial status are unnamed (Philodamus' daughter, Annius' daughter, Malleolus' mother and grandmother) while women who appear in public forfeit social respectability and so can be named with impunity (Chelidon, Pipa, Nike, Tertia).

Interesting tensions emerge, however, to complicate these neat distinctions. Without father or husband, a Roman citizen woman such as Annaea is vulnerable to publicity (and can therefore be named) during the transaction of her financial affairs, even when she has secured permission from relatives and tutors (2.1.43.111). This vulnerability reflects the conventional Roman view of financial transactions, with their proximity to coin, as sordid. Nonetheless, Cicero's record of the name Annaea is precious evidence for the capacity of Roman citizen women to make wills that reflect their testamentary wishes. This evidence can be paralleled in Cicero's correspondence, which details Terentia's financial transactions and illuminates the paradoxical respectability of Annaea's attempts to work around the *lex Voconia* in order to provide for her child.

Other evidence in the *Verrines* for Roman women's financial wherewithal may be furnished by Cicero's repeated references to Chelidon's house, which we have to this point considered only in relation to his damning portrait of Verres' administration of his magistracies in brothels. But Cicero's very insistence on the setting of Chelidon's house (e.g. *meretricis domum*, 2.1.50.137) as the site of Verres' transaction of official business is of considerable interest for the implication that she owned or rented a Roman townhouse (*domus*) large enough to accommodate men, not just in bedrooms but also in public rooms. Nor is this the only information we can glean from the *Verrines* about Chelidon's financial wherewithal. For while denouncing Verres' dedication to Venus Erycina of a silver Cupid holding a torch stolen from a prominent Sicilian, Cicero observes that Verres' own resources could have financed the offering to Venus, 'especially as that very year [he] had had a legacy from Chelidon' (*praesertim cum tibi illo ipso anno a Chelidone uenisset hereditas*, 2.2.47.116), and he later insinuates that this legacy included many choice works of art (2.4.32.71). Indeed, it is clear that her

---

**49** My discussion thus supports the argument of Hillard 1989.

moveable property, much of which may have come to her by way of payment for sexual services, was both rich and extensive.⁵⁰

The very ease and informality of Cicero's remarks about Chelidon's wealth imply that the legal disabilities to which *infames* such as *meretrices* were subject in classical Rome did not include the inability to make a will or leave moveable property where they pleased.⁵¹ Inscriptional and juridical evidence suggests, moreover, that the legal and financial disabilities to which they were subject were connected not with their receipt of payment in gifts (like respectable citizens), but rather with their receipt of payment in coin (felt to be sordid). The light these passages shed on the legal capacity and testamentary practices of subaltern women is often overlooked, but opens up fascinating avenues of inquiry. Was Chelidon Verres' freedwoman? Did she have a legal Roman name, Verria Chelidon? Was her bequest to Verres the bequest of a freedwoman to her patron?⁵²

Finally, we may consider the contrasting evidence of Verres' administrative practices in Lampsacus and Sicily for Greek women's participation in public life. We may safely set aside Cicero's comic characterization of Pipa and Tertia as 'lady tax collectors' in Sicily, though there is every reason to believe that they took an interest in their husbands' financial schemes, as we know that Terentia and other elite Roman women did in this period.⁵³ Cicero's upright Greek provincial Philodamus articulates the well-known rule that respectable Greek women did not attend male drinking parties.⁵⁴ Yet his arrangement of an exclusively Roman male dinner party contrasts with the Greek custom of all-male dining; it is surprising that he invited none of his fellow citizens to meet the visiting Roman dignitaries over dinner. Philodamus' banquet also stands in strong contrast to the Roman practice of inviting husbands with their wives to dinner parties, such as seems to

---

50 On prostitutes' earnings, see Gardner 2008 [1986], 250–3; more nuanced discussion in McGinn 2004, 14–77. On the legal position of prostitutes generally, see McGinn 1998.
51 On women's rights of inheritance and bequest, see Gardner 2008 [1986], 163–203; on the limitations of freedwomen's financial rights under guardianship and in inheritance, see Perry 2014, 83–8. Neither discusses courtesans' (or prostitutes') rights of inheritance and bequest specifically; but for freedwomen's rights of inheritance and bequest, see Gardner 2008 [1986] 168–9, 191, 194–6; Perry 2014.
52 While all women in classical Rome were required to obtain their *tutor*'s consent to make a valid will, freedwomen were further restricted in their capacity for testamentary disposal by the fact that their patron was their *tutor legitimus* and had first claim on the estate if they died intestate: see Gardner 2008 [1986], 168; Perry 2014, 84–5. Plutarch records another instance of a prostitute's bequest to a Roman politician in his *Life of Sulla* (2.4); on Roman republican politicians' connections with prostitutes, see McGinn 2004, 54 n. 285, 91–2 n. 80.
53 Treggiari 2007; Bielman 2012; Brennan 2012.
54 On the violence associated with such parties, see McGinn 2004, 88–92.

have been Verres' habit — perhaps shocking to provincial sensibilities — in Sicily. Yet the evidence that Cicero preserves for Sicilian women's keen interest in their husbands' political maneuvering during Verres' governorship can be paralleled among elite Roman women in this period,[55] and might best be interpreted as an indication of the values that Cicero, the jurors, the broader Roman community, his provincial clients, and indeed all Roman provincials could share.

## Works Cited

Alexander, M.C. (1976), 'Hortensius' Speech in Defense of Verres,' *Phoenix* 30, 46–53.
Alexander, M.C. (1990), *Trials in the Late Roman Republic, 149 B.C. to 50 B.C*, Toronto.
Austin, R.G. (ed.) (1964), *Pro M. Caelio oratio*. 3$^{rd}$ ed., Oxford.
Badian, E. (1983), *Publicans and Sinners. Private Enterprise in the Service of the Roman Republic*, Ithaca, NY.
Baldo, G.B. (1999), 'Enna: un paesaggio del mito tra storia e religio', in: G. Avezzù/E. Pianezzola (eds.), *Sicilia e magna Grecia. Spazi reale e spazio immaginario nella letteratura greca e latina*, Padua, 17–57.
Baldo, G.B. (ed.) (2004), *M. Tulli Ciceronis, In C. Verrem Actionis Secundae Liber Quartus (De Signis)*, Florence.
Balsdon, J.P.V.D. (1938), 'History of the Extortion Court at Rome 123–70 B.C.', *PBSR* 14, 98–114.
Beard, M. (2014), *Laughter in Ancient Rome: on Joking, Tickling, and Cracking Up*, Berkeley.
Bielman, A. (2012), 'Female Patronage in the Greek Hellenistic and Roman Republican Periods', in: James/Dillon 2012, 238–48.
Boatwright, M.T. (2011), 'Women and Gender in the Forum Romanum', *TAPA* 141, 105–41.
Brennan, T.C. (2012), 'Perceptions of Women's Power in the Late Republic: Terentia, Fulvia, and the Generation of 63 BCE', in: James/Dillon 2012, 354–66.
Brunt, P.A. (1980), 'Patronage and Politics in the *Verrines*,' *Chiron* 10, 273–89.
Butler, S. (2002), *The Hand of Cicero*, London/New York.
Carcopino, J. (1919), *La loi de Hiéron et les Romains*, Paris.
Citroni Marchetti, S. (1986), 'L'avvocato, il giudice, il "reus" (la psicologia della colpa e del vizio nelle opera retoriche e nelle prime orazioni di Cicerone),' *MD* 17, 93–124.
Connolly, J. (2007), 'Virile Tongues: Rhetoric and Masculinity', in: W. Dominik/J. Hall (eds.), *Blackwell Companion to Roman Rhetoric*, Malden, MA, 83–97.
Corbeill, A. (1996), *Controlling Laughter: Political Humor in the Late Roman Republic*, Princeton.
Cox, C.A. (2012), 'Women and Family in Menander', in: James/Dillon 2012, 278–87.
Craig, C. (1985), 'Dilemma in Cicero's *Divinatio in Caecilium*,' *AJP* 106, 442–6.
Crook, J.A. (1986), 'Women in Roman Succession', in: E. Rawson (ed.), *The Family in Ancient Rome: New Perspectives*, Ithaca, NY, 58–82.
Dickison, S.K. (1992), *Cicero's Verrine Oration II.4*, Detroit.

---

[55] Bielman 2012.

Dinter, M.T. (2019), 'Fathers and Sons', in: M.T. Dinter (ed.), *Cambridge Companion to Roman Comedy*, Cambridge, 173–87.
Dixon, S. (1985), 'Breaking the Law to do the Right Thing: the Gradual Erosion of the Voconian Law in Ancient Rome', *Adelaide Law Review* 9, 519–34.
Dubouloz, J./Pittia, S. (eds.) (2007), *Sicile de Cicéron: Lectures des* Verrines, Paris.
Edmondson, J./Keith, A. (eds.) (2008), *Roman Dress and the Fabric of Roman Culture,* Toronto.
Edwards, C. (1993), *The Politics of Immorality in Ancient Rome,* Cambridge.
Edwards, C. (1997), 'Unspeakable Professions: Public Performance and Prostitution in Ancient Rome', in: J.P. Hallett/M.B. Skinner (eds.), *Roman Sexualities*, Princeton, 66–95.
Flower, H.I. (2003), 'Memories of Marcellus: History and Memory in Roman Republican Culture', in: U. Eigler/U. Gottter/N. Luraghi/U. Walter (eds.), *Formen römischer Geschichtsschreibung von den Anfängen bis Livius: Gattungen, Autoren, Contexte*, Darmstadt, 39–52.
Frazel, T.D. (2004), 'The Composition and Circulation of Cicero's *In Verrem*,' *CQ* 54.1, 128–42.
Frazel, T.D. (2009), *The Rhetoric of Cicero's* In Verrem, Göttingen.
Gardner, J.F. (2008[1986]), *Women in Roman Law and Society,* New York.
Geffcken, K.A. (1973), *Comedy in the* Pro Caelio: *with an appendix on the* in Clodium et Curionem, Leiden.
Greenwood, L.H.G. (ed.) (1928), *Cicero, The Verrine Orations*, 2 vols., Cambridge, MA.
Gruen, E.S. (1968), *Roman Politics and the Criminal Courts, 149–78 B.C.,* Cambridge, MA.
Gunderson, E. (2000), *Staging Masculinity: the Rhetoric of Performance in the Roman World,* Ann Arbor, MI.
Hallett, J.P. (2014[1984]), *Fathers and daughters in Roman society: women and the elite family,* Princeton.
Henderson, J. (2018[1987]), *Aristophanes*: Lysistrata, Oxford.
Henderson, M.I. (1951), 'The Process *De Repetundis*', *JRS* 41, 71–88.
Hillard, T. (1989), 'Republican Politics, Women and the Evidence', *Helios* 16, 165–82.
Hunter, R.L. (1985), *The New Comedy of Greece and Rome,* Cambridge.
Innocenti, B. (1994), 'Towards a Theory of Vivid Description as Practiced in Cicero's *Verrine Orations*,' *Rhetorica* 12, 355–81.
James, S.L./Dillon, S. (eds.) (2012), *A Companion to Women in the Ancient World*. Malden, MA/ Oxford.
Keith, A. (2018), 'Historical Roman Courtesans', in: R. Berg/R. Neudecker (eds.), *The Roman Courtesan: Archaeological Reflections of a Literary Topos*, Rome, 73–86.
Leigh, M. (2004), *Comedy and the Rise of Rome*, Oxford/New York.
Lintott, A.W. (1981), 'The *leges de repetundis* and Associated Measures under the Republic', *Zeitschrift der Savigny-Stiftung für Rechtsgeschichte* 98, 162–211.
Marshall, A.J. (1989), 'Ladies and Law: the Role of Women in the Roman Civil Courts', in: C. Deroux (ed.), *Studies in Latin Literature and Roman History*, Collection Latomus 207, Brussels, 35–54.
McClintock, A. (2013), 'The *Lex Voconia* and Cornelia's Jewels', *Revue Internationale des droits de l'Antiquité* 60, 183–200.
McDermott, W.C. (1977), 'The Verrine Jury', *RhM* 120, 64–75.
McGinn, T.A.J. (1998), *Prostitution, Sexuality, and the Law in Ancient Rome*, New York/Oxford.
McGinn, T.A.J. (2004), *The Economy of Prostitution in the Roman World*, Ann Arbor, MI.
Milnor, K. (2014), *Graffiti and the Literary Landscape in Roman Pompeii*, Oxford.
Mitchell, T.N. (1986), *Cicero:* Verrines *II.1*, Warminster.
Morrell, K. (2017), *Pompey, Cato, and the Governance of the Roman Empire,* Oxford.

Olson, K. (2008), *Dress and the Roman Woman: Self-presentation and Society*, London/New York.

Perry, M.J. (2014), *Gender, Manumission, and the Roman Freedwoman*, New York.

Peterson, W. (ed.) (1917), *M. Tulli Ciceronis Orationes. III.*², Oxford.

Pritchard, R.T. (1970), 'Cicero and the *Lex Hieronica*', *Historia* 19, 352–68.

Richlin, A. (1997), 'Gender and Rhetoric: Producing Manhood in the Schools', in: W.J. Dominik (ed.), *Roman Eloquence: Rhetoric in Society and Literature*, London.

Rickman, G. (1980), *The Corn Supply of Ancient Rome*, Oxford.

Riess, W. (2012), '*Rari exempli femina*: Female Virtues on Roman Funerary Inscriptions', in: James/Dillon 2012, 491–501.

Rizzo, F.P. (1980), '*Principes ciuitatis* nelle Verrine: Realtà civica e idealità Ciceroniana', *Ciceroniana, Nuova Serie* 4, 211–21.

Schaps, D. (1977), 'The Woman Least Mentioned: Etiquette and Women's Names', *CQ* 27, 323–30.

Treggiari, S. (2007), *Terentia, Tullia and Publilia: the Women of Cicero's Family*, London/New York.

Vasaly, A. (2009), 'Cicero, Domestic Politics, and the First Action of the *Verrines*', *CA* 28, 101–37.

Jacqueline Fabre-Serris
# Identities and Ethnicities in the Punic Wars: Livy's Portrait of the Carthaginian Sophonisba

There are many situations during war (fighting, embassies, and alliances) where ethnic groups become aware of their differences in behavior, ethical values, and beliefs. As a result, they usually emphasize these differences by highlighting their own (real or constructed) characteristic features and arguing that these features played a major role in the successful outcome of the conflicts. The Romans built up a vast empire, in which most of the defeated peoples had been integrated. The question of what had constituted, and did constitute, Roman identity was acute and particularly complex, not only during these successive wars, but afterwards, when the ancient historians sought to retrace the great steps of the Empire by analyzing the various impacts of its conquests on the specificity and evolution of Roman culture. As Feeney has observed, 'What counts as Roman culture is continually being reinvented and redefined as a result of the mutual interaction between the Romans and other peoples with whom they progressively come into contact'.[1]

As scholars have noted, Livy is always seeking to highlight 'Roman' moral values and behaviors, by promoting them as having significantly contributed to the glorious story of Rome. The superiority of the Roman cultural model, based on, among other virtues, the practice of bravery, justice, loyalty and self-control,[2] is thus vaunted as explaining the defeat and justifying the assimilation of the conquered peoples.[3] This perspective is particularly noticeable in Livy's many narratives on the Punic wars. This was the longest and most dangerous period of war for Rome, but also the last one praised by the Augustan writers as illustrating the good practice of *mores* defined as typically Roman.[4] The following wars, conversely, were seen as having paved the way to foreign ways of living, thinking, and behaving, whose influence was deemed negatively decisive on the evolution and crisis of the Roman cultural model.

---

[1] Feeney 2016, 93.
[2] See Moore 1989.
[3] As recalled by Levene (2010, 214), Livy was native of Padua, a city of Cisalpine Gaul that was not fully enfranchised and incorporated into Italy at the time of his birth.
[4] According to Walsh (1996, 189–90), Livy believes that the hidden seeds of moral decline began to be sown in 187 upon the return of Manlius Volso with his army from Asia.

In Livy's time, the topical issue of morality and sexuality had become particularly important since Augustus had launched a policy of return to traditional values, stressing the prevalence of collective interests and advocating for sexual self-regulation.[5] This policy was in direct opposition to the lifestyle described and promoted in the only literary genre invented by the Romans, the love elegy. This new genre was successively practiced by many male poets and even by a female poet, with the result that the elegiac 'lover's discourse' focused on *furor* and advocating for sexual passion, became widespread across the whole of Roman society.

When Livy relates the events from the Numidian leader Masinissa's hasty marriage to Sophonisba (resulting from the fact that he is suddenly sexually aroused by his captive) to Sophonisba's death by suicide, as Levene has shown, the historian uses certain notions relating to ethnicity as a key to understanding the relations between the Romans and the Numidian leaders, Syphax and Masinissa. Both Numidians are subject to their sexual impulses,[6] whereas the *temperantia* ('self-control') embodied by Scipio is peculiarly Roman.

In line with this very illuminating perspective, I will argue that the comparison made by Livy between different behaviors supposedly resulting from the membership in a particular ethnic group also includes the Carthaginians. When relating this episode of the Punic Wars, Diodorus, Appian, and Cassius Dio do not assign an important role to Sophonisba, despite the fact that Masinissa and Syphax become, each after the other, the allies of the Carthaginians because they want to marry her. In their accounts, although Sophonisba is not merely a passive object of desire, she plays only a minor role through her ultimate but ineffective attempt to manipulate Masinissa. I will try to show that Livy, conversely, is the only historian who, in this episode, gives a major role to Hasdrubal's daughter, whom he describes as 'representative' of the Carthaginian enemy. It is indeed no coincidence that Livy calls Sophonisba not only *uxor Syphacis* but also *filia Hasdrubalis Poeni* (30.12.11).[7] In reflecting on identity and ethnicity Livy thus integrates the parameter 'genre' that was playing a more important role in Roman society when he was writing than at the time of the historical events he relates.

---

[5] See Edwards 1993.
[6] Levene 2010, 258–9.
[7] It should be noted that Sophonisba is always identified in relation to the names of her family members, whether by birth or marriage, with the sole exception of when Syphax uses the word *matrona* (on the use of this word in Livy, see Truschnegg 2000).

# 1 Sophonisba and Masinissa: a captive and her victor

We do not know in which historians Livy found the first mention of this episode of the Punic Wars. Some modern critics have suggested as sources Coelius Aniter, by arguing that the latter was interested in portraying women,[8] or Valerius Antias, because of the similarities with the episode of the Celtiberian captive.[9] Regardless, in my study I will take into account the choices made by Livy both regarding the factual elements and his way of telling the story. Regarding the factual elements, the most striking choice, noted by many scholars,[10] is that Livy seems to intentionally ignore what Diodorus, Appian, and Cassius Dio present as 'fact': Sophonisba and Masinissa would have been betrothed or married before the daughter of Hasdrubal was finally given in marriage to Syphax.[11] According to Livy, Masinissa and Sophonisba had never seen each other before meeting in the palace of Cirta, which Livy describes in detail at the beginning of his narra-

---

**8** See, for Coelius Aniter, Burck 1934, 26, De Sanctis 1968, 181, and Walsh 1961, and for Valerius Antias, Soltau 1894, 57 (14.1.4; 7.6).
**9** Sophonisba is mentioned twice in the fragments of Polybius on the Punic War. In the first passage (14.1.4), Scipio, once landed in Africa, tries to make Syphax, who had become an ally of the Carthaginians because of his wife, change sides. In the second passage (14.17.6), Polybius relates that Sophonisba successfully begged her husband not to abandon the Carthaginians.
**10** This divergence between Livy and the other historians is noted by Haley 1989, 174, Johner 1996, 243–4, Kowalewski 2002, 225, and Levene 2010, 236 n. 239.
**11** According to Diodorus (27.7), Sophonisba was first married to Masinissa, then to Syphax, and came back to share Masinissa's life. According to Appian (*Pun.* 10), Masinissa was raised in Carthage and Sophonisba was engaged to him by her father, Hasdrubal. However, to get military assistance from Syphax, as the latter was in love with Sophonisba and began to pillage the territory of Carthage, the Carthaginians gave her in marriage to Syphax, without Hasdrubal and Masinissa knowing it. Consequently Masinissa passed to the side of the Romans. According to Cassius Dio (Zonaras 9.11, 9.13), to get military assistance from Syphax, Hasdrubal gave him her daughter in marriage, even though he had promised her in marriage to Masinissa. For Haley (1989, 174), the effect of Livy's choice 'emphasizes Sophonisba's persuasive skills and Masinissa's impetuosity'. As a result, in Livy, the latter is not, as among the historians for whom he was engaged or married to Sophonisba, in the process of 'recovering his property' (I leave to Haley the responsibility for this formula) and restoring his honor. For Johner (1996, 243–4), because of the version given by Livy, the final episode illustrates above all the weakness of Masinissa, that is also underscored by Scipio's moralizing and haughty intervention.

tive. Regarding Livy's way of telling the story, if we refer to the terminology invented by Genette[12] to analyze 'the forms of narrative', the Roman historian prefers to use, not the 'summary' normally used in a historical narrative, but the 'scene', where the exchange of directly-reported words allows the author to highlight different 'points of view,'[13] while contextualizing them in a particular space.

The first scene imagined by Livy is located in the royal palace of Cirta when, after defeating Syphax, Masinissa is entering the forecourt (*intranti uestibulum*, 30.12.11). The version, chosen or invented by Livy, in which Masinissa and Sophonisba have never met before, allows him to construct a scene inspired by the tragic genre. Like in a tragic play, one of the characters goes towards the other at the very threshold (*in ipso limine*). The reader is in the position of a spectator who attends the meeting between a victor and his captive, in which the captive addresses a request to the victor by attempting to arouse his pity. Sophonisba identifies Masinissa, 'conspicuous both by his arms and the rest of his dress' (*insignem cum armis tum cetero habitu*, 30.12.11), rushes toward him,[14] and launches into a scene of supplication, saying, 'If a captive is permitted in front of the master of her life and her death to lift the voice of a suppliant' (*si captiuae apud dominum uitae necisque suae uocem supplicem mittere licet*, 30.12.12).

## 1.1 A reasoned request

Livy puts a long tirade into the mouth of Sophonisba, in the posture of a pleading woman at the feet of the person to whom, she says, the gods, his *uirtus* ('courage') and his *felicitas* ('good fortune/divine protection') have given all power over her and Syphax (*omnia quidem ut posses ... in nobis*, 30.12.12). This tirade is highly political in its aim and its arguments. Sophonisba begs Masinissa by the royal state in which until recently she and Syphax were also living (*per maiestatem regiam in qua paulo ante nos quoque fuimus*), then by the Numidian race which

---

[12] Genette 1972, 128–44.
[13] I will not endorse the notion of 'tragic story', theorized at the end of the 19th century in the Greek historiography and applied to Livy by Burk in 1934 (see De Franchis 2015). On the other hand, my study is in line with Conte's paper 'Saggio di interpretazione dell'*Eneide*. Ideologia e forma del contenuto', on 'la moltiplicazione dei punti di vista' and its effects: relativise 'la norma epica e la sua significazone ideologica'. This perspective applies, *mutatis mutandis*, given the difference in literary genre, to the historical genre, and is quite enlightening on the effects induced by Livy's narrative choices.
[14] In Cassius Dio, the situation is the opposite: when he sees Sophonisba, Masinissa rushes out to meet her.

Masinissa shares with Syphax (*per gentis Numidarum nomen quod tibi cum Syphace commune fuit*, 30.12.13). To add value to this argument, Livy has used the word *nomen*, which is particularly telling for the Romans. Sophonisba finishes this part of her speech by invoking the gods and hoping that they will be more favorable to Masinissa than they were for Syphax. Only after this cautious and skillful start does she present her request. Sophonisba implores Masinissa to remain her only master and not deliver her 'into the haughty and cruel power of any Roman' (*in cuiusquam Romani superbum et crudele arbitrium*, 30.12.15). The words chosen in Livy are particularly hard (*superbum, crudele, arbitrium*) and scornful (*cuiusquam Romani*). These are the words of an enemy of Rome, who implicitly supposes that her interlocutor could share her judgment. Sophonisba thus specifies that, even if she was only the wife of Syphax, she would prefer to trust the word (*fides*) of a Numidian than to rely on a 'man of another race and a foreigner' (*alienigenae et externi*, 30.12.15). She precisely refers to community of geographical origin that she shares with Masinissa, 'a man born in the same Africa as myself' (*in eadem mecum Africa geniti*, 30.12.15). Livy puts in her mouth the word *fides* ('loyalty, protection, and the word given to ensure it'), expected in the scene of supplication in which a captive attempts to get a promise from a victor. Sophonisba adds that, given her own ethnic and family origin, Masinissa sees[15] what she can expect from the Romans: 'What a Carthaginian, what the daughter of Hasdrubal has to fear from a Roman, you see' (*Quid Carthaginiensi ab Romano* (the juxtaposition of words is striking), *quid filiae Hasdrubalis timendum sit uides*, 30.12.16). She concludes by asking Masinissa again to shield and save her from the *arbitrium* ('arbitrary power') of the Romans and by stating 'by death, if he does not find any other means' (*si nulla re alia potes, morte*, 30.12.16). This imagined speech is intended for the contemporary reader, for whom Livy thus recalls how Rome's enemies view the Roman way of exercising power (*superbum et crudele imperium*), while suggesting that their allies could share this judgment. Independently of his personal reaction towards this critical point of view, the Roman reader could not help but understand, if not approve, the request of Sophonisba: to die rather than become a prisoner.[16] In this episode of the Punic war in which the vital issue for Scipio is to check the fidelity of his Numidian ally, Masinissa, by attributing this request to the 'daughter of Hasdrubal', Livy implicitly emphasizes how implacable was the Carthaginian enemy. In doing so, he also underscores that during war the relentlessness of a people is

---

15   In a very clever way, Sophonisba makes Masinissa take her own point of view.
16   On the ability of Roman historians to put critical speeches in the mouths of Rome's enemies against the Roman Empire, see Adler 2010.

also measured by the way in which the women are committed alongside the men to the continuation of the war. Furthermore the woman staged in this episode is not any woman: Sophonisba belongs to the Carthaginian elite. She is the wife of a king, formerly ally of the Romans, and Livy has often stressed that, as requested by her father, she has played an active role in the defection of his husband.[17]

## 1.2 A speech with seductive gesture

Fictionalising a meeting by creating a typical scene between captive and victor allows Livy to imagine that Sophonisba, whose 'beauty was conspicuous and her age at full bloom' (*forma erat insignis et florentissima aetas*, 30.12.17), had also 'spoken' with her body. While developing a very constructed and controlled discourse, Sophonisba seeks assurances (*fidem*) that Masinissa will not surrender her to any Roman by accompanying her prayers with the usual gestures in these circumstances: she is clasping now his knees, now his hand. At the end, the nature of her speech changes: it becomes 'closer to caresses and flatteries than to the prayers of a suppliant' (*propriusque blanditias iam oratio esset quam preces*, 30.12.17). *Blanditiae* belongs to elegiac vocabulary. But it is also the case for *fides*, used when a lover wants to ensure that he will remain faithful to his beloved until the death. I give as an example this line of Propertius 2.20.18: *ambos una fides auferet, una dies* ('a single faithful love, a single day shall take us both away').[18] For explaining Masinissa's reaction to Sophonisba's words and gestures Livy combines two types of interpretation (30.12.18):

> ... non in misericordiam modo prolapsus est animus uictoris, sed ut est genus Numidarum in Venerem praeceps, amore captiuae uictor captus.
>
> ...the heart of the victor let himself go and was move not only to pity, but, as the Numidian race has (natural) propensity for sexual desire[19], the victor was captivated by love of his captive.

If the 'nature' specific to his race is supposed to make the Numidian victor an easy target for a woman who would 'use her charms', the reversal of the initial scene

---

17 See further below.
18 See also Tibullus 1.9.32; 10.19; 2.2.11; 3.4.4, 64, 6.46, 49 and Propertius, 1.1.16.
19 As noted by Haley 1990, 377, '*uenus* is used by Livy only of barbarians or, in the case of Flamininus, of a Roman acting in a barbaric fashion (39.43.5)'. According to Haley, Livy's depiction of the Numidians is unique and he could have drawn a general conclusion about Numidians, based apparently upon the specific example of Masinissa.

in which a captive is begging her victor (what is expected from the victor is only that he yields to pity) is described in terms referring to the vision Livy's contemporary reader has of love. The discourse about love which prevails at this time in Rome originates in the elegiac genre, in which, because of his amorous *furor*, the man becomes subject to the woman, her slave or captive. By combining this way of describing the phenomenon of love with an ethnic explanation (the temperament specific to the Numidian race), Livy provides his reader with two Roman reading grids. This is not the first time Livy uses these two keys for reading at the same time, but it is perhaps the passage in which this double use is the most explicit. In 29.23.4, according to Livy, Hasdrubal is planning to use the same ethnic feature to push Syphax into the Carthaginian camp. The Carthaginian leader, too, would have deemed the inability to control his sexual impulses as specific to the Numidians: ... *Hasdrubal,* **ut accensum cupiditate** *— et sunt ante omnes barbaros* **Numidae effusi in Venerem** *—, sensit, uirginem a Carthagine arcessit maturatque nuptias* ('... on perceiving that he was fired with passion — and more than all barbarians the Numidians totally indulge in sexual pleasures — he summoned the maiden from Carthage and hastened the wedding'). Hasdrubal also relies on another ethnic feature (on which the Carthaginians agree with the Romans): the unreliability of the Barbarians.[20] 'Remembered ... how naturally characterless and fickle are Barbarians' (*memor... quam* **uana et mutabilia** *barbarorum ingenia essent*, 29.23.6), shortly after her wedding, Hasdrubal tells his daughter to make use of caresses to hasten the defection of her husband, when Syphax was always 'fired by his new-found love' (*accensum recenti amore*, 29.23.7). In 30.7.8, when staging the relations between Sophonisba and Syphax, Livy describes Sophonisba making use not only of caresses, but also of prayers, i.e. the two means she will use later in the scene with Masinissa: *cum uxor non iam ut ante* **blanditiis**, *satis potentibus ad animum amantis, sed* **precibus** *et* **misericordia** *ualuisset, plena lacrimarum obtestans ne patrem suum patriamque proderet* ... ('since his wife no longer prevailed, as before, by caresses, effectual enough for the heart of a lover, but by prayers and moving entreaty, imploring him, her eyes filled with tears, not to betray her father and her city...'). Livy is the sole historian to use an ethnic argument to explain the behavior of Masinissa and Syphax. The other historians emphasize the skill of Sophonisba, and especially her ability to use her charm,[21] by advancing only this gendered explanation in which the woman is

---

[20] Regarding the Roman perception of the Numidians, see Dauge 1981, 48, 64, 74, 80–1, 91.
[21] For Diodorus (27.10), Sophonisba is a dangerous woman, beautiful and skillful, able to manipulate men. He describes her as 'expert in various tricks' (τοῖς τρόποις ποικίλη) and 'able to

considered responsible and blamed. The solution Masinissa finds to keep his commitments (*promissi fidem praestaret*, 30.12.19) is to immediately marry Sophonisba and thus eliminate her status of prisoner that gives Laelius and Scipio full power over her. Laelius takes this marriage very badly, but he is persuaded by Masinissa to defer to Scipio's decision. Livy transports his reader to the Roman camp.

## 2 Scenes in the Roman camp

I will be brief on the first scene. Livy gives his reader a first point of view on Syphax through the eyes of soldiers who come to see the arrival of the defeated king. Once again, he uses a Roman grid by explicitly referring to the 'spectacle of the triumph': *omnis uelut ad spectaculum triumphi multitudo effusa est* ('all the rank and file poured out, as though they were to witness a triumph', 30.13.1). In a short span on time, the space of the camp is made similar to a street in Rome during the triumphs: *praecedebat ipse uinctus; sequebatur grex nobilium Numidarum* ('First came Syphax in chains, followed by a company of noble Numidians', 30.13.2). The sight of the king in chains gives rise to many comments. The soldiers, in amplifying their own victory, do their best to magnify the greatness of Syphax (*magnitudini*) and the fame of his race (*famaeque gentis*, 30.13.2).

The second scene imagined by Livy takes place when Syphax is brought before Scipio at headquarters. Like on a theatre stage, a military leader and his enemy meet in a private space for the first time after the defeat of the latter. According to Livy, Scipio is deeply moved by the reversal of fortune Syphax has experienced[22] and by the memory (*recordatio*) of everything that should have sealed a lasting alliance: the guest hospitality (*hospitii*), the exchanged handshake (*dextraeque datae*), the compact made for their states, and that made in a private capacity (*foederis publice ac priuatim iuncti*, 30.13.8). Hence the question Scipio asks Syphax:[23] why has Syphax rejected 'the alliance with Rome' (*societatem ... Romanam*) and taken the aggressive in war (30.13.9–10)? The narrative choice of the 'scene' (with the sequences: memory and emotion, question, response) emphasizes the interpretation of the events that Livy ascribes to Syphax.

---

obtain everything' (πᾶν ἐξομηρεύσασθαι δυναμένη). For Cassius Dio (Zonaras 9.13), she is a woman using magical charms (μαγγανείας).
22 On the reversal of fortune as a tragic topic, see Feldherr 1998, 30.
23 That is a question that Appian (10.27) and, Cassius Dio (Zonaras 9.13) also put in the mouth of Scipio.

The latter acknowledges 'having committed a fault' (*peccasse*) and 'lost his reason' (*insanisse*) ... by taking a Carthaginian woman as wife. He ascribes his defection to the influence of Sophonisba, whom he describes as 'a fury and a scourge' (*furiam pestemque*, 30.13.12; *pestem ac furiam*, 30.13.14). The words used by Syphax are extremely strong when he describes the behavior of Sophonisba after her marriage (30.13.12):

> Illis nuptialibus facibus regiam conflagrasse suam; illam furiam pestemque omnibus delenimentis animum suum auertisse atque alienasse, nec conquiesse donec ipsa manibus suis nefaria sibi arma aduersus hospitem atque amicum induerit.

> From those nuptial torches his palace has taken fire; that fury and scourge by all her blandishments had unbalanced and alienated his mind, and she had never rested until with her own hands she had herself put on him guilt-stained arms against a guest-friend and a personal friend.

This answer shows the bad faith of Syphax, who denies any liability and presents Sophonisba as responsible for his change of alliance. However, this answer is disqualified insofar as Livy explicitly ascribes it both to Syphax's hatred for Masinissa and to his jealousy: *haec non hostili modo odio sed amoris etiam stimulis, amatam apud aemulum cernens, cum dixisset...* ('But speaking thus, not only out of hatred as an enemy but also under the goad of jealousy, as he saw his beloved in the possession of his rival ...', 30.14.1).[24] Instead of acknowledging his own incapability to control his sexual impulses, which is the interpretation usually put forward by Livy to explain the unreliability of the Numidians, Syphax is blaming Sophonisba. Nevertheless, Livy puts words into the mouth of Syphax that can make his version of the facts credible (for a Roman reader). As in the case of the expression *captus amore*, Livy probably got an explanatory model from the literature of his time. The word *furia* was previously applied by Vergil to Amata, the wife of the king Latinus, when describing how she played a decisive role in the

---

24 Diodorus (27.10) relates, as a fact, that Sophonisba tries to make Masinissa change sides. Because Scipio treats him with care and respect, Syphax reveals this endeavor to him, urging Scipio to be on his guard, and Laelius makes similar comments. Diodorus underscores that Sophonisba was 'a partisan of the Carthaginian cause' (οὖσα δὲ Καρχηδονίων συμμαχὶς), daily urging Masinissa, with many requests, to revolt from Rome, for she was indeed a woman 'deeply devoted to her country' (ἦν γὰρ ἡ γυνὴ δεινῶς φιλόπατρις). See also Appian (10.27) who describes her as 'passionately attached to her country' (φιλόπατρις δ'ἐστὶν ἰσχυρῶς). According to him, either Syphax was telling the truth or he was moved by jealousy and a desire to hurt Masinissa as much as possible.

breaking of an earlier alliance.²⁵ The fury Allecto infects Amata whose mind has been gradually 'heated up' as a result of 'her female²⁶ wrath and fear' (*femineae ardentem curaeque iraeque coquebant*, 7.345). Amata, hostile to the Trojans, because she wants her daughter to be married to Turnus, gives herself over to unbridled madness (*sine more furit*, 7.377) and drags along the other matrons whose minds the furies are also inflaming (*furiis accensas pectore matres*, 7.392). The word *pestis*, also put into the mouth of Syphax, is used by Vergil about Allecto when she is hiding in the woods, just before she intervenes by calling the men to action with a trumpet (7.505). Syphax adds that there is a consolation in his misfortunes. The 'same fury and scourge' had passed into the house of his greatest enemy, Masinissa, a man neither wiser nor more morally steadfast than himself, who was less on guard owing to his youth, and whose marriage showed more foolishness and lack of discipline than his own. Scipio is very concerned about Syphax's version of the facts. Livy adds a psychological interpretation to explain why the Roman general severely judges Masinissa. His behaviour seems to Scipio particularly shameful/ignominious (*foediora*) because he personally is not at all, and never was, sensitive to feminine charms (*quod ipsum in Hispania iuuenem nullius forma pepulerat captiuae*, 'because in Spain, in spite of his youth, he has himself never been smitten by the beauty of any captive', 30.14.3). Is this a character trait, as suggested by Livy, and/or a cultural trait? Scipio will use the second option as an argument in his private meeting with Masinissa. Livy relates this meeting under the form of a scene that takes place soon after the arrival of the latter with Laelius in the Roman camp.

## 3 Scipio and Masinissa or how to secure the loyalty of a doubtful ally?

All the historians agree that Scipio was concerned with ensuring the fidelity of his Numidian ally. Masinissa and Syphax had both shifted camps since the beginning of the war between the Romans and the Carthaginians. According to

---

**25** According to Mineo (2013, 58–61), Livy's book 27 was written after 17 BCE. Mineo indeed argues that Livy would have created a clear analogy between the expiatory ceremonies of 207, organized by the Decemviral College (27.37) and the secular Games that took place in 17 BCE. If one agrees with this analysis, the book 30 is also posterior to 17 BCE and therefore to the publication of the *Aeneid*.
**26** This gender notation, negatively oriented, is not reused by Livy, but the reader may have it in mind.

Levene,[27] Livy uses two standard images: 'Syphax is the unreliable 'barbarian', Masinissa 'the quintessentially loyal ally''. How does Scipio manage, in Livy' narrative, to ensure that Masinissa will not follow the same path than Syphax? The Roman comments on the concept of alliance (between peoples) by stating that it previously implies friendly relations between their leaders. According to him, the desire that Masinissa would have to forge close links with him (*ad iugendam mecum amicitiam*, 'to cement a friendship with me', 30.14.4) could be ascribed to the fact that Masinissa would have seen in him 'some good qualities' (*aliqua … bona*). As a result, the Numidian leader would have placed all his hopes in Scipio's loyalty and good faith (*in fidem meam*). Scipio is apparently projecting some ideal motivations onto his current ally as a way of suggesting he comply with them. Among all the virtues on account of which Masinissa could have sought his friendship, those of which Scipio says he is most proud are 'his restraint and his continence' (*temperantia et continentia*[28] *libidinum*, 30.14.5). Insofar as both these qualities are the exact opposite of abandonment to sexual impulses,[29] regarded (by the Romans) as a Numidian ethnic feature, Scipio is trying to explain to Masinissa what is necessarily involved in seeking both his friendship and an alliance with Rome. This means adopting self-control and the ability to restrain desires, both qualities the Romans urged be performed in every circumstance, and even considered as more praiseworthy than military glory (30.14.6–8):

> Hanc te quoque ad ceteras tuas eximias uirtutes, Masinissa, adiecisse uelim (…) Qui eas (uoluptates) temperantia sua frenauit ac domuit multo maius decus maioremque uictoriam sibi peperit quam nos Syphace uicto habemus.

> It is this one, Masinissa, I would like you to have also added to all your other remarkable virtues (…). Who has bridled and tamed his pleasures by practicing temperance, has acquired a much greater glory and obtained a greater victory than that brought us by the defeat of Syphax.

---

**27** Levene 2010, 247–8.
**28** According to Moore (1989, 80), *continentia* is used only once by Livy in this passage, where the self-control inherent in this notion applies especially to the control of sexual desires.
**29** As noted by Moore (1989, 78), '*temperantia*, like *moderatio* and *modestia*, means self-control, but it is more specific than the other two words in referring to the control of impulses or desires by reason'.

Moore argues that Livy presents *temperantia* as a peculiarly Roman virtue while closely associating it with the Cornelii Scipiones.[30] It is therefore not surprising that the historian puts into the mouth of Scipio a declaration in which the latter suggests as a model his own behavior. Should we see in it, in the broadest sense, the challenge of the Roman conquest? To share, through military campaigns, the Roman model, as living practice and/or ideal with the peoples who have chosen to fight alongside Rome? Anyway, if Scipio was expecting such behavior from Masinissa, are his expectations met? Scipio asks Masinissa to deliver Sophonisba by giving a legal argument:[31] after Syphax's defeat, she is part of the spoils of war and has to be sent to Rome, where 'the senate and the Roman people would have the right to judge and decide the case of her who is alleged to have estranged from us an allied king and driven him headlong into war' (*senatus populique Romani de ea iudicium atque arbitrium esse quae regem socium nobis alienasse atque in arma egisse praecipitatem dicatur*, 30.14.10).[32] In conclusion Scipio again urges Masinissa to 'control his feelings' (*uince animum*, 30.14.11).

As noted by Kowalewski,[33] Scipio's speech first elicits physical reactions in his interlocutor: 'redness' and 'tears' (*rubor, lacrimae*), to be taken as signs of a violent emotion. Then Masinissa's response is brief (30.15.1):

> ... et cum se quidem in potestate futurum imperatoris dixisset orassetque eum ut quantum res sineret fidei suae temere obstrictae consuleret – promisisse enim se in nullius potestatem eam traditurum ...

> ... and after saying that he, on his part, would be 'under the power of the general' and begging him to let him take action, as far as possible, regarding the word he had thoughtlessly given: he had indeed promised not to hand her over to any man's power...

According to Levene,[34] Masinissa seems to accept Scipio's suggestion to exchange his ethnic behaviour as a Numidian (subjected to his sexual impulses), for the Roman model (based on self-control) that Scipio asks him to take on. But, in fact Masinissa actively 'manipulates' Scipio when he requests to be allowed to keep the promise made to Sophonisba as far as possible, while remaining vague about what it may mean in practice. In my opinion, Masinissa is not really suggesting

---

**30** Moore (1989, 79) notes that Livy praises Cn. Scipio twice for his *temperantia*, once alone (25.36.16), once along with his brother Publius (38.58.6). Here (30.14.5) the great Scipio emphasizes his own *temperantia*. T. Gracchus reminds Scipio of his previous *temperantia* in 38.56.11.
**31** See, on this point, Kowalewski 2002, 231.
**32** It should be noted that Scipio does not name Sophonisba.
**33** Kowaleswski 2002, 232.
**34** Levene 2010, 258–9.

that he will take Scipio's moral advice. By using the expression *in potestate*, he suggests that he has no option but to obey the Roman general. However, at the same time, he asks for some room to maneuver by using an ambiguous expression, *ut quantum res sineret fidei suae temere obstrictae consuleret* ('to have such regard as the case permitted for the promise he had rashly given', 30.15.1).

Again, Livy attributes to Masinissa a series of physical reactions: 'many sighs and moans' (*cum crebro suspiritu et gemitu*, 30.15.3), all noisy signs of deep emotion, which can be heard all around his tents. This emotion, likely more uncontrolled than exhibited, is apparently to be interpreted as the audible expression of struggles with his impulses and desires. After this struggle with himself is ended 'by one very loud groan' (*ingenti ad postremum edito gemitu*, 30.15.4), Masinissa instructs 'a slave he trusts' (*fidum e seruis*) to bring poison to Sophonisba along with a message. Insofar as Livy summarizes the content of Masinissa's message and relates Sophonisba's answer by using direct speech (Livy quotes the answer she gives the slave to be transmitted to his master), the reader is in fact provided with a final scene, although in two parts.[35]

## 4 Masinissa and Sophonisba: the epilogue

Masinissa begins by talking about the promise made to Sophonisba: he 'would have preferred to keep his first promise, which a husband owed to his wife' (*Masinissam libenter primam ei fidem praestaturum fuisse quam uir uxori debuerit*, 30.15.5). Since 'those who have the power' (*qui possint*) deprive him (*adimant*) of his 'capacity to decide freely' (*eius arbitrium*), he fulfills his second commitment not to let Sophonisba fall into the power of the Romans (*in potestatem Romanorum*) 'alive' (*uiua*, 30.15.6). Both key points should be emphasized in this message imagined by Livy. The first point is that 'his' Masinissa implicitly claims the con-

---

[35] Nothing similar can be found in Diodorus (27.7), according to whom Masinissa forces Sophonisba to commit suicide. 'He went himself to her tent, handed his wife a deadly poison, and forced her to drink it'. In Appian (10.28), 'Masinissa gave her a dose of poison by allowing a choice between suicide and captivity. Then he left her and mounted his horse. She showed the cup to her nurse, told her not to weep for her since she died gloriously, and drank the poison'. Cassio Dio (Zonaras 9.13) puts into the mouth of Masinissa a speech in direct discourse that is an astonishing mix of sentimentality and politic realism. He says to Sophonisba that 'if his own death could ensure her freedom and protection, he would die with joy, but that, since this is not the case, he sends her to where he and all men will one day go'.

cern for *fides* as the main rule of his conduct, which seems to contradict the reputation of unreliability previously ascribed to the Numidians. The second important point is Masinissa's insistence on Roman *potestas* when he analyses his current situation. The Romans are in a position of force: they are the masters ... at least as far as he is concerned. This statement is aligned exactly with his proclaiming allegiance to Scipio: *in potestate futurum imperatoris*. It is precisely the situation refused by Sophonisba, who asked him to prevent her from falling into the power of the Romans. Masinissa concludes that 'mindful of her father, his position of general, her native city, and of the two kings to whom she had been married, she should decide for herself' (*Memor patris imperatoris patriaeque et duorum regum quibus nupta fuisset, sibi ipsa consuleret*, 30.15.6).

The answer ascribed by Livy to Sophonisba is brief (30.15.7): 'I receive this wedding gift (she says) and not without gratitude, if there is nothing better a husband has been able to bestow upon his wife' ('*accipio*' inquit '*nuptiale munus, neque ingratum, si nihil maius uir uxori praestare potuit*'), and incisive: 'but tell him this: it would have been better for me to die if I had not married at my funeral' ('*hoc tamen nuntia, melius me morituram fuisse si non in funere meo nupsissem*' (30.15.7). The historian makes it very clear that, according to him, Sophonisba saw in her marriage to Masinissa only what she had asked him for: a way not to be handed over to the Romans. In this way, Livy excludes any possibility of reciprocity for Sophonisba in the sexual attraction that has made Masinissa choose this option. In sexual matters the Carthaginians are the alter egos of the Romans: they do not mix sexual desires and politics. Sophonisba's second marriage with Masinissa is thus explained only by its military and political context, as was also the case for her first marriage with Syphax. Livy then describes Sophonisba's death with a brief comment: 'with as much pride/ferocity as she had spoken, she accepted the cup and emptied it without giving any sign of trouble' (*non locuta est ferocius quam acceptum poculum nullo trepidationis signo dato impauide hausit*, 30.15.8). Sophonisba's lack of emotion contrasts with the blushing, crying, sighing, and moaning attributed to Masinissa. As for the adverb *ferocius*, it is tempting to see in it a way of referring to Horace's verses on Cleopatra's suicide, described as a death *deliberata*[36] (1.37.25–32):

> ausa et iacentem uisere regiam
> uoltu sereno, fortis et asperas
>     tractare serpentes, ut atrum
>     corpore conbiberet uenenum,

---

[36] If Livy's book 30 was written after 17 BCE, it is chronologically possible that Livy alludes to Horace's *Odes* 1, published c. 23 BCE.

> deliberata morte *ferocior*;
> saeuis Liburnis scilicet inuidens
> > priuata deduci superbo,
> > > non humilis mulier, triumpho.

> She dared to look at her royal palace in ruins, with a serene face, and courageously handle the fearsome snakes to soak her body with dark venom, made more proud/ferocious by having resolved to die. She certainly prevented cruel Liburnians from leading her, a woman who was not of humble birth, as a simple private individual to be included in the triumph.

The proposal that Livy might refer to Cleopatra has been put forward by several critics: Martin, Toppani, Haley, and Kolawewski.[37] In doing so, he would allude to the fate that, like Cleopatra, Sophonisba was trying to avoid: being included in a triumph in which she, the daughter of a general, member of one of the most powerful families in Carthage, would have been reduced to the status of prisoner and ordinary citizen. Although their situations are different — Cleopatra's royal palace is in ruins, Carthage has not yet been defeated — using the adverb *ferocius* to allude to the Horatian expression *deliberate morte ferocior* is a way of suggesting the reader bring together and compare two female figures, each representative of intractable enemies of Rome. Both face death with courage, impassivity, and above all, since it is the word common to both Horace's and Livy's descriptions, with an exceptional degree of ferocity.

## 5 Rewards to Masinissa after Sophonisba's death

When hearing what has happened, Scipio seeks to console Masinissa in private, then in public. He praises him widely and gives him magnificent presents. In Livy's narrative, Scipio specifies that there is no higher distinction among the Romans than a triumph, and that those who get the triumph have no more magnificent array than that of which Masinissa 'alone of all foreigners' (*unum omnium externorum*, 30.15.12) is deemed worthy by the Roman people.[38] These honors

---

[37] See Martin 1941/1942, 124 n. 3; Toppani 1978/1979, 574, n. 25; Haley 1989, 178–80; Kowalewski 2002, 239. The parallels that Kowalewski draws between the death of Sophonisba, that of Lucretia, and the suicides of Roman wives who preferred to follow their husbands into death (2002, 238), in my opinion, are not relevant, on the one hand because the circumstances are very different, and on the other hand because the use of the adverb *ferocius* is rather negative, regardless of the fact that it probably echoes Horace's poem.

[38] As noted by Levene (2010, 258), Syphax too had received similar gifts from the Senate at a time when he was assumed to be a reliable ally (27.4.8–9).

soothe the mind of the king (*honoribus mollitus regis animus*, 30.15.14), but above all are taken by him as auguring well for his future in Numidia. Livy underscores that Masinissa's mind is 'roused towards the hope of reigning soon over all Numidia, now that Syphax has been eliminated' (*erectusque in spem propinquam sublato Syphace omnis Numidiae potiundae*, 30.15.14). In other words, Masinissa's grief is driven away and replaced by another interest. However, it is likely that this hope was ancient. Masinissa uses no word referring to an alliance (never, for example, the word *amicitia*, as Scipio does), but twice uses the expression *in potestate*, first when he talks with Scipio, and then in his message to Sophonisba. Apparently indifferent to Scipio's discourse on moral values that should be shared between the Romans and their allies, Masinissa only takes into account power relations and tries to manage his own geo-political interests as best possible. If he agrees to respect the authority of the Romans and succeeds in overcoming his sexual impulses, it is probably because, since the beginning, he is driven by the hope of benefiting from his loyalty during the war,[39] and not by any desire to conform in his military and sexual behavior to the Roman model embodied by 'his friend' Scipio.

Furthermore, as underlined by Levene, Masinissa appears to be a man of his word (*fides*), with the particularity that he exerts this *fides*, not as a loyal ally, but as a husband (*uir*) towards his wife (*uxor*).[40] The attitude towards his wife attributed by Livy to Masinissa may perhaps be also explained as a — secondary — effect of the superimposition of the figure of Cleopatra on that of Sophonisba. From the proclamation of marital *fides* attributed to Masinissa and from Livy's use of a reading key provided by the elegiac discourse to describe his way of yielding to Sophonisba's charms (the victor taken by his captive), it may be concluded that Antony probably stands behind the portrait of the Numidian chief. Antony has indeed been presented as an example of the complete submission experienced by the elegiac lover.[41] In elegy 3.11, Propertius attributes to Cleopatra the

---

**39** Polybius indicates that Masinissa's military campaign in Numidia was intended to add, with the help of the Romans, the kingdom of Syphax to the one he had inherited (15.4.4).
**40** There has been much debate about the meaning of the word *fides*, which, depending on the context, can represent a virtue or simply something more mundane and concrete (see Becker, cols. 801–19 and Flurl 1969, 67–9). As underlined by Moore (1989, 35), 'no virtue plays as important a role in Livy's work as does *fides*'. Moore notes that *fides* is especially used as the quality which leads one ally to defend another against an enemy (38), but also that 'in many passages *fides* is explicitly devotion to the duties which arise from a specific agreement or promise' (42). Here these two types of *fides* may seem to enter in competition; if this is the case, Masinissa clearly gives priority to the obligations implied by his promise made to his wife.
**41** Griffin 1977.

intention to submit to Rome, requested 'as the price of her/their shameful union/marriage'⁴² (*coniugii obsceni pretium*, 31). When Propertius regrets that the City trembled in front of a woman, among the memories of its glorious past, in contrast he recalls in strong position 'Scipios' fleet ... the spoils won from Hannibal, and tokens commemorating Syphax's defeat' (*Scipiadae classes (...) Hannibalis spolia, et uicti monumenta Syphacis*, 67, 69). What does it mean to say that Antony and the elegiac lovers stand behind Masinissa's portrait in Livy? The self-control epitomized by Scipio was clearly no longer relevant for the Romans who felt in tune with the elegiac discourse on love and passions, and, to varying extents, with the lifestyle embodied by Antony. For his part, in rewriting the Roman history by interpreting the past in the light of current events, Livy appears to be in accordance with the position adopted by Antony's political opponent, Augustus. As argued by critics,⁴³ he was a supporter of the *Princeps* and his attempt to revitalize so-called Roman cultural features in order to base his policy on a return to the past, restore Roman moral tradition, and give legitimacy to his power.

# 6 Conclusion

To come back to Sophonisba, Livy interprets this relatively secondary and little-known figure of the Punic wars in the light of the Rome's recent history and Cleopatra's personality. That is one of the reasons why he describes the daughter of Hasdrubal as a skillful seductress, guided solely by political motivations: love of her fatherland and hatred of Rome. By the superimposition of the figure of Cleopatra on that of Sophonisba, Livy implicitly points out the fact that Cleopatra was driven solely by political reasons and would have seen in her love affair with Antony only the opportunity to defend Egypt's interests.⁴⁴ Livy also stresses the ferocity of character of these two foreign queens which would be expressed, with particular intensity, at the time of their death. This ferocity is easier to understand in the situation of Cleopatra who is boldly manipulating dangerous snakes. As the Egyptian queen is about to receive their venom without showing the slightest sign of fear, should the reader conclude that ferocity is also a female feature... as a manifestation of the 'wild' nature of women, *ferox* belonging to the same word

---

**42** On the status of the relationship between Cleopatra and Antony, see Ager 2013.
**43** See for example Mineo 2014.
**44** This was also the case in her relations with Caesar (See Gruen 2011 on Cleopatra's alleged extended stay in Rome before Cesar's death).

family as *fera* and *feritas*?[45] In the case of Sophonisba, the notation is less appropriate as she is only about to drink a poisonous beverage. If courage and impassivity in the face of death are both values shared with their victors, Cleopatra's and Sophonisba's conducts differ from the practice of the same virtues in the Roman style precisely because of this ferocity, emphasized by Horace and Livy. In both cases, it is tempting to suppose that this particular feature, related to the female sex and gender, is also to be taken as a marker of savagery/ barbarity of the enemies of Rome, even when these enemies could appear as 'the most similar in the dissimilar', as was the case for the Carthaginians compared to the Romans, and even more for the composite troops, partly Egyptian, partly Roman, who fought at Actium and at the siege of Alexandria.

## Works Cited

Adler, E. (2001), *Valorizing the Barbarians: Enemy speeches in Roman historiography*, Austin.
Ager, S. (2013), 'Marriage or Mirage? The phantom Wedding of Cleopatra and Antony', *CPh* 108.2, 139–55.
Burck, E. (1934), *Die Erzählungskunst des Titus Livius*, Berlin.
Conte, G.B. (1984), *Virgilio, Il genere e i suoi confini*, Milano.
Dauge, Y.A. (1981), *Le Barbare: Recherches sur la conception romaine de la barbarie et de la civilisation*, Bruxelles.
De Franchis, M. (2015), 'L'épisode de Sophonisbe chez Tite-Live, 30.12–15: un morceau d'histoire tragique ?', in: V. Naas/M. Mahé-Simon (eds.), *De Samos à Rome: personnalité et influence de Douris*, Paris, 303–28.
De Sanctis, G. (1968), *Storia dei Romani*, III.2, Firenze.
Edwards, C. (1993), *The politics of Immorality in Ancient Rome*, Cambridge.
Feeney, D. (2016), *Beyond Greek: the Beginnings of Latin Literature*, Cambridge.
Feldherr, A. (1998), *Spectacle and Society in Livy's History*, Berkeley.
Flurl, W. (1969), Deditio in fidem: *Untersuchungen zu Livius und Polybius*, Diss. Munich.
Griffin, J. (1977), 'Propertius and Antony', *JRS* 67, 17–26.
Genette, G. (1972), *Figures III*, Paris.
Gruen, E. (2011), 'Cleopatra in Rome: Facts and Fantasy', in: M. Miles (ed.), *Cleopatra: a Sphinx revisited*, Berkeley, 37–53.
Haley, S. (1989), 'Livy's Sophonisba', *C&M* 40, 171–81.
Haley, S. (1990), 'Livy, Passion and Cultural Stereotypes', *Historia* 39, 375–81.
Johner, A. (1996), *La violence chez Tite-Live: mythographie et historiographie*, Strasbourg.
Kowalewski, B. (2002), *Frauengestalten im Geschichtswerk des T. Livius*, München.
Levene, D. (2010), *Livy on the Hannibalic War*, Oxford.

---

**45** The etymology given for *ferox* n the *TLL* (6.1.566–560) is *feritas*, defined as *uitae, morum consuetudo similis moribus ferarum* ("kind of life, character similar to those of wild animals").

Martin, J.M.K. (1941/1942), 'Livy and Romance', *G&R* 11, 124–9.
Mineo, B. (2013), 'Tite-Live et la politique apollienne d'Auguste', *DHA* 8, 39–64.
Mineo, B. (2014), 'Livy's Political and Moral Values and the Principate', in: B. Mineo (ed.), *A Companion to Livy*, Oxford, 125–38.
Moore, T. (1989), *Artistry and Ideology: Livy's Vocabulary of Virtue*, Frankfurt am Main.
Soltau, W. (1894), *Livius' Quellen in der III. Dekade*, Berlin.
Toppani, I. (1977/1978), 'Una regina da ritrovare. Sofonisba e il suo tragico destino', *AIV* 136, 561–78.
Truschnegg, B. (2000), 'Die Semantik wichtiger Termini zur Bezeichnung für Personen weiblichen Geschechts bei T. Livius', in: R. Rollinger/C. Ulf (eds.), *Geschlechterrollen und Frauenbild in der Perspektive antiker Autoren*, Innsbruck, 299–344.
Walsh, P. (1961), *Livy: his Historical Aims and Methods*, Cambridge.
Walsh, P. (1996), 'Making a Drama out of a Crisis', *G&R* 43, 188–203.

# Part III: Cleopatra's Survival and Metamorphosis in Roman Poetry

Florence Klein
# Gendered Intertextuality: Feminizing the Alexandrian Models in Propertius' Actian Poetry

Intertextuality can be a way for a culture to appropriate another — foreign — culture, with a mix of respectful admiration and imperialist domination: it is now widely recognized that when some Augustan poets, writing after the Roman conquest of the Ptolemaic kingdom, echo Alexandrian literary models (Callimachus, Posidippus or Theocritus for example), they also use their intertextual appropriation as a form of triumphant imperialism, parallel to that contingent upon military conquest. They do so especially when writing the praise of their patron by following the template of Alexandrian poets celebrating their Ptolemaic sovereigns. In the context of the defeat of Egypt, the apparent paradox of a poetry borrowing its models from the defeated nation is only superficial: the literary models get twisted to inform, and thus enhance all the more, the praise of the Roman conquerors of these sovereigns' very descendants.[1] One famous example is the beginning of *Georgics* 3: the poet claims that, in order to commemorate Octavian's military achievements, and his Eastern conquests in particular, he will construct a temple in an Italian setting, with the *princeps* in its centre. He himself will drive a chariot drawn by hundred horses and preside over games which are to supplant those at Olympia and Nemea: all Greece will leave Alpheus and the 'groves of Molorcus' to compete in these Italian games set up and supervised by the poet.[2] Whereas Probus' testimony had already allowed scholars to interpret this apparent periphrasis for Nemea as an erudite allusion to Callimachus, the discovery and publication of the Lille Papyrus in the late 1970s enabled Richard Thomas to better understand what is at stake in this not-so-purely ornamental

---

[1] See for example Barchiesi 2011, 532–3, with bibliography (n. 40); Acosta-Hughes/Stephens 2012, 204f. See also, e.g., for an analysis of the intertextual reception of Callimachean models in *Aeneid* 8, as 'an aspect, not only of Rome's Hellenisation in the literary sphere, but also of its aggressive disruption and uprooting of Hellenistic cultural narrative', O'Rourke 2017. As O'Rourke states it in his conclusion, 'the encomium of Augustan supremacy in *Aeneid* 8 overturns Callimachus' […] celebrations of the Ptolemaic dynasty in the demise at Actium of the last of the Ptolemaic queens'.

[2] Vergil, *Georgics* 3.19–20, *Cuncta mihi, Alpheum linquens lucosque Molorci, / cursibus et crudo decernet Graecia caestu*.

Callimachean allusion: the periphrasis is to be read as a specific reference to Callimachus' *Victory of Berenice* (the inner panel of which was an epyllion staging the farmer Molorcus), the encomiastic poem for the queen's victory in a chariot race that was situated at the opening of the third book of his *Aetia* (that is to say at the same relative point of the *Georgics* where Vergil choose to evoke Octavian's victory over the East).[3] The allusion to the groves of Molorcus is thus a way for the Roman poet to signal his appropriation of (and his victory over) the Callimachean epinicion for the Ptolemaic queen. Precisely as he evokes Octavian's triumph after Actium and the defeat of Egypt, he replaces the praise of an Egyptian queen, Berenice II, with the praise of the conqueror of her descendant. Thus, the literary appropriation by which the Roman poets pay reverential homage to their Alexandrian models also functions as a display of their domination, and a reduplication, on the literary level, of the military conquest: the poetic models of Ptolemaic Alexandria appear as a spoil and their authors as captives subservient to Roman poetry (and empire).

Now, it is also interesting to observe that Vergil's reference to Callimachus' encomiastic poem enables him to replace a feminine (Alexandrian) leader, as the subject of the encomium, with a male (Roman) one. Are we in some way invited to read the Vergilian allusion as a contrastive one, that retrospectively highlights the femaleness of the Egyptian defeated model? If a complex set of literary allusions is obviously to be read not only as an act of homage, but also as a display of domination over a foreign culture, how is this domination enhanced by a kind of 'feminization' of the dominated culture? Or, to put it otherwise, to what extent is the intertextual appropriation of the 'Other', the 'Foreigner' — i.e. for the Roman, the poetry written in Greek in Hellenistic Alexandria — articulated with a gendered view of the latter?[4]

It is not unusual for Roman poets to metaphorically express their appropriation of the Greek/Alexandrian culture in gendered terms, as can be illustrated, for example, by Catullus' importation of another Callimachean poem praising the queen Berenice, the *Plokamos*, translated in Latin verses in c. 66. As Regina Höschele and Elizabeth Young have shown, the Catullian text can be read as an allegorical tale of its own genesis:[5] thus, as the lock of Berenice protests against its separation from the head of her queen, its sorrow "appears to register a protest

---

[3] Thomas 1983.
[4] See O'Rourke 2011: 'In an orientalist context even the idea of male superiority plays handmaid to occidental geopolitical hegemony' (§ 5).
[5] Höschele 2009; Young 2015, 139–65.

against the violence to which the fragmented *Aetia* has been subjected in translation".⁶ Now, it is well known that Catullus strongly 'gendered' his Hellenistic model: whereas the Callimachean πλόκαμος ('lock') was of ambivalent gender,⁷ its Roman translator feminized it without leaving any ambiguity. Consequently, as the now undoubtedly feminine *coma* complains about the manhandling to which she has been subjected, with phrasing that evokes the rape of a virgin taken away "unwillingly" (*inuita*) from her sisters,⁸ the metapoetic reading of the text figures the intertextual relationship as a strongly gendered one, with the Roman imitator placing himself, with regard to his Alexandrian model, in the position of the male conqueror of a (beloved) female captive.⁹ The representation of the appropriated culture as 'female' enhances the domination of the appropriating one.¹⁰

This overlap of ethnicity and gender in the representation of a 'gendered intertextuality', underlining (or exaggerating, or even retrospectively creating) the femaleness of the appropriated Alexandrian poetic model should be all the more interesting in the case of Augustan poets writing about Rome's (and Octavian's) victory at Actium. As the poets praise Octavian's defeat of Egypt by modeling themselves on the poetry of the defeated culture of (earlier) Ptolemaic Alexandria, the parallelism between the military contest narrated in their texts and the poetics of the imperialist appropriation of the Alexandrian models is all the more striking. Now, the former is (famously) articulated with the overlapping structures of gender and 'orientalism':¹¹ the poetic tales focus on the victory over Cleopatra, the foreign queen who became 'the personification of effeminate and conquered Asia' in the discourses of the West.¹² Their archetype, the Vergilian *ecphrasis* of Aeneas' Shield, pictured Antony's fleet as characterized by its strong

---

6 Young 2015, 147.
7 See Harder 2012 *ad loc.*, with bibliography on the diverging interpretations of the lock's gender.
8 Cat. 66, 39–40; 51–2.
9 Young 2015; Klein forthcoming.
10 Of course, the respective power of male and female is more complex and qualified, in Catullus' work or elsewhere, but there is nonetheless an overlap between the two categories. After all, it is no coincidence, I suggest, that we encounter the same formula to designate the relationship between Roman and Greek cultures in Horace, *Ep.* 2.1.156, *Graecia capta ferum uictorem cepit*, and the male-female ones (see for example, Propertius 3.11.16, on Penthesilea and Achilleus, *uicit uictorem candida forma uirum*).
11 The system of signifiers denoting the 'Other' by which the West has sought to dominate the East. On Orientalism, see Said 1985, and for a stronger emphasis on the gender component of Orientalism, see Yegenoglu 1998.
12 Wyke 2002, 209.

associations of Foreign and Feminine,[13] and they all tend to equate the relation of West to East (or Rome to Egypt) with that of male to female.[14] The issue in question is thus: in such a loaded political and literary context, how does this account of the battle against Egypt, structured as it is with the overlap of ethnicity and gender, affect the Augustan poet's representation of their Alexandrian literary models within those very same 'Actian' poems?

I want to raise this issue by considering two cases in Propertius' poems narrating the Actian victory as both a Roman and a male conquest over Cleopatra, the foreign Egyptian woman.

I will first examine elegy 3.11, where a catalogue of domineering Eastern women culminates in the contemporary example of Cleopatra as the supreme threat to Roman male and Western values, eventually leading to the final praise of Augustus who has released Rome from such a threat. As in Vergil's proemium of *Georgics* 3, the encomiastic section praising Augustus is modeled on the praise of a Ptolemaic Queen, in that case Arsinoe II Philadelphus. I will focus on this other case of replacement – from a female Egyptian leader to the male Roman conqueror of her very descendant – that allows Propertius to duplicate, on the literary level (his own intertextual relationship with an Hellenistic poet), the overlap of ethnicity and gender that articulates the telling of the battle itself.

I will then broaden the perspective by asking whether this (as we shall see, tendentious) contrastive allusion to the Alexandrian literary model's femaleness also functions when the Augustan poet imitates a Ptolemaic encomium praising not a queen, but a male sovereign: do we still encounter a similar process of aggressively gendered intertextuality, highlighting the femininity of the appropriated Hellenistic model? I want to suggest that we do, by reexamining poem 4.6, where Propertius appropriates the Callimachean *Hymns* that praise king Ptolemy II Philadelphus. How, in that case, does the Roman poet still manage to feminize his Alexandrian model, and to what effect?

---

**13** Vergil, *Aen.* 8.685–8; 704–8. On the Vergilian confrontation of male versus female under the banner of West versus East as binary opposite, see Quint 1993.
**14** Regarding Cleopatra on that matter, see Wyke 2002. For an analysis of Propertius' reaction to Vergil's reduction, see O'Rourke 2011.

# 1 Propertius 3.11

Propertius 3.11 appears at first as a paradoxical poem that begins with a traditional elegiac stance: the male lover's subjection to a woman.[15] To resonate with his own erotic situation, the poet enumerates a list of dominant women, who all happen to be linked with the East: Medea, powerful princess of Colchis (9–12); Penthesilea from lake Maeotis, queen of the Amazons who was killed by Achilles but then *uicit uictorem* – conquered her male conqueror as he fell in love with her beauty (13–16); Omphale, the Lydian girl who enslaved Hercules (17–20); and finally Semiramis, queen of Niveneh and founder of Babylon, whose mighty achievements are evoked by Propertius (21–6). With this catalogue of foreign women who have in different ways exercised power and control over men, the poem strongly emphasizes the overlap of ethnicity (Eastern) and gender (female) that culminates with the next (and last) example: Antony's subjection to Cleopatra, and through them the threat of a Roman subjection to Barbarian Egypt. But with the lengthy evocation of Augustus' victory at Actium that follows, the poem moves from its initial endorsement (i.e. the idea that the male enslavement by a woman is prevalent and fully understandable) to its very opposite: the celebration of a Roman male leader, Augustus, for having defeated Cleopatra, the scandalous Egyptian woman who had threatened Rome.

> Quid, modo quae nostris opprobria nexerit armis,
>     et, famulos inter femina trita suos,
> coniugii obsceni pretium Romana poposcit
>     moenia et addictos in sua regna Patres?
> Noxia Alexandria, dolis aptissima tellus,
>     et totiens nostro Memphi cruenta malo,
> tris ubi Pompeio detraxit harena triumphos
>     tollet nulla dies hanc tibi, Roma, notam.
> Issent Phlegraeo melius tibi funera campo,
>     uel tua si socero colla daturus eras.
> Scilicet incesti meretrix regina Canopi,
>     una Philippeo sanguine adusta nota,
> ausa Ioui nostro latrantem opponere Anubim,
>     et Tiberim Nili cogere ferre minas,
> Romanamque turbam crepitanti pellere sistro
>     baridos et contis rostra Liburna sequi
> foedaque Tarpeio conopia tendere saxo,
>     iura dare et statuas inter et arma Mari!

---

[15] See Heyworth/Morwood 2011 for the detailed analysis summed up here (and below).

> Quid nunc Tarquinii fractas iuuat esse secures,
>   nomine quem simili uita superba notat,
> si mulier patienda fuit? cane, Roma, triumphum
>   et longum Augusto salua precare diem!

> What of her who of late has fastened disgrace upon our arms, and, a woman who fornicated even with her slaves, demanded as the price of her shameful union the walls of Rome and the senate made over to her dominion? Guilty Alexandria, land ever ready for treason, and Memphis, so often blood-stained at our cost, where the sand robbed Pompey of his three triumphs no day shall ever wash you clean if this infamy, Rome. Better had your funeral processed over the Phlegrean fields, or had you been doomed to bow your neck to your father-in-law! To be sure, the harlot queen of licentious Canopus, the one disgrace branded on Philip's line, dared to pit barking Anubis against our Jupiter and to force the Tiber to endure the threats of the Nile, to drive out the Roman trumpet with the rattling sistrum and with the poles of her barge pursue the beaks of our galleys, to stretch effeminate mosquito-nets on the Tarpeian rock and give judgement amid the arms and statues of Marius. What profit now is it to have broken the axes of that Tarquin whose proud life gave him a title derived from it, had we been fated to bear a woman's yoke? Sing out your triumph, Rome, and, saved, pray long life for Augustus.[16]

Now, as Alison Keith writes about this passage, "the inclusion of a series of (Greek words for) Egyptian place names (Alexandria, Memphis, Canopus, Nile), people (Philip of Macedon, father of Alexander), gods (Anubis), religious paraphernalia (Isis' rattle, the *sistrum*), and cultural icons (the Nile-barge, *baris*, and its poles, *conti*, along with the mosquito nets) in Propertius' verse entails the verbal subjugation of Greek-speaking Egypt to Latin-speaking Rome":[17] the Otherness of Egyptian culture gets (linguistically) appropriated into the Roman empire. At the same time, throughout this lively evocation of the differences between Roman and Egyptian cultures, the latter is embodied in the feminine nature of her queen, designated as a woman[18] in highly sexualized and offensive terms: simply put, she is a prostitute (30, *famulos inter femina trita suos*; 39, *meretrix regina*). Because of the intersection of the two notions of ethnicity and gender, as in Vergil's *ecphrasis* of the Shield of Aeneas, the opposition becomes mainly formulated in terms of 'female' vs 'Roman', be it in the summary of the threat in the beginning

---

**16** Prop. 3.11.29–50 (edited and translated by G.P. Goold). For an alternative reading of the first line, see Heyworth/Morwood 2011, *ad loc*.
**17** Keith 2008, 152.
**18** We know that Propertius avoids mentioning Cleopatra by name for more than one reason; nonetheless the choice of the words *femina* (30) and *mulier* (49) to designate her obviously create a strongly gendered vision of the battle.

of the passage: 30–2, ... *femina* ... **Romana** *poposcit moenia*, or, later, in the celebration of Cleopatra's defeat by Augustus, as in line 49: ... *si* **mulier** *patienda fuit? cane,* **Roma***, triumphum*. The narrative obviously crystalizes into the opposition 'woman' *vs.* 'Rome', which clearly shows the overlap of ethnic and gendered identities in play.

Now, what about the appropriation of Alexandrian poetry in the Augustan poet's verses? After this triumph of Augustus' (masculine) 'Rome' over the (foreign) 'woman' has led to an enumeration of the male heroes that have warranted Rome's greatness (in obvious contrast with the dominant Eastern Women at the beginning of the poem), Propertius ends his poem by addressing a sailor: whether he is about to make for the sea, or set out from it, he shall always remember Augustus.

> At tu, siue petes portus seu, nauita, linques,
>     Caesaris in toto sis memor Ionio.
>
> But do you, sailor, whether you enter or leave harbor, remember Caesar over all the Ionian sea.[19]

As Gregory Hutchinson first suggested,[20] this final praise of Augustus as the Actian victor is modeled on an epigram by Posidippus celebrating Arsinoe II Philadelphus. This poem, belonging to the section called *Anathematika* ('Dedications') of the 'Milan Papyrus', commemorates the dedication of Arsinoe's temple at Cape Zephyrion by the admiral Callicrates of Samos:

> καὶ μέλλων ἅλα νηῒ περᾶν καὶ πεῖσμα καθάπτειν
>     χερσόθεν, Εὐπλοίαι 'χαῖρε' δὸς Ἀρσινόηι,
> πό]τνιαν ἐκ νηοῦ καλέων θεόν, ἣν ὁ Βοΐσκου
>     ναυαρχῶν Σάμιος θήκατο Καλλικράτης
> ναυτίλε, σοὶ τὰ μάλιστα· κατ' εὔπλοιαν δὲ διώκει
>     τῆσδε θεοῦ χρήιζων πολλὰ καὶ ἄλλος ἀνήρ·
> εἵνεκα καὶ χερσαῖα καὶ εἰς ἅλα δῖαν ἀφιεὶς
>     εὐχὰς εὑρήσεις τὴν ἐπακουσομένην.
>
> When you are about to cross the sea in a ship and fasten a cable from dry land, give a greeting to Arsinoe Euploia, summoning the lady goddess from her temple, which Samian Callicrates, the son of Boiscus, dedicated especially for you, sailor, when he was nauarch. Even

---

19 Prop. 3.11.71–2.
20 Hutchinson 2002, 5.

> another man in pursuit of a safe passage often addresses this goddess, because whether on land or setting out upon the dread sea you will find her receptive to your prayers.[21]

Following Hutchinson's suggestion, Heyworth comments: "Arsinoe has been replaced by the conqueror of her descendant: Rome is learning to treat its rulers as Alexandria treated the Ptolemies; and significant within the poem is that a male leader has replaced a female, the elegist's world turned upside-down." Like Vergil modeling his celebration of Octavian's triumph over Egypt in the proemium of *Georgics* 3 on the Callimachean *Victoria Berenices*, Propertius appropriates an Alexandrian text praising a female royal as an intertext for his own praise of Augustus' victory over another Egyptian queen. This allusive game creates an implicit contrast between the Augustan poet and his Alexandrian/'Egyptian' model by highlighting the preeminence of the feminine in the latter's text.

But it is important, I think, to point out the tendentiousness of this contrastive allusion that retrospectively emphasizes the femaleness of its model. Indeed, if it is true that the Ptolemaic queens, Arsinoe II and Berenice II in particular, were quite prominent in the court ideology,[22] it must be remembered that the poets writing about those female leaders often underline what could appear as masculine strengths: for example, Callimachus underscores Berenice's character and courage in the *Lock of Berenice*, while in the *Victory of Berenice*, the implicit comparison with Heracles, victorious over the Nemean Lion, might play with the meaning of her name "Victory-Bringing".[23] As to Arsinoe, Suzan Stephens notes that Posidippus organizes his epigram collection, as we have it on the Milan Papyrus, in order to associate the queen with Alexander the Great "via several strategically placed poems that move us from the great Persian king Darius to Alexander, who defeated the Persians, to the Ptolemies."[24] Moreover, if one reads the Posidippean epigrams as a sequence of poems whose succession creates meaning, as one should, one must take into account the fact that the piece imitated by Propertius belongs to the 'Dedications' section which begins with a poem picturing Arsinoe II as a warrior, holding the accoutrements of battle, with spear and shield, and sweating — an obvious allusion to Athena.

> Ἀρσινόη, σοὶ τοῦτο διὰ στολίδων ἀνεμοῦσθαι
>     βύσσινον ἄγκειται βρέγμ' ἀπὸ Ναυκράτιος,
> ὧι σύ, φίλη, κατ' ὄνειρον ὀμόρξασθαι γλυκὺν ἱδρῶ

---

21 Posidip. Pell. Ep. 39 AB (translation from S. Stephens).
22 See Gutzwiller 1992; Prioux 2011.
23 See Prioux 2011, 210–1 for examples.
24 Stephens 2004.

ἤθελες, ὀτρηρῶν παυσαμένη καμάτων·
ὣς ἐφάνης, Φιλάδελφε, καὶ ἐν χερὶ δούρατος αἰχμήν,
    πότνα, καὶ ἐν πήχει κοῖλον ἔχουσα σάκος·
ἡ δὲ σοὶ αἰτηθεῖσα τὸ λευχέανον κανόνισμα
    παρθένος Ἡγησὼ θῆκε γένος Μακέ[τη.

Arsinoe, to you is dedicated this *bregma* of linen from Naucratis with folds to be caught by the wind, with which you, dear lady, in a dream wished to wipe your sweet sweat, after ceasing from your sharp toils. You appeared, Philadelphus, holding a spear in your hand, Lady, and with a hollow shield on your arm. The girl, Hêgêsô, a Macedonian in lineage, at your request, dedicated this white strip.[25]

Although Propertius does not appear to allude directly to this epigram in his poem 3.11, he must have known it well: in fact, he seems to have it in mind as he describes again the battle of Actium in poem 4.6 (to which I shall return later) and evokes another Egyptian queen, Cleopatra, holding a spear (4.6.22, *pilaque femineae turpiter apta manu*, "javelins were ill-suited to a womanly hand").[26] One must note that this very evocation of the warrior-queen with her spear is strongly gendered (***femineae** manu*) and, for that reason, condemned (*turpiter*): this could be read as an implicit correction of Arsinoe's usurpation — at least, according to the Roman poet — of masculine attributes of martial greatness in Posidippus' epigram 36 (cf. especially lines 5–6). Thus, if we contend that Propertius knew (and disapproved of) the Alexandrian poet's way of blurring the gendered identity of the Ptolemaic queen, whose 'masculine' qualities are positively enhanced, his appropriation of the fourth poem of the same section in his poem 3.11 appears as a way to both disclose and rectify this blurring: by replacing the Posidippean celebration of Arsinoe with the praise of a male leader, Augustus, as the defeater of an Egyptian queen, Cleopatra, whose femaleness is firmly underlined, Propertius points out the gendered ambiguity of his literary model and, simultaneously, corrects it by reassigning a contrasting opposition between the victorious male (Roman) leader and the defeated female (Egyptian) queen (along with her effeminized lover).

Obviously, Propertius' condemnation of Cleopatra is not to be read primarily as a direct denunciation of Arsinoe herself (after all, the former is said to be — so it seems — the one (exceptional?) disgrace of the dynasty descending from Philip,

---

[25] Posidip. Pell. *Ep.* 36 AB.
[26] I borrow the translation from De Brohun 2003, 216. This parallel has been pointed out to me by one of the anonymous readers of this chapter; I warmly thank him/her for this suggestion.

the father of Alexander the Great);[27] yet the means by which the Augustan poet aggressively underlines Cleopatra's femininity, with sexual innuendo, could in some way target the earlier Ptolemaic queen as well. One can consider in particular the wording of the line 39, *incesti meretrix regina Canopi* ('the harlot queen of licentious Canopus'). For a Roman reader of Hellenistic poetry, Canopus is associated with the shrine of Arsinoe founded at the Cape Zephyrion — the very temple whose dedication by Callicrates is the topic of the Posidippean epigram imitated by Propertius at the end of his own poem. Furthermore, in the *Lock of Berenice*, Callimachus designates Arsinoe Aphrodite Zephyritis as "the inhabitant of Canopus",[28] and in Latin poetry, the word appears in Catullus' translation of Callimachus' poem:

> Ipsa suum Zephyritis eo famulum legarat
> Graiia Canopeis incola litoribus.
>
> Zephyritis herself had sent her servant for that purpose,
> The Greek inhabitant of the coast of Canopus.[29]

Thus, when Propertius uses the word Canopus to disparage the Egyptian queen defeated by Augustus, it might lead the way to the intertextual allusion to queen Arsinoe as she is celebrated in Posidippus' epigram 39 AB: as the goddess of cape Zephyrion, near Canopus. Then, the adjective *incestus* applied to Canopus could, on a proper sense, include in the condemnation Arsinoe II Philadelphus, whose very name designates her as the lover of her sibling: the violent and sexualized rhetoric that thoroughly reduces Cleopatra to her female identity can thus also tendentiously affect the memory of the Ptolemaic queen praised by Posidippus in the epigram imitated (and twisted) by Propertius.

But there is more: beyond the female royal that was celebrated by the Hellenistic poets with a much more qualified view of her femaleness, we might suggest that this 'genderization' also affects the whole Alexandrian culture and literature that was appropriated by the Roman poets. Indeed, it is significant that, whereas Cleopatra herself is not named, but obviously alluded to, in the beginning of the section, the first feminine proper noun that the reader encounters there is 'Alexandria', as if the poet did, in some way, use one for the other: the city and its

---

[27] Prop. 3.11.40, *una Philippei sanguinis usta nota*. But, as Heyworth 2011 puts it (*ad loc.*), "The text and meaning of this line remain very uncertain."
[28] Call. *Aetia Fr.* 110 Pf, 57–8, αὐτή μιν Ζεφυρῖτις ἐπιπροέ[ηκε(ν) / .... Κ]ανωπίτου ναιέτις αἰγιαλοῦ, "Zephyritis herself had sent him on his way, / ... who lives on the coast of Canopus".
[29] Cat. 66.57–8.

queen.³⁰ This equivalence is also strongly supported by the reduction of the narrative as a direct opposition between Rome, on the one hand, and Cleopatra, on the other:³¹ this direct opposition facilitates the latter's assimilation to the city of Alexandria, and, from a Roman point of view, its cultural and poetic legacy. Such an equation could give a particular (and provocative) weight to the adjective *trita* that disparages Cleopatra's so-called sexual depravity.³² In metapoetic contexts, the word *tritus* can function as a Callimachean signpost, to signal Latin equivalents of the "untrodden paths" (κελεύθους ἀτρίπτους) that the poet claims to follow in the programmatic *Aetia* prologue.³³ Hence the paradox of an Alexandrian poetry that would be called *trita*, a poetry which the male (poetic) conquerors reuse as booty for their praise of the Roman Empire. In that sense, it appears that the whole literary culture of Hellenistic Alexandria, the male Roman poet's spoil and captive (as Cleopatra is for Augustus), gets included in Propertius' strongly gendered and orientalist rhetoric.

## 2 Propertius 4.6

The imperialist appropriation of Hellenistic models is also to be read in the poem 4.6, an aetiological poem explaining the temple of Palatine Apollo as founded for the god's aid at Actium and modeling itself, for a great part, on the *Hymns* of Callimachus, mostly 2 and 4 — two hymns that include political eulogies and mention, more or less explicitly, Ptolemy II Philadelphus.³⁴ Propertius outbids his Alexandrian model: with elegy 4.6, the whole poem takes the form of a panegyric, celebrating Augustus' victory over Egypt.³⁵ Moreover, as he embraces this new

---

30 Prop. 3.11.29–33. See p. 119 for the text.
31 For example, l. 49 opposing *mulier*, i.e. Cleopatra, and *Roma* (see *supra*, p. 121). Moreover, one can consider that the poet addresses Roma (in the vocative case) in lines 49–50 (*cane, Roma, … et precare…*) just before addressing Cleopatra in line 51 (***fugisti** tamen in timidi uaga flumina Nili*): this coordination of addressees places the city of Rome and the Egyptian queen on the same level. Also note that a few lines later, Cleopatra herself addresses Roma (55, *Non hoc, Roma, fui tanto tibi ciue uerenda!*).
32 Prop. 3.11.30, *famulos inter femina trita suos*. On the sexual meaning of the adjective, see Adams 1990, 183.
33 Call. Aetia, fr. 1 Pf, 27–8. Cf Lucr. 1.926–7, *auia Pieridum peragro loca nullius ante / **trita** solo. Iuuat integros accedere fontis…*; Manilius 50, *omnis ad accessus Heliconis semita **trita** est.*
34 See Pillinger 1969; Cairns 1984 = 2007, Heyworth 1994, 59–62, Acosta-Hughes/Stephens 2012, 257.
35 On the scholarly reception of this poem in praise of Augustus, see Cairns 2007, 222–3.

and lofty subject, Propertius exhibits the generic disruption at stake: according to his previous programmatic statements, indeed, the elegiac poet was not supposed to sing of wars, *canere bella*.[36] Whereas in elegy 3.1, the poet, claiming to be Callimachus' and Philitas' heir, dismissed anyone daring to "detain Phoebus in arms",[37] this is now literally what he does, staging the god as a formidable warrior fighting for Rome; yet he emphasizes his *aemulatio* all the more with the very same Hellenistic poets:

> Serta Philiteis certet Romana corymbis,
> Et Cyrenaeas urna ministret aquas.

> Let the Roman garland rival the ivy crown of Philitas and let the pitcher pour out pure water of Callimachus.[38]

As Cairns writes, "[the] prologue professes allegiance to Callimachus and Philetas and constitutes a literary programme derived from them";[39] true, but the verb *certare*, in the warlike context of the poem, suggests that what is at stake is not only the depiction of Augustus' defeat of Ptolemaic Egypt, but at the same time, the Roman poets' victory over – and appropriation of – the poetic legacy of the defeated country.

So, whereas the praise of Roman military victories, and especially the battle of Actium, is exactly the kind of topic that was rejected in his earlier *recusationes* of the epic genre,[40] the poem's centerpiece famously consists of a description of the battle against Cleopatra's Egypt. Scholars have pointed out its masculinist view of the events.[41] Following in the footsteps of Vergil's ecphrasis of the Shield and his own elegy 3.11, Propertius, here again, depicts Actium as a "battle of the sexes",[42] opposing for example the "javelins ill-suited to a *womanly* hand",

---

**36** Prop. 2.10.8, *bella canam, quando scripta puella mea est*. In 4.6, Propertius self-consciously recalls this previous *recusatio* by assessing *bella satis cecini* (l. 69). On the exhibition of the generic tension at stake, see DeBrohun 2003. Moreover, as has been noted, the poet will not even stop singing wars after line 69: lines 74–84 stage poets at the symposium singing of recent wars, against the Sygambri, Ethiopians, or evoking the Parthians (see Heyworth 1994, 62 sq; Keith 2008, 165).
**37** Prop. 3.1.1-2, *Callimachi Manes et Coi sacra Philitae, / in uestrum, quaeso, me sinite ire nemus*; 7: *a ualeat, Phoebum quicumque moratur in armis*.
**38** Prop. 4.6.3-4.
**39** Cairns 2007, 223.
**40** Cf. e.g. Prop. 2.34.61-2, *Actia Vergilium custodis litora Phoebi, / Caesaris et fortis dicere posse ratis*, and the analyses of Miller 2004. See also Prop. 2.15.43-6.
**41** E.g. Hutchinson 2006, calling it a "very male poem".
**42** See e.g. DeBrohun 2003, O'Rourke 2011.

(*pilaque **femineae** turpiter apta manu*) — that could be interpreted as a denunciation and correction of Alexandrian poets' valorization of Arsinoe II's martial (/'masculine' strengths)[43] — to the "standards that have learned to conquer for their *father*land" (*signaque iam **patriae** uincere docta suae*).[44] It is striking how, in this perspective, the word *patria*, "fatherland", resumes the overlap of ethnicity and gender in Propertius' account of the battle.[45] Such an overlap is also to be seen in the line that sums up the outcome of the war, *uincit **Roma** fide Phoebi: dat **femina** poenas*:[46] as in elegy 3.11, the direct opposition between a city, Rome, and a woman, the queen of Egypt, contributes to the embodiment of Alexandria — and its cultural legacy — as female. The question is thus: how does this strongly gendered vision of the battle itself affect the Augustan poet's representation of the literary model that he appropriates and advertises as his defeated booty, in a literary duplication of the military battle engaged against Alexandria?

After the beginning of the poem, which imitates the *Hymn to Apollo* (where the poet appears as a priest making sacrifice for the same god) and signals his borrowing by a number of allusions, the account of the Actian battle focuses on the appearance of Apollo standing over Augustus' ship, uttering a prophecy and addressing the latter as 'savior of the world', while his enemies are characterized by chaotic forces that overturned land masses into the sea: these, as Acosta-Hugues and Stephens highlight, are familiar from Callimachus' *Hymn to Delos*, where Apollo *in utero* prophesied Philadelphus' ability to rule, signaled by a contemporary military event: his defeat of the Gauls.[47] As they put it: "Apollo, who was Callimachus' patron deity, both personal and civic, has turned to support the enemy." In the light of this reading, I want to interpret Propertius' evocation of the god changing sides to rally Octavian's Rome.

...
cum Phoebus **linquens** stantem se uindice **Delon**
  (non tulit iratos mobilis ante Notos)
Astitit Augusti puppim super...

---

43 See *supra*, p. 123.
44 Prop. 4.6.21–4, with DeBrohun 2003, 218.
45 Yet, DeBrohun 2003, believes that in 4.6. "Cleopatra's role as 'woman' is highlighted much more than her role as 'Easterner'" (217). I rather agree with O'Rourke 2011 on the fact that the poem articulates closely a male perspective on Cleopatra's femaleness and "the interrogation, if not valorization, of occidental hegemony".
46 4.6.57, "Phoebus keeps faith and Rome conquers: the woman' pays penalty".
47 Acosta-Hughes/Stephens 2012, 257.

> ... when Apollo, leaving Delos, which stands firm under his protection (once it was a moving island, powerless before the anger of the winds), stood over Augustus' ship...[48]

With a metapoetic perspective, one could argue that the move of Apollo 'leaving Delos', *linquens Delon*, to join Augustus thematizes the god's poetic transfer from the Callimachean *Hymn to Delos* (where he voiced the poet's praise of Ptolemy) to Propertius' celebration of the Roman leader's victory over Egypt. Now, it is striking that this very formula echoes another thematization of the same kind of poetic transfer: in the proemium of *Georgics* 3, Vergil claimed that Greece would 'leave the groves of Molorcus' (that is to say: the Callimachean epinician to Berenice) to attend to the Italian games set up by the poet to celebrate Octavian's triumph:

> Cuncta mihi, Alpheum **linquens lucos**que **Molorci**,
> cursibus et crudo decernet Graecia caestu
>
> For me all Greece will leave Alpheus and the groves of Molorcus, to compete in the foot race and with the brutal boxing glove.[49]

With similar wording (*linquens lucos... Molorci*; *linquens... Delos*), Propertius seems to highlight his Vergilian legacy and align his appropriation of Callimachus' *Hymns* with Vergil's appropriation of Callimachus' encomiastic poetry for the queen Berenice II. But here, the appropriated Alexandrian model celebrated a male Ptolemaic sovereign... This might be even more interesting, since one can track the same genderization at play, even without a female Egyptian leader.

As DeBrohun has noted,[50] the interruptive *cum* that marks Apollo's apparition on the battle field recalls its use in elegy 3.3, where the god halted the elegiac poet willing to compose an epic, in an obvious rewriting of the god's intervention as Callimachus' poetic patron in the *Aetia* prologue (3.3.13–14, ***cum*** *me Castalia speculans ex arbore Phoebus / sic ait aurata nixus ad antra lyra*).[51] But in fact, this intratextual echo underlines the change in Apollo's appearance, from the 'Callimachean' peaceful lyre-player to the formidable warrior fighting on Augustus' side.

---

**48** Prop. 4.6.27–9.
**49** Vergil, *Georgics* 3.19–20, translation by H.R. Fairclough, revised by G.P. Goold, Loeb Classical Library, 1999 (revised edition).
**50** DeBrohun 2003, 221.
**51** "When Phoebus observed me from the Castalian wood, and said, as he leaned upon his golden lyre beside the cave...".

> Non ille attulerat crines in colla solutos
>   Aut testudineae carmen inerme lyrae,
> Sed quali aspexit Pelopeum Agamemnona uultu,
>   Egessitque auidis Dorica castra rogis,
> Aut quali flexos soluit Pythona per orbes
>   Serpentem, imbelles quem timuere deae.
>
> He had not come with his locks streaming over his shoulders or brought the unwarlike melody of the tortoise lyre, but with aspects as when he looked upon Pelopean Agamemnon and emptied the Greek camp upon the insatiable pyre, or as when he put to rest throughout its winding coils the serpent Pytho, the terror of the peaceful Muses.[52]

That the god fighting in the battle should have a warlike look is not surprising; but the negative in the beginning, ***non ille attulerat crines in colla solutos***, should prompt us to think that the poet signals here a specific difference with his model: I want to argue that he is actually self-consciously marking a correction of the *Hymn to Apollo*, which was marked out, from the beginning of the poem, as one of Propertius' appropriated poetic models.

Indeed, the Callimachean hymn offers us an androgynous representation of the god as beardless, with youthful locks dripping balm:

> Καὶ μὲν ἀεὶ καλὸς καὶ ἀεὶ νέος· οὔποτε Φοίβου
> Θηλείαις οὐδ' ὅσσον ἐπὶ χνόος ἦλθε παρειαῖς,
> Αἱ δὲ κόμαι θυόεντα πέδῳ λείβουσιν ἔλαια
>
> And indeed he is ever fair and ever young. Never so much as a beard has come to Phoebus' tender cheeks. His hair drips flagrant oils upon the ground.[53]

By claiming that Apollo comes at Actium without those very locks streaming over his shoulders, Propertius highlights the contrast between his representation of the god and Callimachus' one. He thus implicitly points out the adjective Θηλείαις in the latter's text. Obviously in its Callimachean context the word means that Apollo's cheeks are soft, tender (since his beard has not yet coarsened); but it could also evoke the feminine. This latter meaning, and with it the alleged femininity of the god, is retrospectively emphasized by Propertius precisely even as he overtly corrects it: when Apollo turns to support the Roman army, in a Roman poem, he can't keep his Callimachean androgynous look.

---

[52] Prop. 4.6.31–6. On this passage, see Mader 1990. For the duality of Apollo as lyre-player/bowman as embodiment of Propertius' generic choices, with references to the poet's previous picturing of the 'Callimachean' god, see DeBrohun 2003, Miller 2004.

[53] Call. *H.* 2.36–8. See Stephens 2015.

Now one must note, again, the tendentiousness of this retrospective emphasis. Indeed, Propertius strongly contrasts the feminine look denied to 'his' Apollo, as opposed to the Apollo of Callimachus, with the god's victory over the serpent Pytho (the contrast is underlined by the use of the verb *soluere* in the beginning and end of the passage, cf. *non ille attulerat crines in colla* **solutos soluit** *Pythona... serpentem*).[54] But the *Hymn to Apollo* did in fact narrate the slaying of the monster, as one can see especially in lines 100–2:

> Πυθώ τοι κατιόντι συνήντετο δαιμόνιος θήρ,
> αἰνὸς ὄφις. Τὸν μὲν σὺ κατήναρες ἄλλον ἐπ' ἄλλῳ
> βάλλων ὠκὺν ὀϊστόν...,

> When you were going down to Pytho a demonic beast, a dire serpent. You slew him, shooting one swift arrow after another![55]

Moreover, the place Pytho, named after the killing of the monster, is mentioned just before Apollo's androgynous look:

> **Πυθῶνί** κε τεκμήραιο.
> Καὶ μὲν ἀεὶ καλὸς καὶ ἀεὶ νέος· οὔποτε Φοίβου
> Θηλείαις οὐδ' ὅσσον ἐπὶ χνόος ἦλθε παρειαῖς,
> Αἱ δὲ κόμαι θυόεντα πέδῳ λείβουσιν ἔλαια

> You would find proof of this [Apollo's richness] in Pytho. And indeed he is ever fair and ever young. Never so much as a beard has come to Phoebus' tender cheeks. His hair drips flagrant oils upon the ground.[56]

Thus, when Propertius appears to correct his Callimachean model by opposing Apollo's virility and warlike look as the defeater of Pytho to the effeminate unshorn lyre-player, this correction is a tendentious one, that retrospectively overstates his model's feminine and unwarlike traits in order to create a sharper contrast between the Roman and male winner of the military *and* poetic contest and his Alexandrian political enemy / literary model. Propertius enhances the Callimachean Apollo's effeminacy — or, so to say, his *mollitia* — purposely denying

---

[54] This 'contrastive echo' is noted by Miller 2004, 82 after the remind that, as suggested by Rothstein, "*soluit* hints at the rotting dissolution of the beast's body encoded in its name).
[55] Call. *H.* 2.100–2. Moreover, in the surrounding lines (97–104) Callimachus insists on the fact that this warlike episode is the very origin of the way the god is hymned, just before the famous final metapoetic part, where Apollo appears as the protector of the poet attacked by Envy (105–112).
[56] Call. *H.* 2.35 8.

that the god's androgynous look in the Hellenistic model was actually strongly linked with his martial exploits and his use of arms.

Now, after this masculinist view of the Actian battle, and its poetic counterpart including a tendentious feminization of the Alexandrian model being one of the spoils conquered from an hegemonized Egypt, Propertius suddenly disarms Apollo, the victorious god, and gives him back his lyre for peaceful choruses, calling for a banquet in a 'soft' grove (*molli luco*)[57] with seductive roses, expensive wine and imported Cilician perfume: but, as has been noted, in this seemingly more orthodox erotic-elegiac metapoetic setting, the poets attending the symposium are invited to sing of (other) contemporary wars and Roman victories.[58] Yet this should not surprise us. As Alison Keith has shown, "the theme of their song and the leisure in which they sing are predicated on Augustan conquest, as are the luxury products they enjoy at the banquet";[59] to these I would add 'poetic softness' itself, the Callimachean (supposedly) feminine quality of song appropriated by their Roman conquerors. This can be seen in the very beginning of the poem, to which one shall go back:

> Serta Philiteis certet Romana corymbis,
>   et Cyrenaeas urna ministret aquas.
> **Costum molle** date et blandi mihi turis honores,
>   Terque focum circa laneus orbis eat.
> [...]
> Ite procul fraudes, alio sint aëre noxae:
>   Pura nouum uati laurea **mollit** iter.

> Let the Roman garland rival the ivy crown of Philitas and let the pitcher pour out pure water of Callimachus. Give me soft unguents and offerings of appeasing incense, and thrice about the hearth let the woollen fillet be twined. [...] Deceit, far hence begone; let mischief dwell another sky: a pure spray of laurel smoothes for the priest a path he has not trodden before.[60]

As Propertius announces his disruptive choice of an epicized topic, the victory over Egypt, and the form of panegyric, and glosses this change of inspiration, calling it a "new way", *nouum iter*, he insists on his own imperialist appropriation of one of the spoils conquered: Callimachus' poetry (and the claim of the *nouum*

---

**57** Prop. 4.6.71, *candida nunc molli subeant conuiuia luco*. On the use of *mollis* in Propertius' poetry to signal his Callimachean legacy and the latter's association with the feminine, see Klein 2012.
**58** Prop. 4.6.69–84.
**59** Keith 2008, 165.
**60** Prop. 4.6.3–6; 9–10.

*iter* itself obviously functions as an allusive signpost). As he clearly evokes the *Hymn to Apollo* in these prefatory lines,[61] he points out his literary model's *mollitia* — which will later be embodied in the retrospective and tendentious construction of Callimachean Apollo's purely feminine look and demeanour, by contrast with the male and warlike 'Roman' Apollo — as the template that enables him to sing Augustus' military exploits. Like the alluring and exotic goods that came to Rome with the imperial conquest, a feminized Alexandrian poetry that offers the pattern for celebrating the Roman conqueror of Egypt, is presented as a booty highlighting the Roman (literary as well as military) hegemony.

If the poetics of allusion can thus be read not only as an act of homage, but at the same time as an aggressive, imperialist move, it seems that, particularly in the loaded context of Actian poetry – with its constant overlap of ethnicity and gender, and its reduction to the conflict as a Roman victory over a Foreign woman — the reconstruction of Hellenistic models as 'feminine' and the set of tendentious allusions and corrections by which their femaleness is emphasized help the Roman poets to assess their own domination over the hegemonized Alexandrian culture.

## Works Cited

Acosta-Hughes, B./Stephens, S. (2012), *Callimachus in Context: From Plato to the Augustan Poets*, Cambridge/New York.

Adams, J.N. (1990), *The Latin Sexual Vocabulary*, Baltimore.

Barchiesi, A. (1997), 'Otto punti su una mappa dei naufragi', *MD* 39, 209–26.

Barchiesi, A. (2011), 'Roman Callimachus', in: B. Acosta-Hughes/L. Lehnus/S. Stephens (eds.), *Brill's Companion to Callimachus*, Leiden/Boston, 511–33.

Cairns, F. (1984), 'Propertius and the Battle of Actium (4.6)', in: A.J. Woodman/D.A. West (eds.), *Poetry and Politics in the Age of Augustus*, Cambridge, 129–68 and 229–36 = (2007) in: *Papers on Roman Elegy. 1969–2003*, Bologna, 220–61.

Conte, G.B. (1986), *The Rhetoric of Imitation. Genre and Poetic Memory in Virgil and Other Latin Poets*, Ithaca/London.

Conte, G.B. (2017), *Stealing the Club from Hercules: On imitation in Latin Poetry*. Berlin/Boston.

Damer, E.Z. (2014), 'Gender Reversals and Intertextuality in Tibullus', *CW* 107, 493–514.

DeBrohun, J.B. (2003), *Roman Propertius and the Reinvention of Elegy*, Michigan.

Fantuzzi, M./Hunter, R. (2004), *Tradition and Innovation in Hellenistic Poetry*, Cambridge.

---

[61] See Heyworth 2011, 61 for the details.

Fowler, D. (2002), 'Masculinity under Threat? The Poetics and Politics of Inspiration in Latin Poetry', in: E. Spentzou/D. Fowler (eds.), *Cultivating the Muse. Struggles for power and inspiration in classical Literature,* Oxford, 141–59.
Gamel, M.K. (1998), 'Reading as a Man: Performance and Gender in Roman Elegy', *Helios* 25, 79–95.
Gildenhard, I./Zissos, A. (2004), 'Ovid's *Hecale*: deconstructing Athens in the *Metamorphoses*, *JRS* 9, 47–72.
Green, E. (1998), *The Erotics of Domination. Male Desire and the Mistress in Latin Love Poetry*, Baltimore/London.
Green, E./Ancona, R. (eds.) (2005), *Gendered Dynamics in Latin Love Poetry*, Baltimore.
Gutzwiller, K. (1992), 'Callimachus' *Lock of Berenice*: Fantasy, Romance, and Propaganda', *AJPh* 113, 359–85.
Harder, A. (ed.) (2012), *Callimachus: Aetia (2 vols.)*, Oxford/New York.
Heyworth, S. (1994), 'Some allusions to Callimachus in Latin poetry', *MD* 33, 51–79.
Heyworth, S.J./Morwood, J.H.W. (2011), *A Commentary on Propertius, Book 3*, Oxford.
Hinds, S. (1998), *Allusion and Intertext: dynamics of appropriation in Roman poetry*, Cambridge.
Hinds, S. (2001), 'Cinna, Statius and 'Immanent Literary History' in the Cultural Economy', in: E.A. Schmidt (ed.), *L'Histoire litteraire immanente dans la poésie latine.* (Entretiens sur l'Antiquité Classique 47), Vandoeuvres-Geneva, 221–57.
Höschele, R. (2009), 'Catullus' Callimachean *Hair*-itage and the erotics of Translation', *RFIC* 137, 118–52.
Hunter, R. (2006), *The Shadow of Callimachus: Studies in the reception of Hellenistic poetry at Rome*, Cambridge.
Hutchinson, G. (2002), 'The New Posidippus and Latin Poetry', *ZPE* 138, 1–10.
Hutchinson, G. (2006), *Propertius, Elegies Book 4*, Cambridge.
Janan, M. (2001), *The Politics of Desire: Propertius IV*, Berkeley.
Keith, A. (2008), *Propertius: Poet of Love and Leisure*, London.
Klein, F. (2013), '*Mollis* — ἁπαλός : la démarche féminine des vers poétiques dans l'élégie romaine et ses modèles hellénistiques', *Eugesta* 3, 264–81.
Klein, F. (forthcoming), 'Objets arrachés/femmes enlevées : le rapt des vierges et les images du transfert culturel dans les poèmes 64, 65 et 66 de Catulle', in: H. Harich-Schwarzbauer (ed.), *Women and Objects* (IPHIS, Gender Studies in des Altertumswissenschaften), Trier.
Mader, G. (1990), 'The Apollo Similes at Propertius 4.6.31–36', *Hermes* 118, 325–34.
Miller, J.F. (2004), 'Propertian reception of Virgil's Actian Apollo', *MD* 52, 73–84.
Miller, J.F. (2009), *Apollo, Augustus, and the Poets*, Cambridge.
Nelis, D. (2005), 'The Roman Callimachus: structure and coherence in the Propertian corpus' in: A. Kolde/A. Lukinovich/A.-L. Rey (eds.), κορυφαίῳ ἀνδρί. *Mélanges offerts à André Hurst*, Geneva, 235–48.
Newman, J.K. (1997), *Augustan Propertius: The Recapitulation of a Genre*, Hildesheim.
O'Rourke D. (2011), "Eastern' Elegy and 'Western' Epic: reading 'orientalism' in Propertius 4 and Virgil's *Aeneid*', *Dictynna* 8.
O'Rourke, D. (2017), 'Hospitality narratives in Virgil and Callimachus: the ideology of reception', *Cambridge Classical Journal* 63, 118–42.
Pillinger, H.E. (1969), 'Some Callimachean Influences on Propertius, Book IV', *HSCP* 73, 171–99.
Prioux, E. (2011), 'Callimachus' Queens', in: B. Acosta-Hughe /L. Lehnus/S. Stephens (eds.), *Brill's Companion to Callimachus*, Leiden/Boston, 201–24.

Quint, D. (1993), *Epic and Empire: Politics and Generic form from Virgil to Milton*, Princeton.
Rabinowitz, N./Richlin, A.(1993) (eds.), *Feminist Theory and the Classics*, New York.
Said, E.W. (1978), *Orientalism*, New York.
Stephens, S. (2004), 'For You, Arsinoe...', in: B. Acosta-Hughes/E. Kosmetatou/M. Baumbach (eds.), *Labored in Papyrus Leaves: Perspectives on an Epigram Collection Attributed to Posidippus (P. Mil. Vogl. VIII 309)*, Washington DC, 161–76.
Stephens, S. (2015), *Callimachus, The Hymns. Edited with Introduction, Translation, and Commentary by Susan A. Stephens*, Oxford.
Sweet, F. (1972), 'Propertius and Political Panegyric', *Arethusa* 5, 169–75.
Thomas, R.F. (1983), 'Callimachus, the Victoria Berenices, and Roman Poetry', *CQ* 33, 92–113.
Thomas, R.F. (1986), 'Virgil's *Georgics* and the Art of Reference', *HSCP* 90, 171–98.
Wyke, M. (1992), 'Augustan Cleopatras: Female Power and Poetic Authority' in: A. Powell (ed.), *Roman Poetry and Propaganda in the Age of Augustus*, 81–140, rev. as M. Wyke (2002), '*Meretrix regina*: Augustan Cleopatras', in: *The Roman Mistress*, Oxford, 195–243.
Yegenoglu, M. (1998), *Colonial Fantasies. Towards a Feminist Reading of Orientalism*, Cambridge.
Young, E.M. (2015), *Translation as Muse. Poetic Translation in Catullus' Rome*, Chicago/London.

Andrew Feldherr
# Caesar or Cleopatra? Lucan's Tragic Queen

The broad appeal of scholarly attempts to recover the 'real' Cleopatra is not difficult to explain. As it becomes harder to inhabit the world mapped by the polarizing rhetoric of Augustus' triumph, which founds the historical and conceptual Roman empire on the defeat of the Eastern female, the recovery of Cleopatra as an authentic subject seems to offer a way to challenge this image from within. However, from their Augustan beginnings, depictions of Cleopatra have themselves posited a real queen within, or beyond her image. Horace's 'Cleopatra Ode' shows us the queen herself 'daring to gaze' (1.37.25) on the spectacle of her defeat while Vergil by contrast presents her as a viewer trapped within a representation, the central panel of Aeneas' shield. When she 'does not yet look back at the twin serpents approaching from behind' (8.697), her limited vision tragically opposes that of reader/viewers who know how her story will end, not least from having seen similar scenes depicted at an actual triumph.[1]

In both of these works, juxtaposing the real, unnamed queen with the representation of her defeat directs attention to the process of becoming Cleopatra. Lucan's *Pharsalia*, a crucial stage in the reception of that Augustan image, moves in the opposite direction. It returns us to an earlier point in the queen's life to show that she is already Cleopatra.[2] And Lucan's own concern with the representation of Cleopatra reveals itself in the very fact that this is likely the first extant poetic text where she is named.[3] The queen's belated debut in verse is often explained on metrical grounds. The four short syllables of Cleopatra make it difficult to incorporate in many meters, and Vergil's reluctance to allow a mute and a

---

[1] Fundamental studies of Cleopatra in Augustan poetry include Gurval 1998 and Wyke 2002, 197–243. A fuller description of how Horace and Vergil focalize the imagery and ideology of Octavian's triumph through the figure of Cleopatra will be found in Feldherr 2010 and 2014, 295–8. For an important interpretation of how Cleopatra's death was 'theatricalized' in the *Carmen de Bello Actiaco*, see Keith 2000, 119–22.
[2] Pathbreaking literary interpretations of Lucan's Cleopatra include Becher 1966, 117–22, Zwierlein 1974, and the brief but rich discussion by Ahl 1976, 225–7. Among Important recent treatments are Sannicandro 2010, 101–27, Turner 2010, Pyy 2011, and Ambühl 2015, 129–34 and 369–402.
[3] Another candidate is 'Seneca's' epigram 69.3. See Schmidt 1986, 103–4, and Becher 1966, 115 n. 2. For the most recent arguments on the date and authenticity of these poems, see Breitenbach 2010, 116, who regards the collection as a unified Gedichtbuch from the second century CE, and Dingel 2007, 33, who argues that it is an assemblage containing many poems probably or possibly by Seneca.

liquid to lengthen the preceding syllable discourages him from naming her. Lucan's looser prosody, moving in the direction of Cole Porter's 'Cleopatterer', removes the obstacle. Yet this is unlikely to be simply a metrical problem, nor perhaps even an accident of survival. For Lucan does not just happen to include her name: Cleopatra appears no fewer than nine times in the final two books of the poem. It has also been suggested that there was a kind of taboo against naming this dangerous foe during the Augustan period.[4] I rather think the point of calling her instead a 'queen' (*regina*), a 'destructive prodigy' (*fatale monstrum*), or an 'Aegyptian wife' (*Aegyptia coniunx*) was to use these fearsome predicates to consolidate the significance and identity of this figure. For Lucan, looking back from his place in literary history, the queen has become 'Cleopatra'; the name alone can summon up the associations that the earlier generation of poets constructed for her. Conversely, looking forward from the time frame of the represented events, the act of naming her gives the sense that his is 'the' Cleopatra who attracts all those damning metonyms.

If the effect of representing the queen in contexts like the Actian triumph was to mark the conclusion of the danger she posed and to contain her influence by presenting her as 'other' and un-Roman, the very context in which Lucan depicts her takes her beyond those limits. For Lucan describes Cleopatra's success rather than her defeat and places her not at the ending point of civil war but at the start of the dynasty that replaced it. Indeed the scene Lucan presents, more than an example of what Barchiesi (1993) calls 'a future reflexive allusion', appears as the *aition* for the later chapter of civil wars and the whole Augustan condemnation of Cleopatra: 'that night gave her this courage' (*hoc animi nox illa dedit*, 10.68). Lucan shows Cleopatra as the lover not of Augustus' rival but of his father, an alternative mother, so to speak, of a counterfactual dynasty that continues the legacy of Alexander rather than conquering it.[5] And in re-imposing this uncannily familiar Cleopatra on the story of Rome's imperial origins, Lucan gives Cleopatra a particularly vivid presence by evoking the medium of dramatic performance. He makes the myth of Cleopatra real not only by showing us the queen before the image, but by superimposing that image on reality, by putting the mythical Cleopatra as a symbol of un-Roman otherness back into history, and by making her a figure for the reality of the present and its own reliance on the power of illusion.

---

[4] Fordyce 1977, 281, also Berti 2000, 96. See esp. Chaudhuri 2012.
[5] The contemporary political force of Lucan's invective against Cleopatra is especially stressed in Schmidt 1986, 107. As an anonymous referee suggests, 'Lucan takes a hint from Dido's wish for a 'little Aeneas' (*paruulus Aeneas*, *Aen.* 4.328–9), a foreshadowing of the 'little Caesar' Caesarion'; see Eidinow 2003, 264–7.

The first section of this paper will demonstrate in general terms the Neronian presence within the figure of Cleopatra while the second will argue that Lucan evokes the medium of tragedy to convey that presence. The conclusion then considers how this mimetic strategy might affect responses to the linked representation of gender and ethnicity in the episode.

Before beginning this argument, a summary of what happens in this generally less-studied section of the poem is in order. The short answer is very little. Lucan is well known for avoiding the consequences of civil war by deferral and regression, as if not telling the story of civil war can keep it from happening.[6] Thus even though Rome and the future are the goals for the rivals in the civil war, the forward movement of the poem's plot takes the form of a geographical and temporal retreat. Pompey's trajectory pushes him back to the Eastern lands where he won so much glory, and Caesar follows.[7] As the tenth book begins, he reaches the ultimate origins of 'Magnus' in the tomb of Alexander the Great. Next on the scene is Alexander's ersatz descendant Cleopatra, who sneaks into the palace where Caesar is lodged. She has to sneak in because the affections of her brother and intended husband, Ptolemy, have been alienated by the nefarious eunuch Pothinus. Cleopatra's regaining her position depends on her persuasion, which becomes her seduction, of Caesar. Caesar may eventually yield but Lucan does not. Cleopatra's arrival prompts 25 lines of invective on the part of the narrator, which prepares us to see Cleopatra in action (10.59–84). She delivers a cunningly effective speech, her only utterance in the poem (10.85–104), but Caesar would not have been persuaded unless her appearance came to the aid of her words, leading into a fantastical banquet that continues for more than two hundred lines, most of it taken up with a digression on the origins of the Nile (10.107–331). Yet as in the similarly extended banquet between Aeneas and Dido that seems to delay the *Aeneid* through two whole books, here too a lot is going on simultaneously.[8] In Vergil, Dido is being worked on by desire and is so setting the stage for the love and betrayal that will lead to lasting hatred between Rome and Carthage. Here desire's alter ego, Pothinus, persuades Ptolemy to make an attack on Caesar himself.

As can be seen from the previous summary, the beginning of book 10 thematizes questions of origins, from the explicit discussion of the sources of the Nile,

---

**6** See esp. Masters 1992, 1–10.
**7** See Ahl 1976, 183–4 and Rossi 2000.
**8** Zwierlein 1974, 61–6 gives a brilliant analysis of the Vergilian reminiscences in Lucan's banquet scene. For further comparison of the effect of the two banquets, see Ahl 1976, 227–8.

to the sense that the banquet replays the starting point for the plot of the *Aeneid*.[9] Caesar has come from the site of Troy, the simultaneous starting point for his family, Roman history, Aeneas' journey, and the tradition of epic narrative itself. But he found nothing familiar there. By contrast when he reaches the always topsy-turvy land of Egypt, he encounters an alternative set of 'real' origins for his own power in the reviled legacy of Hellenistic monarchy.[10] Hence perhaps the way that origins are so closely connected with things that are supposed to be ending. For this was at once the site of Magnus' death and the source of his name and public image. The paradox of the Nile lies in its flowing between hemispheres, so that while its origin is unknown in one place, its ending is a mystery in another (*hic quaeritur ortus, illic finis aquae*, 10.301–2). In following literally in Magnus' footsteps, Caesar will begin to appropriate an Alexandrian legacy that turns out to be inseparable from a decadent Ptolemaic present. Lucan's description of Caesar's 'eager descent' into the 'cave' of Alexander's tomb (10.19), creates a kind of catabasis, with invective against a foreign tyrant taking the place of Anchises' praise of Roman *duces*. And the subsequent image of the 'boy king' Ptolemy (*rex puer*), coming not from Pella but the Pelusiac Nile to meet Caesar suggests at once a decline that might be similarly traced between Caesar and his own 'unwarlike' (*imbellis*) descendant but also the revenant power of the past (10.53–4).[11]

Cleopatra's subsequent appearance adds a literary dimension to this impression of a return from the dead. Those who remember Horace's ode may note that the queen enters the narrative by coming back into the selfsame palace whose 'destruction she dared to look upon' in the poem's finale (*ausa et iacentem uisere regiam*, 1.37.25). Should they remember her ending at this new beginning in Lucan's poem, or does the textual succession from the Augustan poets to their Neronian imitator signal a rebirth of Cleopatra from the ashes of her imperial destruction? The description of that palace as Emathian with its echo of Lucan's own first line suggests the restarting of the next civil war, between Antony and Octavian at the site of Pompey's death.[12] But Cleopatra's influence survives civil war as well. Plutarch (*Ant.* 87.4) ends his life of Antony with a list of his descendants which soon becomes uncannily identical with the Julio-Claudian dynasty,

---

9 On beginnings and closure in book 10, see Rossi 2005. Pp. 238–43 in particular treat allusions to *Aeneid* 1 in this section of the poem.
10 Rossi 2005, 245–52 gives an excellent analysis of how Lucan unmasks Alexander as a forerunner for the Caesars. For Alexander as a model specifically for Nero, see Tracy 2014, 94–6 with further bibliography.
11 On Ptolemy as a figure for Nero, see McCloskey/Phinney 1968.
12 Ahl 1976, 225.

though with an emphasis on its maternal connections. Nero, Antony's descendant in the fifth generation through Agrippina, ends the series with a bang by killing off the mother who won him power and 'came near destroying the Roman empire through madness and folly'.

A temporal model that ends Cleopatra's story not with Actium but with Nero highlights how Lucan is doing more than developing the ambiguous potential of Cleopatra to conjure up the future, latent in her cautionary role in Horace's ode. The very fact that he does so from the perspective of that future gives his reading a particular authority. At the same time, of course, the general condemnation of the Neronian regime as foreign, effeminate, and incestuous draws on the very rhetorical strategies used to castigate Cleopatra.[13] In the rest of this paper I want to illustrate the particular techniques Lucan uses to confuse the foreign past and the Roman present and to make clear that this confusion operates in two directions: Nero is already immanent in Cleopatra, but Cleopatra can be re-visualized as Nero. Familiar aspects of anti-Neronian invective are re-written as projections, indeed fulfillments of the represented Cleopatra, while the real presence of a Neronian model for the queen, revises and undoes attempts to write her off as a defeated 'other' by anchoring her connection to the historical 'now'.

Although there is no specific reference to Nero in the passage, the velcro-like capacities of both figures to attract all the attributes that the Romans ever feared or rejected, allow for an easy conceptual slippage between the regimes of Nero and Cleopatra. When Cleopatra describes the love between brother and sister Caesar is urged to restore, we might think not just of the generic charges of incest that accrue around the bad Julio-Claudians, but the specific dynastic marriage of brother and sister that cemented Nero's link to the family of his adopted father

---

13  The polemical portraits of Nero we find in Suetonius, Tacitus, and Dio should not be confused with historical reality. However, different approaches to their obvious bias have different implications for the crucial question of whether the basic lines of this invective would have been available to Lucan's audience. One alternative, summarized in Grau 2018, looks to the demonization of Nero to legitimize his Flavian successors as the ultimate source of this negative image and therefore encourages skepticism about the possibility that the familiar charges against the emperor had much contemporary resonance. Another, adopted especially in Champlin 2003, 52, while fully accepting the polemical aims of the sources, highlights the continuities between these later interpretations and the known facts of Nero's reign. Thus Champlin shows how some behaviors that could be the targets of invective were polyvalent and possessed their own kind of logic. Space prevents a full discussion of the issue, but my premise throughout this discussion will be that the negative portrayal of Nero found in later sources forms an inevitable flipside of the strategies he used to define his authority and that the hostile constructions of his actions found in the sources would likely have been available during his lifetime. There was of course a resistance to Nero, and I assume that its account of Nero drew on similar stereotypes.

Claudius.¹⁴ Change a few of the names, and Cleopatra's lament about being alienated from the affections of her husband/brother could be transposed into an *Octavia*. More specifically Alexandrian images came to play a crucial role in the characterization of Nero's reign. The emperor was notoriously fond of Alexandria, and Woodman (1992) has argued that Tacitus' description of his own paradoxical fêtes portrays a Rome that has indeed been replaced by the city it once feared as a rival. More recently, Champlin has suggested that these later charges were not simply the work of polemicists influenced by the Augustan imagery of decadence epitomized by Cleopatra.¹⁵ Rather the emperor himself seems to have deliberately evoked his rakish but glamorous ancestor, Mark Antony. If this is so, then the 'authorship' of Nero's Alexandrian imitations becomes as confusing as the question of whether Cleopatra was the model for characterizing Nero, or Nero for Cleopatra. Was the emperor's own attempt to play Antony countered/complemented by the re-mobilization of the Augustan condemnation of that figure? From the perspective of such perennial public relations wars, we can understand the resemblance between Cleopatra and Nero not only in terms of Lucan's engagement with Augustan *auctores* but as already written by another hidden author, the emperor Nero himself.

All these doublings, maskings, and revelations, however, are not just free-floating hermeneutic challenges that could be developed for any later Cleopatra, as a dangerously paradoxical and elusive figure. Rather, the attention Lucan gives to the themes of disguise, illusionism, and re-doubled identity forms part of a strategy to super-impose reality and representation thanks to two essential attributes of Neronian culture with which they may be connected and that play a crucial role in characterizing the epoch, luxury and theatricality. In the discussions that follow, my focus will be on two moments when Cleopatra's very body becomes a means of summoning up the visual presence of Neronian Rome, first her seductive presence at the banquet and then, in the next section of the paper, her initial appearance in the poem.

I previously described how notions of dynastic decline were incestuously repeated, or anticipated, as origins, and this superimposition suggests another kind of alternative imperial history. For a passage in Tacitus' *Annales* makes it

---

**14** For discussion of how Nero's domestic life inverts that of the dynasty's founder Augustus, see Milnor 2005, 295–304. Particularly important for my argument is her emphasis on this inversion as a feminization of the dynasty.
**15** Champlin 2003, 171–7. For more on Nero's Alexandrianism in connection with this passage, see Tracy 2014, 259–71.

clear that the reign of the Julio-Claudians is precisely co-extensive with the history of luxurious dining itself, which lasted from Actium to the next civil war in 69 (3.55). Lucan, in referring to 'luxury not yet handed on to Roman generations' (*nondum translatos in Romana saecula luxus*, 10.110), seems to evoke a similar historical chronology.[16] The seductive banquet begins after 'peace has been achieved' (10.107), and the sense that this *pax Iulia* prospectively re-writes the Augustan empire to come emerges from the spatial as well as temporal reach of *luxus*. Luxury provides a new motive for conquest and as such a new origin for the empire, one that springs from bodily desire and manifests itself in bodily pleasures. Not only does the description of 'a multitudinous throng of attendants and a nation of servants' (*famulae numerus turbae populusque minister*, 10.127) suggest that the banquet contains an imperial population, but it revises and challenges the military history of its attainment. 'Caesar would say he never saw such red hair in the fields of the Rhine' (10.130–1). He would say that if he were to compose a new *Gallic Commentaries* as an erotic romance.

The sense of this scene as an anachronistic glimpse of the future retrojected into the violence of the civil war picks up on another crucial aspect of luxury that will introduce the final theme of the talk. Luxury is deceptive: various kinds of discourses from annalistic history to stoic sermons like Seneca's letters and the satirical attacks on luxurious freedmen reinforce the notion that the flashy surfaces of wealth distract the eye from what really matters, *uirtus*, and a prominence in society that must be earned, not bought.[17] Hence, in a connection that will be important for the last stage in my argument, Pliny will describe how the ornaments that first transformed Roman houses to palaces were originally themselves stage sets (*HN* 36.116). An obvious symptom of luxury was its divergence from nature: in the old days, as Seneca puts it, no embossed ceilings loomed above, but the stars glided over men lying in the open air (*Ep.* 90.42). The emphasis on luxury as the deceptive and artificial visual intrusion of a false image upon reality matches the elaborate illusionism of the Roman visual arts, exemplified by the simulation of precious materials through fake surfaces. But, as often, Lucan gives a new, antithetical twist to this topos in order to keep luxury from being what it seems in ever new and more inventive ways. The encrusted surfaces of a Roman palace may appear to be recalled in Cleopatra's palace, but they are not because

---

**16** See Tracy 2014, 54–6, and, for an account of the banquet as inflected by 'contemporary concerns with luxury and ostentatious display', Turner 2010, 206–7.

**17** *Loci classici* in historiography include Sallust *BC* 11, Livy *praef.* 11, and Cato's speech against the repeal of the *lex Oppia* (34.2–4). For the various aspects of the theme, including the emphasis on artificiality, see Edwards 1993, 137–72.

here the luxury deceives by being real. 'The house did *not* shine with slices of marble, with only a surface veneer. Not inactive, the agate supported itself, and porphyry and onyx were trod upon, spread out through the whole hall: nor does Ethiopian ebony cover the vast columns; it takes the place of cheap oak – it is the support, not the ornament (*forma*) of the home' (10.114–9).

The paradox of a form that is no mere appearance brings us back to Cleopatra herself, who takes her place as the visual centerpiece of this description and concentrates in her own 'beauty painted beyond measure' (*immodice fucatam formam*, 10.137) the semantic contradictions of the whole ensemble: for while Cleopatra would appear at first glance not to be what she seems, a dyed surface, the adornments simultaneously reveal and conceal. The garment she wears has the special property of transparency: an already over the top Chinese silk has been laboriously loosened by an Alexandrian acuity with textiles, so that her gleaming breasts 'shine through Sidonian stuff' (10.142). The process further makes the garment reveal its wearer, for the loosening of the threads (10.147) echoes the first emergence of Cleopatra within the text, with the loosening of the harbor chains (10.57). The Sidonian element of the line denotes the purple dye that adds a further ethnic color to this Eastern confection. But its obvious evocation of Dido not only recalls another original sin, it also sets the bodily presence of the queen in opposition to this merely literary ornament.[18] Cleopatra may be a Dido, in fact she may be 'the' Dido, that is the historical figure who inspired and emerges from the Vergilian myth. Or Dido might merely be the costume for the role she has been made to play by Lucan.

The problem of role-playing and the suggestion of a real presence behind a mythical impersonation link Cleopatra as the embodiment of the deceptive power of luxury with the related idea of theater. And to make this connection more prominent I turn in this section of the paper to Lucan's first description of Cleopatra's appearance. For this passage too features an uncertain, even paradoxical, visual sign that makes Cleopatra seem to be two things at once.

It would require little textual prompting to visualize Cleopatra as a theatrical presence. Her own self-presentation relied heavily on spectacle. Plutarch, who was extremely interested in the visual impressions made by this figure, presents her first meeting with Antony as a naval pageant – the famous prototype for the Shakespearean description of her barge. But the important point about this episode is that it involves not just spectacle but mimesis: Cleopatra is playing Aph-

---

[18] Pyy 2011, 89.

rodite, with her handmaidens accessorized as Nereids (*Ant.* 26). Conversely, Cleopatra herself was an attested subject for a particular form of dramatic spectacle, the pantomime, which represented episodes from chaos down to Cleopatra the Egyptian (Luc. *Salt.* 37), and, for what it is worth, Lucan himself is said to have composed '14 pantomimes' (*salticae fabulae XIV*, *Vit. Vaccae*, p. 336.19 Hosius). Now it may well be that the theatricalization of Cleopatra in accounts like Plutarch's itself depends on a tradition of seeing her depicted in the theater. But this is precisely my point: whether or not such performances on Cleopatra's part were authentic, and perhaps even more so if their authenticity was debated, the synthesis between Cleopatra as an actress herself and a subject portrayed by actresses creates a cultural environment that blurs the distinction between representation and reality.

In Lucan's poem the theatrical dimension is highlighted in two ways, first through a literary allusion, which is then itself made more vividly present to the audience through a representation of theatrical practice. The most vexed intertextual moment in this part of the epic comes just after Cleopatra's appearance in the palace. Lucan amplifies her presence with a series of appositional phrases, one of which terms her 'the deadly Erinys of Latium' (10.59), a reminiscence of the much-debated 'Helen episode' of *Aeneid* 2, where Helen of Troy is called 'the common Erinys of Troy and her own *patria*' (2.573).[19] Since the allusion is so apt for Cleopatra, whose threat embraces both Rome and her native Egypt, and since Helen of Troy herself appears two lines later, when Lucan characterizes Cleopatra not by metonymy but by an explicit comparison to 'the Spartan' woman (10.61), scholars have used this as evidence if not for the authenticity of the Vergilian passage then to establish a *terminus ante quem* for its appearance in the text.[20]

However, as Annemarie Ambühl has shown in considerable detail, the Vergilian intertext provides just one stage in a literary tradition that goes further back to Greek and Roman tragedy.[21] Propertius could speak of 'tragic Furies' (*tragicae Erinyes*, 2.20.39), and the specific comparison of Helen to a fury has explicit parallels in tragedy, beginning with Aeschylus' description of her as the 'Erinys

---

**19** On the connections between Lucan's Cleopatra and Helen, see Becher 1966, 118–9, Schmidt 107–9, and Berti 2000, 97–9. Cf. also Goossens 1946, 277–8, and the lapidary formulation of von Albrecht 1970, 276 n. 1: 'hinter Caesar steht Alexander, hinter beiden Achilleus, der vor dem Kampf mit Hektor (*Il.*, 22.25–32) mit einem Unstern verglichen wird. Hinter Cleopatra steht Helena, ...'.
**20** See esp. Bruère 1964, 267 ('Lucan knew the Helen episode in its present context'), Murgia 2003 (the Helen episode in the *Aeneid* was composed in imitation of Lucan himself), and Conte 2006 (the passage derives from a first draft by Vergil that was suppressed by his editors).
**21** Ambühl 2015, 129–34.

whom brides lament' (*Ag.* 749).²² In Latin, Cicero preserves a fragment of Ennius, attributed to a tragedy about Alexander, appropriately enough, but the Trojan one, in which Cassandra looks forward to the judgment of Paris and its consequence, the coming of Helen to Troy (*Div.* 1.114).²³ And the situation of that Alexander, whose function as judge (*iudicium*) is stressed by Ennius (fr. 14.48 Jocelyn), anticipates the verdict to be rendered by the successor of the other Alexander, Caesar, between Ptolemy and Cleopatra.²⁴ The corruption of this judge (10.106) proleptically figures Cleopatra as both Aphrodite (cf. 10.75), winner of the contest, and Helen, the bribe that secured her victory.²⁵

Ambühl uses these references to the tragic Helen to unlock a striking series of mythical parallels linking Cleopatra's potential effect on Rome to the fall of Troy itself. But the importance of the narrative content of these tragic episodes for Lucan's theme is complemented by an evocation of the theater as a medium through which that distant, foreign past becomes confused with the audience's here-and-now. These tragic echoes also function in a metaliterary sense to characterize the effects of the character within the narrative, and of the narrative itself. Cleopatra 'terrified' the Roman Capitolium (10.63), and her appeal to Caesar with its 'feigned grief' (*simulatum dolorem*, 10.82–3) resembles a *miseratio*. If Cleopatra evokes the emotions of tragedy, for the dynamics of Lucan's narrative these parallels alert us to a characteristically tragic discrepancy in knowledge between the characters and the poetic voice. Cicero quotes the Ennius passage as an example of prophetic language, and Lucan's ability to see the consequences of this deed in hindsight makes him a Cassandra-like presence in his own narrative, denouncing the vice and folly of characters who, of course, cannot hear him (cf. *ignaro Caesare*, 10.58). And the lines between these temporal perspectives blur in a confusing way when Lucan moves from Cleopatra's actual accomplishments to her ultimately unrealized intentions. She would indeed terrify the Capi-

---

22 See esp. Conte 2006, 160 n. 1. Parallels to Aeschylus and Ennius are also noted in Schmidt 1986, 108: also Eur. *Or.* 1389.
23 On the relationship of this play to the Euripidean *Alexandros*, see Timpanaro 1996.
24 Many stages in Paris/Alexander's career are blended in Caesar's encounter with Cleopatra: Sannicandro 2014, 55–7 also compares Caesar's dalliance here to Paris' in *Iliad* 6. Ambühl 2015, 152–3 further develops this.
25 If, as Conte 2006, 163, shows, it is typical of Lucan that he cites Vergil 'antiphrastically', with significant verbal variations, he does the same with Ennius. Helen there is not only designated as 'one of the Furies', *Furiarum una*, but also referred to by her ethnic identity: '*Lacedaemonia mulier*' ('Spartan woman'). Lucan calls Cleopatra an Erinys and Helen *Spartana* (which Conte takes as a variation of the indisputably Vergilian *Lacaena* in 2.601).

tol, at least when read through Horace, but her aspiration to lead Caesar in triumph is shown to be vain by the same Horatian allusion, where Octavian has identical plans for her (*deduci*, 1.37.31). And the 'uncertain outcome' at Actium seems to hint that Cleopatra might win (*dubius casus*, 10.66). These 'counterfactual' elements of Lucan's invective move us from perceiving the terrible consequences of this encounter to dreading them. Even those who know how it all ought to end are brought back to a turning point in the fortune of world history.

There is also a particularly tragic effect to the layered comparison of Cleopatra both to Helen and an Erinys that is lost when we describe her with a cliché like 'fatal beauty'. For Erinyes were easily visualized figures notable for the horror inspired by their theatrical representation, while Helen, another tragic character, was their visual antithesis. When Lucan says that Helen destroyed Argos and Troy with her 'destructive appearance' (*facie ... nocenti*, 10.61), it is a further Vergilian echo, but in addition to the allusive links to Ennius my reading has emphasized, there is another reason to think specifically of a tragic performance here. Helen in the *Aeneid* is directly present, but in Lucan's passage she only emerges through the visage of Cleopatra, or rather we see Cleopatra wearing her mask. Allusion here becomes a kind of impersonation that develops into a full-blown tragic performance. Not only was a royal palace, the setting in which she appears, the typical tragic stage set, but Lucan may have remembered from the last lines of Caesar's own *Commentarii* that the part of the palace where he had first been housed adjoined a theater, which also gave entrance to the port (*B. Ciu.* 3.112). A recollection of this passage may make Cleopatra's own entrance even more theatrical, or rather blur the difference between a real palace and a real theater. After the poet compares her to Helen, she seems to take on the role herself. She makes her entrance, 'trusting in her appearance', and the details of that appearance, its combination of beauty and gloom (*tristitia*), create a specifically visual manifestation of paradox. Indeed the attention to Cleopatra's hair, disarrayed as if she had torn it, not only facilitates her fury-like role as an inspirer of revenge, it recalls one of the distinctive physical aspects of the Erinyes, their disordered serpent hair.[26] As later Caesar will be moved not by her words but her 'baleful beauty' (*incesta facies*, 10.105), exactly the noun used to describe Helen's appearance earlier (10.61), so we see her precisely in the redoubled form of a combined mask of beauty and horror.

Cleopatra, then, does not just use deception and illusion to trick Caesar; she is playing a role, and what is more a doubled one, as an Erinys masquerading as Helen of Troy. The particular tragic mask she wears in itself helps connect her

---

[26] On the seductive power of Helen's hair in tragedy, see Ambühl 2015, 131.

performance to the themes of illusionism raised by luxury. Helen too was a famously seductive figure, but also one famous for not being what she seemed. What Paris had abducted was according to tragedy, simply an εἴδωλον. But paradoxically, where Helen really was is precisely where Cleopatra is now, on the island of Pharos, which as we have seen becomes both the stage set and the mythical locale such a set depicts.²⁷ When we say Cleopatra is playing Helen, on the one hand it makes her an image of an image, but geographically we are much closer to the real Helen than in the scenes imagined by Vergil or Ennius. An awareness of tragedy as a medium which Lucan evokes, rather than a repertoire of mythical narratives to which he alludes, matters thematically because the sense of physical presence it creates disorders the relationship between present and past and representation and reality.

We can relate this new exploration of the tension between reality and illusion also to the doubled vision produced by Lucan's complex temporal perspectives on the action. First of all, that reduplicated mask combining the terror of a Fury and the appeal of Helen, neatly divides according to whether we see her as Caesar does or with authorial hindsight. The terror of the scene all comes later; what Cleopatra shows Caesar is only beauty. Yet, as I have suggested, a tragic vision of this Erinys has the effect of undoing what we know will happen, of returning us to the presence of Cleopatra and of turning the Caesars into a tragic dynasty whose ancestral guilt returns in time. And this sense of reversing history becomes all the more compelling when we see not Cleopatra playing Helen, but as Helen herself. For in addition to undoing the difference made by the historical defeat of Cleopatra at Actium, reifying this counterfactual drama collapses the past by making Caesar an Alexander, indeed two Alexanders, either of whom may be called a 'fortunate plunderer' (*felix praedo*, 10.21), forming part of an *Ilioupersis* theme that knits together the impending fall of Rome and the fall of Troy.²⁸ That was precisely the cyclical link between myth and history that Augustan propaganda claimed to have broken, but it was also a story that the Neronian present loved to tell, being the subject of epics by both the poet and the emperor.

If Lucan's rant at Cleopatra's appearance turned him into a sort of tragic Cassandra, we might take comfort in bringing down the curtain by remembering that, while Cassandra was right in predicting that Helen would destroy Troy, it

---

**27** A point also observed by Ambühl 2015, 132, who goes on to note that references to Proteus later in the book (10.509–11) recall his presence at the beginning of Euripides' *Helen*. She does not, however, discuss the phenomenological effects of Helen's characterization as εἴδωλον ('image').
**28** See Ambühl 2010 and 2015, 287–368.

was possible to claim that Lucan was wrong since Cleopatra would not destroy Rome, provided that she was defeated by Augustus. But to see Cleopatra back again in the present, to imagine that there was no difference between her Alexandria and Rome, between the imaginary, allegorical world Lucan described and the lived reality of Nero, gives a new authority to those tragic premonitions. Even her oft-repeated, and evidently Alexandrian, name takes on, in hindsight, an imperial echo. For that prosodically problematic syllable *patr-* which Lucan succeeds in incorporating within his hexameters gains additional emphasis in Cleopatra's own words. Her single speech features the cognate '*paternus*' twice, and Cleopatra also tells Caesar to 'read the last words of her dead father' (*summa perempti uerba patris*, 10.92–3). Reading the end of her own name in this context recalls that it was designed to preserve the reputation of her fathers.[29] So too Nero, like all Caesars bears the name of his ultimate 'father', though here it is also a feature he shares with his distant mother.

The way the name and face of Cleopatra call up the reality of Nero possesses another very up-to-date aspect thanks to the increasing importance of theatrical performance in the emperor's own construction of his power. His experimentation with a variety of performance genres was a gradual and complex process, and Lucan did not live to see its fullest manifestation, Nero's appearance on the public stage in the fully mimetic media of tragedy and pantomime, a practice which began only during the last years of his reign.[30] Nevertheless it is plausible, at least as the basis of a thought experiment, that Lucan would have been aware of the tendencies leading Nero not just to claim public attention in the already controversial role of a citharode[31] but to activate the double vision by which the emperor would be seen both as a glamorous performer and as the manifestation of distant figures of myth, especially given that Nero's public appearances were often prepared for with more intimate private performances. If, then, Lucan's poem allows us to see Cleopatra not just as an acting queen but as if in a theatrical performance, the guise in which in pantomime she may well have been a real presence on the contemporary stage, her trajectory meets up with the emperor's practice of taking on the fictive identities of his characters. An awareness of gen-

---

**29** Chaudhuri 2012, 224–6 identifies similar wordplay at *Aen.* 8. 696: *regina in mediis patrio uocat agmina sistro* ('in the middle, the queen calls her troops with her native rattle').
**30** For an overview of the chronology, and the problems our evidence presents, see Champlin 2003, 68–77 and Bartsch 1994, 4, both with notes and further bibliography; Bartsch's whole treatment of the political and ideological implications of a performing emperor is fundamental.
**31** On the distinctiveness of citharodic performance and its implications for Nero, see Power 2010, 3–181.

der difference further enhances this pattern of illusionistic overlap, for while Cleopatra would, in pantomime, conventionally have been played by a man, Nero's repertoire conspicuously included female roles (Suet. *Nero* 21.3; Dio 63.9.5).[32] Reading Lucan's theatrical queen from this vantage point encourages the sense that we are not so much seeing Cleopatra made to resemble Nero as the face of the Neronian present emanating through a text about the past. We can no longer tell whether we are seeing the perfect construction of an illusion, Cleopatra come back to life, or the real staging of that illusion, Nero becoming Cleopatra.

A particularly significant aspect of Nero's career as a performer is its connection not only with his notorious relationship to his own mother but with mothers more generally. The graffito that placed Nero in the sequence of mythical matricides after Alcmaeon and Orestes (Dio 61.16.2) anticipates roles he was later to play on stage.[33] And his first public appearance as a citharode took place just after her death and was linked to his liberation from the constraint she imposed. So too his female roles included famous mothers, including eventually Canace (Suet. 21.3, Dio 63.10.2). Niobe, an over-reaching mother punished by the lyre-playing god, was the role he chose for his semi-public debut as a citharode at the second Neronia, a debut that may have taken place already in 64.[34] Nero's stage career taken as a whole, with his later *Oedipus* taken into account, as a reflection of his real-life story, gave him a context at once to avenge his mother, but also to become her. The simultaneous distance and identity such performances construct in relation to Nero's own origins also provide a suggestive model for interpreting his conceptual interpenetration with Cleopatra, another tragic mother sometimes read as a historical original for the Niobes that populated Augustan temples to Apollo. As 'then' joins uncomfortably with now, Nero can be identified simultaneously with his historical namesake Caesar, or that figure's literary prototype, and his own real ancestor, Antony, or, finally, as the already incestuous seducer of both, Cleopatra. He thus becomes the mother via Egyptian Caesarion, or the father as Roman Antony, of a dynasty whose unreality becomes all the more marked by the theatrical scaffolding surrounding its myth of origins but whose own embrace of theatricality emphatically asserts its presence and authority.

---

**32** On Nero's theatrical impersonations of women, see Milnor 2005, 295–6.
**33** Champlin 2003, 96–107.
**34** Suet. *Nero* 21.1–2. This anticipatory second Neronia is uniquely attested by Suetonius. See the discussions in Bradley 1978, 133–4, who accepts Suetonius' evidence, and Champlin 2003, 74–5, who does not.

The loss of distinction between male and female that comes when we see Cleopatra as Nero aligns the three axes of difference elided in the episode, those of gender, of ethnicity, and of temporality. The interaction between gender and ethnicity had been set out in Cleopatra's first speech to Caesar: the reversal of gender roles that must be explained to a Roman are the norm in Egypt (*nullo discrimine sexus reginam scit ferre Pharos*, 'Alexandria can endure a queen with no distinction made of sex', 10.91–2).[35] While the prospect of Cleopatra ruling in Rome has been displaced into an alternate reality, Cleopatra would hardly be the first to rule the cities of the Nile. But the element I want to stress in conclusion is time: from the Augustan perspective, so vehemently adopted by the narrative voice, it is history that creates the '*discrimen*', but also the difference that makes history. Actium established Rome as a place where women do not reign, but the ability to evoke gender to characterize the 'other' defines the consequences of that battle. And so those who maintain a consciousness of time will be secure in the knowledge of Cleopatra's defeat and the various battles that separate Ptolemies from Caesars, Caesar from Pompey, Augustus from Antony, and prevent the incestuous coupling of Nero with someone who was not, after all, his ancestor.

This in turn leads to some reflections on Lucan's narrative technique. As I mentioned before, the main action of book 10 is inaction, a delay[36] that prevents any of these distinctions from being made. If tragic performance blends then and now and imposes an Alexandrian disorder on the present, the emotional responses most associated with it, pity and fear, similarly map alternatives for the audience's awareness of time and gender. I suggested that in the representations of Horace and Vergil, Cleopatra opened out a vision at variance with their audience's own. To feel pity for a queen's change of state created the prospect of seeing destruction from within and operated as a corrective to victory which protected the Romans from the full moral consequences of that victory. Yet Caesar does not seem able to see as Cleopatra sees, and this breakdown in identification is doubly surprising. *Clementia* was his secret political weapon. Moreover, the substance of her speech, a plea for aid against the illegal and degrading challenges of a rival, recalls one Caesar himself made to his troops when he first appears in his *Bellum Ciuile* (1.7). This inability to recognize himself in another may at once be a reminder of his mastery. Lucan's uncle Seneca insists that *clementia*, unlike the tragic emotion of pity (*misericordia*), does not debase the one who feels it but emphasizes his higher, imperial status (*Clem.* 2.5–6). The absence of pity, especially in the master of *clementia*, then, affirms the superiority of conquest

---

**35** Pyy 2011 notably places the emphasis on gender rather than ethnicity in Lucan's treatment.
**36** See Berti 2000, 16–21.

entailed in what we might call the official image of Cleopatra, and this reflects an ideal distance between the Romans and the tragic spectacles that ornamented their triumphs.

It was the central premise of Lucan's view of history that the battle of Pharsalus had changed everything by condemning all who followed after it to slavery (7.641). To turn Caesar into an Antony seems at first an attempt to undo that past by using the gendered rhetoric on which the empire was founded against him. A recognition not only of Caesar as 'father' of empire but of Nero as already present at the moment of its conception would accomplish something more, pointing out that the ideology of empire has been undone by the reality of empire. Yet those ideologies of gender encoded by Actium are also available to characterize Lucan himself. His intervention in the narrative at the moment of Cleopatra's appearance makes him doubly a Cassandra. The warnings of the 'Roman disaster' (*Romano... malo* 10.60) to come from Cleopatra's adultery would hardly have dissuaded a Caesar. And for a contemporary audience, this rehearsal of the terrors of the Augustan Cleopatra may seem false as well, whether because the Romans did ultimately defeat Cleopatra and thwart her plans, or conversely because it is the triumphal rhetoric itself which has failed: Cleopatra does rule at Rome in the person of Nero. Another voice available to be heard as Lucan's is that of Cleopatra herself. After all, to hold the character Caesar in Egypt with Alexandrian learning and sensuality serves Lucan's aims for his narrative as much as Cleopatra's dynastic strategy. And the indignation she voices at being unfairly stripped of her former fate (10.88) recalls not only Caesar's justification of civil war but Lucan's complaint against the destiny that has compelled him to live after Pharsalus. If Lucan's own presence in Cleopatra is recognized as a way of advertising his debasement, this provides a very uncomfortable stopping point for a reading of the episode. For it suggests that the poet is not so much resisting the polemical associations of the foreign and female with defeat enshrined by Actium as wielding them for his own ends. If Lucan, at best, cannot escape the logic of imperial triumph, its power extends to his readers in the present. Certainly my own attempt to discover a resistant voice in Lucan has only reinforced the difficulty of escaping the polarities of gender and race. Paradoxically, however, if there is in the poem a glimpse of an Alexandrian world 'without difference' (*nullo discrimine*), it may only be made available in the tragic mask that at once combines Cleopatra and Nero and asserts their own priority to the imperial age as well as to whatever representation Lucan may offer of them.

# Works Cited

Ahl, F. (1976), *Lucan: An Introduction*, Ithaca, N.Y.
Albrecht, M. von (1970), 'Der Dichter Lucan und die epische Tradition', *Lucain: Entretiens Hardt* 15, 267–308.
Ambühl, A. (2010), 'Lucan's 'Ilioupersis' — Narrative Patterns from the Fall of Troy in Book 2 of the *Bellum Civile*', in: N. Hömke/C. Reitz (eds.), *Lucan's* Bellum Civile: *Between Epic Tradition and Aesthetic Innovation*, Berlin, 17–38.
Ambühl, A. (2015), *Krieg und Bürgerkrieg bei Lucan und in der griechischen Literatur*, Berlin.
Barchiesi, A. (1993), 'Future Reflexive: Two Modes of Allusion and Ovid's *Heroides*', *HSCPh* 95, 333–65.
Bartsch, S. (1994), *Actors in the Audience*, Cambridge, Mass.
Becher, I. (1966), *Das Bild der Kleopatra in der griechischen und lateinischen Literatur,* Berlin.
Berti, E. (2000), *M. Annaei Lucani: Bellum Civile Liber X*, Florence.
Bradley, K.R. (1978), *Suetonius'* Life of Nero: *An Historical Commentary*, Brussels.
Breitenbach, A. (2010), *Die Pseudo-Seneca-Epigramme der Anthologia Vossiana: Ein Gedichtbuch aus der mittleren Kaiserzeit,* Spudasmata 132, Hildesheim.
Bruére, R.T. (1964), 'The Helen Episode in *Aeneid* 2 and Lucan', *CPh* 59, 267–8.
Champlin, E.J. (2003), *Nero*, Cambridge, Mass.
Chaudhuri, P. (2012), 'Naming *Nefas*: Cleopatra on the Shield of Aeneas', *CQ* 62, 223–6.
Conte, G. (2006), 'Questioni di metodo e critica dell'autenticità: Discutendo ancora l'episodio di Elena', *MD* 56, 157–74.
Dingel, J. (2007), *Senecas Epigramme und andere Gedichte aus der* Anthologia Latina, Heidelberg.
Edwards, C. (1993), *The Politics of Immorality in Ancient Rome*, Cambridge.
Eidinow, J.S.C. (2003), 'Dido, Aeneas, and Iulus: Heirship and Obligation in *Aeneid* 4', *CQ* 53, 260–7.
Feldherr, A. (2010), 'Dionysiac Poetics' and the Memory of Civil War in Horace's 'Cleopatra Ode'', in: B. Breed/C. Damon/A. Rossi (eds.), *Citizens of Discord: Rome and its Civil Wars*, Oxford, 223–32.
Feldherr, A. (2014), 'Viewing, Myth, and History on the Shield of Aeneas', *ClAnt* 33, 281–318.
Fordyce, C.J. (1977), *P. Vergili Maronis* Aeneidos *Libri VII–VIII*, Oxford.
Goossens, R. (1946), '*Ferum victorem cepit*: Observations sur les sources grecques des quelques passages d'auteurs latins', *Latomus* 5, 275–91.
Gowers, E. (1994), 'Persius and the Decoction of Nero', in: J. Elsner/J. Masters (eds.), *Reflections of Nero: Culture, History and Representation*, Chapel Hill, N.C., 131–50.
Grau, D. (2017), 'Nero: The Making of the Historical Narrative', in: S. Bartsch/K. Freudenburg/ C. Littlewood (eds.), *The Cambridge Companion to the Age of Nero*, Cambridge, 261–75.
Gurval, R. (1998), *Actium and Augustus: The Politics and Emotions of Civil War*, Ann Arbor.
Keith, A. (2000), *Engendering Rome: Women in Latin Epic*, Cambridge.
Lada-Richards, I. (2007), *Silent Eloquence: Lucian and Pantomime Dancing,* London.
Masters, J. (1992), *Poetry and Civil War in Lucan's* Bellum Civile, Cambridge.
McCloskey, P./Phinney, E. (1968), 'Ptolemaeus Tyrannus: The Typification of Nero in the *Pharsalia*', *Hermes* 96, 80–7.
Milnor, K. (2005), *Gender, Domesticity, and the Age of Augustus*, Oxford.
Murgia, C. (2003), 'The Date of the Helen Episode', *HSCPh* 101, 405–26.

Power, T. (2010), *The Culture of Kitharôidia*, Washington, D.C.
Pyy, E. (2011), 'The Conflict Reconsidered: Cleopatra and the Civil War in the Early Imperial Epic', *Arctos* 45, 77–102.
Rossi, A. (2000), 'The *Aeneid* Revisited: The Journey of Pompey in Lucan's *Pharsalia*', *AJPh* 121, 571–91.
Rossi, A. (2005) '*sine fine*: Caesar's Journey to Egypt and the End of Lucan's *Bellum Civile*', in: C. Walde (ed.), *Lucan im 21. Jahrhundert,* Munich, 237–60.
Sannicandro, L. (2010), *I personaggi femminili del* Bellum Civile *di Lucano*, Rahden, Westf.
Sannicandro, L. (2014), 'Der 'dekadente' Feldherr: Caesar in Ägypten (Luc. 10)', *Mnemosyne* 67, 50–64.
Schmidt, M.G. (1986), *Caesar und Kleopatra. Philologischer und historischer Kommentar zu Lucan 10, 1–171*, Frankfurt.
Timpanaro, S. (1996), 'Dall' *Alexandros* di Euripide all' *Alexander* di Ennio', *RFIC* 124, 5–70.
Tracy, J. (2014), *Lucan's Egyptian Civil War*, Cambridge.
Turner, A.J. (2010), 'Lucan's Cleopatra', in: A.J. Turner/J.H. Kim On Chong-Gossard/F. Juliaan Vervaet (eds.), *Private and Public Lies*, Leiden, 195–209.
Voisin, J.-L. (1987), 'Ex oriente sole (Suétone, *Ner.* 6): D'Alexandrie à la Domus Aurea', in: *L'urbs: espace urbain et histoire (Ier s. ap. J.C.)*, Actes du colloque international organisé par le Centre national de la recherche scientifique et l'École française de Rome, Rome, 8.–12. mai 1985, Collection de l'École Française de Rome 98, Paris, 509–43.
Woodman, A.J. (1992), 'Nero's Alien Capital: Tacitus as Paradoxographer (*Annales* 15.36–7)', in: A.J. Woodman/J.G.F. Powell (eds.), *Author and Audience in Latin Literature*, Cambridge, 173–88.
Wyke, M. (2002), *The Roman Mistress*, Oxford.
Zwierlein, O. (1974), 'Cäsar und Kleopatra bei Lucan und in späterer Dichtung', *A&A* 20, 54–73.

Part IV: **Love, Oriental Ethnicity and Gender in Roman Literature**

Federica Bessone
# The Indiscreet Charm of the Exotic: *Amores Peregrini* as Explorations of Identity in Roman Poetry

This paper investigates the forms in which Roman poetry represents the charm and otherness of the exotic, analysing the theme of foreign *eros* in a selection of examples. I will deal with tales of *amores peregrini* both as a contact between different cultures, which puts to the test — and sometimes puts in crisis — their foundations, and as a perturbing individual experience, that can lead to the loss of gender identity. In the experience of *eros*, as in other experiences of personality formation (e.g., education on the fringes of civilisation),[1] confrontation with Otherness — cultural, geographical and ethnic — contributes to the construction of gender, national, or individual identities, putting into play, and disputing, the definition of their boundaries.[2] Studying the literary codification of these 'irregular' experiences in Latin poetry through the category of the exotic — with its connotations of attraction and danger, of charm and transgression — allows us to trace the developments of cross-cultural discourse within the Late Republican and Imperial Ages in the forms of lyric, elegy, and epic. The entanglement between eroticism and exoticism, associated with notions of oriental luxury, excess, and moral corruption, transposes historical conflicts and cultural tensions onto the level of myth, adopting and complicating mainstream and normative representations of ethnic and gender identity.

---

[1] In the oral version of this contribution I dedicated the second part (*Vite ai margini: primitivismo, instabilità di genere, identità 'nazionali'*) to Camilla in the *Aeneid*, Parthenopaeus in the *Thebaid* and Achilles in the *Achilleid*, different heirs to Numanus Remulus insofar as they are brought up in the wild. The primitivistic and singular traits of these exceptional creatures, endowed with an outstanding individual identity and a problematic gender identity (inverted, indefinite, or exasperated), become part of a proudly claimed ethnic identity — 'the Italics', 'the Arcadians' — or of a wider 'national' identity: 'the Greeks', of whom the Thessalian Achilles is the greatest (*The Best of the Achaeans*). The warrior maiden, *decus Italiae*, challenges traditional gender identities, but has her own role in the construction of the complex Roman national identity represented in the *Aeneid*, resulting from the integration of Italics, Arcadians, and Trojans; Achilles, hypervirile on the Pelion, and feminised in Scyros (like a Paris), becomes an all-round hero, not only *decus... Pelasgi / nominis* (Ov. *Met.* 12.612–3), but a model for Rome (and its emperor): a binational, or better, a supranational hero, fit to represent — with his complex identity — an ecumenical empire, which has absorbed Greece and Asia together into itself.
[2] Cf. Parca/Tzanetou 2016, 155–9.

Erotic attraction is an extreme form of cognitive experimentation in what is similar and 'other', and proves all the more revealing when the Other is supposed to be the antipole of the Self: for every culture, 'inventing the barbarian' means uncovering itself, in its own repressed or rejected aspects. By representing mythical passions which draw distant worlds near to one another, poetic discourse brings out cultural stereotypes and literary conventions, and lays them bare: as it shows the nature of ideological simplifications or propagandistic formulas, it invites us to reflect on the instrumental use of ethnographic or gender clichés, on political readings of history or social structures, and finally, on the literary codification of those very stereotypes.

In ancient culture, foreign loves outline a map of historical relationships, ethnic conflicts and wars between continents. In the opening of his *Histories*, Herodotus traces the causes of the war between the Greeks and Persians back to alternating abductions of women between Europe and Asia (Hdt. 1.1–4: Io, Europe, Medea, Helen).[3] Mythical tales of erotic unions which link distant countries have for the ancients a founding role: myth motivates history and transposes the primary forces that drive human action into fabulous narration.

Roman poetry inherits from the Greek world a literary trope of international relationships established by *eros*, and rethinks it in new forms, within a changed cultural and historical context. In the Late Republican Age, Laevius' lyric explores, through experiments in style, the psychic world of women, letting feelings of jealousy be expressed with nuances of envious hostility for ethnic and ethical diversity. A fragment of the *Protesilaudamia*, studied by Vincenzo Tandoi and Marco Fantuzzi,[4] gives voice to the heroine's fear that the charm of Asian women may exercise an irresistible attraction on Protesilaus:

>           aut
> nunc quaepiam alia te †illo†
> Asiatico ornatu affluens
> aut Sardiano aut Lydio

---

[3] Hdt. 1.4: 'Thus far it was a matter of mere robbery on both sides. But after this (the Persians say) the Greeks were greatly to blame; for they invaded Asia before the Persians attacked Europe. 'We think', say they, that it is wrong to carry women off: but to be zealous to avenge the rape is foolish: wise men take no account of such things: for plainly the women would never have been carried away, had not they themselves wished it. We of Asia regarded the rape of our women not at all; but the Greeks, all for the sake of a Lacedaemonian woman, mustered a great host, came to Asia, and destroyed the power of Priam. Ever since then we have regard<ed> the Greeks as our enemies'. The Persians claim Asia for their own, and the foreign nations that dwell in it; Europe and the Greek race they hold to be separate from them' [tr. G. Rawlinson].
[4] Tandoi 1992; Fantuzzi 1995.

> fulgens decore et gratia
> pellicuit

> ...or now some other woman, gorgeous in Asian adornment, of Sardis or Lydia, shining with beauty and grace, has seduced you. (Laev. fr. 18 Courtney)[5]

The '*aria* of jealousy' by Laodamia refashions, with inverted gender roles, the seduction exercised on the Spartan Helen by the Asian Paris: the Trojan War multiplies the occasions of explosive contact between cultures whence it originated, and each new reformulation of the Trojan matter revisits that traditional theme.

The general distrust of the foreigner gets more acute when it is reinforced by ethnographic clichés, which are perpetuated and renewed with changing historical circumstances: thus in Greece, from the 5th century on, the literary prejudice against the 'barbarian' Paris assimilates the Trojan War to the Persian Wars;[6] and, in Late Republican and Imperial Roman poetry, suspicion of oriental luxury prolongs the debate on the Hellenisation of *mores* following military conquests. In Laevius' fragment, the ethnic-geographic adjectives (*Asiatico... Sardiano... Lydio*), which are loaded with the connotations of refinement associated with those countries since archaic Greek lyric, and are exhibited perhaps as a memory of Sappho,[7] evoke a world that Rome has come to know well: '...Sardi, la Lidia e il regno di Pergamo erano luoghi divenuti celebri nell'Urbe (non meno dei tesori di Attalo III), dopo essere entrati a far parte della provincia d'Asia, nel 129 a.C. Ben presto la storiografia moralistica avrebbe ravvisato in questi primi contatti dei Romani con l'Oriente asiatico – *loca amoena, uoluptaria* (Sall. *Cat.* 11.5; Flor. 1.47.7) – l'inizio di ogni decadenza dei *mores*' (Tandoi 1992, 115 n. 15).

The link between oriental luxury and erotic enticement is the same which, in the Augustan Age, will be stigmatised by Propertius in Elegy 1.2.1–6:

> Quid iuuat ornato procedere, uita, capillo
> > et tenuis Coa ueste mouere sinus,
> aut quid Orontea crines perfundere murra,
> > teque peregrinis uendere muneribus,
> naturaeque decus mercato perdere cultu,
> > nec sinere in propriis membra nitere bonis?

---

[5] = 18 Morel, Traglia, Büchner = 21 Blänsdorf. At line 2 Blänsdorf 2011[4] prints *ilico*, proposed by Tandoi after Osann and Knoche (other conjectures in the apparatus).

[6] See, after Hall 1989, Erskine 2001, 73–82 and *passim*.

[7] Cf. Sapph. 16.19 V.; 39; 98.10–1 μιτράναν... ποικίλαν ἀπὺ Σαρδίων ('a multi-colored mitre from Sardis'); 96.1 and 6; Anacr. 158 Λυδοπαθής ('refined like a Lydian'); Page 1951, 69; Tandoi 1992, 116, 118; Courtney 1993, 133–4. Fantuzzi 1995 sees in the 'nostalgia/gelosia' of Laevius' fragment a precise memory of Sappho, fr. 96 V.

What avails it, my love, to step out with coiffured hair and flutter the sheer folds of a Coan dress? What avails it to drench your locks with Syrian perfume and to vaunt yourself in foreign finery, to destroy your natural charm with purchased ornament, preventing your figure from displaying its own true merits? [tr. G.P. Goold]).

In that hyper-traditionalist text, the poet-lover rejects for Cynthia *peregrina munera*, the foreign adornments by which her beauty would be put up for sale: the elegiac *puella*, when she appropriates Coan fabrics and myrrh from the Syrian Orontes, assimilates to an oriental courtesan, exercising her seduction thanks to the luxury goods imported into the capital of the empire.[8]

But let us go back to Laodamia's fears. Blame of foreign loves, with their evil consequences, spreads from the epic-tragic paradigms of Medea and Helen to the world of love poetry and, in the wake of Laevius and Catullus, pervades the laments of Ovid's *Heroides*: the *perfidus hospes* — who can come from Greece itself, even from the most civilised Athens — is a stock character of 'elegy in the feminine' (his literary role is defined by Helen in *Ep.* 17.191–2) and *amores peregrini* are a recurrent cause of jealousy and scandal.[9]

There is more. The double *Heroides*, as we know, rewrite a mythical story from two conflicting perspectives: the epistolary couple lends itself to a discussion of myth which reproduces famous debates of ancient culture, and brings them into the Augustan Age. Here we again find Paris and Helen (*Heroides* 16 and 17); and here the traditional charges addressed to both, for the role of foreign wealth in inducing the 'abduction', are transformed into a boast of wealth as a means of erotic persuasion.[10] Ovid presupposes the bad reputation of Helen, often blamed by tradition for letting herself be seduced by Paris' Trojan splendour: so Hecuba attacks her in Euripides' *Trojan Women*[11] and so the Polyphemus of the

---

**8** Prop. 1.2.1–6: Keith 2008, 153–4. Cf. Prop. 3.13 and see Stok 2012, 161–2 (also 166–70 on Propertius' oscillation between prejudice and relativism in the approach to ethnic otherness).
**9** Ov. *Ep.* 17.191–2: *certus in hospitibus non est amor: errat, ut ipsi, / cumque nihil speres firmius esse, fugit*, 'Uncertain is the love of strangers; it wanders, like themselves, and when you expect nothing to be more sure, it flees' [tr. Showerman/Goold]. Cf. Della Corte 1969; Perutelli 1997. On love for the stranger as a cause of jealousy and resentment by local suitors, or as a source of slander and hostility by one's own people, from Nausicaa to Apollonius' Medea, from Vergil's Dido to that of the *Heroides*, from Phyllis' epistle (*Ep.* 2) to the Scylla episode in *Met.* 8, see Piazzi 2007 on *Ep.* 7.123–4 (p. 241); see also *infra*, n. 17.
**10** Cf. Bessone 2003, 153 n. 17; 164–5 and n. 49; 180–1.
**11** Eur. *Tro.* 987–97, esp. 991–7: 'So when you caught sight of him in gorgeous foreign clothes, ablaze with gold, your senses utterly forsook you. Yes, for in Argos you had moved in simple state, but, once free of Sparta, it was your hope to deluge by your lavish outlay Phrygia's town, that flowed with gold; nor was the palace of Menelaus rich enough for your luxury to riot in' [tr. E.P. Coleridge].

Cyclops defames her, in a vulgar key.¹² Paris' epistle plays ironically on this well-known theme. The luxury imputed to the Phrygian prince by Graeco-Latin tradition is exploited here as a rhetorical instrument of seduction: Paris' *suasoria*, in line with Ovid's erotic ideology, extols *cultus* against *rusticitas*, and opposes Troy to Sparta, as the Augustan poet opposes contemporary Rome to Archaic Rome.¹³

The modernising language of the *Ars Amatoria* is reused here to provide myth with a modern look: Paris' argumentations, with the comparison between the simplicity of Sparta and the splendour of Troy, retrace the Augustan comparison between the past and present of Rome. Praise of golden buildings and temples worthy of gods (*Ep.* 16.179–80, *innumeras urbes atque aurea tecta uidebis / quaeque suos dicas templa decere deos*, 'Unnumbered cities and golden dwellings you will see, and temples you would say fit well their gods') echoes the Imperial discourse on the passage from clay gods to golden temples – the temples in which the gods themselves delight, like Janus in the *Fasti* (Ov. *Fast.* 1.223–6, '*nos quoque templa iuuant, quamuis antiqua probemus, / aurea: maiestas conuenit ipsa deo. / laudamus ueteres, sed nostris utimur annis: / mos tamen est aeque dignus uterque coli*', 'We, too, are tickled by golden temples, though we approve of the ancient ones: such majesty befits a god. We praise the past, but use the present years; yet are both customs worthy to be kept').¹⁴ The magnification of the luxury of Trojan dwellings, by which 'One household, any one you choose, will show a city's wealth' (*Ep.* 16.188, *una domus quaeuis urbis habebit opes*), echoes the Late

---

**12** Eur. *Cycl.* 182–6: CH. 'The traitoress! She saw the parti-colored breeches on the man's legs and the gold necklace around his neck and went all aflutter after them, leaving behind that fine little man Menelaus' [tr. D. Kovacs]. Cf. Napolitano 2003 on 175–7 and Seaford 1988 on 182–6 for the attribution of the trousers typical of contemporary Persians (ἀναξυρίδες) to the Phrygian Paris. On the theme see also Gerchanoc in this volume.
**13** Ov. *Ep.* 16.33–4: *nec uenio Graias ueluti spectator ad urbes: / oppida sunt regni diuitiora mei*, 'Nor am I come as one to see the sights of Grecian towns – the cities of my own realm are wealthier'; 177–96 (esp. 177–8: *regna parens Asiae, qua nulla beatior ora est, / finibus immensis uix obeunda tenet*, 'my father governs the realm of Asia, than which no land has greater wealth'; 187–8: *o quotiens dices 'quam pauper Achaia nostra est'! / una domus quaeuis urbis habebit opes*, 'Ah, how often will you say: "How poor is our Achaia!". One household, and any one you choose, will show a city's wealth'; 191–4: *parca sed est Sparte, tu cultu diuite digna; / ad talem formam non facit iste locus. / hanc faciem largis sine fine paratibus uti / deliciisque decet luxuriare nouis*, 'But a niggard land is Sparta, and you deserve keeping in wealth; with fairness such as yours this place is not in accord. Beauty like yours it befits to enjoy rich adornment without end, and to wanton in ever new delights'). Cf. *Ep.* 17.63–6; 221–4. For other effects of anachronism in the epistolary couple, cf. Michalopoulos 2006, *Introduction*, 35–6 and n. on 16.187–8, *pauper Achaia*.
**14** Cf. Green 2004 *ad loc.*; Pittà 2015 on Var. *De Vita p.R.* fr. 6 (= 15 R.; 295 Salvadore).

Republican and Imperial debate on the legitimation of private luxury:[15] the scandalous equation *domus/urbs* returns in the *Fasti* as a moralistic condemnation of the *luxuria* of Vedius Pollio, whose sumptuous mansion (*urbis opus domus una fuit*, 'The single house was like the fabric of a city', *Fast.* 6.641) was taken down by Augustus, who had inherited it.[16]

From the splendour of the city, to that of the house, to that of the individual: here at last is the climax of Paris' argument. The luxury which Troy allows to a woman can be inferred from that of the Trojan men: 'When you look on the garb of the men of our race, what garb, think you, must be that of the daughters of Dardanus?' (*Ep.* 16.195–6, *cum uideas cultus nostra de gente uirorum, / qualem Dardanias credis habere nurus?*). The hero's words, the high point of the section, agree with the — provocative — apology of modernity uttered by the love teacher in the *Ars Amatoria* and *Medicamina* (Ov. *Ars* 3.107–8: *corpora si ueteres non sic coluere puellae, / nec ueteres cultos sic habuere uiros* 'If women of old did not so cultivate their bodies, the women of old had not lovers so cultivated' [tr. Mozley-Goold]; cf. *Med.* 23–4: *nec tamen indignum: sit uobis cura placendi, / cum comptos habeant saecula uestra uiros,* 'Nor is that a fault: you must be anxious to please, for men love elegance in these times of ours'; 25–6). At the same time, Paris' apology dangerously borders on the invectives of moralists, and their scandal of men's refinement which now surpasses that of women, as Seneca will say (Sen. *Nat.* 7.31.2: *adhuc quidquid est boni moris extinguimus. leuitate et politura corporum muliebres munditias antecessimus, colores meretricios matronis quidem non induendos uiri sumimus,* 'We are still doing our best to extinguish any spark of virtue that is left. By the smoothness and polish of our bodies we men have

---

**15** See La Penna 1989; Romano 1994; in particular on buildings and houses, Edwards 1993, ch. 4 (pp. 137–72).

**16** Ov. *Fast.* 6.639–48, cf. 639–44: *disce tamen, ueniens aetas: ubi Liuia nunc est / porticus, immensae tecta fuere domus; / urbis opus domus una fuit, spatiumque tenebat, / quo breuius muris oppida multa tenent. / haec aequata solo est, nullo sub crimine regni, / sed quia luxuria uisa nocere sua*, 'But learn, you coming age! Where the Livian portico now is, there were the roofs of a vast house. One house was the work of a city, and occupied a space greater than than many towns contained within their walls. This was levelled to the ground, not for any charge of treason but because its luxury seemed to be harmful' [tr. A. and P. Wiseman]. The scandal of the *domus* equal to *urbes*, already raised in Republican debate (Sall. *Cat.* 12.3, *domos atque uillas... in urbium modum exaedificatas*, 'mansions and villas extended to the size of cities' [tr. J.S. Watson]) and continued under the Empire (Sen. *Ep.* 90.43, *non habebant domos instar urbium*, 'They did not have houses matching towns in size' [tr. C.D.N. Costa]), will get particular prominence in relation to the Domus Aurea: cf. Mart. *Sp.* 2.4 *unaque iam tota stabat in urbe domus*, 'and in the whole city there was only one house standing', with Coleman 2006 *ad loc.*

outdone the refinements of women; we have adopted the colours of harlots, that even an honest woman would not put on' [tr. J. Clarke]).

Ovid updates the traditional charges against Paris' effeminate softness for the Augustan Age, and rebuts them with the cutting edges of his modernising ethics, not without an ironic smile: indeed, the excess of luxury identifies a feminisation of the male still stigmatised by Imperial culture.

Thus we touch on a key point of our discussion. Private luxury (particularly luxury of the person) is still, in the age of Augustus, considered an attack on codified social and gender roles; only in the Flavian Age, with the occasional poetry by Martial and Statius, and in oxymoronic celebratory rhetoric, will a eulogy of wealth, even of luxury, as moral virtue develop: this is the virtuous and exhibited wealth of exemplary married couples, like Pollius Felix and Polla, or Stella and Violentilla[17] — but, once again, without concessions to masculine *cultus*. For a good part of Augustan culture, the excess of refinement, associated with oriental peoples and dangerously imported into Rome, is a corrupting force, a reprehensible lack of measure:[18] immoderate refinement can confuse a *puella*, or a *matrona*, even with a *meretrix*; and, as in Greek culture, the same excess of refinement can reduce a *uir* to a *semiuir*. If *eros* is the most powerful agent of a metamorphosis, and even of an exchange of gender roles (as I have tried to show elsewhere),[19] luxury, associated with *eros*, enhances that destabilising effect by adding another element of 'immoderation'.

The love teacher himself, in the third book of the *Ars*, warned the *puellae* away from men who are well-groomed and elegant like dandies, womanisers who can have more men than the *puellae* themselves (Ov. *Ars* 3.437–8: *femina quid faciat, cum sit uir leuior ipsa / forsitan et plures possit habere uiros?*, 'What can a woman do when her lover is smoother than herself, and may perhaps have more lovers than she?'; cf. 443–8). And, between the lines of his epistles, Paris appears to us, here also, as the fop of tradition, blamed for the care of his looks since Homer, even before taking on the barbarous traits of the luxurious oriental (Hom. *Il.* 3.39 [Hector]: 'Δύσπαρι, εἶδος ἄριστε, γυναιμανές, ἠπεροπευτά', 'evil-hearted Paris, fair to see, but woman-mad, and false of tongue' [tr. S. Butler]; cf. Hor. *Carm.* 1.15.13–4 '*nequiquam Veneris praesidio ferox / pectes caesariem grataque feminis / imbelli cithara carmina diuides...*, 'Vainly shall you, in Venus' favour

---
17 Cf. Newlands 2002, 124–38; Rosati 2006.
18 Cf. Hardie 2014, 57: 'Ancient moralists often characterize the luxury endemic to an advanced urban civilization as infection by the vices of the Other, and in particular, in classical antiquity, by the decadence and effeminism of the Orient'.
19 Bessone 2015.

strong, / your tresses comb, and for your dames divide / on peaceful lyre the several parts of song'; 19–20 *tamen, heu, serus adulteros / crinis puluere collines'* 'those adulterous locks, though late, / shall gory dust deface' [tr. J. Conington]).

The modern category of the exotic, applied to *eros* in order to investigate the literary motif of foreign loves, is useful for detecting the cracks in gender, social, or national identity caused by an 'extreme' erotic experience, in both a geographical and cultural sense. The barbarian otherness of Paris exemplifies a persistent paradox in ancient culture: the excess, of luxury or *eros*, equates a womaniser to a half-man — a γυναιμανής to a *semiuir*.

Foreign charm is a fundamental ingredient of love stories, not limited to the ancient ones. And, in Latin poetry, *peregrinus amor* becomes a codified literary motif. The adjective that defines it, *peregrinus* (already used by Horace for Helen, then by Seneca for Medea),[20] is what comes closest to our category of 'exotic', for its connotations of charm mixed with risk, attraction with blame. Ovid, the only classical poet who employs it often, refers it, among other things, to the Phrygian Pelops, conqueror of Hippodamia, and lets it be used in an insulting tone by Medea, who in the *Heroides* calls Jason *peregrinus latro*.[21] Attributed to women (or men) of geographically and culturally distant, or even extreme, countries, the epithet sometimes implies a perturbing notion of refinement and foreign luxury.

In the first of the *Heroides*, Penelope fears erotic adventures by Ulixes in his peregrinations:[22] *Ep.* 1.75–6, *haec ego dum stulte metuo, quae uestra libido est, / esse peregrino captus amore potes* ('While I live on in foolish fear of things like

---

**20** Hor. *Carm.* 3.3.18–21 *Ilion, Ilion / fatalis incestusque iudex / et mulier peregrina uertit // in puluerem...*, 'Oh Ilium, Ilium, wretched town! / The judge accurst, incontinent, / and stranger dame have dragg'd thee down'; 25–6 *iam nec Lacaenae splendet adulterae / famosus hospes*, 'No more the adulterous guest can charm / the Spartan queen'; Sen. *Med.* 114–5 *tacitis eat illa tenebris, / si qua peregrino nubit fugitiua marito*, 'Let her pass in silent gloom who steals away to wed with a foreign husband' [tr. F.J. Miller], on which cf. Boyle 2014 *ad loc.*
**21** Catul. 1, Lucr. 0, Verg. 1 (1), Hor. 4 (1), Tib. 0, Prop. 1 (1.2.4 cit. *supra*), Ov. 29 (13). Cf. *Ep.* 8.70 *uecta peregrinis Hippodamia rotis* (= *Ars* 2.8), 'Hippodamia was borne away in the car of the stranger'; 12.111 *uirginitas facta est peregrini praeda latronis*, 'My maidenly innocence has become the spoil of a pirate from overseas' [tr. Showerman/Goold]. For the association of *peregrinus* with the blame of foreign loves see Barchiesi 1992 on *Ep.* 1.76; Bessone 1997 on *Ep.* 12.111 (moreover on 29 *hospitio*; 31); on Sen. *Med.* 114–15 cf. the previous n. and, on the use of the adj. in Verg. *A.* 11.772 for Chloreus' adornment, with which Camilla falls in love, see *infra* in the text. Cf. Ap. Rh. 3.795 (Medea imagines the Colchian women's contempt) ἥ τις κηδομένη τόσον ἀνέρος ἀλλοδαποῖο, 'The maid who cared so much for a stranger' [tr. R.C. Seaton]; Ov. *Met.* 7.39 *nescio quis... aduena*, 'some nameless stranger' [tr. A.D. Melville].
**22** Cf. Barchiesi 1992 on v. 76, who recalls that Ulysses' love affairs were probably treated in Laevius' *Sirenocirca*.

these, you may be captive to a stranger love'). Ovid exploits the conventionality of the motif for ironical effects: the author alludes to Ulysses' 'forced' stay, not at a foreign woman's, but even at a goddess', while Penelope fears the exotic refinement of the rival, to whom her husband 'maybe even *tells* how rustic a wife *he has* — one fit only to dress fine the wool' (*Ep.* 1.77–8, *forsitan et narres, quam sit tibi rustica coniunx, / quae tantum lanas non sinat esse rudes*).

But the motif of *peregrinus amor* can be associated more specifically with the ethnographic cliché of oriental luxury — and the gender inversion it entails. In *Heroides* 9, as she writes to Hercules after the arrival of the captive Ioles, Deianira recalls with scandal the previous adventure of the hero with Omphale, queen of Lydia:[23]

> haec mihi ferre parum: peregrinos addis amores,
>   et mater de te quaelibet esse potest.
> Non ego Partheniis temeratam uallibus Augen
>   nec referam partus, Ormeni nympha, tuos;
> non tibi crimen erunt, Teuthrantia turba, sorores,
>   quarum de populo nulla relicta tibi est.
> Una, recens crimen, referetur adultera nobis,
>   unde ego sum Lydo facta nouerca Lamo
>
> Is this too little for me to endure? You add to it your stranger loves, and whoever will may be by you a mother. I will say nothing of Auge betrayed in the vales of Parthenius, or of thy travail, nymph sprung of Ormenus; nor will I charge against you the daughters of Teuthras' son, the throng of sisters from whose number none was spared by you. But there is one love — a fresh offence of which I have heard — a love by which I am made stepdame to Lydian Lamus (*Ep.* 9.47–54).

In the series of Hercules' 'foreign loves', the one set in soft Lydia stands out for its piquant notoriety, and is selected to emphatically occupy the central part of the epistle.[24] Omphale's story is that which changes the Greek superhero and *supermacho* into a slave to a *domina*, and makes him a paradigm of elegiac *seruitium*

---

[23] On Hercules' and Achilles' transvestism as an exploration of gender polarity and a rite of passage, finally reasserting the hero's masculinity, as well as gender hyerarchies, see Cyrino 1998.

[24] And to ironically prefigure Deianira's involuntary victory over Hercules, who will succumb once again, and definitively, to a woman, for the sending of the poisoned robe: cf. Casali 1995, 16–7; nn. on 55–118, 71, 115.

*amoris* (as already in Propertius).²⁵ In this emblematic story, the Orient, corrupted and corrupting, is responsible for a loss of identity and a sensational confusion of gender roles.

This is the scandal denounced by Deianira in *Heroides* 9: the exchange of arms and jewels between Hercules and Omphale, he, degraded in the female *cultus*, she, triumphant in front of the mirror:

55–63 Maeandros ...
        uidit in Herculeo suspensa monilia collo...
        non puduit fortis auro cohibere lacertos
           et solidis gemmas opposuisse toris?...
        ausus es hirsutos mitra redimire capillos!...

65–6 nec te Maeonia lasciuae more puellae
        incingi zona dedecuisse putas?...

69–72 si te uidisset cultu Busiris in isto,
        huic uictor uicto nempe pudendus eras!
   detrahat Antaeus duro redimicula collo,
        ne pigeat molli succubuisse uiro!

100–4 haec tu Sidonio potes insignitus amictu
        dicere? non cultu lingua retecta silet?
   **se quoque nympha tuis ornauit Iardanis armis**
        **et tulit a capto nota tropaea uiro!**

115–18 **femina** tela tulit Lernaeis atra uenenis,
        ferre grauem lana uix satis apta colum,
   instruxitque manu claua domitrice ferarum,
        **uidit et in speculo coniugis arma sui**

The Meander... has seen hanging from the neck of Hercules... bejewelled chains! Felt you no shame to bind with gold those strong arms, and to set the gem upon that solid brawn? You have not shrunk from binding your shaggy hair with a woman's turban!...

---

**25** Prop. 3.11.17–20: *Omphale in tantum formae processit honorem, / Lydia Gygaeo tincta puella lacu, / ut, qui pacato statuisset in orbe columnas, / tam dura traheret mollia pensa manu*, 'Omphale, the Lydian girl who bathed in Gyges' lake, won such renown for her beauty that he who had set up his pillars in the world he had pacified plucked with his brute hands soft tasks of wool'; 4.9.47–50: '*idem ego Sidonia feci seruilia palla / officia et Lydo pensa diurna colo, / mollis et hirsutum cepit mihi fascia pectus / et manibus duris apta puella fui*', 'I have also performed menial service dressed in a Sidonian gown and completed my daily stint at the Lydian distaff; a soft breastband once confined my shaggy chest, and for all my rough hands I proved a likely girl'.

And do you not think that you brought disgrace upon yourself by wearing the Maeonian girdle like a wanton girl?...
Had Busiris seen you in that garb, he whom you vanquished would surely have reddened for such a victor as you. Antaeus would tear from the hard neck the turban-bands, lest he feel shame at having succumbed to an unmanly foe;
These deeds can you recount, gaily arrayed in a Sidonian gown? Does not your dress rob from your tongue all utterance? **The nymph-daughter of Iardanus has even tricked herself out in your arms, and won famous triumphs from the vanquished hero;**
A woman has borne the darts blackened with the venom of Lerna, a w o m a n scarce strong enough to carry the spindle heavy with wool; a woman has taken in her hand the club that overcame wild beasts, **and in the mirror gazed upon the armour of her dear husband!**[26]

Revisited from the elegiac perspective of the wife, the myth of Hercules acquires a new side, and an unexpected correlative.[27] The subdued hero is matched by a winning woman who inherits his 'trophies', and struts with them; through the use of military language for the queen's *toilette* (she 'adorns herself with weapons', *se... ornauit armis*, as he is 'decorated' with a Sidonian robe, *Sidonio... insignitus amictu*),[28] the reversal of roles is complete: *Ep.* 9.105–6, *i nunc, tolle animos et fortia facta recense: / quod tu non esses, iure uir illa fuit* ('Go now, puff up your spirit and recount your brave deeds done; *what you were not, a man, rightly was she*').[29] Often, the topos of the 'conqueror conquered'[30] serves to define the greatest heroes, conquered by women of different worlds: Agamemnon and the barbarian slave Cassandra,[31] Achilles and the Amazonian queen Penthesilea. Here, that paradox characterises the hard Hercules subdued by a lascivious Maeonides — and makes 'soft' Lydia an upside-down world.

This is only one example among many of the cultural extraneity which the stories of foreign loves reveal and enhance: in them, the otherness of the 'barbarian' element often manifests itself in an inversion of gender roles, even in the form of less enjoyable excesses, like savagery and intra-familial violence. As Thebes, in Attic tragedy, dramatizes Athens' *alter* ego, so the extremes of the world, or the marginal enclaves, at each time represent for ancient societies the

---

[26] In defence of the transmitted *sui* at line 118, against *mei* by Shackleton Bailey printed by Showerman/Goold 1977² (who translate 'of my husband'), see Casali 1995, *ad loc.*
[27] Frequent, on the contrary, is the representation of Hercules who, dressed as a woman, spins wool: *Ep.* 9.73–80; cf. *Ars* 2.219–20 and n. 25.
[28] Cf. Casali 1995 on *ornauit* and *tropaea* (and, before, on *insignitus*); moreover at 117 *instruxit* (which is in contrast with the gesture of looking at oneself in the mirror).
[29] Here I accept *quod*, printed by Casali 1995, while Showerman/Goold 1977² print *quo*, conjectured by Palmer, and translate: 'she has proved herself a man by a right you could not urge'.
[30] On which see Casali 1995, 12–13 and on v. 2 *uictorem uictae*.
[31] Cf. Briguglio 2019 (originally a paper given at the Lille conference).

'other' which is the obscure part of the self. In the tales of *amores peregrini*, erotic peregrinations put alternative worlds into contact, and bring to light uncomfortable truths. The 'barbarian' Medea, imported from Colchis, is the heroine who reveals to Greece the potentialities of the female, because — as she herself says in Euripides — 'In all other matters a woman is full of fear, cowardly in regard to battle and unable to look upon weaponry of iron; but when she finds herself to have been wronged in her marriage bed, no mind is more murderous than hers' (Eur. *Med.* 263–6 [tr. following Mastronarde 2002]); while in Lemnos, the island of the warrior-women killers of the males, the arrival of the Argonauts is what restores the 'norm' of relations between the sexes, in a marginal community that — like a social laboratory — has experienced a subversion of gender roles.[32]

Conversely, *amores peregrini* often problematise the values of a civilisation that wants to represent itself as central, normative, and exemplary. The cruel abandonment of a woman on a deserted island by Theseus is a blatant denial of Athens' celebrated *clementia*, as Catullus 64 suggests (Catull. 64.137–8, '*tibi nulla fuit clementia praesto, / immite ut nostri uellet miserescere pectus?*', 'Had you no clemency there, that your pitiless bowels might show me compassion?' [tr. L.C. Smithers]).[33] Similarly, Jason's betrayal sanctions the loss of αἰδώς 'in great Greece', as the chorus states in Euripides' *Medea*: 'The magical power of an oath has gone, and Shame is no more to be found in wide Hellas: she has taken wing to heaven' (βέβακε δ' ὅρκων χάρις, οὐδ' ἔτ' αἰδὼς / Ἑλλάδι τᾷ μεγάλᾳ μένει, αἰθερία δ' ἀνέπτα, Eur. *Med.* 439–41 [tr. D. Kovacs]). The reputation of Greece as a land of superior culture and civilisation, which Ovid lets Medea yearn for in the monologue of *Metamorphoses* 7 (and of which the faithless will be so impudent as to remind her in tragedy),[34] is just that which the love story with Jason destroys,

---

**32** On the parallel crimes, and gender transgression, by Medea and the Lemniads cf. Bessone 2015, 133–4. On Medea as 'the stranger par excellence', standing 'on the other side of any boundary drawn around what is normative', and representing 'the ultimate Other for Greece', see Cowan 2010.

**33** Bessone 2011, 143–4.

**34** Ov. *Met.* 7.48–61: '*tibi se semper debebit Iason, / te face sollemni iunget sibi,* **perque Pelasgas / seruatrix urbes matrum celebrabere turba**. */ ergo ego germanam fratremque patremque deosque / et natale solum uentis ablata relinquam? / nempe pater saeuus,* **nempe est mea barbara tellus**, */ frater adhuc infans; stant mecum uota sororis, / maximus intra me deus est.* **non magna relinquam, / magna sequar: titulum seruatae pubis Achiuae / notitiamque loci melioris et oppida quorum / hic quoque fama uiget cultusque artesque uirorum** */ quemque ego cum rebus, quas totus possidet orbis, / Aesoniden mutasse uelim, quo coniuge felix / et dis cara ferar et uertice sidera tangam*, 'Jason shall owe himself always to you, and you shall be his bride; **you shall be hymned on every mother's tongue in every town of glorious Greece — Jason's deliverer!** —. So shall I sail away and leave for ever sister and brother, father, gods and home?

driving the chorus' women to claim a new literary configuration of the relationships between sexes:³⁵

> Backward to their sources flow the streams of holy rivers, and the order of all things is reversed: men's thoughts have become deceitful and their oaths by the gods do not hold fast (ἀνδράσι μὲν δόλιαι βουλαί, θεῶν δ' / οὐκέτι πίστις ἄραρεν). The common talk will so alter that women's ways will enjoy good repute. Honor is coming to the female sex: no more will women be maligned by slanderous rumor. The poetry of ancient bards will cease to hymn our faithlessness (ἀπιστοσύναν). Phoebus lord of song never endowed our minds with the glorious strains of the lyre. Else I could have sounded a hymn in reply to the male sex (ἐπεὶ ἀντάχησ' ἄν ὕμνον / ἀρσένων γέννᾳ). The long expanse of time can say many things of men's lot as well as of women's. (Eur. *Med.* 410–31)

We know well how the tale of a foreign love, of an illustrious *hospes* arrived in his peregrination at an alien royal palace and struck by passion, lends itself to exploring and constructing an identity, individual and 'national', personal and gender, literary and heroic, and how this pattern of mythical narrative can comprise a complex reflection on history: we know this from the *Aeneid*. Vergil's national *epos* stages the tragedy of Dido as an *aition* of the Punic wars and, in the encounter between the Trojan exile and the queen exiled from Tyre, mirrors the cultural confrontation between Rome and Carthage, their ethnic polarisation. As recent studies have shown, Augustan discourse as a whole reprises fifth century Athenian discourse, inventing its own barbarians: it constructs past and present enemies of Rome — from the Punic to the Parthian Wars, through the Civil Wars presented as wars against the Orient — in the same way as Greek literature constructed the Persian enemy.³⁶ In a superimposition of myth and history, Latin

---

**In truth** my father's cruel, **my native land is barbarous**, my brother still a child, my sister shares my hopes. The mightiest god is in my heart! **Great things I shall not leave, great things I go to. Glory shall be mine — to have saved the youth of Greece! And I shall know a better land and cities whose fair fame lives even here, and arts and elegance** and him, my love, whom I would never leave for all the wide world holds, beloved Jason. He'll be my husband; men shall call me blest. Fortune's darling: my head shall touch the stars!'. Cf. Eur. *Med.* 534–44: IA. 'But in return for saving me you got more than you gave, as I shall make clear. **First, you now live among Greeks and not barbarians, and you understand justice and the rule of law, with no concession to force** (πρῶτον μὲν Ἑλλάδ' ἀντὶ βαρβάρου χθονὸς / γαῖαν κατοικεῖς καὶ δίκην ἐπίστασαι / νόμοις τε χρῆσθαι μὴ πρὸς ἰσχύος χάριν). All the Greeks have learned that you are clever, and you have won renown. **But if you lived at the world's edge** (εἰ δὲ γῆς ἐπ' ἐσχάτοις ὅροισιν ᾤκεις), there would be no talk of you. May I have neither gold in my house nor power to sing songs sweeter than Orpheus if it is not my lot to have high renown!'.

35 Cf. Bessone 2018.
36 Hardie 2007a, 136; Spawforth 1994, 240–2, on which Giusti 2018, 27.

poetry depicts Cleopatra's Egypt, or Dido's Carthaginians, in the same manner in which tragedy represented the Persians, or the Trojans-as-Persians, making them the opposite of Athenian ideals.

Vergil's epic discourse, however, does not just confirm ideological clichés, like oriental luxury or Carthaginian *perfidia*; rather, it unearths in a problematic way a deeper and more complex truth, as Elena Giusti has clarified: namely, that the proto-Roman Aeneas, with his Phrygian traits (an aspect which is never obliterated), is more similar to the 'enemy' than the propagandistic polarisation between Rome and Carthage, credited in official versions of history, prompts one to expect.[37] The liaison with the oriental queen reactivates in the figure of Aeneas, 'a second Paris' (*Paris alter*, A. 7.321), all the connotations of softness and effeminate luxury attributed to the Phrygians by an ethnographic cliché well alive even in the *Aeneid*, and thus complicates the problematic role of the Trojan element in the formation of Rome's national identity.[38] Vergil's fourth book suggests that the accomplished, or idealised, Roman identity, which is so often opposed to the negative pole of the Carthaginians, is an ideological construction, or at least a gradual acquisition, and one which always needs be re-affirmed, as the hero's painful formative stage at Dido's royal palace teaches. The same epic narrative, moreover, evokes the more recent experience of the evil liaison with an oriental queen, letting Cleopatra be glimpsed in Dido,[39] and Antony in the dangerously orientalising traits of Aeneas: in Carthage, the ancestor of Augustus, and 'man of providence', is temporarily transformed into (or made to regress to) a *uir uxorius*, effeminate, indolent, and luxuriously dressed in oriental fashion.

The wars of conquest of the Republican Age, and the civil war itself from which the Augustan regime was born, are thus alluded to in the mythical narrative of a *peregrinus amor*, which is also a poetic reflection on historical reality, on external and internal political relations, on the (remote or recent) past and the present of Rome. As Herodotus suggests at the outset of his *Histories*, troubled

---

**37** Giusti 2018 studies the construction of the Carthaginians in the *Aeneid* as 'Other' to the Romans, and Trojans, and at the same time as similar to them, and analyses the implications of this fluctuation (traced back to the Republican Age) for the Augustan reconstruction of Rome's history.
**38** Cf. esp. *A*. 4.261–4. On the paradox by which 'In Roman literature of the Late Republic and Early Empire 'Phrygian' is both a label for the Trojan origins of Rome and a term for the barbarian Other', see Hardie 2007b, 93. For Vergil's problematic representation of the cultural-historical process leading to the construction of Roman identity, cf. Hardie 1998, 69–71; Ando 2002; Syed 2005; Reed 2007 and 2010; Barchiesi 2009, esp. 100–2; Fletcher 2014.
**39** Bibliography in Giusti 2018, 14 n. 54.

loves for foreign women — not only abductions, but betrayals or abandonments — outline a map of international relationships or historical and political tensions between peoples; and the poetic representation of inter-ethnic tensions can hint to the reality of intra-ethnic strife. In Vergil, as in Euripides or Apollonius, as in Laevius, Catullus and Ovid, lovers from different worlds engage with ethnographic clichés in extreme conditions and 'test' the limits of reciprocal differences, trespassing into one another's territory: they thus discover inedited sides of themselves and sometimes lose, or nuance and problematise, their own identity — gender, individual, or national.

But this might be the subject of wider research. Let us go back, from the love story at the heart of the *Aeneid*, to a marginal example from the same poem: back to the adjective *peregrinus*, to close on a problematic note. In her contribution to the previous *Eugesta* conference in Lille, Alison Sharrock dedicated insightful pages to Camilla: Vergil features her as an accomplished commander figure, a true military leader of the Italians; and 'what brings about her downfall is simply a fatal moment of lost concentration, when Camilla pursues the "heroic" masculine goal of magnificent spoils (*rather than* a womanish love for finery)' (Italics mine).[40]

In the moment when the 'Phrygian weapons' of Chloreus, covered with purple and gold even more than the Volscan queen, captivate her, the narrator leaves open an alternative, between the intention of the warrior woman to dedicate the spoils in a temple, and that of putting on the captured gold, as a huntress. Suspended between the two roles, Camilla tracks that one enemy throughout the array, 'blind' and 'reckless', and 'burns with a feminine love for booty and spoils' [tr. mine], *femineo praedae et spoliorum ardebat amore* (*A*. 11.778–82 *hunc uirgo, siue ut templis praefigeret arma / Troia, captiuo siue ut se ferret in auro / uenatrix, unum ex omni certamine pugnae / caeca sequebatur totumque incauta per agmen / femineo praedae et spoliorum ardebat amore...*, 'Him the maiden, whether to deck the temples with Trojan arms or to parade herself in captured gold as huntress followed him alone unseeing out of all the combat of the battle and incautiously through all the array blazed with a womanly love of booty and spoils' [tr. N. Horsfall]).

Syntax and word order in the line merge the various elements in an inextricable whole, the 'spoils' with the 'booty', and the 'feminine love' with both objects — the contact *femineo praedae* puts in the foreground what would seem the second option ('venatorial' and seemingly frivolous), but the frame *femineo*...

---

**40** Sharrock 2015, 159–68 (quotation from p. 159).

*amore* embraces the two genetives in a hendiadys. And, as Alison Sharrock observes, 'both options are within the range of heroic behavior and do *not* imply the actions of a woman going shopping' (Italics by the author).[41]

That adjective remains, *femineus* — just one trait, but one which has the force of an enigma: as Alison Keith has shown, modern critics eschew it, ancient commentators exploit it, in order to insert the character back into the gender stereotypes from which Vergil has exceptionally subtracted it.[42] The only *eros* attributed to Camilla (in this, akin to the Amazons to whom she is compared) is the 'love' for booty and spoils; and her only professed trait of 'femininity' is this heroic love for the insignia of victory. The narrator closes the character story recalling its presentation in the catalogue, and repeats the adjective — *femineus* — which marked there, in a negative sentence, the refusal of female activities in favour of war: *bellatrix, non illa colo calathisue Mineruae / femineas adsueta manus, sed proelia uirgo / dura pati*, 'a warrior, her woman's hands not used to the spindle and yarn-basket of Minerva, but a girl tough enough to stand battle' (*A.* 7.805–7 [tr. N. Horsfall]).

Until the end, Camilla remains a paradox. Oxymoronic combinations define her: in the catalogue, *proelia uirgo*...; in the 'aristeia', *femineo praedae et spoliorum*... — as if, here too, the feminine element could take on a concessive, and paradoxical, nuance: 'she burnt with a — woman's! — love for booty and spoils'; 'she burnt with love for booty and spoils, although a woman' (a potentiality exploited by Ahl 2007: 'hot, but with feminine tastes, in her passion for booty and plunder'). Or, if one wants to respect syntax, neglecting the contact between words (and translating according to tradition), 'blazed with a womanly love of booty and spoils' [Horsfall]: where, however, 'womanly' is not a synonym of 'irrational', as Servius wanted,[43] nor a disparaging epithet; rather, it is an oxymoronic connotation, exalting taste conjoined with bravery: the feminine style of a 'love for booty and spoils' which is the mark of the warrior (a 'something more' which, unfortunately, in this moment proves fatal to the heroine).[44] By a further paradox, in her 'womanly love' for the precious spoils, the Italian warrior woman appears more virile than her effeminate Phrygian enemy.

---

[41] Sharrock 2015, 160.
[42] Keith 2000, 27–32.
[43] Serv. *ad loc.*: *inpatienti, irrationali*. Cf. Horsfall 2003, and now McGill 2020, *ad loc.*
[44] Cf. now McGill 2020 on 782, quoting Liv. 34.7.8 and observing: 'Camilla confounds the distinctions drawn in Livy as a woman who could win spoils, but who is also attracted to sumptuous attire'.

But there is another key epithet in Camilla's 'aristeia': this is *peregrinus*. The adjective opens the six-line sentence which describes the sophisticated clothing of the Trojan warrior-priest, *ipse peregrina ferrugine clarus et ostro* (11.772), 'bright in foreign rust-red and purple' [tr. mine]. The literal translation of *peregrinus* = 'foreign' (with the additional connotation of foreign charm, 'exotic') is the only one which maintains the different narrative functions of the adjective: in *peregrina* the point of view of the omniscient narrator and that of the character in action, the Volscan queen who is here the internal focalizer, are combined. Among recent translations, Horsfall and Ahl do not retain the multi-functionality of the term, but privilege the narrator's point of view, opting for a rendering in a realistic-commercial tone, or even an explanatory-geographical one: 'bright in imported rust-red and purple' (Horsfall); 'resplendent himself in Iberian rust-red and purple' (Ahl). But here Vergil's text does more: it signals, so to speak, an exoticism within the exoticism, and suggests its potentiated seductive effect; *peregrina ferrugo* (like *ostrum*, itself *peregrinum*) is a 'foreign' element for the Phrygian warrior himself, and 'doubly' foreign for the Volscan queen, as well as for Vergil's reader; an element, then, of further exotic charm. *Ferrugo* is a tincture from Spain, which in the outfit of the Trojan warrior adds to purple, the arrows from Gortyna, the horn from Lycia, gold, linen, embroidery, and the barbarian 'trousers', *barbara tegmina crurum* (A. 11.772–7 *ipse peregrina ferrugine clarus et ostro / spicula torquebat Lycio Gortynia cornu; / aureus ex umeris erat arcus et aurea uati / cassida; tum croceam chlamydemque sinusque crepantis / carbaseos fuluo in nodum collegerat auro, / pictus acu tunicas et barbara tegmina crurum*, 'Chloreus himself, bright in imported rust-red and purple, despatched Cretan arrows from a Lycian bowl. On his shoulders, the seer had a golden bow and his helmet was golden. With tawny gold he had gathered the rustling folds of his cotton cloak into a knot; his undershirts and the barbarian coverings of his limbs were ornamented by the needle' [tr. N. Horsfall]).

The erotic potential of the foreign element acts in this scene in the form of the charming power of an object, a detail of clothing, one among many: the prominence of *peregrinus*, here, loads the adjective with the connotations of exotic charm, irresistible and dangerous, which, we have seen, are proper to it. Even on the battlefield, foreign refinement — a ruin for men and women — can exercise a (literally) fatal attraction.

# Works Cited

Ahl, F. (transl.) (2007), *Virgil, Aeneid*, Oxford.
Ando, C. (2002), 'Vergil's Italy: Ethnography and Politics in First-Century Rome', in: D.S. Levene/ D.P. Nelis (eds.), *Clio and the Poets. Augustan Poetry and the Traditions of Ancient Historiography*, Leiden/Boston/Köln, 123–42.
Barchiesi, A. (ed.) (1992), *P. Ovidii Nasonis Epistulae Heroidum 1–3*, Firenze.
Barchiesi, A. (2009), 'Roman Perspectives on the Greeks', in: G. Boys-Stones/B. Graziosi/Ph. Vasunia (eds.), *The Oxford Handbook of Hellenic Studies*, Oxford, 98–113.
Bessone, F. (2003), 'Discussione del mito e polifonia narrativa nelle Heroides. Enone, Paride ed Elena (Ov. Her. 5 e 16–17)', in: M. Guglielmo/E. Bona (eds.), *Forme di comunicazione nel mondo antico e metamorfosi del mito: dal teatro al romanzo*, Alessandria, 149–85.
Bessone, F. (2011), *La Tebaide di Stazio. Epica e potere*, Pisa/Roma.
Bessone, F. (2015), 'Love and War: Feminine Models, Epic Roles, and Gender Identity in Statius's *Thebaid*', in: J. Fabre-Serris/A. Keith (eds.), *Women and War in Antiquity*, Baltimore, 119–37.
Bessone, F. (2018), 'Storie di eroi, scrittura di eroine. Storia e critica letteraria nelle Heroides', in: P. Fedeli/G. Rosati (eds.), *Ovidio 2017. Prospettive per il terzo millennio*. Atti del Convegno internazionale (Sulmona, 3/6 aprile 2017), Teramo, 181–213.
Biehl, W. (ed.) (1989), Euripides, *Troades*, Heidelberg.
Blänsdorf, J. (ed.) (2011⁴), *Fragmenta poetarum Latinorum epicorum et lyricorum*, Stutgardiae/Lipsiae.
Boyle, A.J. (ed.) (2014), *Seneca, Medea*, Edited with Introduction, Translation, and Commentary, Oxford.
Briguglio. S. (2019), 'La geografia dell'adulterio. Ruoli sessuali, mito e tensioni di genere nell'Agamemnon di Seneca', *Maia* 71, 699–710.
Coleman, K.M. (ed.) (2006), *Martial: Liber Spectaculorum*, Edited with Introduction, Translation, and Commentary, Oxford.
Courtney, E. (ed.) (1993), *The Fragmentary Latin Poets*, Oxford.
Cowan, R. (2010), 'A Stranger in a Strange Land: Medea in Roman Republican Tragedy', in: H. Bartel/A. Simon (eds.), *Unbinding Medea. Interdisciplinary Approaches to a Classical Myth from Antiquity to the 21st Century*, Abingdon/New York, 39–52.
Cyrino, M.S. (1998), 'Heroes in D(u)ress: Transvestism and Power in the Myths of Herakles and Achilles', *Arethusa* 31, 207–41.
Della Corte, F. (1969), 'Perfidus hospes', in: *Hommages à Marcel Renard*, Bruxelles, vol. I, 312–21 (= *Opuscula* IV, Genova 1973, 29–38).
Erskine, A. (2001), *Troy between Greece and Rome: Local Tradition and Imperial Power*, Oxford.
Fantuzzi, M. (1995): 'Levio, Saffo e la grazia delle fanciulle lidie (Laev.fr. 18)', in: L. Belloni/G. Milanese/A. Porro (eds.), *Studia classica Iohanni Tarditi oblata*, 2 vols., Milano, I, 341–7.
Fletcher, K.F.B. (2014), *Finding Italy: Travel, Nation and Colonization in Vergil's Aeneid*, Ann Arbor.
Giusti, E. (2018), *Carthage in Virgil's Aeneid. Staging the Enemy under Augustus*, Cambridge.
Green, S.J. (ed.) (2004), *Ovid, Fasti 1: A Commentary*, Leiden/Boston.
Hall, E. (1989), *Inventing the Barbarian: Greek Self-definition through Tragedy*, Oxford.
Hardie, Ph. (1998), *Virgil*, Cambridge.

Hardie, Ph. (2007a), 'Images of the Persian Wars in Rome', in: E. Bridges/E. Hall/P.J. Rhodes (eds.), *Cultural Responses to the Persian Wars: Antiquity to the Third Millennium*, Oxford, 127–43.
Hardie, Ph. (2007b), 'Phrygians in Rome / Romans in Phrygia', in: G. Urso (ed.), *Tra Oriente e Occidente. Indigeni, Greci e Romani in Asia Minore*, Milano, 93–104 (http://www.fondazionecanussio.org/atti2006/06Hardie.pdf).
Hardie, Ph. (2014), *The Last Trojan Hero: A Cultural History of Virgil's Aeneid*, London/New York.
Heslin, P. (2005), *The Transvestite Achilles: Gender and Genre in Statius' Achilleid*, Cambridge.
Horsfall, N. (ed.) (2000), *Virgil, Aeneid 7. A Commentary*, Leiden/Boston/Köln.
Horsfall, N. (2003), *Virgil, Aeneid 11. A Commentary*, Leiden/Boston.
Keith, A. (2000), *Engendering Rome. Women in Latin Epic*, Cambridge.
Keith, A. (2008), *Propertius. Poet of Love and Leisure*, London.
La Penna, A. (1989), 'La legittimazione del lusso privato da Ennio a Vitruvio', *Maia* 41, 3–34.
Labate, M. (2010), *Passato remoto. Età mitiche e identità augustea in Ovidio*, Pisa/Roma.
Mastronarde, D.J. (ed.) (2002), *Euripides, Medea*, Cambridge.
McGill, S. (ed.) (2020), *Virgil, Aeneid, Book XI*, Cambridge.
Michalopoulos, A.N. (ed.) (2006), *Ovid Heroides 16 and 17. Introduction, Text and Commentary*, Cambridge.
Napolitano, M. (ed.) (2003), *Euripide, Ciclope*, Venezia.
Newlands, C.E. (2002), *Statius' Silvae and the Poetics of Empire*, Cambridge.
Page, D.L. (1951), *Alcman: The Partheneion*, Oxford.
Parca, M./Tzanetou, A. (2016), 'Introduction: Gender, East, and West in Classical Antiquity', *CW* 109, 155–64.
Perutelli, A. (1997), 'Il tema del perfidus hospes nella poesia erotica antica', in: M. Domenichelli/P. Fasano (eds.), *Lo straniero*, Atti del convegno di studi, Cagliari, 16–19 novembre 1994, 2 vols., Roma, vol. I, 331–37.
Piazzi, L. (ed.) (2007), *P. Ovidii Nasonis, Heroidum Epistula VII. Dido Aeneae*, Firenze.
Pittà, A. (ed.) (2015), *M. Terenzio Varrone, De vita populi Romani: introduzione e commento*, Pisa.
Reed, J. (2007), *Virgil's Gaze: Nation and Poetry in the Aeneid*, Princeton.
Reed, J. (2010), 'Vergil's Roman', in: J. Farrell/M.C.J. Putnam (eds.), *A Companion to Vergil's Aeneid and its Tradition*, Malden, MA/Oxford/Chichester, 66–79.
Reed, J. (ed.) (2013), *Ovidio, Metamorfosi, Volume V, Libri X–XII*, Milan.
Romano, E. (1994), 'Dal De officiis a Vitruvio, da Vitruvio a Orazio: il dibattito sul lusso edilizio', in: *Le projet de Vitruve. Objet, destinataires et réception du De architectura, Actes du colloque international de Rome (26–27 mars 1993)*, Rome, 63–73.
Rosati, G. (2006), 'Luxury and Love. The Encomium as Aestheticisation of Power in Flavian Poetry', in: R.R. Nauta/H.-J. van Dam/J.J.L. Smolenaars (eds.), *Flavian Poetry*, Leiden/Boston, 41–58.
Seaford, R. (ed.) (1988), *Euripides, Cyclops*, with Introduction and Commentary, Oxford.
Sharrock, A. (2015), 'Warrior Women in Roman Epic', in: J. Fabre-Serris/A. Keith, *Women and War in Antiquity*, Baltimore, 157–78.
Showerman, G./Goold, G.P. (eds. and transl.) (1977$^2$), *Ovid, Heroides and Amores*, with an English translation by G. Showerman, Second edition revised by G.P. Goold, Cambridge, Mass./London.

Spawforth, A. (1994), 'Symbol of Unity? The Persian-Wars Tradition in the Roman Empire', in: S. Hornblower (ed.), *Greek Historiography*, Oxford, 233–47.
Stok, F. (2012), 'Barbari e alterità etnica nelle Elegie di Properzio', in: R. Cristofoli/C. Santini/F. Santucci (eds.), *Properzio fra tradizione e innovazione. Atti del convegno internazionale, Assisi–Spello, 21–23 maggio 2010*, Assisi, 155–72.
Syed, Y. (2005), *Vergil's Aeneid and the Roman Self: Subject and Nation in Literary Discourse*, Ann Arbor.
Tandoi, V. (1992), 'Dalla Protesilaudamia di Levio alle Heroides ovidiane', in: F.E. Consolino/G. Lotito/M.-P. Pieri/G. Sommariva/S. Timpanaro/M.A. Vinchesi (eds.), *Scritti di filologia e di storia della cultura classica*, Pisa, 112–27.

Judith P. Hallett
# Latin Literary Lenses on Phoenician Female Speech

My paper analyzes Latin literary portrayals of two fictional women, both represented as 'Phoenician', to consider what their distinctive modes of self-expression may imply about Roman views of the relationship between gender and Phoenician ethnicity. The comic playwright Plautus identifies the first, a young brothel slave, as Phoenician quite literally, by her name — Phoenicium — in his *Pseudolus*, datable to 191 BCE.[1] Vergil emphasizes that the second, the Carthaginian queen Dido, is an exile from Phoenicia in his epic *Aeneid*, written over 150 years later.[2] I will spotlight some similarities between the language and concerns assigned these female characters, taking into consideration their dissimilarities as well: not only their contrasting social circumstances but also the different literary genres embraced, and different ideological perspectives adopted, by the Roman authors who 'put words in their mouths.'

I will acknowledge the representation, by Roman writers beginning with Plautus himself, of all Phoenicians, male and female, as masters of verbal artifice, and at times verbal deception, inasmuch as this mode of stereotyping helps to account for one of the major similarities between these two women. But central to the specific resemblances between them is Phoenicium's specialized 'job' function: that of gratifying the sexual tastes and thereby raising the self-esteem of her cultured elite male customers like Calidorus — young master of the title character Pseudolus — who patronize her owner, the pimp Ballio. Her conduct in this re-

---

[1] For the date of Plautus' *Pseudolus*, attested in the *Didascalia* — M IUNIO M FIL PR VRB AC ME, 'When Marcus Junius, son of Marcus, was *praetor urbanus*, performed at the Megalensia' — see Willcock 1987, 95, who cites Livy 36.36 as evidence that Marcus Junius Brutus (ancestor of Julius Caesar's assassin in 44 BCE) was praetor in charge of this festival honoring the *Magna Mater*, that year. As Starks 1999, 258 n. 8 observes, Franko 1994, argues that Roman authors contemporaneous with the still existent city of Carthage often distinguished their use of the terms 'Carthaginian' and 'Punic' according to the purpose at hand. *Carthaginiensis* was the more neutral, civic, political term while *Punicus* and *Poenus* could describe other cultural or ethnic associations. As the *Pseudolus* takes place in Athens, Plautus is not necessarily representing Phoenicium as a Carthaginian and, with her name, seeks to underscore these 'other cultural and ethnic associations.' Vergil's frequent references to Dido as *Phoenissa*, discussed below, reminds his readers that she has fled to Carthage as an exile and should be judged as a Phoenician.
[2] For the date of Vergil's *Aeneid*, see, e.g. *Vita Vergili* 30–41.

gard has affinities with the role Dido assumes towards Aeneas: that of a knowledgeable, sympathetic listener, keen to make him feel understood, and motivated by physical passions that ultimately cause her undoing. The emotional work that these women perform helps explain their representations, comic and tragic, as similarly preoccupied with, and skilled at voicing, desires for shared erotic fulfillment and demands that their lovers value their erotic investments. Yet their Phoenician ethnicity also helps to account for the emotional work that they perform, and the emotions that they elicit.

Finally, I will connect the portrayals of Phoenicium and Dido with those of erotically preoccupied and demanding women in two first century BCE Latin literary texts: Book Four of Lucretius' *De Rerum Natura*, and the elegies of the Augustan female poet Sulpicia. Scholars have long investigated Vergil's evocations of Lucretius in depicting Dido, and explored how Vergil's characterization of Dido informs Sulpicia's own self-representation. But the possibility that Vergil, Sulpicia, and Lucretius knew, and allude to, Plautus' comic representation of Phoenicium casts a new light on their writings, and on their relationship to an earlier dramatic text about an actual female 'love slave'. The differences between these, comic and epic, Phoenician women on the one hand, and an aristocratic Roman woman such as Sulpicia on the other, throws into clearer relief what Romans regarded as distinctive about Phoenicians generally and these Phoenician women in particular.

# 1 Plautus' Phoenicium

The *Pseudolus* opens with the title character, a male Athenian slave, reading aloud, for his young master Calidorus (as well as the theatrical audience), a letter from Phoenicium. Pseudolus thereby launches the dramatic plot without benefit of a traditional expository prologue. Her female voice, represented as written but impersonated orally, is the creation of a male playwright, disembodied on stage, and channeled in this scenario through a male actor playing a male slave. Unlike other female sex-slaves and workers in Plautine comedies, Phoenicium never actually appears on stage as a speaking character.[3] Even so, the words of her letter provide her with a dramatic, albeit distanced, presence.

---

[3] Indeed, Phoenicium is totally silent when she does appear, and is addressed by name, at line 1038. For female speech in Roman comedy generally, see Adams 1984.

I have translated this opening scene, lines 3–78, into English; my discussion will examine relevant words and passages in the Latin text as well:

Pseudolus: If I could have gotten a better idea from you with your mouth shut, master, what sorrows hurt you so wretchedly, I would gladly have saved the effort of two men—of me asking you and you answering me. Since that cannot happen now, obligation forces me to ask you. Answer me: what's the reason that you, after being a virtual vegetable for many days now, keep carrying these writing tablets with you, wash them with your tears, and don't let anyone in on what you're thinking? Speak up, so that I might know as well as you know what I don't know.
Calidorus: Pseudolus, I am wretchedly wretched.
PS: May Jupiter keep you from that condition.
CA: This has no relevance to Jupiter's sphere of judgment. I am suffering under the reign of Venus, not Jupiter.
PS: Is it allowed for me to know what the problem is? In the past you considered me your closest consultant in your thinking processes.
CA: That's my intention now.
PS: Give me an idea of what's bothering you. I will help—with money or work or good thinking.
CA: Take these writing tablets and from reading them tell yourself what unhappiness and concern make me waste away!
PS: Your wish will be my command. But what's this, I ask you?
CA: What's this?
PS: As I ascertain, these letters are seeking to produce children; since they climb on top of each other.
CA: Are you now joking with a joke?
PS: Indeed by Pollux I believe that unless the Sibyl manages to read these letters, no one is able to make sense out of them.
CA: Why do you speak disparagingly of charming letters on charming tablets, written by a charming hand?
PS: By Hercules I plead, what hands do hens have? For a hen has certainly written these letters.
CA: You are annoying to me. Read the tablets or hand them back.
PS: Why, I'll read them through. Pay attention in my direction.
CA: It's not here.
PS: Then you summon it.
CA: Why I will keep my mouth shut, you summon it from the wax; for my attention is now there, and not inside of me.
PS: I see your girlfriend for hire, Calidorus.
CA: Where is she? I appeal to you.
PS: Stretched out, on the tablets and lying as if in bed on the wax.
CA: May the gods and goddesses to you with all in their power—
PS: Be protectors of course.
CA: Just like grass of midsummer I stood tall for a while: suddenly I rose up, suddenly I withered.
PS: Keep your mouth shut while I read the tablets.

CA: Fine, why don't you read, then?
PS: 'Phoenicium sends good wishes to her lover Calidorus, through wax and wood and letters as intermediaries, and seeks good wishes from you, as she is weeping, with trembling mind, heart, and breast.'
CA: I'm done for, Pseudolus, nowhere do I find good wishes of the kind I can send back.
PS: What good wishes do you mean?
CA: Of a moneyed persuasion.
PS: Do you want to send her good wishes in the form of money in return for good wishes on a wooden tablet? Please consider what kind of business you're doing.
CA: Just read the text: now I'll arrange for you to know, from the tablets, how suddenly I need to have money found.
PS: 'A pimp has sold me, abroad, to a Macedonian soldier for twenty minae, my darling: and before he departed from here, this soldier had given fifteen minae: now only five minae hold up the sale. For that reason the soldier left a pledge, his own portrait from his ring stamped in wax so that whoever might bring him a pledge resembling his might at the same time send me with it, and the day for this transaction has been appointed beforehand, the very next festival of Dionysus.' Why, that's tomorrow!
CA: My day of destruction is almost here, unless there's some kind of help for me in you.
PS: Let me read the words through.
CA: Fine with me, for I seem to myself to be having a conversation with her; read: now you mix sweet and bitter together for me.
PS: 'Now our love affairs, ways, routines, joking, playing, talking, sweet conversation, close cuddlings of loving bodies, on delicate little lips soft little bites ... of our secret passionate rites, little squeezing of slightly stiffening nipples, a dragging apart, a tearing apart, a devastation of all these pleasures for me and likewise for you is coming, unless there are good wishes for me toward you or for you toward me. I have taken care that you may know all of these matters I have known of: now I will try to determine what you do by way of loving and what you do by way of pretending. Farewell.'
CA: That's wretchedly written, Pseudolus.
PS: O, most wretchedly.
CA: Why aren't you weeping, then?
PS: I have eyes made of pumice stone: I am not able to beg them to trickle even one single tear.
CA: What's the problem?
PS: Our race has always been dry eyed.[4]

According to Roman epistolary convention, Phoenicium's words, reported — with frequent interruptions — from lines 41–73, begin with a seemingly detached statement, referring to their subject in the third person, and using, in line 43, the third person singular verbs *mittit* and *expetit*.[5] But they, and the responses to them,

---

[4] I follow the text of Willcock 1987. All translations are my own; those of the *Pseudolus* are from Hallett 2011.
[5] For the use of the third person singular — in the phrase *salutem dicit* — as a standard feature of Roman epistolary salutations and greetings, see Lanham, 1975, and s.v. *salus* in Glare 1982,

express strong emotions. Most notably, words associated with 'sad feelings'— the adjective *miser*, its adverb *misere*, and the noun *miseria* — loom large in Plautus' characterization of Calidorus, Phoenicium's letter, and the reactions her words evoke. In line 3 Pseudolus tries to ascertain what miseries (*miseriae*) afflict his lovesick master so miserably (*tam misere*); in 13 Calidorus declares 'I am miserably miserable' (*misere miser sum*) and in 21 he insists that Pseudolus read Phoenicium's letter to understand 'what misery (*miseria*) and unhappiness make him grown weak'. In line 74, after Pseudolus reads the letter, Calidorus judges it *misere scriptum*; Pseudolus *miserrume*. Finally, in line 80 Calidorus terms himself *miser* too.

In line 74 Calidorus clearly uses *misere*, the positive form of the adverb, to judge the letter as written 'sadly, full of sorrowful feelings' and hence as emotionally wrenching for him. I have argued, however, that Pseudolus employs *miserrume*, the superlative form, in a different sense, to mean written 'most wretchedly', mocking both its style and feigned sentiment.[6] Indeed, the word *miserrume* culminates a critique of both Phoenicium's letter and Phoenicium herself in which Pseudolus has engaged from the very start of the scene, through a series of sexist jokes that ridicule her handwriting, sexual promiscuity, and financial rapacity.

The letter's content and style warrant scrutiny. After claiming to be 'weeping with trembling mind, heart and breast', Phoenicium reports that her pimp will sell her for twenty *minae* to a Macedonian soldier from abroad unless Calidorus can purchase her himself. Then, after describing their mutual pleasures in the past, she concludes, in lines 71 through 73, with a financial ultimatum: '[an end] of all these pleasures (*uoluptatum*) for me and likewise for you is coming, unless (*nisi*) there are good wishes for me toward you or for you toward me'.

Phoenicium's description of the erotic joys she has shared with Calidorus — what she has done to earn this money — features a striking collocation of Latin words. Their most eye and ear catching feature is the abundance of nouns, a few evidently *hapax legomena*, words for the occasion and never attested anywhere else in extant Latin literature. Some are abstract, others concrete. Several, such as *morsiunculae* (soft little bites) and *oppressiunculae* (close cuddlings), are diminutives. Most are, repetitively, in the nominative case. She frequently omits

---

1685; the latter, under 8 ('used in various formulas of greeting'), cites Plautus, *Bacchides* 34 as the earliest attestation of this third person singular phrase. The noun *salus* itself figures in both Phoenicium's letter and the reactions to it, but she does not employ the phrase *salutem dicit*.

6 See Hallett 2011, 179–80; the commentary by Willcock 1987, 100, does not say anything about *misere* and *miserrume* here, much less interpret the superlative in an ironic fashion.

connective words (asyndeton), uses alliteration lavishly, and often repeats initial or medial consonants in two or more adjacent words, in such phrases as *sermo, suauisauiatio* in line 65 and *distractio discidium* in 70. The prominence of rhyming, illustrated by the final syllables of *amores, mores, consuetudines* in line 64 and *papillarum horridularum* in 68, merits mention too: both phrases exemplify homoeoptoton, words in the same case with the same terminations. Finally, we should note the pairs of abstract terms fairly close in meaning to one another, if not precise synonyms, a stylistic peculiarity known as 'padding': *mores* and *consuetudines* in 64 and *distractio, discidium*, and *uastatio* in 70.[7]

Nevertheless, as I have argued, Phoenicium's manner of verbal expression, with its inventive language and plethora of rhetorical devices, when recalling the erotic pleasures she and Calidorus have shared, is routinely extolled when employed by Roman males in Roman oratory, such as Plautus' contemporary the elder Cato.[8] The well born, educated, utterly smitten Calidorus judges the words of Phoenicium as emotionally moving and exquisitely wrought. But the middle-aged slave Pseudolus cynically dismisses them as emotionally exploitative, overly extravagant in style and materialistically motivated: he faults them because she is a young female sex slave pressuring a lovesick male youth for money. I have contended, too, that Plautus' later characterization of Phoenicium's pimp Ballio implies that she has acquired these verbal resources — erotic vocabulary, figures of speech — and her facility for issuing financial ultimata by listening to Ballio in his own brothel.[9]

For in lines 225–9, in concluding a lengthy "soliloquy" overheard with horror by both Pseudolus and Calidorus, Ballio addresses and threatens Phoenicium. He

---

[7] Hallett 2011, 180; see also Willcock 1987, 98–100.

[8] See Hallett 2011, 182 ff. "At *Noctes Atticae* 13.15.11–14, Aulus Gellius quotes some interminably long sentences from two orations by one of Plautus's contemporaries, the elder Cato, prefacing and illuminating Cato's words with laudatory remarks by his contemporary Favorinus about how the use of multiple synonyms enriches meaning, because they are heard multiple times.... Cato's words display many of these same features, in both combination and abundance: alliteration (*tantam trucidationem, scio solere* ), rhymed phrase endings (*excellere ... augescere* ), new coinages (*incondemnatis*; see *OLD* s.v.), and above all 'padding.' A double standard for assessing men's and women's words evinces itself yet again."

[9] Hallett 2011, 190–1 "Through the language that Plautus assigns Ballio here, the playwright also implies that the pimp's words, and style of communication, have heavily influenced those of his brothel slave Phoenicium. As noted earlier, her letter, like Ballio's speech, abounds in unusual nouns (both diminutive and invented), verbal padding, and stylistic and sound effects such as asyndeton, anaphora, and rhymed endings. In addition, her letter resembles Ballio's addresses to her and another female brothel slave in its issuance of an ultimatum through the employment of a 'nisi' clause."

illuminates why Phoenicium is portrayed as speaking and indeed writing in this literarily ambitious way by calling her the 'sexual darling of the top-drawer men' (*deliciae summatum uirum*), those of refined intellectual sensibilities. Calidorus has earlier signalled his own membership in that number at 38–9: by evoking the lyrics of Sappho, in poetically arranged Latin words, when voicing his feelings for Phoenicium: 'Just like grass of midsummer I stood tall for a while: suddenly I rose up, suddenly I withered' (*repente exortus sum, repentino occidi*).[10]

Ballio's lines addressing Phoenicium at 225–9 resemble his earlier menacing remarks to Phoenicium's fellow female brothel slaves, threatening brutal physical punishment if they do not maximize the profits from their specialized clienteles.

> Ballio: You moreover, who always are on the point of counting up money to pay for your freedom, you only know how to make an arrangement, but you do not know how to pay what has been arranged, Phoenicium. I say these things to you, the darling of the top-drawer men: unless today the entire store of household provisions is brought to me from the estates of your male friends, tomorrow you, Phoenicium, will visit the brothel shed with a hide of Phoenician purple.

Significantly, Ballio's addresses to each of these slaves (as well as his male slaves) end in an ultimatum like the one Phoenicium issues to Calidorus threatening in lines 228–9: 'unless (*nisi*) today the entire store of household provisions is brought to me from the estates of your male friends, tomorrow you will visit the brothel shed with a hide of Phoenician purple, Phoenicium (*Phoenicium poeniceo corio*)'.[11] This ultimatum includes an etymological figure punning on Phoenicium's name that her educated clients would doubtless appreciate: the adjective *poeniceus*, here describing the scarlet and violet hue of her beaten body if she fails to meet Ballio's expectations, designates the red/purple color associated with dyed Phoenician textiles.[12]

The combination of the adjective *poeniceo* with Phoenicium's name emphasizes her origins from a nation that, as Josephine Crawley Quinn has recently documented, Plautus and other Romans regarded as masters of verbal artifice and

---

10 Hallett 2006, 40, on the echo here of Sappho 31 Lobel-Page, lines 14–16.
11 See Hallett 2011, 191, 'Prior to addressing Phoenicium, Ballio likewise speaks to three of his other female brothel slaves in a similarly menacing and abusive tone, associating each with a different group of paying customers.... Significantly, Ballio issues ultimata with the word *nisi* at five earlier points in this same speech: at lines 135, 143, and 144, when threatening all the male slaves, and at lines 178 and 183, when threatening all the females.'
12 See Glare 1982, 1521, s.v. *puniceus*; Plautus also describes the results of flogging with this same adjective at *Rudens* 1000.

often deception. In Quinn's words: 'The most famous example [of associating the Phoenicians with untrustworthy language] comes in the first ever use of the phrase usually rendered in English as 'Punic Faith,' which is of course to say lack of faith, in Sallust's *Jugurthine War*, written in the 40's BCE. Here *punica fides* is ascribed not to a Phoenician of any kind but the Mauretanian king Bocchus: 'But I find that Bocchus more from *punica fides* than for the reason he claimed lured both the Roman and the Numidian (i.e., Jugurtha) with the hope of peace'. Despite the vagueness of the language they used, Roman period authors did inherit from western Greeks the stereotype of the Carthaginians as deceptive, encouraged of course by the Punic Wars. For Plautus in the third century 'a true Carthaginian knows every language but cunningly pretends not to', and the late republican rhetorical handbook dedicated to Gaius Herennius quotes a speech of presumably second century date claiming that the Carthaginians were confirmed treaty-breakers. And again, this stereotype of Carthaginians was sometime extended to Phoenicians as a whole in Roman contexts: according to Diodorus, a false treaty made by a Roman embassy with King Perseus of Macedon in 172 BCE led some of the older Roman senators to reflect that 'it was not fitting for Romans to imitate Phoenicians, so as to overcome their enemies through deception and not through virtue'. Views about Phoenicians' deception [were] expressed by Cicero, and a little later we have Livy's famous description of Hannibal's *perfidia plus quam punica* or 'more than Phoenician perfidy'.[13]

Phoenicium's words to Calidorus about their mutual erotic pleasures in the past, then, are justifiably suspected by Pseudolus as insincere and emotionally exploitative. They operate chiefly as a sales pitch. Yet they also function as a form of effective verbal therapy, aimed to make Calidorus feel erotically desired as well as desiring. While we soon learn that Phoenicium's training under Ballio in his brothel has prepared her well for entrepreneurial self-advertising, her therapeutic deployment of love-language apparently originated elsewhere: at least it contrasts to Ballio's weaponizing of his words merely to insult and threaten others. She resorts to this description of shared physical joys to sell herself, threatening an impending rupture in their relationship so as to secure Calidorus' financial support and protection. As merely an enslaved Phoenician girl prostitute, not the

---

**13** Quinn 2018, 58: the relevant passages are Sallust, *Iug.* 108.3, Plautus, *Poen.* 112ff., *Rhet. Her.* 4.20, Diod. Sic. 30.7, Livy 21.49.9 and 42.47.7. Plautus' *Poenulus* also represents a Carthaginian woman, Giddenis, actually speaking in the Punic tongue, although her circumstances are radically different from those of Phoenicium (and Dido). For Plautus' ethnic humor in this play, which 'presents the wonderful irony that Plautus may have gotten a Scipio responsible for Carthage's military defeat to produce his comedy that left the Carthaginian soldier standing tall at the end of his conflict with a [cowardly Greek] bigoted soldier,' see Starks 2000.

freeborn daughter of an Athenian male citizen, she is of course ineligible to marry him.[14]

## 2 Vergil's 'Phoenician Dido'

Vergil's *Aeneid* recalls Homer's *Odyssey* by depicting its hero as narrating his adventures at a royal banquet, just as Odysseus does at the Phaeacian court. So, too, like Odysseus, who apparently crafts his story telling there with a woman listener, Queen Arete, primarily in mind, Aeneas directs his recollections at Dido. Aeneas also resembles Odysseus, who loves and leaves two independent and sexually experienced women, the goddesses Circe and Calypso, in his erotic interactions with Dido. Nevertheless, Odysseus never shares his actual military experiences at Troy with a female erotic partner, not even his wife Penelope after they have reunited. Aeneas, however, shares his, traumas and all, with Dido, at the importuning of Dido herself: after Aeneas' mother, the love goddess Venus, has schemed to have one of her other sons, the love god Cupid, inflame Dido with unquenchable passion for Aeneas.[15]

The final lines of *Aeneid* 1.748–56, represent Dido as first asking for details about both the Trojans for whom Aeneas fought and his Greek foes, then demanding (*dic*) to hear, from the beginning, about the misfortunes of his entourage and his own wanderings.

Likewise unfortunate Dido prolonged the night with conversation of different kinds and imbibed deep drafts of love, asking many questions about Priam, many about Hector; now with what arms Memnon had come, now what the horses of Diomedes were like, now how great Achilles was. 'Please tell and relate from the very beginning, guest, the treacheries to us, "she said, "and the misfortunes of your Greeks and your wanderings; now the seventh summer already carries you wandering on all these shores and seas.'

The second book of the *Aeneid* opens where the first left off, with Aeneas' response to Dido's request. In lines 1–13 Aeneas immediately characterizes the

---

[14] See Rosivach, 1998, for the legal status of the different types of women with whom 'young men fall in love' in Plautine and Terentian comedy.

[15] See Hallett 2016, as well as Doherty 1995, for the different female audiences of Odysseus' different autobiographical narratives; Hallett underscores the differences between Odysseus' various audiences and Vergil's Dido, with whom Aeneas shares not only information about his traumatic travels that Odysseus tells the women of the Phaeacian court and his erotic partners but also his military experiences.

narrative that Dido has demanded from him as 'a grief that must not be spoken about' (*infandum dolorem*):

> All fell silent and, eager to listen, continued to focus on Aeneas. At that point father Aeneas began to speak from his lofty couch, 'Queen, you demand that I revive a grief that must not be spoken about, how the Greeks utterly annihilated the resources of Troy and its pitiable kingdom, most heartbreaking events which I myself witnessed and of which I was a great part. Who of the Myrmidons and Dolopians or what soldier of harsh Ulysses would refrain from tears in describing such things? And now the dewy night in the sky rushes down into the sea and the falling stars urge on dreams. But if you are compelled by so great a love to learn about our own misfortunes and to hear, briefly, the final agony of Troy, although the mind shudders to remember and retreats because of sorrow, I will begin.'

Yet he speaks about it nonetheless, presuming that Dido's request to share his emotionally fraught experiences stems from an intellectual desire (*amor*) to learn about his own misfortunes (*casus cognoscere nostros*), and subtly soliciting her as a therapist.

Aeneas finishes his narrative at the end of Book 3. At the opening of Book 4, Vergil portrays Dido as yielding to a different kind of *amor*, the passion for Aeneas aroused by Venus and Cupid, thereby breaking her vow to remain faithful to her dead husband Sychaeus. But Dido only consummates their relationship physically after Aeneas has recounted his military experiences at Troy and similarly heroic deeds in his travels. As she relates to her sister Anna at 4.12–14, while listening she has become impressed not only with his physically appealing qualities but also the wars, 'fought to the finish' (*bella exhausta*) that he narrated in epic fashion (*canebat*).

> Indeed I believe nor is my belief groundless, that he is of divine ancestry. Cowardice reveals ignoble spirits. By what fates has he been tossed! What wars, fought to the finish, did he narrate heroically!

And Vergil depicts Aeneas as sharing with Dido the details of what he has gone through on multiple occasions: first at the court banquet, later after she, at her sister's urging, offers Carthage as his new home. Indeed, at 4.74–9 Vergil describes Dido as out of her mind (*demens*), as she repeatedly (*iterum*) demands that Aeneas repeat what he told her previously about his Trojan toils, and repeatedly (*iterum*) hangs on his every word, simultaneously functioning as both therapist and lover:

> Now Dido guides Aeneas with her through the middle of the fortifications, and shows him the resources of the Phoenician settlement, and the city in preparation, and she begins to speak and stops in mid-conversation; now she seeks the same banquets as the day wanes,

repeatedly, out of her mind, demands to hear about the Trojan toils and repeatedly hangs on his words as he narrates them.

Significantly, at 1.446–97, before Aeneas actually meets Dido, he ascertains her compassionate and informed interest in his painful military past. Almost immediately upon arriving in Carthage he encounters, and responds tearfully to, scenes from the Trojan War on a temple she is building to the goddess Juno. Lines 450–2 portray him as emotionally strengthened by what he sees almost at once:

> In this grove for the first time a newly offered sight alleviated his fear, here for the first time Aeneas dared to hope for security and to feel more confident about his shattered fortunes.

Shortly after this therapeutic moment, in 459–62, Vergil depicts Aeneas' sight of the Trojan king Priam, viewed through his tears, as fostering his recognition that struggles and sufferings such as his own are valued by others and validated by human emotion:

> He stopped in his tracks, weeping. 'What place now', he says, 'Achates, what region on earth is not full of our toil? Behold, Priam; here there are also rewards for merit; there are tears for human experiences and human sufferings touch the heart'.

Finally, at 488, Aeneas finds himself represented on the temple, struggling against his military foes, in a scene illuminating the relevance of these past battles to his own present circumstances: 'he saw himself, too, caught up among the Greek chieftains' (*se quoque principibus permixtum agnouit Achiuis*).

The scenes depicted on Dido's temple hence establish her as knowledgeable about Aeneas' own traumatic experiences, specifically the Trojan War in which he himself fought and whose outcome has created unspeakable grief. Hence they alert Aeneas that Dido will be a good listener, and source of emotional support, when he shares his experiences with her personally. Aeneas reaps further therapeutic benefits from what evolves into an erotic liaison with Dido. Recounting his actual military experiences to a compassionate lover energizes and sustains him emotionally. But while Vergil represents Dido's love as positively transforming the invisible war wounds in Aeneas' heart, mind and spirit, at the same time he depicts Dido as rendered emotionally wounded, unable to continue living. Owing to Aeneas' abandonment of her at the height of their love affair, and ingratitude for her trusting, therapeutic efforts to heal him, she takes her own life.[16]

---

[16] Hallett 2016; for other ancient versions of Dido's story, which often refer to her as Elissa, see Starks 1999 and Quinn 2018, 114–6.

The language that Vergil employs to describe Dido, and assigns to Dido, like that which Plautus uses for and ascribes to Phoenicium, underscores Dido's preoccupation with mutual erotic fulfillment, and closely associates it with both her own unhappiness and her Phoenician, female identity. It does not, however, characterize her as invariably deceptive in her use of language and thereby embodying a negative stereotype associated by the Romans with Phoenicians, one that Plautus to my mind evokes in his portrait of Phoenicium.[17] Yet Vergil nonetheless represents Dido as employing words to obtain an emotional hold over Aeneas, much as Phoenicium does in the *Pseudolus*. Owing to the differences between the language of Plautine comedy and Vergilian epic, Vergil does not echo, or have Dido's speeches echo, many of the words that describe or are attributed to Phoenicium, other than the adjective *miser*, and the adjective and nouns concluding her letter to Calidorus at line 44, where Phoenicium describes herself as *lacrumans titubanti animo, corde et pectore*, 'weeping with trembling heart, mind and breast.' But even without a large number of specific verbal echoes, Vergil's Dido recalls Phoenicium in her acknowledgment, however euphemistic, of her sexual appetites, verbal artifices and frequent lack of trustworthiness.[18]

In 1.344, when briefing Aeneas on Dido's background, Vergil's Venus uses the genitive plural noun *Phoenicum* itself, 'of the Phoenicians', for the wealth of Dido's late husband Sychaeus; the line proceeds to describe Dido's reciprocated erotic feelings for Sychaeus with the phrase *magno miserae dilectus amore*, 'adored with great passion by his unhappy wife', applying the adjective *miser* to Dido: *Phoenicum, et magno miserae dilectus amore*, 'Her husband was Sychaeus,

---

**17** See Bednarowski, 2015, which examines how stories of deceit in *Aeneid* 2 and 3 influence perceptions of the relationship between Aeneas and Dido, pointing out that Dido is both deceived by Aeneas and Venus, and — with Juno — deceives him in Book 4. Starks 1999, argues that Dido breaks the stereotypes that a Punic-hating audience would expect, taking issue with earlier studies that stress Dido's 'negative' Punic traits such as Horsfall, 1973/74, Piccaluga 1979 and Hexter 1982; indeed, he maintains that Vergil transfers Punic stereotypes to Aeneas. Yet he acknowledges that in a few instances 'Dido appears to conform to the stereotypical role of deceptive Punic woman, but these moments need not be understood as destructive of the non-stereotypical Dido which Vergil has constructed.'
**18** In discussing the stereotype of the 'passionate Numidian' in Livy, Haley 1990, 379 remarks: 'It is striking, however, that Vergil, Livy's closest literary contemporary, chose not to emphasize or exploit [this stereotype] in the *Aeneid*. This is not due to the absence of the Numidians; they are cited in the catalogue of Dido's hostile neighbors (*Aen*. 4.41) where they are described as 'unrestrained' (*Numidiae infreni*). Nor is passion lacking; passion is clearly the central motif of Book 4. Vergil preferred to make Dido, the Carthaginian queen, the victim of passion. Passion is for Vergil, as for Livy, the mark of a barbarian; it is certainly not a positive trait."

richest in land of the Phoenicians, and adored with great passion by his unhappy wife'.

In describing Dido's lovesick reaction and thwarted desire for a mutually gratifying, permanent sexual relationship with Aeneas, Vergil proceeds to use the adjectives *miser* and *infelix* for her repeatedly. Not only does he have Venus use *miserae* for Dido at the aforementioned 1.345, but also has Juno use, in the superlative form, *miserrima*, at 4.117–8, when proclaiming 'Aeneas together with most unhappy Dido are preparing to go into a wood to hunt' (*Venatum Aeneas unaque miserrima Dido/in nemus ire parant*).

As we have seen, he refers to Dido as *infelix* at 1.749 as she 'imbibed deep drafts of love,' asking Aeneas questions about his experiences in the Trojan War; as we will see, he calls her *infelix* as well as *Phoenissa* at 1.712–4 as she succumbs to her passion. At 4.529–32 Vergil also characterizes her as both *infelix animi* and *Phoenissa* as she seethes over Aeneas' abandonment of her:

> But Phoenician Dido, unhappy of mind, is not ever released into her dreams and does not welcome the night with her eyes and heart: her concerns double and passion, resurfacing again, storms, and surges on a great tide of angry feelings.

Vergil uses the feminine adjective *Phoenissa*, 'of Phoenicia' for Dido at other times as well, again in the context of her erotic interactions with either Aeneas or Sychaeus. At 1.670 Venus calls Dido *Phoenissa* when asking her son Cupid to make Dido fall in love with "his brother" Aeneas; at 1.714, Vergil refers to her as *Phoenissa* when observing that, at the banquet with Aeneas, 'the unhappy (*infelix*) Phoenician woman, doomed to impending destruction, is unable to satisfy her mind and burns (*ardescit*) by gazing.' Finally, in Book 6, when depicting Aeneas' encounter with Dido in the underworld, Vergil refers to her as *Phoenissa* in line 450, has Aeneas address her as *infelix* in line 456, and, in 474, represents her husband Sychaeus as sympathizing with her anxieties and reciprocating her passion: *respondet curis aequatque Sychaeus amorem*.[19]

In attempting to dissuade Aeneas from abandoning her, Dido, like Plautus' Phoenicium, recalls the amorous bond she and Aeneas have shared. But, in accordance with the decorous conventions of epic diction as well as her lofty birth and mature years, Dido does not enumerate the physical details of mutually pleasurable couplings in graphic fashion, nor insist on repayment for her sexual services. Rather, she characterizes those couplings as respectable monogamous

---

**19** As an anonymous referee has observed, it is significant that Dido, who has vainly tried to use words in holding on to Aeneas and his love, refuses to speak to him in the underworld. He, and the reader, are longing for her words, as is the reader.

marriage, for which she is owed devotion and support. She invokes marital ties as well as her own physically and emotionally vulnerable situation in her appeal to him at 4.314–8, citing 'these tears (*per... has lacrimas*), and your right hand pledged in marriage (*dextram tuam*), our marital union (*conubia nostra*), wedding ceremonies undertaken (*inceptos hymenaeos*).' Aeneas responds in 332–9 by denying that he ever held out the prospect of marriage or entered into marital arrangements.

Dido also is represented, and represents herself, as, like Plautus' Phoenicium, owing to her passion for Aeneas, tearful, physically shaky, and affected in mind, heart and breast (*animo, corde, pectore*). As we have observed, at 4.314 she appeals to Aeneas through her tears. Earlier, at *Aeneid* 4.22, when confessing her love to her sister Anna, she characterizes her mind as 'wavering' with *animumque labentem*; Vergil describes her at line 30 as, having spoken in this way, filling her breast with tears that have sprung up (*sic effata sinum lacrimis impleuit obortis*). Earlier still, at 1.717–9, when depicting how the sight of Cupid, disguised as Ascanius, embracing Aeneas, captures Dido's affections, Vergil refers to her as clinging to this sight with her eyes and her entire heart (*haec oculis, haec pectore toto*), and, as she fondles the boy in her lap, unaware in her unfortunate state (*miserae*) of how great a god nestles there. At 722, moreover, recounting how Cupid drives away Dido's love for Sychaeus, and reawakens her mind and heart, long unstirred and unaccustomed to such feelings (*iam pridem resides animos desuetaque corda*).[20]

Curiously, a rhetorical question that Dido earlier, at 4.307–8, poses to Aeneas, after accusing him of concealing his planned departure from her shores, employs a third person singular verb, and speaks of herself in the third person, much as Phoenicium does at the start of her letter: 'Does not our love (*amor*), nor the right hand given at one time in marriage (*data dextera quondam*), nor Dido about to die in a cruel death hold (*tenet*) you, you (repeated *te*) here?' Both *tenet* and Dido's name impart an impersonal, distancing tone to a highly emotional demand. So does Dido's use of the third person for Aeneas, in a series of rhetorical questions, when she addresses him in 369–70: 'He did not lament (*ingemuit*) at

---

**20** At *Aeneid* 4.535 Dido also uses the verbal form *experiar*, 'I will try', employed by Phoenicium at line 73 in issuing an ultimatum to Calidorus 'to determine what [he does] by way of loving and by way of pretending.' Here, however, Dido asks Aeneas, rhetorically, if she is to try to regain the affections of her earlier suitors now that Aeneas has abandoned her and made her a laughing stock, to insure her survival in her hostile political environment. While Dido is not claiming to test the sincerity of Aeneas' love as Phoenicium is that of Calidorus, both seek to be protected from harm – sale to a foreign soldier in Phoenicium's case, safety for herself and her kingdom in Dido's.

our weeping, did he? He did not move (*flexit*) his gaze, did he? He did not, emotionally overcome, shed (*dedit*) tears or take pity (*miseratus est*) on his lover, did he?'

Curiously, too, Dido attests to her own erotic desire when seeking advice from her sister Anna at the start of Book 4, with the fire imagery of a *uetus flamma* in 23. Yet she does not speak of her own physical passion for Aeneas, or their mutual pleasures, when reproaching him directly for his, treacherous, abandonment of her. And while she, like Phoenicium, threatens Aeneas with the prospect of dire outcomes if he leaves her, she does so more subtly than Phoenicium and Ballio, who introduce their ultimata by the conjunction *nisi*, 'unless', followed by verbs in the future tense. Instead, at 4.320–6, she forecasts what his departure will do to her: weakening her own, and her city's, ability to survive in the face of resentment from her own people, hatred from neighboring nations, military threats posed by King Iarbas and her own brother, giving her no other option than death.

## 3 Phoenicium and Dido, Lucretius and Sulpicia

Jacqueline Fabre-Serris identifies various Epicurean philosophical elements prominent in Vergil's representation of Dido's passion for Aeneas, ascribing them to the elegies of Cornelius Gallus, and Gallus' own careful reading of Lucretius' *De Natura Rerum*.[21] While Pamela Gordon's analysis of Dido as an Epicurean figure does not discuss Vergil's debt to Gallus and Roman elegy, she does call attention to Vergil's use of vocabulary and themes from Lucretius' epic when describing the banquet Dido holds for Aeneas and the Trojans in *Aeneid* 1.[22] I would add another Lucretian 'buzzword' in Book Two: *cognoscere*, implying Dido's commitment to enlightened philosophical pursuits, in Aeneas' aforementioned characterization of Dido as motivated by a love to learn about his misfortunes and Troy's final agony. It looms large in Vergil's own tribute to Lucretius at *Georgics* 2.490, *felix qui potuit rerum cognoscere causas*, 'fortunate is he who has been able to understand the causes of things.'

Scholars have contended, too, that the Augustan elegist Sulpicia pointedly evokes, so as to distinguish herself from, Vergil's Dido in such poems as 9 and 13. As I have observed, the former recalls Vergil's portrayal of Dido's and Aeneas' hunting expedition at *Aeneid* 4.129–59, particularly in its use of the unusual noun

---

21 Fabre-Serris 2008, and 2018.
22 See Gordon 2012, 60–72.

*indago* for a hunting net in line 7, use of the noun *uenus* for sexual activity, and representation of her lover as, like Aeneas' son Ascanius, a boy in pursuit of a boar. As Alison Keith has argued, in lines 2 and 9 the latter evokes Vergil's portrait of Dido's obsession with her reputation, *fama*, later in the same book.[23]

These contentions — about Vergil's use of Lucretian language and themes to represent Dido as an Epicurean, and about Sulpicia's use of Vergilian language and themes to evoke and yet distinguish herself from Dido — have particular relevance to recent and forthcoming interpretations of Lucretius by Erin McKenna Hanses as well as the studies by Fabre-Serris contending that Sulpicia's elegies, like Vergil's epic, appear to evoke those of Cornelius Gallus.[24] Hanses has suggested that Sulpicia identifies herself with women depicted at Lucretius' *De Rerum Natura* 4.1192–208, for achieving the shared erotic pleasures, *communia... gaudia*, they are said to seek, and not merely feigning love (*ficto amore*). Hanses views Sulpicia as echoing Lucretius' Epicurean contemporary Philodemus as well: by heralding — at 11.6–7, and 12.8 — her shared passion, love, bonds (*mutuus ignis...mutuus amor...mutua uincla*) and pleasures, both sexually and philosophically. Vergil's Dido, of course, seeks, but cannot sustain, a mutually pleasurable relationship of body and mind with Aeneas, one that involves shared governance of the Phoenician colony she has founded.

Yet Hanses would also link both Lucretius' depictions of women seeking shared erotic pleasures with men, and Sulpicia's self-representation as enjoying shared erotic pleasures with her lover, to Phoenicium's description of the erotic joys she and Calidorus have shared in Plautus' *Pseudolus*. Hanses thereby would connect these women with Vergil's Dido too. Phoenicium refers to the physical pleasures she enumerates with the plural of the noun *uoluptas*; Lucretius recalls her enumeration of these joys at 4.1193, in portraying a female who seeks mutual pleasure as 'having embraced a man's body and joining it with her body' (*conplexa uiri corpus cum corpore iungit*). That Lucretius would have been familiar with Plautus' *Pseudolus* and its portrayal of Phoenicium is highly plausible, inasmuch as his contemporary Cicero not only celebrates the performance by the great actor Roscius in the role of Ballio but also appears to evoke the Latin text of Phoenicium's letter as well as other portions of the play.[25]

---

**23** See Hallett 2002, and Keith 1997. In elegy 12, where Sulpicia addresses and honors the goddess Juno, she may also be recalling Vergil's portrayal of Dido's devotion to this same goddess.
**24** E. Hanses 2018, and *per litteras*.
**25** M. Hanses 2020. In commenting, for example, on *Pro Caelio* 6, where Cicero remarks that, upon becoming an adult male, *obterendae sunt omnes uoluptates, relinquenda studia delectationis, ludus, iocus, conuiuium, sermo paene est familiarum deserendus*. (All lust has to be abandoned; all pursuits of pleasure have to be left behind; play, joke, and dinner party, almost all

The resemblances Hanses detects between the Sulpicia's elegies and Plautus' depiction of Phoenicium are endowed with metapoetic as well as philosophical resonances: both Plautus and Sulpicia associate the wax tablets on which these women write their words of love with their physical, erotic behavior. Indeed, Sulpicia seems to have derived the pseudonym for her lover. Cerinthus, from words for 'wax' in both Latin and Greek.[26] Both Phoenicium and Sulpicia attempt, as do the women in Epicurus' garden, to take charge of their own sexuality. What is more, elegies 8, 10, and 12, all of which describe Sulpicia (and her lover) in the third person singular, may endeavor to evoke Phoenicium's detached, 'epistolary' mode of addressing Calidorus.[27] They summon to mind as well Dido's use of third person verbs when talking about herself and to Aeneas. One could also interpret as therapeutic Sulpicia's reassuring words to Cerinthus at 10.15–16: 'put away your fear, Cerinthus, this god does not harm lovers. Only love her always, your girl is safe' (*pone metum, Cerinthe: deus non laedit amantes/tu modo semper amas; salua puella tibi est*). What is more, one might read her statement in poem 16 — confronting Cerinthus about his relationship with a lowly prostitute — about those 'with her interests at heart' (*solliciti*) as a veiled but self-assertive ultimatum.

But the resemblances shared by Plautus' Phoenicium and Vergil's Phoenician Dido with Sulpicia — and with the Lucretian female also desirous of mutual pleasure — are offset by powerful differences. Plautus and Vergil represent their two Phoenician female characters as, although disparate in age and social class, similarly skilled at communicating with and emotionally manipulating male partners through talking, listening, and seeking mutual sexual accommodation.[28] Yet even if Sulpicia's words, and employment of words, recall earlier literary portraits of Phoenicium and Dido, she never represents herself or her lover as

---

conversation with friends, have to be forsaken), he notes that 'Cicero's *ludus, iocus, conuiuium, sermo* is almost identical to similar lists in Plautus's *Pseudolus* and *Bacchides* (*iocus, ludus, sermo, suauisauiatio*, 'joke, play, conversation, sweet-kissing,' Plaut. *Pseud.* 65 = *Bacch.* 116).' Cicero attests to his familiarity with Plautus' *Pseudolus* at *Pro Roscio* 7.20, when describing how Roscius played the pimp Ballio, a detail about the play's later popularity suggesting that Vergil was also acquainted with its text.

**26** See Roessel 1990, as well as Sulpicia's own claim in 13.7–8 that she would not entrust what she has written to sealed tables (*signatis tabellis*) so that no one would read them before her lover.

**27** Sulpicia's poems describing her in the third person are 8 (*est/uult/agit/mouit/componit/soluit/compsit/est/urit/uoluit/urit/uenit/est/possideatque/est*); 10 (*est/est/cogitat*); and 12 (*dat/est/compsit/staret/relegat/uelit/praecipit/rogat/uritur/uelit*).

**28** To be sure, seductive and deceptive speech by female characters who are not Phoenician figures in both Roman comedy and Latin love poetry: at Ovid, *Amores* 1.8.103–4, the procuress

unhappy — with the adjectives *miser* or *infelix* — when making erotic appeals or demands. In contrast, both Phoenicium and Dido seek to elicit pity, and are depicted as both experiencing and generating sorrow, and as victimized by misfortune, in their erotic relationships.

What is more, both Phoenicium and Dido also partake of negative stereotypes applied by Plautus himself and subsequent Roman writers to Phoenician men. By using adjectives that emphasize their ethnic identities as well as by attributing them with emotionally manipulative words, Plautus and Vergil depict these verbally talented women as representing a foreign population rightly distrusted for words, and hence ethics, of little worth. Finally, Sulpicia's poems exude a self-confident, socially entitled air hardly surprising in a member of Rome's entrenched elite. It differs sharply from the insecure tone permeating the words assigned to the young brothel slave sold into Athenian slavery and the mature queen exiled to North Africa: both far from their "Phoenician" homeland, both in desperate need of validation, whether in the form of purchase or legitimate wedlock, to survive, and dependent on their words as well as their bodies to do so.[29]

# Works Cited

Adams, J.N. (1984), 'Female Speech in Latin Comedy,' *Antichthon* 18, 43–77.
Bednarowski, K.P. (2015), 'Dido and the Motif of Deception in *Aeneid* 2 and 3,' *TAPA* 145, 135–72.
Doherty, L.E. (1995), *Siren Songs: Gender, Audiences and Narrators in the* Odyssey, Ann Arbor.
Fabre-Serris, J. (2008), *Rome, l'Arcadie et la mer des Argonautes: essai sur la naissance d'une mythologie des origines en Occident. Mythes, imaginaires, religions*, Villeneuve d'Ascq.
Fabre-Serris, J. (2018), 'Love and Death in Propertius 1.10, 1.13 and 2.15: Poetic and Polemical Games with Lucretius, Gallus and Vergil,' in: S. Frangoulidis/S. Harrison (eds.), *Life, Love*

---

Dipsas advises 'let your tongue be of help, and cover up your mind — say flattering words and do harm; wicked poisons lurk under sweet honey' (*lingua iuuet mentemque tegat — blandire nocequelimpia sub dulci melle uenena latent*). But other similarities between Phoenicium and Dido encourage according special attention to their Phoenician identity: both share, as an anonymous referee has underscored, exile and dependency on men who might be called unreliable. Furthermore, one might liken Dido's helpless situation created by the conspiracy of the all-powerful goddesses Juno and Venus against her to the plight of Phoenicium, under the control of a sadistic pimp.

**29** My thanks to Jacqueline Fabre-Serris, Erin McKenna Hanses, Josephine Crawley Quinn, John H. Starks, Jr. and the two anonymous referees of this essay for their very helpful suggestions on earlier versions of this paper.

and *Death in Latin Poetry. Studies in Honor of Theodore D. Papanghelis*, Trends in Classics Supplementary Volumes, vol. 61, Berlin, 37–50.

Franko, G.F. (1994), 'The Use of *Poenus* and *Carthaginiensis* in early Latin Literature,' *CP* 89, 153–8.

Glare, P.G. (1982), *Oxford Latin Dictionary*, Oxford.

Gordon, P. (2012), *The Invention and Gendering of Epicurus*, Ann Arbor.

Haley, S.P. (1990), 'Livy, passion and cultural stereotypes,' *Historia* 39, 375–81.

Hallett, J.P. (2002), 'The eleven elegies of the Augustan elegist Sulpicia', in: L.J. Churchill/P.R. Brown/E. Jeffrey (eds.), *Women Writing Latin from Roman Antiquity to Early Modern Europe*, vol. 1: *Women Writing Latin in Roman Antiquity, Late Antiquity, and the Early Christian Era*, New York/London, 45–65.

Hallett, J.P. (2006), 'Gender, Class and Roman Rhetoric: Assessing the Writing of Plautus' Phoenicium (*Pseudolus* 41–73),' *Advances in the History of Rhetoric* 9, 33–54.

Hallett, J.P. (2011), 'Ballio's Brothel, Phoenicium's Letter, and the Literary Education of Greco-Roman Prostitutes: The Evidence of Plautus' *Pseudolus*,' in: A. Glazebrook/M.M. Henry (eds.), *Greek Prostitutes in the Ancient Mediterranean 800 BCE–200 CE*, Madison, WI, 172–96.

Hallett, J.P. (2016), 'Can Love Alleviate the Unseen Wounds of War? Erotic and Therapeutic Encounters en Route 'Home' from the Trojan Conflict,' in: A. Setaoli (ed.), *Apis Matina: Festschrift Carlo Santini*, Trieste, 354–65.

Hanses, E.M. (2018), 'Lucretius and the Origins of Roman Love Elegy,' Diss. Fordham University.

Hanses, M. (2020), *The Life of Comedy after the Death of Plautus and Terence: The Reception of Roman Comoedia in Latin Literature of the Late Republic and Early Empire*, Ann Arbor.

Hexter, R. (1992), 'Sidonian Dido,' in: R. Hexter/D. Selden (eds.), *Innovations of Antiquity*, New York/London, 332–84.

Horsfall, N. (1973/1974), 'Dido in Light of History,' *PVS* 13, 1–13.

Keith, A. (1997), '*Tandem Venit Amor*: A Roman Woman Speaks of Love,' in: J.P. Hallett/M.B Skinner (eds.), *Roman Sexualities*, Princeton, 295–310.

Lanham, C. (1975), *Salutatio Formulas in Latin Letters to 1200: Syntax, Style, and Theory*, Hildesheim.

Piccaluga, G. (1979), 'Fondare Roma, domare Cartagine: un mito delle origini,' *Atti del 1 Congresso Internazionale di Studi Fenici e Punici*, Rome, 409–24.

Quinn, J. (2018), *In Search of the Phoenicians*, Princeton.

Roessel, D. (1990), 'The Significance of the Name Cerinthus in the Poems of Sulpicia,' *Transactions of the American Philological Association* 120, 243–50.

Rosivach, V.J. (1998), *When a Young Man Falls in Love: The Sexual Exploitation of Women in New Comedy*, London/New York.

Starks, J. (1990), '*Fides Aeneia*: the Transference of Punic Stereotypes in the *Aeneid*,' *CJ* 94, 255–83.

Starks, J. (2000), '*Nullus Me Est Hodie Poenas Poenior*: Balanced Ethnic Humor in Plautus' *Poenulus*,' *Helios* 27, 163–86.

Willcock, M.M. (ed.) (1987), Plautus, *Pseudolus*, Bristol/Oak Park, Illinois.

Alison Sharrock
# Babylonians in Thebes: Some Ovidian Stories of Barbarians and Foreigners

## 1 Geography and ethnography

Ovid's *Metamorphoses* paints on a broad temporal canvas, exploring the world from its first origins to the poet's own time (*Met.* 1.1–4). The poem has an almost equally wide-ranging spatial canvas, in which that major structural building block of epic, the journey, causes the narrative line to criss-cross the known world.[1] The poem thus takes the totalising claims of epic to new heights, making not only a universal history but also a kind of universal geography out of its myriad stories of metamorphosis.[2] For all its universalist perspective, however, the poem has been relatively little studied from the point of view of ethnography. The question for this paper is how the geographical range and local specificity of the poem's many parts work with — or against — the fluidity of identity which is now conventionally seen in the medium and the message of the poem. In a world in which difference and sameness are always at issue, what role does the representation of ethnic variation play? Do the major themes of the poem look different in different parts of the world? Or are personhood, love, metamorphosis, artistry, and suffering presented as universals?

One role that could be expected of ethnic variation is what I call an 'Othering' effect. This is construction of the people, customs, and places of distant lands as 'different', in such a way as to create by opposition a sense of self-identity and communal identity for the 'us' who view the 'others' as Other,[3] a process which has been theorised in postcolonial discussion of Western 'Orientalising' readings of and attitudes to Eastern cultures.[4] The *Metamorphoses* looks at the world overwhelmingly to the east and south of Rome. In part this easterly gaze will be a side-

---

[1] Pavlock 2009, 49; Holzberg 1998, 90–1. I am grateful to the editors and the anonymous readers, whose suggestions have greatly improved this piece, and to Julene Abad del Vecchio for her help in the production of it. The text of Ovid is quoted from Tarrant 2004. Translations are my own unless otherwise stated.
[2] On universal history and Ovid, see Wheeler 2002; Galinsky 1975, 3, although he plays down the role of geography; Solodow 1988, 24.
[3] Hall 1989.
[4] For a programmatic statement of Orientalism, see Said 1978, 12. It is a process which involves the flattening out of local variation in the geography and ethnography of Other. In reference to

effect of the existing mythographic material on which Ovid draws, but equally it is in keeping with the dominant construction in Augustan Rome of Other as Eastern, a perspective with huge progeny in Western literature and culture. In what ways does this narrative eye see similarity and difference in the nations and peoples of the world?[5]

I am going to suggest that, in some cases, there is considerably more similarity and less difference in the representation of Others than we might expect. While there are indeed examples of the representation of Others as different, there are also extensive cases of domestication, of the ironing-out of differences between self and other from an ethnic or geographical perspective. I shall concentrate on the stories told by the daughters of Minyas in *Met.* 4. First, however, I shall briefly explore the range of the poem's ethnographic outlook by examining some examples of ethnic stereotyping.

## 2 Who is a barbarian?

There are a small number of characters in the poem who play to geographical stereotypes in fairly predictable ways, especially the monstrous tyrant and vicious rapist Tereus, appropriately from Thrace.[6] The story includes a rare case of an explicit connection made between a people and a behaviour (*Met.* 6.458–60):

>     sed et hunc innata libido
> exstimulat, pronumque genus regionibus illis
> in Venerem est; flagrat uitio gentisque suoque.

> But both his inborn lust stimulates him [Tereus], and also the race in those regions is prone to Venus; he burns by his own vice and that of his race.

---

the Classical world, for Vergil and Propertius, see O'Rourke 2011; Parker 2011 expands on Said's paradigms, calling for a more nuanced reading of the 'orientalising' Indians, Egyptians and Parthians of Aeneas' shield in book 8; for a discussion of similar issues in Silius Italicus, see Keith 2010. For slippage between and conflation, in Roman perceptions of the world, of places which we now regard as clearly distinct, see Schneider 2016, who interprets the 'confusion' between Ethiopia and India as, rather, a form of knowledge.

**5** There is not space here to explore the complexity caused by the implied author being expelled, along with the flesh and blood author, to the shores of the Black Sea sometime during the composition of the *Metamorphoses*.

**6** For Thrace as barbaric, see Hdt. 5.1–10, an excursus on their unusual customs; modern scholarship on the Thracians as a barbaric tribe includes Marazov 2011, 132–5.

Investigation of the direct terminology of barbarism within the poem shows both conventional and rather more surprising usages. Of the 12 examples I have counted of *barbarus* and cognates within the poem, three apply unsurprisingly to Medea (7.53, 7.144, 7.276). Four occur in the Tereus episode: the two referring to Tereus himself (6.515 and 6.533) are likewise straightforwardly Othering, but in the case of the first instance, introducing the episode at 6.423, it is barbarian hordes (*barbara ... agmina*) who are attacking Athens and are repelled by the arch-barbarian, the Thracian Tereus, illustrating that while it may take one to fight one, the process of doing so confounds the difference between civilisation and barbarism. The final example from that story, when Philomela weaves the story of her suffering on a *barbarica ... tela* ('barbarian loom', 6.576), might constitute a transferred epithet but additionally foreshadows the barbaric revenge which the Athenian sisters exact on Tereus, thus playing out the confounding of the difference with which the story began.

Two other instances in the poem belong to a quasi-universalising discourse of civilisation over barbarism, in which Graeco-Roman culture is identified with civilising forces. The first comes at the end of Calliope's song of Ceres, when the Scythian King Lyncus is given the epithet *barbarus* (5.657) as he plots to kill the Athenian Triptolemus and to usurp credit for Ceres' gift of agriculture. The second (11.162) characterises Pan's rustic song which pleases the foolish Midas more than does that of Apollo. The straightforward dichotomy between Apolline high culture and barbarian alternatives is somewhat undermined by the description of the god, as he is about to perform, bedecked with Indian and Tyrian luxury (11.165–9).

The remaining three examples problematise the relationship between Graeco-Roman hegemony and the barbaric world. The last one comes in the picture of world domination prophesied for Roman Augustus by a highly partisan Jupiter, as Julius Caesar is about to be assassinated. After foretelling a version of Vergil's Roman victory over Egypt (15.826–8; see below for the Vergilian version), Jupiter sums up the Augustan achievement (*Met*. 15.829–31):

quid tibi barbariam gentesque ab utroque iacentes
Oceano numerem? quodcumque habitabile tellus
sustinet, huius erit; pontus quoque seruiet illi.

Why should I enumerate to you the barbarian world and the nations lying by either Ocean? Whatever habitable place the earth sustains, will belong to him; the sea also will serve him.

The two previous instances of *barbarus* or cognates occurring after the transition into proto-historic time with the move to the Trojan cycle[7] both apply to Aeneas' Trojans, on their way to founding Rome. The first, at 14.163, is spoken by the Greek Macareus, when he describes his surprise at seeing Achaemenides with the Trojans, in a 'barbarian ship'; the second describes the sword of Aeneas which kills Turnus and so brings to an end Ovid's 'little *Aeneid*' (14.574) — and, in Vergilian intertext, ultimately founds Rome. Although one could envisage the 'barbaric sword' as focalised by Turnus, it is spoken by the primary narrator.

To explore further the way in which the *Metamorphoses* uses Vergilian depictions of the Eastern Other, I dwell briefly on a passage which expresses that Other in apparently simplistic terms. The goddess Isis has a fine tradition of Orientalising representation in Latin literature.[8] When the pregnant Telethusa is instructed by her husband to expose the child if it is female, she is visited by a dream of Isis in full 'exotic' regalia and told to rear the child (*Met.* 9.686–94).

> ...cum medio noctis spatio sub imagine somni
> Inachis ante torum pompa comitata sacrorum
> aut stetit aut uisa est; inerant lunaria fronti
> cornua cum spicis nitido flauentibus auro
> et regale decus. cum qua latrator Anubis
> sanctaque Bubastis uariusque coloribus Apis,
> quique premit uocem digitoque silentia suadet;
> sistraque erant numquamque satis quaesitus Osiris
> plenaque somniferis serpens peregrina uenenis.

> ...when in the middle of the night in the image of sleep the daughter of Inachus, accompanied by her ritual procession, either stood or seemed to do so; on her forehead were moon-shaped horns, with ears of corn yellow with shining gold, and royal beauty. With her, barking Anubis and holy Bubastis and multicoloured Apis, and he who suppresses the voice and urges silence with his finger: the rattles were there and Osiris never sufficiently sought and the foreign snake filled with sleep-inducing poison.

This traditional picture of Egyptian religion evokes the *Aeneid*'s most extreme moment of Othering, in the highly nationalistic depiction of Antony and Cleopatra on the Shield of Aeneas (*Aen.* 8.685–8; *Aen.* 8.696–700):

---

[7] Previous to this moment, the last example of a *barbarus*-cognate was the reference to Pan's song (11.162).

[8] For Isis's exoticism, see Propertius 2.33a; Ovid, *Am.* 2.13.7–14 (Isis and the Nile); Tibullus 1.3.23–34 (Isis vs. Penates); for the cult of Egyptian gods not allowed within the Pomerium during Augustus' reign, see Cassius Dio 53.2.4; for Agrippa's curtailment of Egyptian rites that were proliferating in Rome, again Cassius Dio 54.6.6.

> hinc ope barbarica uariisque Antonius armis,
> uictor ab Aurorae populis et litore rubro,
> Aegyptum uirisque Orientis et ultima secum
> Bactra uehit, sequiturque (nefas) Aegyptia coniunx.

On this side Anthony with barbarian resources and variegated arms, victor from the peoples of the Dawn and the shore of the Red Sea, draws with him Egypt and the strength of the East and furthest Bactra, and is followed (unspeakable!) by his Egyptian wife.

> regina in mediis patrio uocat agmina sistro,
> necdum etiam geminos a tergo respicit anguis.
> omnigenumque deum monstra et **latrator Anubis**
> contra Neptunum et Venerem contraque Mineruam
> tela tenent.

The Queen in the middle calls on her troops with her ancestral rattle, and does not yet see the twin snakes behind her back. The monstrosities of gods of every race and **barking Anubis** hold their weapons against Neptune and Venus and against Minerva.

The collocation *latrator Anubis* occurs in only these two passages in classical Latin poetry,[9] while the explicit designation of something as 'barbaric' is one of only four examples in the *Aeneid*.[10] The snake and the rattle appear in both, as does the Queen/goddess surrounded by her possession. But the context could hardly be more different. On the Vergilian shield, the gods of Rome, supported by the weight of Roman military might, are opposed to — and will conquer — the chaotic, variegated (one might almost say 'metamorphic'), Eastern crowd. In the Ovidian dream, the exotic Eastern goddess, introduced by a patronymic (*Inachis*) which reminds us that she — Isis — began her metamorphic story as one of the earliest victims of heartless divine erotic attention.[11] Now, moreover, she appears to a respectable but lower-class Cretan pregnant wife in order to put to rights the disorder in the household created by the expectant father's economic misogyny. She does so ultimately by redirecting the disruptive female-to-female love, experienced by the resultant progeny, towards the gendered norms of Graeco-Roman society. When Iphis becomes a man, s/he immediately takes on the attributes and

---

**9** There are, in addition, three examples in the *Anthologia Latina* and one in Prudentius.
**10** The other three examples are: *Aen*. 1.539, spoken by Ilioneus regarding his reception by Dido's people, so by proto-Roman (but non-Greek) regarding proto-Carthaginian; 2.504, Aeneas' description of the palace of Priam; and 11.777, of the clothing of Chloreus, focalised by the Italian Camilla.
**11** See *Met*. 1.583: *Inachus unus abest* ('[the river] Inachus was the only one to be absent').

signifiers of masculinity, in a way that seems to cancel out the gender fluidity that we might have expected from the Egyptian goddess (9.787–90).

## 3 Thebes, Bacchus, and the Other

A useful locus for examining potential ethnic Othering and representations of peoples and places in the poem is the episode of the daughters of Minyas, who tell tales to pass the time as they sit weaving, while the other Theban women celebrate the rites of the new god Bacchus. Several of the stories are of Babylonian provenance, one of which was immortalised by Shakespeare as the inset story of Pyramus and Thisbe within *A Midsummer Night's Dream*,[12] while others include the Carian Salmacis, whose spring causes hermaphroditism, and most of the rejected stories also come from the East. The Minyeides should be in nearby Orchomenus, but Ovid has found it convenient to glide over that fact, keeping the focus on Thebes. While Thebes itself might seem a candidate for some degree of Othering, at this stage in the poem Thebes is where the narrative happens to be. Thebes has already produced the first epic hero of the poem, in the form of Cadmus, as well as some of the most memorable metamorphic stories (Narcissus and Echo, Actaeon). At this stage, at a time long before the rise of Rome and differentiation between Romans and Greeks, Thebes stands as nothing more than the Greek city which is currently acting as the anchor for the super-narrative.[13]

Ovid, moreover, suppresses other aspects of the existing myth of the Minyeides, which would make the women considerably more threatening than in the story as he tells it. According to Antoninus Liberalis (10), the daughters of Minyas, maddened by terrifying manifestations of Bacchic power, tore apart the son of one of them and then fled to the mountains before being transformed into nocturnal birds.[14] It could be thought that Ovid has suppressed the dismemberment because he has just told the story of Pentheus, but similar stories not rarely stand next to each other in the *Metamorphoses*. Rather, the comparison with alternative myth shows the remarkably stable and domesticated representation of the women.

---

[12] Since the story is active in the plot of *Romeo and Juliet* and features in *Merchant of Venice*, it clearly had great resonance for Shakespeare and his audience. See Bate 1993, 130.
[13] For the structural role of Thebes, see Hardie 1990; Rosati 2009, esp. 125–8. Janan 2009 is a challenging study of Ovid's Thebes, framed as both Rome and the human universal. The classic work on the Othering of Thebes as an anti-Athens is Zeitlin 1986.
[14] See also Aelian *Varia Historia* 3.42.

It is Bacchus, rather than the Minyeides, who has most potential to represent the Other in the wider context of this episode. His epiphany as a disruptive new god has already caused conflict with Pentheus, in which the latter attempts to present the former as strange, foreign, and threatening, but at the same time weak and effeminate, in contrast with his own earthborn virility,[15] as his long speech at 3.531–63 indicates (*Met.* 3.531–7):

> 'quis furor, anguigenae, proles Mauortia, uestras
> attonuit mentes?' Pentheus ait 'aerane tantum
> aere repulsa ualent et adunco tibia cornu
> et magicae fraudes, ut quos non bellicus ensis,
> non tuba terruerit, non strictis agmina telis,
> feminae uoces et mota insania uino
> obscenique greges et inania tympana uincant?...'

> 'What madness, snake-born men, offspring of Mars, has struck your minds?' Pentheus says, 'are mere bronzes struck by bronze so powerful, and the flute with its hooked horn and magic tricks, that those whom neither the sword of war nor the trumpet has terrified, nor battlelines with their drawn weapons, might be conquered by feminine cries and madness driven by wine and obscene crowds and empty drums?...'

The Othering of Bacchus, however, is limited. Despite the fact that the god was not raised in Thebes, as was the autochthonous descendant Pentheus, nonetheless they are cousins. Bacchus is also home-grown, a son of Thebes returning in expected triumph to his people. Moreover, the narratorial hymn to Bacchus (4.9–30) in which the Minyeides refuse to join, for all its Eastern and Indian exoticism, is focalised through the people of Thebes and is also explicitly Greek (*Met.* 4.13–6).

> additur his Nyseus indetonsusque Thyoneus
> et cum Lenaeo genialis consitor uuae
> Nycteliusque Eleleusque parens et Iacchus et Euhan,
> **et quae praeterea per Graias plurima gentes nomina, Liber, habes.**

> To these is added Nyseus and unshorn Thyoneus and along with Lenaeus sower of the festive grape, and Nyctelius and father Eleleus and Iacchus and Euhan, and **all the other names which you, Liber, have throughout the Greek peoples**.

The traditional celebration of Bacchus as conqueror of India appears during the hymn not to orientalise Bacchus but to orientalise the East precisely as Other to him: *Oriens tibi uictus adusque/ decolor extremo qua tingitur India Gange* ('yours

---

[15] One might see a hint of Romanness in his robust, bellicose attitude, as is argued also by Janan 2009, ch. 6.

is the conquered Orient as far as coloured India is dyed in furthest Ganges', 4.20–1). Likewise, at the end of the Theban cycle, Bacchus' achievement over *debellata... / India* ('conquered India', 4.605–6, using a highly charged Vergilian word, cf. *Aen.* 6.853) brings solace to his metamorphosed Theban grandparents Cadmus and Harmonia. Although the Indian connection may perhaps be hinted at through the epithet Nyseus (4.13, above),[16] it looks more like a military honorific title such as Africanus than an epithet implying Indian identity.[17]

## 4 Women who weave

Bacchus is certainly threatening in *Metamorphoses* 3 and 4, but not simply as the Eastern Other as which Pentheus attempts to portray him; and the risks can be managed by proper Greek (Graeco-Roman) religion. The Minyeides, however, insist on staying with their looms (*Met.* 4.31–6).

> 'Placatus mitisque' rogant Ismenides 'adsis,'
> iussaque sacra colunt; solae Minyeides intus
> intempestiua turbantes festa Minerua
> aut ducunt lanas aut stamina pollice uersant
> aut haerent telae famulasque laboribus urguent.
> e quibus una leui deducens pollice filum...

> 'Placated and kindly' the daughters of Ismenus ask 'be present,' and they worship the rites as ordered; alone the Minyeides inside, disturbing the festival with untimely Minerva, either draw out the wool or turn the threads with the thumb or stick to their loom and encourage the maidservants in their work. One of them drawing down the thread with a light thumb...

Despite the explicit untimeliness of their work and its disruption of the festival (the latter a particularly Roman concern), it is hard not to see the Minyeides as

---

[16] The epithet Nyseus, according to Rosati 2007, 247, with no Greek equivalent and not occurring before Ovid, derives from Mount Nysa, the locality of which is debated but generally thought to be in India.

[17] It would nonetheless be appropriate to note that the Eastern and Southern associations of Bacchus can work both ways, presenting him both as Western conqueror and as exotic Easterner, hence his usefulness, to both friends and enemies, as a model for Alexander and for Mark Anthony. See Rosati 2007, 249.

Roman 'good women'.[18] Being opposed to the accommodation to Bacchic excess made by the people of Thebes and apparently by the narrator (4.9–13), the attitude of the Minyeides exposes the risks and anxieties around ecstatic religion as it arose in Roman history in the Bacchanalia affair. Whether Greeks are 'them' or 'us' as regards the Roman 'I-eye' of the *Metamorphoses* is variable: here the Greeks, the Thebans, both worshippers of Bacchus and Minyeides – are 'us'. In addition, the Minyeides are, as is well known, ciphers for Ovid as implied author of the poem. They are the first straightforwardly human variant speakers of the *Metamorphoses*' stories, the first storytelling group, the first in a series of women who weave (followed by Arachne and Philomela), and do so with explicitly metapoetic presentation.[19]

The tales told by these respectable Theban ladies are remarkable in a number of ways, especially for their various aspects of female agency, from the likeable Thisbe to the aggressive Salmacis. They also include a great deal that is not, or not straightforwardly, Greek.

## 5 The first Minyeid: Pyramus and Thisbe

The unnamed first sister rejects a set of stories that are all of Syrian/Babylonian provenance (4.44–51): Derceto is a version of the Syrian goddess of love who, out of shame at falling in love with a mortal man, turned herself into a fish; her daughter Semiramis is the famously erotic and exotic Babylonian queen; the nymph who turned strangers into fish before undergoing the same metamorphosis herself also appears to derive from Eastern stories.[20] The subject chosen by the

---

**18** Rosati 2007, 252 also associates the Minyeides with Roman tradition here, while Salzman-Mitchell 2005, 99 says that Leuconoe 'rewrites herself (and her sisters) in the figure of Leucothoe, who acts as a fantasy about what they believe are good and desirable woman would be like in the eyes of the male viewer'.
**19** Wheeler 1999, 182; Sharrock 2002, 213. On the Minyeides as narrators and ciphers for Ovid see Janan 1994, 427 n. 3; Myers 1994, 80; Rosati 2007, 252 and 255. Heath 2011 is a wide-ranging discussion of the association between weaving, women's narratives, and the transmission of Graeco-Roman myth.
**20** Rosati 2007, 254–5. Duke 1971 lists several exotic goddesses and minor divinities of Eastern origin who may be implicated in the stories rejected by the Minyeid. Perdrizet 1932 develops a number of interesting links for the rejected stories. For the third rejected story, that of the fishy Naiad, he refers to stories in Herodotus 3.19 on the fish-eaters from the city of Elephantine, an island on the Nile, and in Diodorus 3.14–9 about a similar people living on the coast around the

Minyeid, Pyramus and Thisbe, has no extant precedent in Latin literature, but may have a relationship with a Greek tradition, to be explored below, which, if so, would mean that it should be set in Cilicia, rather than in Babylon. It seems to be agreed that Ovid himself is responsible for the move of Pyramus and Thisbe from Cilicia in Asia Minor to Babylon in Mesopotamia.[21] While it is possible that they have moved to Babylon because Ovid found them in a book of Babylonian stories, as Duke suggests, the move can be interpreted in its own terms: that it contributes to the characterisation of the Minyeid, torn between Eastern exoticism and universalist romanticism. Her story, as told, expresses both her desire for such Eastern exoticism and her domestication of that fantasy world. It produces a world in which Semiramis is not the embodiment of the exotic dream, nor the sexually voracious Eastern Queen of legend as she appears in *Am.* 1.5.11, but is a marvelous builder who is credited with Babylon's lofty brick walls (4.57–8).[22] It is a world in which the Babylonian lovers seem remarkably familiar.

The story of Pyramus and Thisbe is unusual in a number of ways. Not only is the unnamed Minyeid the first straightforwardly human variant speaker in the poem,[23] but her heroine Thisbe is the first — and almost the only — human female to pursue her own desires, which she does within a context of mutual love directed towards marriage. This is one of the few stories in the poem of a fully consensual relationship, with as near to equality and personal choice on the part of both lovers as is possible within the world of the *Metamorphoses*. Moreover, it offers almost nothing in the way of Othering. In comparison with what we might expect of a Babylonian story, and with what may be an existing more exotic metamorphic myth, Ovid and his unnamed Minyeid make Pyramus and Thisbe in fact remarkably ordinary, domesticated, and bourgeois.

The Minyeid introduces her protagonists as explicitly Eastern as well as beautiful (*Met.* 4.55–8).

> Pyramus et Thisbe, iuuenum pulcherrimus alter,
> altera, quas Oriens habuit, praelata puellis,

---

Arabian Gulf, who live very primitive lives and eat literally nothing but fish. According to Perdrizet, they are actually identified with the fish and may, in mythic terms, be reflected in the stories of metamorphosis.

**21** Rosati 2007, 257. Tarrant 2005, 67 remarks on a mild irony in calling Pyramus and Thisbe little-known compared with the others, 'since as far as we can determine they were no more familiar to Ovid's audience than the story that is chosen in preference to them.' On the poetics of *praeteritio* in Ovid, see Cowan 2011.
**22** I thank an anonymous reader for this point.
**23** Rosati 2007, 256.

> contiguas tenuere domos, ubi dicitur altam
> coctilibus muris cinxisse Semiramis urbem.

> Pyramus and Thisbe, the one the most beautiful of young men, the other preferred before all the girls which the Orient possesses, had next-door houses, where Semiramis is said to have surrounded the high city with brick walls.

Semiramis is potentially highly exotic and has already appeared, elliptically, in the rejected stories, turning into a dove (47–8), while the high walls of Babylon were one of the great wonders of the ancient world. The setting places the story in this exotic location, to be reinforced later by the mention of Ninus' tomb. The beauty of the young people, and the terms on which it is introduced, however, are no different from those in any number of Ovidian stories. What is unusual is their next-door houses, indeed attached houses sharing a party wall. Most stories with any domestic reference in the poem are rather more palatial, such as the dwelling of the daughters of Cecrops, king of Athens.[24] Here, however, we are in the world of ordinary, perhaps even bourgeois, families (4.59–62). The lovers want to marry, in the normal bourgeois way, except that their parents object – this is the middle-class world of New Comedy.

There are hints also of the world of Roman Elegy, although the relationship between the couple is more like that of the novel than of elegy, where love on the girl's part is a rarity and mutuality exists only in the imagination of the poet-lover. Elegiac, however, is the communication through nods and signs (4.63–4). Another elegiac element in the story is its focus on the barrier, putting this couple in the position of quasi-paraclausithyron.[25] A house wall divides the lovers, but there is a tiny chink in the barrier (*Met.* 4.65–70).

> fissus erat tenui rima, quam duxerat olim
> cum fieret, paries domui communis utrique.
> id uitium nulli per saecula longa notatum
> (quid non sentit amor?) primi uidistis amantes
> et uocis fecistis iter, tutaeque per illud
> murmure blanditiae minimo transire solebant.

---

[24] Other non-aristocratic abodes in the poem are equally interpretable, be it the simple hut of the recipients of theoxeny, Baucis and Philemon, with its hints at Callimachus' *Hecale*, or the *de plebe* home of the anti-aristocratic Arachne. With regard to Pyramus and Thisbe, the house is bourgeois rather than simple, and, in my interpretation, indicates the ordinariness and non-Otherness of the couple.
[25] Perraud 1983.

> The wall which was shared by both houses was riven by a thin chink, which was caused during construction. This fault, noticed by no one through the long ages (what does love not perceive?), you lovers were the first to see and you made a path for your voice, and through it endearments would pass safely with the least sound.

The hole in the wall is highly symbolic and gives delightfully amusing opportunities for less delicate representations than that of Ovid and his Minyeid – as exploited by Shakespeare. The lovers make full use of the opportunities provided, singing a paraclausithyron together in unison (*Met.* 4.73–5).

> 'inuide' dicebant 'paries, quid amantibus obstas?
> quantum erat, ut sineres toto nos corpore iungi?
> aut, hoc si nimium est, uel ad oscula danda pateres!
> …'
>
> 'Jealous wall', they used to say, 'why do you get in the way of lovers? How much would it be for you to allow us to be joined in whole body? Or, if that is too much, if only you would open up enough for us to give kisses!…'

Continuing the quasi-elegiac theme, but with a distinctly non-elegiac complementarity, they agree to *fallere custodes* (85) at night and meet up in the wilderness outside the city, at the landmark immortalised as Ninny's tomb by Shakespeare's 'rude mechanicals'.[26] Nonetheless, it is another reminder of the exotic location, as Ninus was the husband of Semiramis, as well as eponym of Mesopotamian Nineveh. A few lines later (99), when the daring but terrified Thisbe sees the lioness drinking at the spring, she is given the epithet *Babylonia*, but she behaves as any Graeco-Roman girl would do (*Met.* 4.99–101).

> quam procul ad lunae radios Babylonia Thisbe
> uidit et obscurum timido pede fugit in antrum,
> dumque fugit, tergo uelamina lapsa reliquit.
>
> Babylonian Thisbe saw it [the lioness] from afar in the rays of the moon and fled on fearful foot into a dark cave, and as she fled, she left her shawl which fell from her back.

The outcome is that Pyramus sees the bloody shawl and thinks Thisbe has been killed by the lion, so kills himself. When Thisbe returns and finds him dying, she joins him in death, praying that their parents will allow them a kind of posthumous marriage by enabling their remains after cremation to rest in a single urn (166). The story is heavily romanticised, but not in any way Othered, apart from

---

26 On the interactions of domesticity and wildness in the story, see Salzman-Mitchell 2005, 156–7.

its setting. If Babylonians were thought by Greeks and Romans to deal differently with the dead than they do themselves, there is no hint of it here.[27] Indeed, the combined suicide of husband-and-wife has a respectable tradition in Roman history.

The homeliness of Ovid's story is summed up in the notorious broken-pipe simile used for Pyramus' death-wound (*Met.* 4.121–4).

> ut iacuit resupinus humo, cruor emicat alte,
> non aliter quam cum uitiato fistula plumbo
> scinditur et tenui stridente foramine longe
> eiaculatur aquas atque ictibus aera rumpit.

> As he lay on his back on the ground, the blood shot up on high, just as when a pipe is split when the lead is impaired and it casts out a long jet of water, as the thin hole whistles, and bursts the air with its strokes.

Critics have objected to the anachronism of a simile from Roman plumbing applied to a Babylonian suicide.[28] The spurting blood is a shock, certainly, to which the simile contributes in both content and form, but that does not undermine its point. The cognitive dissonance of place and time is precisely part of Ovid's domestication of this story.

As is well known, this is a particularly erotic death, in which the jet of blood and its watery comparison suggest sexual ejaculation. I offer a small addition to this point, by suggesting that there is a hint about reproduction in the play with metamorphosis of colour. Line 4.125 has the *arborei fetus* spattered by the blood and turning black, also the *radix*. It does indeed also hit the *pendentia mora*, so potentially might discolour them at that point, but in the conclusion of the story, we hear that the colour *in pomo* is black, *when it matures* (4.165). That is, the metamorphic effect of the blood is perpetuated in the species.[29] This, then, can be

---

**27** Herodotus has a brief mention (1.198) of an exotic funeral practice among the Babylonians, which involves burying in honey, although he also claims that their rituals are very close to those of the Egyptians. (For which see 2.85–90, 2.36, and 3.12.). Thanks to my colleague Christian Laes for help on this matter.
**28** Newlands 1986 answers the critics. Like Holzberg 1988, 271, Newlands sees the simile as a break with the romantic, novelistic expectations of the story. See also Schmitzer 1993, Gaillard 1997, Shorrock 2003.
**29** As such, this metamorphosis would be similar to that of the flowers coloured by the blood of Ajax, Adonis, and Cyparissus.

seen as a quasi-conception and later birth for the couple (*Met.* 4.125–7; 4.164–5):[30]

> arborei fetus aspergine caedis in atram
> uertuntur faciem, madefactaque sanguine radix
> purpureo tinguit pendentia mora colore.
>
> By the spattering of blood the produce of the tree is turned black, and moistened by the blood the root dyes the hanging mulberries with purple colour.
>
> uota tamen tetigere deos, tetigere parentes;
> nam color in pomo est, ubi permaturuit, ater…
>
> But her prayers touched the gods, touched the parents; for the colour in the fruit, when it has matured, is black…

I return now to the wider tradition of Pyramus and Thisbe, mentioned above, and its potential intertextual implications. According to late evidence, there was a much more exotic — one might even say more Ovidian — Greek version of the story in which the lovers either were or became a river god and a water nymph.[31] Nonnus, at *Dionysiaca* 6.344–55, has the Peloponnesian river Alphaeus (to feature in the next book of the *Metamorphoses*) speak to the Cilician river Pyramus about their respective spring-beloveds (Arethusa and Thisbe), while at *Dion.* 12.70–89 there is a prophecy of various metamorphoses, in which Pyramus and Thisbe are both going to become running water. Nicolaus of Myra[32] relates a version in which Pyramus and Thisbe begin as humans, but Thisbe kills herself because she is pregnant and Pyramus joins her in death, after which they are transformed into the Cilician river and its nearby spring.

A late antique mosaic on the subject implies a similar trajectory for the story, which Knox regards as an existing strand separate from Ovid's version.[33] It is suggested by Stramaglia, however, that the recent earlier dating of PMich inv. 3793 implies that the 'Latin' and 'Greek' strands may not have been quite so separate.[34] The papyrus, now thought to be Hellenistic, carries a Cypriot story with some similarities to Ovid's version, possibly including communication through the wall and a problem with a wild beast. If, as Stramaglia suggests, PMich inv. 3793's

---

**30** I offer this suggestion as an addendum to Keith 2001, on the wordplay of *amor, mors, mora, morum, morus*.
**31** Duke 1971.
**32** Duke 1971, 320.
**33** Knox 1989.
**34** Stramaglia 2001.

story has a connection with the Greek romance tradition, it would be likely that reports of any deaths would turn out to be false. Stramaglia suggests, perhaps rightly, that the references to Semiramis and Ninus in Ovid evoke the world of the Greek novel, since that couple also was the subject of a romance. I would add that the idea of a behind-the-scenes secret passageway for young lovers does occur in New Comedy, for example in Plautus' *Miles* and Menander's *Phasma*. The lovers being 'next-door' to each other is a standard topos of comedy. If a novelistic or comic version existed and was known to Ovid, he has chosen not to follow it to its conclusion, a conclusion that would be very unlikely to be tragic, as it is here. It would be possible that the homely aspects of his tale have some resonance with an account belonging to those lower genres.

Nonnus' two references to Pyramus and Thisbe are worth further consideration, for their differences from as well as similarities with Ovid's.[35] The first, in Book 6, has the river Alphaeus bemoaning the absence of his beloved Arethusa, which he attributes to the nefarious amatory activities of Poseidon. Other rivers are drawn into his lament, including the Cilician Pyramus, who is encouraged to seek his spring-beloved Thisbe in companionship with Alphaeus' own attempts to find Arethusa (*Dion.* 6.347–55).[36]

> Πύραμε, τί σπεύδεις; τίνι κάλλιπες ἠθάδα Θίσβην;
> ὄλβιος Εὐφρήτης, ὅτι μὴ λάχε κέντρον Ἐρώτων.
> ζῆλον ἔχω καὶ δεῖμα μεμιγμένον· ὑδατόεις γὰρ
> ἱμερτῇ παρίαυε τάχα Κρονίδης Ἀρεθούσῃ·
> δείδια, μὴ προχοῇσι τεὴν νυμφεύσατο Θίσβην.
> Πύραμος, Ἀλφειοῖο παραίφασις, ἡμέας ἄμφω
> οὐ Διὸς ὄμβρος ὄρινεν, ὅσον βέλος ἀφρογενείης.
> ἕσπεό μοι φιλέοντι, Συρηκοσίης δ' Ἀρεθούσης
> ἴχνια μαστεύσω, σὺ δέ, Πύραμε, δίζεο Θίσβην.

Pyramos, why this haste? You have left your companion Thisbe—to whom? Happy Euphrates! He has not felt the sting of love. Jealousy and fear possess me together. Perhaps Cronos' watery son has slept with lovely Arethusa! I fear he may have wooed your Thisbe in his flowings! Pyramos is a consolation for Alpheios. The rain of Zeus has not stirred us so much as the arrow of the Foamborn. Follow me the lover, I will seek the tracks of Syracusan Arethusa, and do you, Pyramos, hunt for Thisbe.

---

[35] For a powerful intertextual reading of the relationship between Nonnus and Ovid, see Paschalis 2014.
[36] Text and translation of Rouse 1940.

What we see here, then, is no bourgeois boy and girl as we do in Ovid, though there are clear allusions to other characters (personified male rivers and female springs) and stories (divine erotic pursuit) with strongly Ovidian associations.

The second occurrence comes as part of a remarkably Ovidian ekphrasis in *Dionysiaca* 12. The context is that the divine personification Season has asked her father Helios about the right time for grapes to grow, in answer to which the Sungod points to a set of prophetic tablets, the third of which will answer her question. Any useful didactic lesson is extensively ornamented with highly Ovidian metamorphic decoration, including the herdsman Argos, Harpalyce turned into a bird, tongueless and weaving Philomela, and Niobe turned to stone. And then (*Dion.* 12.84–9):

> **Θίσβη δ' ὑγρὸν ὕδωρ καὶ Πύραμος, ἥλικες ἄμφω,**
> **ἀλλήλους ποθέοντες·** εὐστεφάνοιο δὲ κούρης
> Μίλακος ἱμείρων Κρόκος ἔσσεται ἄνθος Ἐρώτων·
> καὶ γαμίην μετὰ νύσσαν ἀελλοπόδων Ὑμεναίων
> καὶ Παφίης μετὰ μῆλα λεοντείην ἐπὶ μορφὴν
> Ἄρτεμις οἰστρήσειεν ἀμειβομένην Ἀταλάντην.

> **Thisbe shall be running water along with Pyramos, both of an age, each desiring the other.** Crocos, in love with Smilax, that fair-garlanded girl, shall be the flower of love. And after the goal of the stormy marriage-race, after the Paphian's apples, Artemis shall change Atalanta into a lioness and drive her mad.

Next door to Pyramus and Thisbe are Crocus and Smilax, whose story appears among the tales not told by the third Minyeid sister, Alcithoe. In Nonnus, Pyramus and Thisbe become running water, a change which could refer to a metamorphosis earlier than the situation in *Dion.* 6, i.e. *into* river and spring, or it could imply a secondary transformation from water-divinity to simple water, like that of Cyane in *Met.* 5. Whichever we should envisage here, what it is *not* is the kind of domesticated human love story of Ovid and the first Minyeid.

Pyramus and Thisbe have been transferred from Cilicia to Babylon, but are presented in domesticated, homely, and essentially Greek terms. Their story appears in the relatively 'homely' location (from the Graeco-Roman point of view) of the Theban environs. Whether it was Ovid or some earlier text which moved Pyramus and Thisbe from Cilicia further East to Babylon, he has chosen to fix this story there, but to make it completely domesticated and no more foreign than is the Theban setting in which it is told. In doing so, I suggest that he is playing with the interaction of the universal and the particular. It might be that the universal trumps the particular, with love stories being the same the world over, or perhaps this point subsists in the characterisation of the narrator herself, who aims to give expression to a young woman's choice of sexual partner, irrespective of her geographical and cultural origins.

## 6 Leuconoe and Leucothoe

The baton passes to Leuconoe (4.167–8), the sister who, in Antoninus Liberalis' version, was the mother of the dismembered child, but who here receives the least authorial comment of any of the three. She begins her turn with the very well known (*notissima fabula*, 4.189) story of Mars and Venus, familiar from Homer (*Od.* 8.266–366).[37] It functions as a prelude to Leuconoe's more obscure main performance, which is the love of the Sun for the speaker's near-namesake Leucothoe. The story of Leucothoe is not attested before Ovid.[38] The name 'Leucothoe', 'White Smoke', is played out in her eventual metamorphosis into an incense tree, but also has resonance with the Homeric goddess Leucothea, embodiment of the foam on the top of waves.[39] The scent of incense characterises Leucothoe's race (*Met.* 4.209–13):

> gentis odoriferae quam formossima partu
> edidit Eurynome; sed postquam filia creuit,
> quam mater cunctas, tam matrem filia uicit.
> rexit Achaemenias urbes pater Orchamus isque
> septimus a prisco numeratur origine Belo.

[Leucothoe] whom Eurynome, loveliest of the scent-bearing race, bore; but after the daughter grew, as much as the mother overcame all others, so the daughter overcame the mother. Her father Orchamus ruled the Achaemenid cities and he himself numbered seventh in origin from ancient Baal.

---

[37] Janan 1994, 427–8 offers reading of the Minyeides as less domesticated and more independent, as storytellers who 'stage Woman's desire, not as an affair of anatomy or biology, but of knowledge and institutions'. Apropos Leuconoe's version of Mars and Venus, she remarks that the speaker 'jettisons any 'moral' interpretation of the adultery tale. No husband demands recompense, as in Demodokos' version, or regrets his futile intervention, as in *Ars Amatoria*. Leuconoe's tale ends with the subversive power of laughter, which pays no debts nor acknowledges any allegiance to the social concerns that are its foil', 438. Salzman-Mitchell 2005, esp. 152–3, sees them, rather, as constructing themselves as 'good women', while nonetheless claiming 'a voice for themselves, speech being a masculine prerogative par excellence'.
[38] Rosati 2007, 269.
[39] See also Rosati 2007, 315 on the component [-*thoe*] in the names of sea nymphs. Perdrizet 1932.

Although its exact location is, as often, somewhat unclear, this again is a story set in the East,[40] but beyond the introduction of the cast, there is little in the way of local colour. The Sun visits Leuconoe, who is demurely weaving among her maids, in language that alludes closely to that used of the Minyeides themselves (*Met.* 4.218–21):

> thalamos deus intrat amatos
> uersus in Eurynomes faciem genetricis et inter
> bis sex Leucothoen famulas ad lumina cernit
> leuia uersato ducentem stamina fuso.
>
> The god enters the beloved bedroom, having taken the form of her mother Eurynome, and sees Leucothoe among her twelve maidservants by lamplight drawing out the smooth threads with her turning spindle.

With this description compare that of the Minyeides at 4.32–5 (quoted above). So far, so conventional. The story continues with the god's self-revelation, the girl's initial fear but quick acceptance of his attentions, the jealousy of Sun's former lover Clytie and her tale-telling to Leucothoe's father. Is there anything barbaric here? Initially one might think that the reaction of the father, which is to bury his daughter alive, would qualify as an act of barbarity which could 'only happen over there'. Perdrizet links Orchamus' punishment of Leucothoe with evidence of child sacrifice by inhumation in the Levant,[41] and suggests that we should see in Leucothoe's death-by-live-burial an allusion to such a tradition, which, as he points out, is rejected as 'unRoman' by Livy (22.57). I would like to suggest a slightly different interpretation of this valuable connection between Ovid and Livy, and between Eastern and Western forms of punishment and sacrifice.

Livy's story is set in 216 BC, after the disaster at Cannae in the same year. Livy 22.57 opens with the city in panic: 'not only because of the great disasters they had suffered, but also by a number of prodigies, and in particular because two Vestals, Opimia and Floronia, had in that year been convicted of unchastity. Of these one had been buried alive, as the custom is [*uti mos est*], near the Colline

---

**40** Rosati 2007, 276 on lines 208–11 describes Leucothoe as Persian, though Perdrizet 1932, 210 says that the reference to *Achaemenias urbes* is a prolepsis alluding to the conquest of Babylon by Cyrus, and that the setting is in fact Babylonian. Perdrizet also draws attention to Horace *Odes* 1.11, in which the addressee Leuconoe is advised not to rely on Babylonian calculations (about the future).

**41** Perdrizet 1932, 215–6.

Gate, and the other had killed herself.'⁴² Livy reports that these events were regarded as a portent, as a result of which the decemvirs were instructed to consult the Sibylline Books and an envoy was sent to the Oracle at Delphi. On the instruction of the 'Books of Fate', 'some unusual sacrifices were offered' (*sacrificia aliquot extraordinaria facta*). This involved the burial alive of two couples, one Gaulish and one Greek, in each case one male and one female – an act which Livy describes as *minime Romano sacro*. This, no doubt, is in contrast with *uti mos est*, for the punishment of Vestals who lose their virginity. My suggestion is that Ovid/Leuconoe's story is precisely not one of barbaric human sacrifice which could only happen in other places, or very occasionally when Rome, under great pressure and losing touch with its own wisdom and practices, succumbs to foreign rituals. Rather, it is a story much more like that of the Vestal whose burial alive is integral to the Roman sense of self. There are, moreover, parallels in Greek and Roman myth for the daughter who is punished by her father for unchastity, whether by death (effected or escaped) or by incarceration.⁴³ Human sacrifice, even if it occasionally occurs, is widely regarded as unRoman, but the story in *Met*. 4 is not one of sacrifice, rather of punishment. If it is cruel and unusual punishment, it is punishment which is nonetheless regarded as customary (*ut mos est*) by the Romans. The story of Leucothoe shows more sameness than difference from the Roman perspective.

## 7 Alcithoe and the 'female rape'

The third sister also chooses a story from the East, and one which takes female agency to extremes. Alcithoe's Halicarnassan tale of the boy Hermaphroditus, who becomes his eponym as a result of a merger with the nymph Salmacis, has evoked considerable interest in recent scholarship.⁴⁴ My concern here is only with the question of how Alcithoe's performance relates to the domestication of Otherness for which I have argued in the first sister's story, or the questioning of stereotyping through presentation of similarity which I have suggested may be at work in Leuconoe's account of the punishment of Leucothoe. At first sight, the

---

42 I quote the text and translation of Foster 1929.
43 Apollonius provides a summary of examples at *Arg.* 4.1086–95. Roman fathers had at least the theoretical right to kill unchaste daughters, even if they did not often avail themselves of that right. See Caldwell 2015, ch. 2.
44 See especially Nugent 1990; Labate 1993; Robinson 1999; Sharrock 2002; Salzman-Mitchell 2005; Zajko 2009; Romano 2009; Groves 2016.

gender-inversions and troubling 'aggressiveness' of the presentation of Salmacis might encourage us to see a more predictable 'Orientalising' going on in this Carian story — although its setting is considerably less exotic than for either of the other two. A relevant aspect of the story, however, is its potential intertextual connection with Vitruvius' account (2.8.11), which has it that the Halicarnassan spring, and its associated hostelry, had a civilising effect on local barbarians, and that this reality was deformed into the story of emasculinisation.[45] On the one hand, Ovid/Alcithoe chooses precisely *not* to pursue the idea of Salmacis' pool as an aphrodisiac which, when applied in moderate doses, works to turn barbarians into decent husbands. He (she) chooses not to explore the possible positive association between hyper-masculinity and barbarism, together with its inverse, the risk of (negatively valued) soft emasculinisation which comes from civilisation. Scholars have noted that Salmacis disappears from the story, being wholly absorbed by Hermaphroditus. Romano suggests that 'If the story is a coded way of talking about marriage, the question of why Salmacis seems to disappear becomes less pressing.'[46] Perhaps so, but only if Alcithoe is intending to give expression to the loss of identity caused to a woman by marriage in Graeco-Roman culture. If so, she does so in rather shocking terms.

# 8 Conclusion

Ovid sometimes doesn't do what we expect. I have suggested that ethnic identity in the poem is sometimes much less Othered than might be thought likely. Despite the small number of egregious examples of ethnographic stereotyping, much more extensive are cases where stories of exotic provenance are naturalised and domesticated in such a way as to neutralise ethnic difference. It will be up to the reader to decide whether the effect of this neutralisation is to undermine diversity by the imposition of sameness, which allows white European men to speak for everyone, or on the other hand to celebrate universal humanity.

---

**45** Romano 2009; Groves 2016.
**46** Romano 2009, 558.

# Works Cited

Bate, J. (1993), *Shakespeare and Ovid*, Oxford.
Caldwell, L. (2015), *Roman Girlhood and the Fashioning of Femininity*, Cambridge.
Cowan, R. (2011), 'Passing Over Cephisos' Grandson: Literal *Praeteritio* and the Rhetoric of Obscurity in Ovid *Met.* 7.350–93', *Ramus* 40, 146–67.
Duke, T.T. (1970–71), 'Ovid's Pyramus and Thisbe,' *The Classical Journal* 66, 320–7.
Foster, B.O. (trans.) (1929), *Livy. History of Rome, Volume V: Books 21–22*, Loeb Classical Library 233, Harvard.
Gaillard, J. (1997), 'Le Sang de Pyrame', *Cahiers des Études Anciennes* 33, 109–18.
Galinsky, G.K. (1975), *Ovid's Metamorphoses. An introduction to the basic aspects*, Oxford.
Hall, E. (1989), *Inventing the Barbarian: Greek Self-Definition through Tragedy*, Oxford.
Hardie, P.R. (1990), 'Ovid's Theban History: the First 'Anti-*Aeneid*'?', *Classical Quarterly* 40, 224–35.
Heath, J. (2011), 'Women's Work: Female Transmission of Mythical Narrative', *Transactions of the American Philological Association* 141, 69–104.
Holzberg, N. (1988), 'Ovid's 'Babyloniaka' (*Met.* 4.55–166)', *Wiener Studien* 101, 265–77.
Holzberg (1998), '*Ter quinque volumina* as *carmen perpetuum*: the division into books in Ovid's *Metamorphoses*', in: *Materiali e discussioni per l'analisi dei testi classici* 40, 77–98.
Janan, M. (1994), 'There beneath the Roman ruin where the purple flowers grow: Ovid's Minyeides and the Feminine Imagination', *American Journal of Philology* 115, 427–48.
Janan, M. (2009), *Reflections in a Serpent's Eye: Thebes in Ovid's Metamorphoses*, Oxford.
Keith, A.M. (2001), 'Etymological Wordplay in Ovid's 'Pyramus and Thisbe' (*Met.* 4.55–166)', *Classical Quarterly* 51, 309–12.
Keith, A.M. (2010), 'Engendering Orientalism in Silius' *Punica*', in: A. Augoustakis (ed.), *Brill's Companion to Silius Italicus*, Leiden, 355–73.
Knox, P.E. (1989), 'Pyramus and Thisbe in Cyprus', *Harvard Studies in Classical Philology* 92, 315–28.
Labate, M. (1993), 'Storie di instabilità: l'episodio di Ermafrodito nelle *Metamorfosi* di Ovidio', *Materiali e discussioni per l'analisi dei testi classici* 30, 49–62.
Marazov, I. (2011), 'Philomele's Tongue: Reading the Pictorial Text of Thracian Mythology', in: L. Bonfante (ed.), *The Barbarians of Ancient Europe: Realities and Interactions*, Cambridge, 132–89.
Myers, S.K. (1994), *Ovid's Causes: Cosmogony and Aetiology in the Metamorphoses*, Ann Arbor.
Newlands, C. (1986), 'The Simile of the Fractured Pipe in Ovid's *Metamorphoses* 4', *Ramus* 15, 143–53.
Nugent, G. (1990), 'This Sex Which is Not One: Deconstructing Ovid's Hermaphrodite', *Differences* 2, 160–85.
O'Rourke, D. (2011), '"Eastern' Elegy and 'Western' Epic: Reading 'Orientalism' in Propertius 4 and Virgil's *Aeneid*', *Dictynna* 8.
Parker, G, (2011), 'India, Egypt and Parthia in Augustan Verse: the Post-Orientalist Turn', *Dictynna* 8.

Paschalis, M. (2014), 'Ovidian Metamorphosis and Nonnian *poikilon eidos*', in: K. Spanoudakis (ed.) *Nonnus of Panopolis In Context: Poetry and Cultural Media in Late Antiquity*, Berlin, 97–122.

Pavlock, B. (2009), *The Image of the Poet in Ovid's* Metamorphoses, Madison.

Perdrizet, P. (1932), 'Légendes Babyloniennes dans les 'Métamorphoses' d'Ovide', *Revue de l'Histoire des Religions*, 105, 193–228.

Perraud, L.A. (1983), '*Amatores exclusi*. Apostrophe and Separation in the Pyramus and Thisbe episode', *The Classical Journal* 79, 135–9.

Robinson, M. (1999), 'Salmacis and Hermaphroditus: When Two Become One (Ovid *Met.* 4.285–388)', *Classical Quarterly* 49, 212–23.

Rohrer C.C. (1980), 'Red and White in Ovid's Metamorphoses: The Mulberry Tree in the Tale of Pyramus and Thisbe', *Ramus* 9, 79–88.

Rosati, G. (2007), *Ovidio Metamorfosi Voume II, Libri III–IV*, Milan.

Rouse, W.H.D. (trans.) (1940), *Nonnos. Dionysiaca, Volume I: Books 1–15*, Loeb Classical Library 344, Harvard.

Salzman-Mitchell, P.B. (2005), *A Web of Fantasies: Gaze, Image, and Gender in Ovid's Metamorphoses*, Columbus.

Said, E.W. (1978), *Orientalism*, New York.

Schmitzer, U. (1992), 'Meeresstille und Wasserrohrbruch: über Herkunft, Funktion und Nachwirkung der Gleichnisse in Ovids Erzählung von Pyramus und Thisbe (*Met.* 4, 55–166)', *Gymnasium* 99, 519–45.

Schneider, P. (2016), 'The So-Called Confusion between India and Ethiopia: the Eastern and Southern Edges of the Inhabited World from the Greco-Roman Perspective', in: S. Bianchetti/M.R. Cataudella/H.-J. Gehrke (eds.), *Brill's Companion to Ancient Geography: the Inhabited World and Greek and Roman Tradition*, Leiden, 184–202.

Sharrock, A.R. (2002), 'An A-musing Tale: Gender, Genre, and Ovid', in: E. Spentzou/D. Fowler (eds.), *Cultivating the Muse. Struggles for Power and Inspiration in Classical Literature*, Oxford, 207–29.

Shorrock, R. (2003), 'Ovidian Plumbing in *Metamorphoses* 4', *Classical Quarterly* 53, 624–7.

Solodow, J.B. (1988), *The World of Ovid's Metamorphoses*, Chapel Hill.

Stramaglia, A. (2001), 'Piramo e Tisbe di Ovidio? PMich inv. 3793 e la narrativa d'intrattenimento alla fine dell'età tolemaica', *Zeitschrift für Papyrologie und Epigraphik* 134, 81–106.

Tarrant, R.J. (ed.) (2004), *P. Ovidi Nasonis Metamorphoses*, Oxford.

Tarrant, R.J. (2005), 'Roads Not Taken: Untold Stories in Ovid's *Metamorphoses*', *Materiali e discussioni per l'analisi dei testi classici* 54, 65–89.

Wheeler, S.M. (1999), *A Discourse of Wonders: Audience and Performance in Ovid's Metamorphoses*, Philadelphia.

Wheeler, S.M. (2002), 'Ovid's *Metamorphoses* and Universal History', in: D.S. Levene/D.P. Nelis (eds.), *Clio and the Poets: Augustan Poetry and the Traditions of Ancient Historiography*, Leiden, 163–89.

Woolf, G. (2011), *Tales of the Barbarians: Ethnography and Empire in the Roman West*, Chichester.

Zajko, V. (2009), 'Listening with Ovid: Intersexuality, Queer Theory, and the Myth of Hermaphroditus and Salmacis', *Helios* 36, 175–202.

Zeitlin, F. (1986), 'Thebes: Theater of Self and Society in Athenian Drama', in: J.P. Euben (ed.), *Greek Tragedy and Political Theory*, Berkeley, 101–41.

Part V: **Constructing or Deconstructing Female Ethnicity in Late Antiquity**

Therese Fuhrer
# Thessalian Witches: An Ethnic Construct in Apuleius' *Metamorphoses*

Thessaly had a reputation in classical literature as a centre of magical practices. Sorceresses and witches are frequently referred to as Thessalians. In the following, I examine the question of why such texts regard Thessaly as a location of particular magical skills. I will argue that the Thessalian identity of the witches is an ethnic construction which was already known in the classical period (5th century BCE) but was only justified in narrative terms in the Roman literature of the imperial period, 500 years later. I will begin by briefly recapitulating the role played by Thessaly in the (literary) representation of magical practices and how 'the witches became Thessalian', i.e. how the sorceresses managed to acquire a specifically Thessalian identity. I will then focus my analysis on Apuleius' novel *Metamorphoses* and the way in which the text makes use of geographical and ethnic stereotypes. I hope to show that the notion of 'Thessalian witches' is unmasked and thus in effect deconstructed in the Apuleian text.

## 1 Thessaly as a magical landscape

The major figures to whom classical literature assigns magical powers[1] as magicians, sorceresses, or witches[2] were all women: Medea, Circe and — at the level of the gods — Hecate. Medea is a foreigner who comes to Greece from Colchis at the bounds of the known world, the eastern end of the Black Sea.[3] Circe lives on the

---

[1] This article will not discuss the notion of magic or magical practices, which is problematic from a modern (etic) viewpoint, as the texts discussed here are primarily seen as literary constructs. I refer here to Edmonds 2019, 5–19, which regards the phenomenon of classical magic as a "discourse" and as "ritualized activity" and, taking up the approaches of scholars such as James G. Frazer, Henk Versnel and Richard Gordon, who stress the non-normative aspect, which the actors in classical magical discourses often attributed to themselves.

[2] As for the term 'witch' and corresponding terms in modern languages ('Hexe', 'magicienne/sorcière', 'strega', 'maga/bruja' etc.) cf. Paule 2014, 745 and note 1. The Latin terms and quotations are compiled by Burriss 1936, 138–40 (cf. ibid. 140f. on the male counterpart) and by Paule 2014.

[3] On Medea as an "outsider magician", "invasive outsider" and "always in transit" cf. Gordon 1987, 80–2.

mythical island of Aiaia.[4] Hecate, Medea's 'aunt', is ubiquitous but clearly belongs to the realm of darkness and the underworld; she is secretly invoked at lonely crossroads or in obscure places. None of the above are Thessalian. However – in anticipation of the literature of the imperial period — Erictho can also be regarded as a major figure. In the 6th book of the *Bellum ciuile* Lucan locates her in Pharsalos, and thus in Thessaly. She dwells in the mountainous landscape of Northern Greece, which is already a demonic location due to the civil war battle. This demonic connotation is definitively given by Erictho's appearance in the *Pharsalia*.[5] However a more important point here is that all these women come from geographical regions at the edge of the new or civilised world, regions that in the case of Colchis and of Thessaly are toponymically and hence ethnically identified.

The fact that magical practices are performed by women can be understood as part of this strategy of marginalisation: certain women, by virtue of their magical powers may be able to harm men or to help them — only to the detriment of others. The very fact that they possess supernatural powers as well as knowledge of magic and magical practices makes them unconventional. They are often also socially marginalised and old, sometimes ugly, occasionally sexually aggressive. Further, they come from geographically distant countries or topographically remote regions, and were therefore considered culturally and ethnically foreign.[6] Apart from the *topoi* of the old but still sexually interested 'hag' and the construction of ethnic alterity bordering on xenophobia, the stereotypes also include an element of fear of the liminal, or fear of the hard-to-control and therefore sinister power of an unconventional woman over the socially established man.[7] The characteristics of the non-normative and of alterity are thus determined by gender, status, ethnic origin, and age.[8] But even when male protagonists deploy magical

---

**4** Which only Vergil claims in the *Aeneid* is Caieta, close to the Italian coast (*Aen.* 7.10–24).
**5** See the remarks by Ambühl 2016.
**6** On the connection between alterity and space in modern theories of foreignness, cf. Müller-Funk 2016, 24–9; on the mechanisms of the social (and also the narrative) construction of alterity, cf. Wilden 2013, esp. 102–4 on "alterity as the result of power-based figuration".
**7** On the role of the fantastic and of fantastic literature in the generation and heightening of the alien and liminal cf. Müller-Funk 2016, 84f. and 303–10.
**8** Edmonds 2019, 19: "its alterity is marked by various aspects of alterity of the performers, especially their alien status, their gender and their age" and 111: "gender is one of the markers of alterity, along with age, alien origin, and marginal social status, that indicate the extra-ordinary status of the one using magic." Cf. Padel 1983; on the motif of the old witch, cf. Stanley Spaeth 2014.

powers and potions in myths, they are portrayed as outsiders – such as the Centaur (half-horse, half-human) Nessus – or are lumped together with witches and/or associated with Thessaly as an ethnic location.[9] In the real world they are taken to court because they have damaged others by their actions. The most prominent instance of this is Apuleius, who successfully defended himself against this charge.[10]

Why Thessaly of all possible places came to be regarded as a centre of magic and witches is a question that has often been posed by researchers. In classical literature, the following reasons are proposed: the region is richly endowed with plants that are suitable for the production of magical potions and poisons;[11] Medea first comes to Iolcus in Thessaly, where she uses her magical powers to kill Jason's uncle Pelias;[12] Ovid's Medea in the *Metamorphoses* 'travels' among other places to the Thessalian mountains to collect herbs for her lethal magical potions.[13] The motif of 'drawing down the moon' is also specifically located in Thessaly.[14] In Greek literature from the late 5th century BCE onwards, Thessalian women were believed to be endowed with the ability to draw down the moon using a spinning wheel.[15] This *topos* subsequently appeared in Latin literature too.[16] This 'Thessalian trick' now becomes the characteristic feature of all witches and sorceresses. Pliny the Elder refers to a passage in Menander involving a maid who possessed this trick. Her name was Thessala, a case of the ethnonym being used

---

**9** Hor. *Carm.* 1.27.21–2: *quae saga, quis te soluere Thessalis / magus uenenis, quis poterit deus?*; Plaut. *Amph.* 1043–4: (Amph.): *ego pol illum ulciscar hodie Thessalum ueneficum, qui peruorse perturbauit familiae mentem meae*; Schol. Aristoph. *Nub.* 794: Διαβάλλονται οἱ Θετταλοὶ ὡς γόητες. καὶ μέχρι νῦν δὲ φαρμακίδες παρ' ἡμῖν αἱ Θετταλαὶ καλοῦνται.
**10** Cf. the precise overview in Harrison ²2008, 39–88 and recently in Edmonds 2009, 390–6.
**11** Theophr. *Hist. pl.* 9.15.2; Tib. 2.4.55f.; Hor. *Carm.* 1.27.21f.; Ps.-Sen. *Herc. Oet.* 456f.; *Anth. Pal.* 5.205.
**12** Gordon 1987, 81: "Colchis transposes the motif of Thessaly as non-Greek". Cf. also Phillips 2002, 379f. and 386, who argues that Medea's very short sojourn in Thessaly led to Thessaly becoming "the witches' Thessaly".
**13** *Met.* 7.224–7. See Cazeaux 1979, 272f. The scholion to Aristoph. *Nub.* 749 has a version which states that Medea 'threw out a chest of herbs there which took root and grew' (ὅτι Μήδεια φεύγουσα κίστην ἐξέβαλε φαρμάκων ἐκεῖ καὶ ἀνέφυσαν). See also Philipps 2002, 379f.
**14** For this motif cf. Phillips 2002, 382; Edmonds 2019, 19–32.
**15** Aristoph. *Nub.* 749f. (cf. Edmonds 2019, 3f.); Plat. *Gorg.* 513a; Plin. *HN* 30.6f.; Plut. *De Def. or.* 416 E–F; *De Pyth.or.* 400B. Cf. the lists with references in Cazeaux 1979, 268 and Phillips 2002, 382 and 385.
**16** Hor. *Epod.* 5.45; Ps.-Sen. *Herc. Oet.* 467f.; Mart. 9.29.9–12; 12.57.15–7. On the "whirligig, the spinning wheel device that makes a buzzing noise that draws down the moon" cf. Edmonds 2019, 19–21.

as a personal name.[17] An otherwise unknown writer of tragedies by the name of Sosiphanes is said to have attributed the ability to draw down the moon to young Thessalian women in general.[18] Hence, long before Lucan's Erictho, the epithet Thessalian became a stereotypical way of describing sorceresses, so that the combination *Thessala saga, Thessala maga,* or *Thessala uenefica* (rarely *striga*) is simply a synonym for witch,[19] without any reference to this specific geographical and ethnic origin.[20]

Thessalian witches are thus to a considerable degree an ethnic construction: Thessaly at an early stage in the tradition was dubbed a magical landscape. These witches are also the products of female stereotyping which remains influential to this day.[21] The attribution of ethnic origin from Thessaly provides a possibility of excluding certain types of women as ethnically foreign from the 'normal world' while at the same time presenting them as objects of fascination in literature and thus keeping them alive in the collective imagination.

---

**17** Plin. HN 30.7: *ut Menander quoque, litterarum subtilitate sine aemulo genitus, Thessalam cognominaret famulam complexam ambages feminarum detrahentium lunam*; cf. PCG VI.2, p. 127 K-A s.v. Θετταλη. See Cazeaux 1979, 266, Phillips 2002, 381 and Edmonds 2019, 20. Philips and Edmonds clearly wish to use the variant *fabulam* (instead of *famulam*) printed in the text of the Loeb Classical Library (p. 418) ed. by W.H.S. Jones (Cambridge MA 1963); this would mean that Pliny was referring to a comedy entitled *Thessala*.
**18** Sosiphanes *TrGF* I 92, fr. 1. See Phillips 2002, 318. Cf. Edmonds 2019, 19f.: "The Thessalian trick is the sort of thing that people in far off Thessaly do, so that Thessalian women become proverbial as magicians."
**19** Cf. e.g. Prop. 3.24.10. Cf. Edmonds 2019, 400: "Ethnic identity might provide one means: the *magoi* are Persians, witches are Thessalians, while the astrologers are Chaldeans. The Jews specialised in prophecy, Etruscans make the best haruspices, while the Egyptians know ancient secrets" and ibid. 416: "Some kind of alien social location thus appears to be one of the most valid cues for the label of 'magic' throughout the evidence, as the Greeks (for Romans) viewed the ritual activities of those outside their own cultural tradition as non-normative and therefore characterize the non-normative ritual activities in their own communities as alien. As the Greco-Roman cultural tradition develops, certain cues accumulate particular meanings, so that the specific cue of Thessalian or Chaldean or whatever is linked to the particular activity or other circumstantial factors, but any of them can contribute to the plausibility of the label."
**20** Cf. Bowersock 1965, 277; Phillips 2002, 379: "Thessalian acquires the more general sense of 'magical' and loses any geographical determination"; ibid. 382: "on occasions the Roman poets simply use Thessalian as a synonym for what they might otherwise call 'magical'. It is rare for male magicians to be described as Thessalian." However there is a danger of circular arguments; cf. e.g. Gordon 1987, 81: "If there is anywhere that Medea belonged it was in Thessaly, home of witchcraft"; Medea's sojourn in Iolcus contributed to the fact that Thessaly is regarded as the "home of witchcraft".
**21** See Stratton 2007 and Stratton 2014.

## 2 Thessalian Witches in Apuleius' *Metamorphoses*

The following textual analysis is largely based on the spatial concepts of Michel de Certeau, who speaks of the "performative power" of the narrative, which "does what it says" and hence "creates" spaces, and on the work of Henri Lefebvre, who describes how actors moving in real space always also produce "abstract spaces".[22] On the basis of the geographical and toponymic specification of the space of Thessaly, I would now like to focus on how the town of Hypata in the Roman province of Thessaly is represented as a 'witches' town' in Apuleius' *Metamorphoses*. From the outset, the location of the first part of the narrative (*Met.* 1–3) in the 'really existing' town of Hypata and its surroundings creates the combination of extra-textual reality and fictional action that is typical of the ancient novel. Apuleius clearly adopted the location from his model, the (pseudo-)Lucianic *Onos*, which had also been working with this stereotype.[23] The character of the first person narrator and protagonist Lucius exemplifies the way in which a place in the real world can be perceived, described and read – a world which simultaneously contains non-real, invented and surrealistic elements and endows them with a reality of their own. From the start, the first person narrator and protagonist Lucius finds himself in a space identified with toponyms but also in a space shaped by literature.[24]

Lucius, an educated young merchant from Corinth who is always keen to learn, meets a man called Aristomenes and his companion on a journey to Thessaly. As they laboriously make their way through the mountainous landscape Aristomenes recounts his experiences with two witches in the town of Hypata

---

[22] De Certeau 1980; Lefebvre 1991, 229–91 (ch. 4); cf. Spentzou 2018, 23–30; Fuhrer 2015, 87–91; Fuhrer 2018, 197f.

[23] Cf. Ps.-Luc. *Asin.* 1: ἐς Ὕπατα πόλιν τῆς Θετταλίας. In line with Nesselrath 2014 I work on the assumption that the Pseudo-Lucianic *Onos* as well as Apuleius' novel are derived from the *Metamorphoses* of one Lukios of Patrai, who is mentioned by Photios; see van Thiel 1971, 2–21; Mason 1999.

[24] Cf. Rose 2012, 42 who refers to structuralist concepts of spatial theories, in particular spatial semantics and advocates the important role of 'place' in the real world as a category of literary shaping through a focus on specific geographical location. A specific geographical reference endows the text or narrative with a reality content that can be worked with in the fictional action. On Apuleius' technique of semanticisation of the narrative by means of information about the geographical and ethnic origin characters of and of cultural techniques and objects, cf. Fuhrer 2016.

(1.5–19). Aristomenes tells him that he met a man called Socrates in the town. Socrates relates that in Larissa, a town far to the north of Hypata, he was robbed by the sorceress Meroe, who changed refractory people into animals or creatures similar to animals. Socrates then fled from her to Hypata, where he met Aristomenes. Aristomenes recounts that the following night the witch visited the two men in their lodgings in Hypata and used her magical skills to mistreat them (1.7 and 17). This is the first information that Lucius obtains about this town, which he later sets off to visit. He experiences his first adventures there (1.20–8) and the town becomes the starting point of further — this time involuntary — adventures. As a result of a mishap, he is changed into an ass (3.24), then kidnapped by a band of robbers and taken into the mountains (3.28). At this point, the end of book 3, the story leaves the town of Hypata and from then on, the topography of Lucius' journey remains anonymous until he reaches his hometown Corinth, where he re-assumes human form.[25]

Hypata is located on the northern slope of the Oita mountain range. At the time of the probable composition of Apuleius' *Metamorphoses* in the second century CE, Hypata was the main town of the Greek tribe of the Ainianes. It had been a Roman colony since the year 30 BCE.[26] The town (now Ipati or Neopatra, a village with 700 inhabitants) is still located on the southern edge of Thessaly. However right at the start of the novel the character of Aristomenes tells Lucius that Hypata is a *ciuitas* that 'surpasses all of Thessaly' (1.5.4: *quae ciuitas cunctae Thessaliae antepollet*).[27] This is clearly a fiction, as Larissa is a more important town in political, economic and cultural terms and is also the capital of Thessaly.[28] In this context it is noteworthy that in the text Aristomenes is repeatedly

---

**25** In contrast to the narrative of the pseudo-Lucianic *Onos*; the itinerary of the *Onos* is reproduced by van Thiel 1971, 159. On the geographical indeterminacy of the rest of Lucius' journey in Apuleius cf. Zimmerman 2005, 34 and König 2013, in particular 225. Cf. also Fuhrer 2015, 91–4.

**26** Cf. Kramolisch 1998, 799: "Der nachmalige Augustus vereinte den Stamm um 30 v.Chr. mit Thessalia" ("Octavian, soon to become Augustus, united the tribe with Thessaly in about 30 BCE").

**27** See Stählin 1914, 239 and Kramolisch 1998, 799. Cf. also Stählin, *loc.cit.*: "Unter Hadrian scheint die Stadt besonders geblüht zu haben" ('The town seems to have prospered particularly under Hadrian'); the only evidence to underpin this statement are a number of inscriptions testifying to the emancipation of slaves and a reference to arbitration about a border dispute with Lamia.

**28** See Bowersock 1965, 279. The Thessalian capital is not Hypata, as stated by Slater 2008, 240. However he does capture the point of the Apuleian narrative well: "To be the capital of Thessaly is rather like being the Paris of Kazakhstan: Hypata is simply the biggest place in the boondocks."

described as a "liar" by his companion.[29] The narrative thus clearly contains indications of its fictional status, a fact that should discourage historians and interpreters — particularly modern ones — from reading the text as a source of antiquarian information.

As already mentioned, in the classical tradition Thessaly is regarded as the land of magic and of sorceresses,[30] which is why the (newly) Thessalian town of Hypata immediately appeals to the adventure-seeking hero of the novel. However in this respect too Larissa upstages Hypata, as Apuleius makes Larissa the location of two witch stories. Larissa is the scene of two transformations of human beings into animals (1.7–10) and later of Thelyphron's witch story. The most prominent witch-town in Thessaly is probably Pharsalus, where Lucan's *Bellum ciuile* sets the Erictho scene.

**Fig. 13:** Map of Thessaly.

---

**29** 1.2.5 and 1.3.1. Zimmerman produces a classical circular argument when, referring to the article in 'New Pauly', she concludes that Aristomenes is not lying on precisely this point: "il ne ment pas du tout en la désignant comme 'la ville la plus importante de Thessalie'."
**30** Cf. also Bowersock 1965, 278f.; Keulen 2007, 92. The map is from Stamatopoulou 2007, 212.

However, Aristomenes' story fixes in the reader's mind the notion that Hypata is an outstanding town in Thessaly, the domain of witches and their gruesome magical activities, and it is this notion that sets the action of the novel in motion. With their stories and expectations the protagonists of Apuleius' *Metamorphoses* transform the provincial backwater of Hypata, located at the very edge of Augustean Thessaly, into a 'magical' place; indeed, the town has maintained this label in modern research.[31] Friedrich Stählin, author of the RE article, unhesitatingly states that the town of Hypata enjoyed a "special reputation for Thessalian magic".[32]

In the story of the fictional character Aristomenes, the (newly) Thessalian town of Hypata is endowed with the connotation of a place in which the inquisitive and adventure-seeking young man Lucius is likely to have his expectations fulfilled.[33] Lucius is not disabused of his notion that he is now in a 'wonderland', even though his first impressions of the town are rather sobering and trivial — for example the stinginess of his host Milo, who together with his wife Pamphile lives only on the edge of the town, and the pomposity of his former fellow-student Pythias (Book 1). The second book begins with the 'new day' (2.1.1: *sol nouus*): the 'hero' wakes up and looks forward excitedly to the *rara miraque* that he believes are awaiting him "in the middle of Thessaly",[34] which is world-famous for its "magical songs", the very town in which Aristomenes' witch story started (2.1.2):[35]

> reputans me media Thessaliae loca tenere, quo artis magicae natiue cantamina totius orbis consono ore celebrentur, fabulamque illam optimi comitis Aristomenis de situ ciuitatis huius exortam, suspensus alioquin et uoto simul et studio, curiose singula considerabam.

---

**31** Cf. Bowersock 1965, 279: "Neben diesem fabelhaften Ereignis beweist der Reichtum des Milo ... und der Reichtum der Byrrhena ..., und auch andere materielle Details, die man in dem ausführlichen Bericht des Apuleius in größerem Ausmaß findet, dass Hypata eine geschäftige und große Stadt war" ('Besides this fabulous event [i.e. the transformation of Lucius into an ass] the wealth of Milo ... and of Byrrhena ... as well as other material details that are exhaustively reported in Apuleius' account prove that Hypata was a large and busy town'); Zimmerman 2005, 29 (referring to Kramolisch, 1998): "Lucius s'arrête parfois dans d'autres grandes villes de l'Empire, comme Hypata et Corinthe" and ibid. 31: "La ville avait toujours joué un rôle politique important ... sa grandeur n'avait pas cessé de croître"; referring to both quotations Keulen 2007, 154. However, Harrison [2]2008, 41f., esp. note 11, seems closer to the mark: "Hypata has a big name but a small reality." See also Fuhrer 2015.
**32** Stählin 1914, 239, referring to Ps.-Luc. *Onos* 1.
**33** In *Onos* 4 no reason is given to explain why Lukios hopes to find sorceresses in Hypata. At the beginning of Apul. *Met.* Thessaly is described not as a land of magic but as Lucius' business destination (1.2.1. *Thessaliam ex negotio petebam*).
**34** In fact Larissa is located in the "middle of Thessaly", see above 224f.
**35** The text is from Zimmerman 2012, the translation by Kenney [2]2004.

> Being in any case an all too eager student of the remarkable and miraculous, and remembering that I was now in the heart of Thessaly, renowned the whole world over as the cradle of magic arts and spells, and that it was in this very city that my friend Aristomenes' story had begun, I examined attentively everything I saw, on tenterhooks with keen anticipation.

This is followed by a description of a walk around the town but without any mention of specific locations (2.13–5): Lucius *wants* to believe (2.1.2: *et uoto simul et studio*) that what he is seeing in this town is something 'other than what it was' (2.1.3):[36]

> nec fuit in illa ciuitate quod aspiciens id esse crederem quod esset, sed omnia prorsus ferali murmure in aliam effigiem translata.
>
> There was nothing I looked at in the city that I didn't believe to be other than what it was: I imagined that everything everywhere had been changed by some infernal spell into a different shape.

In his perception, everything is the result of metamorphoses (*in aliam effigiem translata*) brought about by 'an infernal spell' (*ferali murmure*).[37] Lucius reads the world as if it is already the result of transformations or is about to be transformed, and so the town seems to him to be a speaking and also a knowing entity. Lucius comes across as a miniature Don Quixote who has read Ovid's *Metamorphoses* and Lucan's *Pharsalia* and who cannot, and does not wish to, distinguish between fiction and reality.[38]

He makes some progress when he meets Lady Byrrhena, his mother's foster-sister:[39] She warns him about Milo's wife with the telling name Pamphile,[40] saying that she is a witch who targets young men such as himself and changes them into animals to keep them with her (2.5.3–8). But this sounds a bit like small town gossip and jealousy on the part of aunt Byrrhena, who has to stand by and watch while the other woman shows a sexual interest in a young Boeotian, not in her

---

**36** On this passage cf. the rather naïve remark by Slater 2008, 240–3, esp. 242: "… it is utterly impossible to draw a picture of the actual city of Hypata from these words … His text is a remarkably visual description of *not* seeing … Lucius describes the city populated with everything *but* citizens."
**37** Transformed in the negative sense by evil witches into a condition not desired by the object of the magic spell, as a punishment or an act of revenge. On the distinction between negative and positive magic — the latter is exercised only by Isis at the end of the story — cf. Frangoulidis 2008, esp. 6–8.
**38** See Fuhrer 2015, 94–100.
**39** On the character of Byrrhena cf. van Mal-Maeder 2001, 91f.; Frangoulidis 2015, esp. 78–81.
**40** 'The All-Loving' or 'Loved-By-All'. See van Mal-Maeder 2001, 118f.; Stamatopoulos 2018, 206.

guest Lucius.⁴¹ Lucius meanwhile has fun with Pamphile's and his host's maid, the attractive and erotically experienced Photis.⁴²

Lucius accepts Byrrhena's invitation to a dinner party (to which Pamphile for obvious reasons is not invited and would not be allowed to participate) and in the course of the meal he steers the conversation around to his favourite subjects – magic and sorceresses. He refers to rumours of desecrated cemeteries, robbed corpses and old women who flit around funeral processions in Hypata (2.20.1–3). But all that happens is that a guest by the name of Thelyphron of Miletus, whose nose and ears have been mutilated, tells a ghost story set in the town of Larissa that all the other guests have already heard (2.20–31). Neither the narrator's home town nor the setting of the story is located in Hypata, and this confirms the experiences recounted so far: Hypata does not appear to be what Aristomenes' tale of the witch Meroe and Byrrhena's warning about man-crazy Pamphile had led the naïve Lucius to believe.

But people from Hypata are aware that they need to offer the guest from Corinth something more than stale old ghost stories. Byrrhena invites her guest Lucius to the annual town festival in honour of the god of laughter, Risus, a kind of carnival – something akin to an April Fool's joke or a Fasching prank – that is due to take place the next day. He is given the task of devising a prank (2.31.2f.) and explicitly agrees to perform this task and to find 'material in which the god may be dressed up in impressive finery.'⁴³ On the way home from the dinner party in a drunken state he slays three wineskins of goat leather, taking them for robbers trying to break into Milo's house (2.32). The next day he is arrested for the triple homicide and paraded through the town (3.2); but the whole thing turns out to be a show trial as part of the Risus festival. Lucius is even officially honoured by the town for his role as an April fool.⁴⁴

---

**41** Similarly in Stamatopoulos 2018, 208 with footnote 23. However, Byrrhena's warnings have at least the effect of whetting Lucius' curiosity, cf. 2.6.1f.: *at ego curiosus alioquin, ut primum artis magicae semper optatum nomen audiui, tantum a cautelae Pamphiles afui ut etiam ultro gestirem ... me uolens ... praecipitare."*
**42** On the figure of Photis cf. May 2015, esp. 69: "Lucius is less interested in sex than in magic ... but it is clear that with Photis Lucius is not able to separate one from the other"; Frangoulidis 2008, 36 and 52–7.
**43** 2.31.3: *'bene', inquam 'et fiet ut iubes. et uellem hercules materiam repperire aliquam quam deus tantus affluenter indueret.'*
**44** The terms carnival and April fool are after van Thiel 1971, 94f., who also refers to the Roman Hilaria. As van Mal-Maeder 2001, 353 persuasively points out, the nature of the conversation corresponds to that typically offered to the audience by the show speaker in the Second Sophistics. The fact that Lucius, in his very explicit promise in 2.31.3 (quoted in footnote 43), tells the people of Hypata and the organisers of the Risus festival that he is informed about the situation and that

Up to now, the town of Hypata has been the setting for a novel in which, as with Pip in the novel by Dickens, Lucius' "great expectations" have not been fulfilled — because they were false. Hypata is not Larissa, is part of modern, not of ancient Thessaly.[45] The only witch in Hypata mentioned by name so far is the sex-mad Pamphile. The cultural events that the town has so far offered are not *magicae artes* but — apart from Lucius' wild sex with Photis — the carnival with the three wineskins of goat leather representing supposed murder victims. The town's inhabitants construct their own imaginative world but at first everything seems to be rather humdrum and harmless.

But then the adventurous young man is after all, like Alice, led into a wonderland (3.13–8): Photis tells him about the voodoo magic practices of her lady Pamphile, who uses them to try to retain the affections of the young Boeotian man that she desires.[46] A mistake on Photis' part means that instead of the Boeotian the three wineskins of goat leather are lured to Milo's house. After confessing to this error, Photis, to make up for it, initiates Lucius into the mysteries of witch magic. This is the first point at which the rather insipid tale resembles a Thessalian witch story. However the witches that now appear do not at all correspond to the stereotype of the old Thessalian woman who draws down the moon or gathers poisonous herbs; on the contrary, they are young, sexually inquisitive and erotically interesting women. Photis enthralls Lucius with her physical charms and good sex. In the transformation scene recounted by Photis (3.21), Pamphile takes all her clothes off and covers her entire body with an ointment so that she can assume the shape of an owl and hunt her lovers. This seems to correspond more to the image of a sex witch (a figment of male fantasies).[47]

Photis' description of the witch's kitchen in Milo's house on the edge of town, in the tower room under the shingle roof, is also instructive (3.17). Here we find many elements that are familiar from literary magical scenes (§ 4: *apparatus so-*

---

he should have known that it was only a show trial, has hardly been noted at all in research (some indications in van Thiel 1971, 93; van Mal-Maeder 2001, 400); see Fuhrer 2015, 99f.

**45** This is underlined by the information on the place of origin of Plutarch (2.1.1: Thessaly instead of Boeotia), with whom the first person narrator invokes a relationship (3.2.3).

**46** On erotic tying or *agoge* magic cf. Frangoulidis 2008, 3; Stamatopoulos 2018, 68 and 229–32; Edmonds 2019, 111f.

**47** As Edmonds 2019, 112 points out, Pamphile corresponds more to the Circe type, which has no connections whatever with Thessaly. Stamatopoulos 2018, 220–3 interprets Pamphile as being in opposition to the Roman matrona ("Pamphile: an anti-*matrona*?"), comparable with Roman female types such as Clodia Metelli, Sempronia or Poppaea Sabina. Thus Apuleius satirically reveals older or contemporary Roman discourses on the figure of the Roman female libertine.

*litus*), with much more thrown in for good measure. In addition to the usual herbs and ointments we are here presented with letters, parts of shipwrecks, human limbs, remains of flesh, the blood of murder victims and the shattered skulls of wild animals: an imaginatively presented pseudo-magical cabinet of horrors which serves to facilitate Pamphile's erotic adventures.[48] Lucius himself does not enter this room but observes Pamphile's enchantments through a gap in the door. Apart from Pamphile herself, only Photis has access to the witch's kitchen. It is Photis who brings Lucius the ointment that later leads to him being bewitched.

What follows is well known. Lucius is turned into an ass, into that which he had previously perceived in inanimate and animate nature in the town: the product of a metamorphosis. But as an ass there is no longer any place for him in the ostensibly magical town of Hypata. He is kidnapped by real robbers, not by transformed wineskins, and he is forced to carry their loot across the mountains. The remainder of the novel — even for the transformed Lucius — no longer takes place in Thessaly. He finds out about the world of magic and witches only from tales told by others.

## 3 Concluding remarks

Thessaly can no longer be regarded as a marginal geographical region in the Roman Empire of the second century BCE. In the *Metamorphoses*, Apuleius further deprives it of its mystique: He displaces the location of the novel's plot to the margins of the province of Thessaly that was not extended this far until the reign of Octavian/Augustus. In Hypata therefore the witches have only been Thessalians since the reign of Augustus. The cliché of the corpse-robbing and ugly old witch is invoked only in the stories within the story.

Hypata's only sorceress is the 'All-Loving' Pamphile whom Apuleius makes into a new type of Thessalian witch. He rejuvenates her and re-defines her existence as a marginal figure in society who lives on the edge of town, disregards bourgeois conventions and is excluded by urban society.[49] She remains a female fantasy figure, a figure created by male narrators and protagonists, but also a figure who manipulates them.

Apuleuis' location in the (newly) Thessalian town of Hypata thus constitutes a questioning of the old tradition of the ethnic identity of the Thessalian witch.

---

**48** See Stamatopoulos 2018, 230.
**49** See Stamatopoulos 2018, 202–10 (cf. ibid. 224–45).

Thessaly as an imagined and indeed imaginary land of sorceresses and witches provides a stage for male fantasies, fantasies on which the novel sets at least geographical limits when Lucius, after the transformation into an ass, leaves the town and enters the anonymous topography for further magic – 'asinine' – adventures.[50]

# Works Cited

## Text and Translation

*Apulei Metamorphoseon Libri XI*, rec. M. Zimmerman, Oxford 2010.
Apuleius, *The Golden Ass*, transl. E.J. Kenney, London ²2004.

## Literature

Ambühl, A. (2016), 'Thessaly as an Intertextual Landscape of Civil War in Latin Poetry', in: J. McInerney/I. Sluiter (eds.), *Valuing Landscape in Classical Antiquity Natural Environment and Cultural Imagination*, Leiden/Boston, 279–322.
Bowersock, G.W. (1965), 'Zur Geschichte des römischen Thessaliens', *RhM* 108, 277–89.
Burriss, E. E. (1936), 'The Terminology of Witchcraft', *CPh* 31, 137–45.
Cazeaux, J. (1979), 'La Thessalie des magiciennes', in: B. Helly (ed.), *La Thessalie*, Lyon, 265–75.
de Certeau, M. (1980), *L'Invention du Quotidien*, vol. 1: *Arts de Faire*, Paris.
Edmonds, R.G. III (2019), *Drawing Down the Moon. Magic in the Ancient Greco-Roman World*, Princeton.
Frangoulidis, S. (2008), *Witches, Isis and Narrative. Approaches to Magic in Apuleius' Metamorphoses*, Berlin/New York.
Frangoulidis, S. (2015), 'Byrrhena and her Household (*Metamorphoses* Books 2–3)', in: Harrison (2015) 75–88.
Fuhrer, T. (2015), ''In jeder Stadt steckt ein großer Roman': Hypata – eine erzählte Stadt in Apuleius' *Metamorphosen*', in: T. Fuhrer et al. (eds.), *Cityscaping. Konstruktionen und Modellierungen von Stadtbildern in Literatur, Film und bildendender Kunst – Constructing and Modelling Images of the City in Literature, Film and Art*, Berlin/Boston, 87–108.
Fuhrer, T. (2016), 'Korinth oder Madauros? Zur Semantik der Herkunftsräume in Apuleius' *Metamorphosen*', in: M. Benz / K. Dennerlein (eds.), *Räume der Herkunft. Fallstudien zu einer historischen Narratologie*, Berlin/Boston, 67–90.

---

50 Cf. Edmonds 2019, 111: "the imagined power of magic is bounded only by the limits of the imagination, so literature tends to depict magic in more extreme ways, as being more out of the ordinary, more inexplicable, more powerful." — I would like to thank Paul Knight for translating this article from German.

Fuhrer, T. (2018), 'Carthage – Rome – Milan: ‚Lieux de passage' in Augustine's *Confessions*', in: W. Fitzgerald/E. Spentzou (eds.), *The Production of Space in Latin Literature*, Oxford, 195–214.

Gordon, R. (1987), 'Aelian's peony: the location of magic in the Graeco-Roman tradition', in: E.S. Shaffer (ed.), *Comparative Criticism 9: Cultural Perception and Literary Values*, Cambridge, 59–95.

Harrison, S.J. (²2008), *Apuleius. A Latin Sophist*, Oxford.

Harrison, S.J., ed. (2015), *Characterisation in Apuleius'* Metamorphoses. *Nine studies*, Newcastle-upon-Tyne.

Keulen, W.H. (2007), *Apuleius Madaurensis. Metamorphoses, Book I. Text, Introduction and Commentary*, Groningen.

König, J. (2013), 'Landscape and Reality in Apuleius' *Metamorphoses*', in: M. Paschalis/S. Panayotakis (eds.), *The Construction of the Real and the Ideal in the Ancient Novel*, Groningen, 219–41.

Kramolisch, H. (1998), 'Hypáta', *DNP* 5, 799.

Lefebvre, H. (1991), *The Production of Space*, transl. by D. Nicholson-Smith, Malden etc.

van Mal-Maeder, D. (2001), *Apuleius Madaurensis, Metamorphoses. Livre II. Texte, introd. et commentaire*, Groningen.

Mason, H.J. (1999), '*Fabula Graecanica*. Apuleius and his Greek Sources', in: Harrison (2015) 217–36.

May, R. (2015), 'Photis', in: Harrison (2015) 59–74.

Müller-Funk, W. (2016), *Theorien des Fremden. Eine Einführung*, Tübingen.

Nesselrath, H.-G. (2014), 'Language and (in-)Authenticity: The Case of the (Ps.-) Lucianic *Onos*', in: J. Martínez (ed.), *Fakes and Forgers of Classical Literature*, Leiden/Boston, 195–205.

Padel, R. (1983), 'Women: Model for Possession by Greek Daemons', in: A. Cameron/A. Kuhrt (eds.), *Images of Women in Antiquity*, London, 3–19.

Paule, M.T. (2014), '*Quae saga, quis magus*: on the vocabulary of the Roman witch', *CQ* 64, 745–57.

Phillips, O. (2002), 'The Witches' Thessaly', in: P. Mirecki/M. Meyer (eds.), *Magic and Ritual in the Ancient World*, Leiden/Boston, 378–85.

Rose, D. (2012), 'Die Verortung der Literatur. Präliminarien zu einer Poetologie der Lokalisation', in: M. Huber et al. (eds.), *Literarische Räume. Architekturen – Ordnungen – Medien*, Berlin, 39–57.

Slater, N.W. (2008), 'Apuleian Ecphraseis: Depiction at Play', in: W. Riess (ed.), *Paideia at Play. Learning and Wit in Apuleius*, Groningen, 237–50.

Spentzou, E. (2018), 'Propertius' Aberrant Itineraries: Fleeting Moments in the Eternal City', in: W. Fitzgerald/E. Spentzou (eds.), *The Production of Space in Latin Literature*, Oxford, 23–43.

Stählin, F. (1914), 'Ἡ Ὕπατα', *RE* 9,1, 236–40.

Stamatopoulos, K. (2018), *Embracing the Occult: Magic, Witchcraft, and Witches in Apuleius' Metamorphoses*, Diss. Göttingen.

Stamatopoulou, M. (2007), 'Thessalian Abroad, the Case of Pharsalos', *Mediterranean Historical Review* 22.2, 211-36.

Stanley Spaeth, B. (2014), 'From Goddess to Hag: The Greek and Roman Witch in Classical Literature', in: Stratton/Kalleres (2014) 41–70.

Stratton, K. (2007), *Naming the Witch. Magic, Ideology and Stereotypes in the Ancient World*, New York.

Stratton, K./D.S. Kalleres (2014), *Daughters of Hecate. Women and Magic in the Ancient World*, Oxford.

Stratton, K. (2014), 'Magic, Abjection, and Gender in Roman Literature', in: Stratton/Kalleres (2014) 152–81.

van Thiel, H. (1971), *Der Eselsroman,* Bd. I: *Untersuchungen*, München.

Wilden, A. (2013), *Die Konstruktion von Fremdheit – Eine interaktionistisch-konstruktivistische Perspektive*, Münster.

Zimmerman, M. (2005), 'Les grandes villes dans les *Métamorphoses* d'Apulée', in: B. Pouderon/D. Crismani (eds.), *Lieux, décors et paysages de l'ancien roman des origines à Byzance*, Lyon, 29–41.

Charles Delattre
# Exemplary Gallic Wives in the *Erotikos* and *Mulierum Virtutes* of Plutarch: Stereotypes and Comparisons

Plutarch's *Mulierum Virtutes* (n° 126 of the Lamprias catalogue) seems, if we trust its title, to propose a strategy of systematic valorisation of women: this anthology of stories draws up a series of striking portraits, which repeatedly highlight the courage of women, individually or in groups. By affirming that women can act bravely, Plutarch particularly targets, among the possible virtues, that which takes its name from the male element of the human species, ἀνδρεία, and strongly asserts the possibility of its application to women, as did other authors of the same period.[1]

Among all the anecdotes reported, we consider the example of the Galatian Camma (§20, 257E–258C): the happy wife of the tetrarch Sinatos, she is persecuted after the death of the latter by the tetrarch Sinorix, her husband's murderer, who wishes to marry her. Finally, during an appointment, she shares with him a cup of poisoned mead, thus causing the almost immediate death of Sinorix, whom she soon follows into the grave — though not without declaring the rightness of her act in the face of the world. Camma's heroism and worthiness are undeniable in the story, and invite us to identify the elements of comparison that Plutarch implicitly invokes: cowardly individuals and courageous personalities, wives and tyrannical individuals, women and men, are all stereotypes against which Camma is literarily constructed.

It is from the perspective of stereotype and comparison that I wish to approach Camma's character, which has already attracted sustained attention in recent years, particularly among specialists in women's history[2] and those who have questioned the notion of ἀνδρεία.[3] Camma's story is indeed a particularly fruitful avenue for approaching not only writing techniques, but also Plutarch's practices of evaluation, collation, parallel, and contrast.

In the Plutarchean corpus, Camma enters into comparison with herself: two accounts of her action, differing in detail, context and interpretation, are found

---
[1] See for example Musonius Rufus (born about twenty years before Plutarch), *On Why Daughters Should Receive the Same Education as Sons*, 4.15.4–11, with the comments by Caldwell 2015, 19–20.
[2] For example Schmitt-Pantel 2009 and Mirón Pérez 2012, who are more interested in Plutarch's ideas about gender relations than in the format and literary nature of his text.
[3] McInerney 2003.

in two distinct treatises from essentially the same period: the *Erotikos* (or *Amatorius*) and the *Mulierum Virtutes*. Moreover, her characterization as a Galatian introduces a regional identity in addition to her gender identity: not only does Plutarch adopt a literary strategy based on a partial theorization of the relationship between men and women, but he also incorporates the paradigm of comparison between Greek identity and barbaric peoples. It is not surprising to find in the case of Camma a writing model on which entire parts of his literary production — the *Parallel Lives* of course,[4] but also non-biographical treatises[5] — are grounded. By reporting anecdotes about courageous women, Plutarch models the contours of an *ethos*; by emphasizing their non-Greek identity, he takes part in a historiographical debate on the value of stereotypes attached to ethnic definitions, and participates, in his own way, in the reformulation of certain regional and national designations that emerged under the Empire.

# 1 Gendered and Ethnicized Comparisons and Stereotypes

To write about the Galatians and Gauls[6] in the imperial era, at a time when they no longer represent a military threat, is to confront a series of stereotypes that combine allusions to historical events and social practices, distorted repetitions of anecdotes and remarks without verification, and projections and fantasy reconstructions. Moreover, these stereotypes are not unified among themselves, and each obeys the particular strategy of the author who deploys them, or even of the passage that highlights them. Thus, in the 4th century AD, Emperor Julian was able to both celebrate the memory of his stay 'in his beloved Lutetia'[7] and

---

**4** See, following Erbse 1956 (repeated with revisions in Erbse 1979), Stadter 1975, 77–85; Pelling 2005, in particular the bibliographical information given pp. 325–6; Humble 2010.
**5** This is the case of three books of *Aitia*, on ritual details explained by etiological anecdotes: the *Quaestiones Romanae* (263D–291C), the *Quaestiones Graecae* (291D-304F), and the *Quaestiones Barbaricae*, of which the Lamprias catalogue has preserved only the memory (n° 139; see Boulogne 2002, 23).
**6** It should be recalled that the distinction between Gauls and Galatians does not exist in Greek, both terms being rendered by the ethnonym Γαλάτης, or possibly by the herodotean Κελτός. The Gauls defeated by the Pergamon kings are in fact Galatians. I will therefore use 'Gaul' and 'Gallic' as a general designation in this article, and 'Galatian' for precise cases.
**7** τὴν φίλην Λουτεκίαν. Yet he almost died there because of a failing brazier: *Misopogon*, 7.

regret — at least by play or coquetry — the influence that 'a Gallic and barbaric muse'[8] would have on him, so much 'the country had barbarized him'.[9]

The memory of the sack of Delphi in 270 BC, like that of the capture of Rome in 390, is sufficient to allow statements, in both Greek and Latin, that reject the Celtic world at the borders of civilization;[10] but many testimonies, either in the literary corpus or in epigraphy, recall that this rejection is not uniform, and that the definition of the Gauls in relation to Greeks and Romans is a complicated issue. Thus, according to Strabo (4.1.5), Massalia, shortly before his time, served as a 'school for the barbarians' in the region (τοῖς βαρβάροις παιδευτήριον), so that these Gauls became 'philhellenes' (φιλέλληνας) to the point of writing their contracts only in Greek. The supposed evolution of the populations of southern Gaul is based here on a double stereotype: necessarily barbaric in origin, they become, by dint of pursuing a typically Greek way of life (school, public oratory, philosophy), quasi-Greek, to the extent that in their linguistic written practices in the drafting of contracts they are no longer distinguished from real Greeks. Eloquence and writing, philosophical reflection, and legal practice define the standard ideal of the Greek to whom the barbarian is opposed, but to whom the barbarian can also claim to assimilate.[11]

Practicing the art of stereotyping thus implies that a comparison is made between a norm (even a temporary one) and its opposite, between an ideal and the same inverted ideal. Some historians persist in drawing a negative portrait of the Gauls. Appian,[12] at least for the Gauls of yesteryear, criticizes their intemperance, their excess weight, and their lack of endurance, and thus focuses on the categories of diet (δίαιτα) and physical exercise (ἄσκησις), the regulated practice of which is implicitly defined as that of the civilized man: the Greek (and Roman),

---

**8** Julian, *Letters*, 9 Bidez/Cumont: Γαλλικὴ καὶ βάρβαρος Μοῦσα. Letter written from Gaul.

**9** Julian, *Letters*, 8 Bidez/Cumont: οὕτως ἐσμὲν ἐκβεβαρβαρωμένοι διὰ τὰ χωρία. Letter written from Gaul by Julien to Eumenes and Pharianos, his former classmates, whom he encourages to continue their intellectual life devoted to study and reflection.

**10** It is also possible for some authors to build a Greek/Roman/Gaul tripartition. See for example Plutarch, *Marcellus*, 3.3.7: '[The Romans] were forced, when the war broke out, to obey oracles from the Sibylline books and buried alive two Greeks, a man and a woman, and similarly two Gauls in the square called the Oxen Market'.

**11** For another example where Roman, Gallic and Greek identities are associated, without necessarily merging, see the case of Q. Trebellius Rufus, from Tolosa, who settled in Athens after a prestigious equestrian career in Gallia Narbonensis, and received citizenship and various honours, including the eponymous archontate (*IG* II², 4193.13–14 et 34–5, with comments by Spawforth 2012, 112–3).

**12** Appian, Fr 7 *apud Excerpta de Virtutibus*, 11, p. 222, *unde* Suidas, *s.v.* ἄδην. It should be emphasized that he evokes the Gauls of the past, not those of his time.

of whom Appian wants to be the representative. Here, the challenge of the stereotype is to build a general portrait, valid for a vast population, without distinction of social group, age, territory, or gender. The comparison (σύγκρισις) establishes a clear distinction, without possible interference (διάκρισις),[13] which leads to a verdict that is equivalent to a judgment (κρίσις).

Other historians bring the practice of stereotyping and comparison back to the population itself by making distinctions within the group under consideration. Diodorus of Sicily, for example, defines Gallic adult women, children and men in a differentiated way. The blond hair of children — here treated as a distinctive morphological sign of the Gauls — is interpreted as a reverse old age (5.32.2): most children are born with 'grey' hair (πολιά), and it is by advancing in age that they see their hair colour evolve to approach that of their father, as if Gallic children were a separate species that evolved against the human species.

As for adult Gallic men (5.32.7), they sleep with each other, their behaviour opposing both the specific pedagogical norms of classical Athenian aristocratic education and the matrimonial regulations in force at the beginning of the imperial era. Finally, Gallic women are the object of a comparison that associates them not with Greek women, but with Gallic men, with whom they compete 'in size' and 'in valour' (5.32.2 : τοῖς μεγέθεσι... ταῖς ἀλκαῖς). Gallic men thus are confronted with a physical and ethical rival, their own wives, and at the same time seek the company of men who are identical to themselves. The set of comparisons allows Diodorus to think of the sexuality of Gallic men not only as a reflection of that of the Greeks, but also as a series of duplications within the population itself. In this particular case, the combination of several polarized criteria (adult/child, male/female, Greek/Gaul, valiant/coward) makes it possible to manipulate stereotypes and multiply possibilities.

We can see how some of the tropes used by Plutarch are in fact commonly employed by historians at the end of the Republic and under the Empire: the gender distinction between men and women, the evaluation of bravery and the definition of a people as a general entity, in opposition to or in alignment with the Greeks and Romans, are constants in historiographical discourse, each historian modulating these different variables as he sees fit.

More generally, it is the very nature of the discourse that is the same: the creation of a stereotype for a community is analogous to the definition of a character (or *ethos*) for an individual.[14] However, Plutarch's characterization of Camma

---

**13** This is the meaning adopted by Xenophon, *Cynegetic*, 4.1.
**14** On this definition of *ethos*, see Gill 1990, with the nuances provided by De Temmerman/van Emde Boas 2017, 8.

seems quite different from those of Appian and Diodorus, and it is worth considering its scope further.

A final example shows how much the tools of stereotyping and comparison, through which Plutarch operates, are part of a general system of representation. These same tools also condition the design of a statuary group, the so-called 'Ludovisi Gaul',[15] which was part of a series commissioned by King Attalus I, in commemoration of his victory over the Galatians in 237 BC. This series was exhibited in two ensembles, one in Pergamos itself and the other on the Acropolis of Athens, where the victory of Attalus was celebrated with a double comparison: winning Greeks were compared to defeated Gauls, and Pergamon Greeks were compared to ancient Athenians. The Athenian monumental complex included statues of Gauls, but also of Persians: the victory of Attalus in the 3rd century was thus assimilated to those of the Medic wars at the beginning of the 5th century, and this on the very territory of Athens.

While the series as a whole works through the comparison between ethnicized types, the statuary group of the 'Ludovisi Gaul' also includes a comparison[16] based on gender identity. The Gaul is not alone: his wife is represented with him. The only difference between them is that she's already dead, and he's holding her body at arm's length. It is curious to note that most contemporary critics and interpreters downplay the presence of women, simply noting what makes them Gauls, especially their hair and clothing. Some, like Frederick Brenk, deny him any heroic act: 'the Galatian chieftain has just killed (murdered?) his wife and is about to kill himself, in heroic Greek art often a depiction of madness'.[17] Not only is suicide, motivated here by despair that borders on madness, deprived of any heroic value,[18] but it is in any case attributed solely to the warrior, making the woman a mere victim.

---

**15** A copy of the 1st century BC statue is now preserved in Rome at the Altemps Museum (Inv. 8608).
**16** The notion of parallelism and comparison has often been used in iconography, but rarely as part of a reflection on the different practices of the ancient σύγκρισις, particularly in its rhetorical dimension. To my knowledge, only Newby 2016 (for example, pp. 67–8) offers a partial interpretation, using methodological elements from Newby 2002.
**17** Brenk 2005, 94.
**18** The case of Ajax, in the iconography and texts, nevertheless makes it possible to show that there is no direct and necessary link between madness and suicide on the one hand, and the absence of heroism on the other.

But why wouldn't the wife have shown her husband the way by committing suicide?[19] Why deny her this ἀνδρεία that Plutarch explicitly claims for women? Isn't it necessary to attribute to the sculptor of the 3rd century BC and to his patron a thesis similar to that of Plutarch under the Empire? Or should we instead see in Plutarch's treatise a new affirmation, such as a divergent reading of what could be the history, attitude, and *ethos* of the woman thus represented?

## 2 Camma in the *Erotikos*

The insertion of Camma's story into Plutarch's *Erotikos* is understandable, as was the case with the dead Gallic woman of the Pergamum sculptor, not only in terms of gendered and ethnicized stereotyping, but also through a series of explicit and implicit comparisons. Camma is not alone in this treatise, to say the least, as her character resonates with a number of others who belong to different registers. Camma first serves as an *exemplum*, and shares this status with another Gallic woman, Empona. But the treatise is also a dialogue, and the interlocutors talk at length about a female character named Ismenodora, who contrasts sharply with Camma not only because she is Greek, but because she is part of the world of the dialogue. Finally, Camma is a possible reflection of Plutarch, who projects himself into the text under his own name: it is he who, in the last chapters, delivers the longest speech celebrating ἔρως, and redefines it beyond doubt.[20] The example provided by Camma is not only attributed to one of the participants, it is assumed by the author.

We can thus see how much the *Erotikos* is a treatise whose writing is based on parallelism and comparison, in a specular construction.[21] The theme addressed in the dialogue, that of eroticism and conjugality, had already been addressed by Plutarch some thirty years earlier with his *Praecepta Conjugalia*,[22] but

---

**19** We can thus think of the anecdote, reported by Pliny the Younger, of the death of Caecina Paetus, which his wife Arria encouraged by stabbing herself first, and by accompanying her gesture with a now famous '*Non dolet, Paete*' (Pliny the Younger, *Letters*, 3.16.6).
**20** Plutarch's speech is actually part of a conversation that is supposed to have taken place shortly after Plutarch's own marriage and the birth of his son Autoboulos, at least thirty years earlier. To complicate this time lag, Autoboulos himself, as an adult, provides the details of this conversation, in which he did not take part, but which was reported to him by his father.
**21** See the general analysis by Frazier 2005–2006.
**22** *Praecepta Conjugalia*/Γαμικὰ παραγγέλματα, 138A–146A. The *Erotikos* is generally dated to the last years of Plutarch's life (115–125 AD): see Jones 1966.

the form and scope of the debate had changed considerably since. The *Praecepta Conjugalia* are indeed a series of remarks and advice that are defined as a hymn song intended to accompany young people who are committed to culture and philosophy. In the *Erotikos*, one of the characters in the dialogue, Autoboulos, is Plutarch's own son and his father's spokesman.[23] He is also the result of a happy marriage, that of Plutarch and his wife Timoxena. Even if Plutarch never cites his own case as an example in the treaty itself, the presence of Autoboulos guarantees the veracity of Plutarch's comments on the benefits of marriage.[24]

Compared to the *Praecepta Conjugalia*, the *Erotikos* introduces a new modulation by associating the question of marriage with the search for a definition of *eros* and organizes a debate that is based, as in the *Amores* of the Pseudo-Lucian, on a comparison between ἔρως for women and ἔρως for men.[25] Plutarch, however, stands out by placing his reflection in another comparison, the one that distinguishes the institution of marriage from the erotic relationship with a man. The men and women in the discussion are first and foremost spouses: Plutarch combines a comparison in terms of gender (men/women) and a comparison in terms of social relations (marriage/erotic), which leads him to a necessary new comparison between desire (ἐπιθυμία) and love itself (ἔρως).

The distinction between ἐπιθυμία and ἔρως is made thanks to the first speaker, Protogenes, who thus sets the terms of the debate.[26] On the one hand, 'the fulfillment of desire is pleasure and jouissance'.[27] On the other hand, 'love attaches itself to a young and well-born soul and finds its fulfilment in moral excellence through friendship'.[28] Without friendship, love withers and turns away from its object, even if this one is most desirable, 'since the latter does not give as a fruit a character conducive to friendship and moral excellence'.[29]

Three key terms that influence each other are thus linked: the conjugal ἔρως is conditioned by a sentimental alliance (φιλία), and is based on the moral excellence

---

**23** Plutarch also defines his *Erotikos*, in a last specular move, as the reflection of the Platonic *Phaedrus* and *Symposium* while reformulating their terms. A presentation on the Platonic *eros* is included in the *Erotikos* (§ 19–20), but it is only one aspect of ἔρως definition that Plutarch wants to give. If Autoboulos is Plutarch's real son, in whom the father is textually reincarnated, Plato is the spiritual father summoned by Plutarch and immediately put at a distance by his emancipated son.
**24** See his *Consolatio ad Uxorem*, 608A–612B.
**25** See Boehringer 2007 for a detailed analysis of the comparison methods in this text.
**26** Protogenes' speech is in fact combined with Daphneus', who redirects and specifies it.
**27** 750E: τέλος γὰρ ἐπιθυμίας ἡδονὴ καὶ ἀπόλαυσις.
**28** 750D: Ἔρως γὰρ εὐφυοῦς καὶ νέας ψυχῆς ἁψάμενος εἰς ἀρετὴν διὰ φιλίας τελευτᾷ.
**29** 750E: εἰ καρπὸν ἤθους οἰκεῖον εἰς φιλίαν καὶ ἀρετὴν οὐκ ἀποδίδωσιν.

(ἀρετή) that it also guarantees.³⁰ It is this erotic-matrimonial system and hierarchy of desires that Camma's story reproduces exactly: to the violent desire of the evil Sinorix, Camma opposes the memory of her conjugal union with Sinatos and shows her virtue by remaining faithful to the sentimental alliance that united them.

But, as we have said, Camma also contrasts with one of the characters in the dialogue who, despite her absence, guides part of the conversation: Ismenodora. At the beginning of the dialogue, the participants in the conversation reported that Ismenodora, a widow of good reputation, wished to marry a young man, Bacchon, and met with hostility from his entourage. The conversation is interrupted after a few exchanges by surprising news: Ismenodora had the young man kidnapped – his active participation in the kidnapping is suspected (775C–D) – and the wedding is about to be celebrated. Although some of the participants in the discussion discredit Ismenodora, others defend her, recall her honorability and put forward the hypothesis that 'a kind of divine breath has really seized this woman, a breath even stronger than human reasoning'.³¹

The final speech (§ 21–25, 766D–771C) therefore develops in a troubled context. After delivering a eulogy of the god Eros (§ 13–18) and a presentation on the Platonic ἔρως (§ 19–20), Plutarch at last makes a polemical apology of conjugal love: it can only be built over time – an essential notion for understanding the role attributed to Autoboulos in this text – and pleasure plays an important role in consolidating the feeling of alliance (φιλία) indispensable to conjugal *eros*. Union is a true 'mixture'³² of feelings, bodies and beings, which implies that both members of the couple demonstrate moral excellence (ἀρετή).

The goal pursued by Ismenodora, the conjugal union with Bacchon, is therefore honourable, even if the means used are surprising. The decency of the young man on the one hand, the exemplary attitude of the widow so far on the other hand, explain that the anecdote only evokes the irony or mockery of participants in the conversation who had a personal interest in seeing Bacchon single. Moreover, the stratagem meets with the noisy approval of others and the assent of Plutarch, even of the god himself: 'Obviously', concludes the treaty, the god Eros

---

**30** Beneker 2008, 693: '*eros* is an essential part of a marriage that is held together by self-control and mutual affection rather than external coercion. (…) Carried to its fullest extent, Plutarch's argument, which takes as its starting point the intelligence and virtue of an individual rather than his or her sex, must conclude that the heterosexual, marital union can be ethically fulfilling for both parties'. See also, for similar conclusions, Aguilar 1990; Nikolaidis 1997; Boulogne 2009–2010.
**31** 755E: ἀλλ' ἔοικε θεία τις ὄντως εἰληφέναι τὴν ἄνθρωπον ἐπίπνοια καὶ κρείττων ἀνθρωπίνου λογισμοῦ.
**32** 769F: κρᾶσις.

'assists with pleasure and benevolence in what is happening'.[33] Indeed, the result of the affair will be a conjugal union that can be expected to be perfect, based on the model of the one that recalls Plutarch himself and his wife. In a comical way, in the *Erotikos*, Ismenodora has taken the initiative to break an unsustainable situation: the dialogue ends, like a comedy, with the celebration of the wedding.

The contrast that the *Erotikos* builds between Camma and Ismenodora is worth more in tone than in substance. By choosing to report two anecdotes in his final speech, one dedicated to Camma and the other to the Gallic Empona, Plutarch introduces two *exempla* which, in a serious way, lead to the same conclusion as the story of Ismenodora: the Galatian Camma and the Gallic Empona know how to show value in affirming their fidelity to their spouses. Camma is initially defined only by her extreme beauty: it is her actions that contribute to making her an exemplary wife. By invoking her deceased husband to justify her crime, Camma proclaims her unfailing fidelity, and her death is in itself exemplary, since she expires 'with firmness and great joy' (εὐθαρσῶς καὶ ἱλαρῶς). Plutarch clarifies the scope of the anecdote by providing an argument in the text itself: 'the well-born woman united by Love to a legitimate husband would bear more easily to be hugged by bears or snakes than to be touched by a stranger and to share her bed'.[34]

Similarly, the second anecdote, dedicated to the Gallic Empona, illustrates the 'community of perfect fidelity'[35] which is characteristic of 'love between spouses':[36] Empona helped to hide her husband Civilis, sentenced to death, and secretly pursued a married life with him, at risk of her life. The reading key provided by Plutarch once again brings attention back to the nature of conjugality: the text is not about women, but about wives, with an ideally 'noble' soul (γενναία) and exemplary conduct. Relying on Gallic women to illustrate the excellence of Greek marriage[37] is possible because it testifies to the universal power of ἔρως, within the limited framework defined by the ideal partners that Plutarch convenes. Camma and Empona justify Ismenodora's attitude, because the author carefully imbues their action with the exemplary conjugality that he endeavours to define.

---

33 771E: δῆλος γάρ ἐστι χαίρων καὶ παρὼν εὐμενὴς τοῖς πραττομένοις.
34 768B: Ἡ δὲ γενναία γυνὴ πρὸς ἄνδρα νόμιμον συγκραθεῖσα δι' Ἔρωτος ἄρκτων ἂν ὑπομείνειε καὶ δρακόντων περιβολὰς μᾶλλον ἢ ψαῦσιν ἀνδρὸς ἀλλοτρίου καὶ συγκατάκλισιν. See Tsouvala 2014, 202.
35 770C: πάσης πίστεως κοινωνίαν.
36 more precisely, 'love for and from a wife', 770C: γυναικείων ἐρώτων.
37 See §23, 768E.

## 3 *Camma in the* Mulierum Virtutes

Probably composed in the same years as the *Erotikos*, the *Mulierum Virtutes* incorporates the same story of Camma. The text is no longer a dialogue, or even a treatise, but an anthology of twenty-seven stories,[38] preceded by an explanatory preface. As Plutarch himself explains, the stories are material he compiled as he read them — there are, in particular, similarities between some stories and passages from the *Parallel Lives*,[39] which material is assembled here and put at the service of a new project.

As with thematic anthologies from the 1st and 2nd centuries AD,[40] it is not a simple accumulation of sheets or note-taking. According to the preface, the compilation was composed on the occasion of the death of a friend, or at least an acquaintance, Leontis, who is described as 'a perfect woman' (ἀρίστη).[41] The anthology is to serve as a *consolatio*, and its recipient is also a woman, Clea.[42]

The preface promises a persuasive, but also pleasant reading, which indicates that the various tales stored in Plutarch's archives have been reworked. This is one of the points that explains the significant differences in writing between Camma's story in the *Erotikos* and that in the *Mulierum Virtutes*.

Plutarch inserts in particular a development dedicated to Camma's 'excellence' (ἀρετή): we move from a simple physical description in the *Erotikos* to complete praise of her virtues: a catalogue that includes her intelligence, her generosity, her benevolence and her kindness, and also the dignity with which she assumed her functions as priestess of Artemis. The amplification helps to define Camma as a perfect wife, and as an admirable woman in every respect. Her generosity towards others is only equalled by her piety, to the point that she becomes

---

[38] Each anecdote is presented independently as a unit, which is reinforced in the manuscript by the insertion of titles and in contemporary editions by the distinction between paragraphs, while binding particles make all the tales a long unified text.
[39] See Boulogne 2002, 37 (n. 204).
[40] Including Plutarch's own *Narrationes amatoriae*, 771E–775E, to which the anthologies of Parthenios of Nicaea and Antoninus Liberalis can be compared, as well as Philo's set of treatises known today under the title *Exposition of the Law*, with the recent commentary of Niehoff 2018, 87f, for portraits of exemplary wives, mothers and daughters.
[41] 242F: she may be the daughter of Publius Memmius Theocles.
[42] Clea is related to Eurydice and Pollianus, the dedicatee thirty years earlier of the *Praecepta Conjugalia*. She could be either their daughter Flavia Clea, to whom Plutarch dedicates his *Isis and Osiris* in the same years (Boulogne 2002, 27–8), or Flavia Clea's grandmother (Puech 1992, 4842–3, and Puech 1994).

the 'ornament' (κόσμος) of the goddess' sanctuary.[43] The action which was the manifest sign of her virtue in the *Erotikos* is also the consequence of it here.

Equally significant, Plutarch changes Camma's attitude in the sanctuary after her husband's murder. While in the *Erotikos*, Camma took refuge in order to dedicate herself to the memory of the deceased, and 'admitted no man to her, although she was sought in marriage by several kings or princes',[44] in the *Mulierum Virtutes* she prepares for revenge: 'she tolerated the crime of Sinorix, not in a pitiful abatement, but with courage and intelligently waiting her time'.[45]

Plutarch here more strongly emphasizes the strategy implemented by Camma. Faced repeatedly with Sinorix's indelicate assaults, she builds a graduated response to his insistence, not to attenuate it, but to excite him.[46] Apparently persuaded by her entourage, she finally gives in and receives Sinorix for the fatal meeting, thus, this time, springing the final trap only after the long delay for preparation — a delay which is a trick in itself. In the *Mulierum Virtutes* version, it is not only the final trick, but all its preparation and Camma's self-control that underline an ἀρετή that they help to define. Far from being defined negatively, her concealment and manipulation refer to her modesty (σωφροσύνη) and intelligence (σύνεσις).

The end of the anecdote, despite very similar circumstances, and sometimes even identical wording, differs significantly on one point. In the *Erotikos*, Camma addresses the deceased Sinat and presents Sinorix's murder both as revenge and as an opportunity to find her husband in death. In the anthology, Camma now addresses Artemis. While she had just soiled the goddess' sanctuary, the young woman directly challenges her by recalling the special bond that unites them ('oh most honoured divinity', 'ὦ πολυτίμητε δαῖμον') and by calling her into a fiction of debate on the validity of her act ('I take you as a witness', 'μαρτύρομαί σε'). Revenge is here again given as Camma main's motivation, but this time with the statement that Camma has not enjoyed life all this time. Sinorix, who was in the *Erotikos* only 'the most evil of men' (κάκιστον ἀνθρώπων), becomes here 'the most unholy of all men' (ὦ πάντων ἀνοσιώτατε ἀνθρώπων), a sign that Camma's

---

[43] Plutarch practices here an *interpretatio Graeca* without mention of local divinity. While Brenk 2005 links this Artemis to the Gallic Epona, by parallel with the Empona who appears in the *Erotikos*, Hofeneder 2004 brings her closer to the Anatolian world (according to him, Camma could even be a Phrygian, not a Galatian name).

[44] οὐδένα προσιεμένη, μνωμένων πολλῶν βασιλέων καὶ δυναστῶν αὐτήν.

[45] φέρουσαν οὐκ οἰκτρῶς καὶ ταπεινῶς ἀλλὰ θυμῷ νοῦν ἔχοντι καὶ καιρὸν περιμένοντι τὴν τοῦ Σινόριγος παρανομίαν.

[46] 'at first, the woman's refusals were not too harsh, then gradually she seemed to soften' (ἦσαν οὖν τὸ πρῶτον ἀρνήσεις οὐκ ἄγαν ἀπηνεῖς τῆς γυναικός, εἶτα κατὰ μικρὸν ἐδόκει μαλάσσεσθαι).

ἀρετή is now interpreted in a context sanctioned by the divinity. The pitiful, even ridiculous death of Sinorix[47] contrasts with the death full of firmness and joy of Camma, who resisted agony as long as she did not know whether Sinorix was dead or not.

If the general meaning of the anecdote is the same in both treaties, Plutarch emphasizes in this second composition the violence of the anecdote, in particular the decisive role played by Camma not only in the assassination of Sinorix, but in the preparation of the plot. This is a common feature of all the notices written in the anthology, whether they are about women in groups (§ 2–15), two women (§ 14–15), or women acting alone (§ 16–28): wives take violent action, either to resolve a dangerous situation or to take revenge. What was envisaged in a comic way for Ismenadora becomes a type of action here, characterized by a spirit of decision and sometimes cunning.[48]

Much more than in the *Erotikos*, Plutarch uniformly encompasses the whole world in his selections in the *Mulierum Virtutes*:[49] Greek women, Persian women and Gallic women act in a similar way, any linguistic or ethnic distinction being erased. As wives or mothers, they take the place of defaulting men when a situation requires it.[50]

The anthology thus establishes a network of possible comparisons, from which ethnic, linguistic or cultural particularities and specificities are excluded. Certainly, the example of Camma is part of a unit (§ 20–3) dedicated to Galatia in the 2nd and 1st centuries BC. This group of four entries therefore constitutes a remarkable subset in the work, in a historical and geographical context where the Greek, Gallic, and Roman worlds meet.[51] The Galatian Chiomara, wife of the tetrarch Ortiagon, a hundred years before Camma's time, was faithful to her husband (§ 22) as Camma is to Sinat. The Sinorix killed by Camma (§ 20) may be the

---

**47** 'the Galatian already felt the poison acting and disturbing his body, and jumped on a chariot in the hope that the bumps and tremors would be beneficial to him' (ὁ Γαλάτης καὶ τοῦ φαρμάκου δρῶντος ἤδη καὶ διακινοῦντος τὸ σῶμα συναισθόμενος ἐπέβη μὲν ὀχήματος ὡς σάλῳ καὶ τιναγμῷ χρησόμενος).
**48** It is to this aspect that Polyaenus has been sensitive when he integrated certain passages of *Mulierum Virtutes* (§ 1–8, 10, 11, 14, 16–20, 24, 25 and 27) into his *Strategemata* (7.47–50; 8.26–71). The hypothesis of an independent loan by Plutarch and Polyaenus from a common source seems unfounded; see Boulogne 2002, 30–1. See Mirón Pérez 2012 for a full description of the women's actions in the *Mulierum Virtutes*.
**49** Marasco 1991, 337–8.
**50** D'Ippolito 1991, 14–18.
**51** Following the victory of Eumenes II of Pergamon over the Galatians, the latter obtained an autonomy guaranteed by the intervention of the Roman Senate.

father of Deiotaros Philoromaios,[52] who escaped the massacre of the Galatian tetrarchs organized by Mithridates,[53] a massacre in which only a girl from Pergamos had the courage to perform the funeral rites for her lover (§ 23). Finally, Stratonice, whose courage is celebrated in §21, is the wife of Deiotaros Philopator, son of Deiotaros and therefore grandson of Sinorix. But the chronological disorder imposed by the sequence of entries aims precisely to break these contextual links to make all wives heroines, not only in the religious sense,[54] but more generally, as members of a 'heroine council' (βουλὴ τῶν ἡρωίδων), as Plutarch puts it in a remarkable expression about Aretaphila (§ 19, 255E).

Plutarch explicitly adopts the category of praise by reporting these different cases. Their accumulation reinforces a thesis stated in the preface: 'the woman about whom we speak the least outside her home, in bad or good',[55] is not 'a perfect woman' (ἀρίστην), contrary to Thucydides' opinion, and her name should not be 'locked' (κατάκλειστον) with a ban on 'leaving the house' (ἀνέξοδον). The examples chosen illustrate that 'both a man's and a woman's virtue are one'.[56]

Like the *Erotikos*, the *Mulierum Virtutes* is not about women in general, but about wives: the only exception is this 'little woman' (γύναιον) from Pergamon, this 'girl' (παιδίσκη) with a big heart who plays the role of Antigone (§ 23), and who behaves almost like a wife, or at least a decent relative. The eulogy here is doubly funereal: it is part of the context of Leontis' death, for which the text is a *consolatio*, and it is a *laudatio*, similar to the one that, 'in the name of the State, gives women as well as men, after their death, the appropriate praise'.[57]

However, the anthology partially escapes this program, or overflows it by its margins. While Plutarch insists, both in the *Erotikos* and in the *Mulierum Virtutes*, on conjugality as a source and consequence of 'moral excellence' (ἀρετή), the violent actions, attacks, assassinations or suicides that are the lot of the women he describes escape the framework of conjugal normality.

While in the *Erotikos* the examples of Empona and Camma still resonate in harmony with the case of Ismenodora, the disjunction is more violent in the anthology between the brutally decisive women of its stories and Clea, the dedicatee and member of Plutarch's close circle, and her family. The first notice can serve as a reading guide for the whole book: it talks about the Trojans who survived

---

52  According to *IG*, II.2, n°3429, if the text provided by the editors is deemed acceptable.
53  Appian, *Mithridatic war*, 46/178.
54  This is the case in § 18 for the Greek Lampsake, who receives 'heroic honours', ἡρωικὰς τιμάς.
55  242E: ἧς ἂν ἐλάχιστος ᾖ παρὰ τοῖς ἐκτὸς ψόγου πέρι ἢ ἐπαίνου λόγος.
56  242F: τὸ μίαν εἶναι καὶ τὴν αὐτὴν ἀνδρός τε καὶ γυναικὸς ἀρετήν.
57  242F: ὥσπερ ἀνδράσι καὶ γυναιξὶ δημοσίᾳ μετὰ τὴν τελευτὴν τοὺς προσήκοντας ἀποδιδοὺς ἐπαίνους.

Ilion — Aeneas is not named — and who wandered to the mouth of the Tiber without deciding to settle there. The installation on the spot is determined by their wives, who by trick and violence burn the ships to prevent any departure. The Trojan woman who inspires the decision is Rhome, whose name anticipates that of Rome, but also underscores the 'strength' (ῥώμη) of these women. The women impose a decision on their husbands, who may be courageous, but are also helpless and uncertain — and they do it sometimes at the price of a revolt. Are they really examples to follow?

Other instances show that the anthology does not function exactly like a reservoir of motives to be imitated,[58] a repertoire of actions that would promote gender equality.[59] Admirable in their ἀρετή, the wives in question push the bounds of behaviour that elicits praise as long as the reader stays at a reasonable distance. Behind the *ethos* of these extremely brave wives is sometimes hidden the type of the weak or treacherous woman: when it comes to the Roman woman Clelia, a particularly famous example of courage, Plutarch indicates 'that admiring in her a strength and audacity superior to those of a woman, Porsenna considered her worthy of a gift proper to a warrior'.[60] And when a cruel decision of the tyrant Aristotimos of Elis must be described, it is 'a vile and womanly act, not that of a leader educated in the handling of business'.[61] Even if these harsh words are attributed to characters in the story, not to the omniscient narrator, they nevertheless contribute to the strengthening of the hierarchy between the sexes. While some women may show courage (ἀνδρεία), their nature does not make them equal to men (ἄνδρες).

The plural of the Greek title, Γυναικῶν Ἀρεταί (*Mulierum Virtutes*), is here to be taken into account: the anthology gathers a plurality of heroic actions, which stage the exceptional to show what *even wives* are capable of, especially when men are lacking. But the plural also emphasizes the diversity of the natures of each person's merit: 'by conforming to the underlying habits, temperament, diet, and the kind of life', the virtue is tinged with 'particular colours'.[62] If there is therefore a singular notion which is ἀρετή, it manifests itself in plural and irreducible forms, which can be admired, but which should not always be imitated.

---

**58** There is also talk of cowardly, vile or cruel women: the mother of Nicocrates, tyrant of Cyrene, is burned alive as punishment after her son has been killed.
**59** The bibliography on *Mulierum Virtutes* rightly emphasizes this point.
**60** 250F: τὴν ῥώμην θαυμάσαντα καὶ τὴν τόλμαν αὐτῆς ὡς κρείττονα γυναικὸς ἀξιῶσαι δωρεᾶς ἀνδρὶ πολεμιστῇ πρεπούσης.
**61** 252D: καὶ λέγων ἀγεννὲς εἶναι καὶ γυναικῶδες, οὐκ ἀνδρὸς ἡγεμονικοῦ καὶ πράγμασι χρῆσθαι μεμαθηκότος τὸ ἔργον.
**62** 243C: ὥσπερ χροιὰς ἰδίας.

It is the same definition of a limited universalism that explains both the selection of foreign examples, Galatians or Persians, and their reduction within a strictly Greek reading framework. On the one hand, we can see in these examples the sign of Plutarch's general benevolence towards individuals (φιλανθρωπία), which unites all disparate peoples in humanity.[63] On the other hand, making all these women Greek wives not only ignores ethnographic specificities, but above all locks all cases into a status considered exemplary, which ensures the promotion of the wife provided that she confines herself to her role as wife. The diversity and individual decisions of the women never appear, of course; they only exist as members of the conjugal couple. In this anthology on women addressed to a woman, it is Plutarch and the husband who, once again, regulate the discourse.

## Works Cited

Aguilar, R.M. (1990), 'La mujer, el amor y el matrimonio en la obra de Plutarco', *Faventia* 12–13, 307–25.

Becchi, Fr. (2009), 'La notion de *philanthropia* chez Plutarque. Contexte social et sources philosophiques', in: J. Ribeiro Ferreira *et al.* (eds.), *Symposium and Philanthropia in Plutarch*, Coimbra, 263–73.

Beneker, J. (2008), 'Plutarch on the Role of Eros in a Marriage', in: A. Nikolaidis (ed.), *The Unity of Plutarch's Work. Moralia Themes in the Lives, Features of the Lives in the Moralia*, Berlin/New York, 689–99.

Boehringer, S. (2007), 'Comparer l'incomparable. La *sunkrisis* érotique et les catégories sexuelles dans le monde gréco-romain', in: B. Perreau (ed.), *Le choix de l'homosexualité. Recherches inédites sur la question gay et lesbienne*, Paris, 39–56.

Boulogne, J. (2002), *Plutarque, Œuvres morales, Traités 17–19* [= 242F–316B], t. IV, Paris.

Boulogne, J. (2009–2010), 'La philosophie du mariage chez Plutarque', in: *Ploutarchos* 7, 23–34.

Brenk, F.E. (2005), 'The barbarian within. Gallic and Galatian heroines in Plutarch's *Erotikos*', in: A. Pérez Jiménez/F. Titchener (eds.), *Historical and Biographical Values of Plutarch's Works. Studies Devoted to Professor Philip A. Stadter by the International Plutarch Society*, Malaga/Logan, 93–106.

Caldwell, L. (2015), *Roman Girlhood and the Fashioning of Femininity*, Cambridge, Ma.

De Temmerman, K./E. van Emde Boas (2017), 'Character and Characterization in Ancient Greek Literature. An Introduction', in: K. de Temmerman/E. van Emde Boas (eds.), *Characterization in Ancient Greek Literature*, Leiden, 1–23.

D'Ippolito, G. (1991), 'Il corpus plutarcheo come macrotesto di un progetto antropologico: modi e funzioni della autotestualità', in: G. D'Ippolito/I. Gallo (eds.), *Strutture formali dei Moralia di Plutarco. Atti del III convegno plutarcheo, Palermo, 3–5 maggio 1989*, Naples, 9–18.

---

[63] See Becchi 2009.

Erbse, H. (1956), 'Die Bedeutung der Synkrisis in den Parallelbiographien Plutarchs', *Hermes* 84, 398–424.

Erbse, H. (1979), 'Die Bedeutung der Synkrisis in den Parallelbiographien Plutarchs', in: *Ausgewählte Schriften zur Klassischen Philologie*, Berlin/New York, 478–505.

Frazier, Fr. (2005–2006), 'L'*Érotikos*. Un éloge du Dieu Éros ? Une relecture du dialogue de Plutarque', *Ploutarchos* 3, 63–101.

Gill, C. (1990), 'The Character-Personality Distinction', in: C.B. Pelling, *Characterization and Individuality in Greek Literature*, Oxford, 1–31.

Hofeneder, A. (2004), 'Kann man Kamma, die Frau des Galatertetrarchen Sinatos, für die keltische Religion heranziehen?', in: H. Heftner/K. Tomaschitz (eds.), *Ad fontes! Festschrift für Gerhard Dobesch zum 65. Geburtstag am 15. September 2004, dargebracht von Kollegen, Schülern und Freunden*, Vienna, 705–11.

Humble, N. (ed.), (2010), *Plutarch's Lives. Parallelism and Purpose*, Swansea.

Jones, C.P. (1966), 'Towards a chronology of Plutarch's works', *Journal of Roman Studies* 56, 61–74.

Marasco, G. (1991), 'Sul *Mulierum uirtutes* di Plutarco', in: G. D'Ippolito/I. Gallo (eds.), *Strutture formali dei Moralia di Plutarco. Atti del III convegno plutarcheo di Palermo 1989*, Naples, 335–45.

McInerney, J. (2003), 'Plutarch's manly women', in: R.M. Rosen/I. Sluiter (eds.), *Andreia. Studies in manliness and courage in classical antiquity*, Leiden, 319–44.

Mirón Pérez, Mª D. (2012), 'Plutarco y la virtud de las mujeres', in: M. González González (ed.), *Mujeres de la antigüedad. Texto e imagen. Homenaje a Mª Ángeles Durán López*, Malaga, 211–58.

Newby, Z. (2002), 'Reading programs in Graeco-Roman art. Reflections on the Spada reliefs', in: D. Fredrick (ed.), *The Roman Gaze. Vision, Power, and the Body*, Baltimore, 110–48.

Newby, Z. (2016), *Greek Myths in Roman Art and Culture. Imagery, Values and Identity in Italy, 50 BC–AD 250*, Cambridge, Ma.

Niehoff, M.R. (2018), *Philo of Alexandria. An Intellectual Biography*, New Haven.

Nikolaidis, A.G. (1997), 'Plutarch on women and mariage', *Wiener Studies* 110, 27–88.

Pelling, C.B.R. (2005), 'Synkrisis revisited', in: A. Pérez Jiménez/F.B. Titchener (eds.), *Historical and biographical values of Plutarch's works. Studies devoted to Professor Philip Stadter by the International Plutarch Society*, Malaga/Logan, 325–40.

Puech, B. (1992), 'Prosopographie des amis de Plutarque', in: W. Haase (ed.), *Aufstieg und Niedergang der Römischen Welt (ANRW)*, t. 2.33.6, Berlin/New York, 4831–93.

Puech, B. (1994), 'Cléa' (art. 134), in: R. Goulet (ed.), *Dictionnaire des philosophes antiques (DPhA)*, vol. 2, Paris.

Spawforth, A.J.S. (2012), *Greece and the Augustan Cultural Revolution*, Cambridge, Ma.

Stadter, P. (1975), 'Plutarch's Comparison of Pericles and Fabius Maximus', *GRBS* 16, 77–85.

Schmitt-Pantel, P. (2009), 'Autour du traité de Plutarque *Vertus de femmes (Gynaikôn Aretai)*', *Clio* 30, 39–59.

Tsouvala, G. (2014), 'Love and Marriage', in: M. Beck (ed.), *A Companion to Plutarch*, Malden/Chichester, 191–206.

Henriette Harich-Schwarzbauer
# *Africa, famula Romae*: Constructions of Ethnic Identity in Claudian's Panegyrics

Claudius Claudianus wrote in Latin and Greek. With regard to his cultural identity, he is associated with Alexandria and an Hellenic culture which was still very much alive there during his time.[1] One specific aspect of his identity is revealed by the bilingualism documented in his work.[2] It is often claimed that he was an Egyptian, though what is meant by 'Egyptian' is never defined. It is noticeable that the lyrical 'I' is rather reserved with statements about his origin. As a panegyrist, Claudian was, after a short stay in Rome, indebted to the ruling family in Milan and then in Ravenna in the years 395–404, at a time of extremely tense relations between Constantinople and the West. This situation is clearly reflected in Claudian's poetry, in that the panegyrist in his epics repeatedly depicts West and East in a polarising manner, his invectives against the East directed not against the ruler Arcadius, but against central political actors in Constantinople, including Rufinus and Eutropius,[3] or volatile allies of the East such as the Moor Gildo. He discredits these individuals on the basis of their ethnic origins. Claudian's concept of gender roles and attributions of identity seems to be laid out in an analogous manner to the dichotomous line of argumentation he applied to the centres of power in Late Antiquity, i.e. the Western and Eastern Roman Empire. Following this assumption, this paper will examine the question of how Claudian interlinked constructions of gender and ethnic attributions with each other on the basis of selected personifications of geographical features. I will focus on the

---

[1] I would like to thank the anonymous reviewer for his/her valuable criticism. Translation Fabian Känzig. This paper was originally authored in German, hence the preference for 'ethnic', 'ethnicity' etc. over 'race'. The terminology differs; depending on the language and cultural context one prefers to speak of 'race' or 'ethnicity'. The fact that 'race' should not be erased from our vocabulary is currently being intensively discussed with strong arguments among specialised scholars. On this topic see the comprehensive and illuminating analysis in McCoskey 2012, 1–34. Attempting to be linguistically correct and sensitive in the use of the word 'race' is natural in the German language in the sense of critical race theory; see note 4.
[2] See Mulligan 2007, 285–310; Charlet 2013, 321–50.
[3] See for example Tougher 2005, 60–73. Regarding Claudian's intention to portray the increasingly strained relationship between Rome and Constantinople by personifying Roma, while using surrogates for Constantinople, see Kelly 2015, 241–64.

question of how the three primary categories of gender, race, and class[4] are poetically spelt out through complementary categories such as body, age, religious affiliation and geographical origin (East – West) in Claudian's panegyrics. Approaches of this kind which integrate elements of intersectionality are still relatively new in research on Claudian and focus on the figure of Stilicho, who represents the masculine ideal.[5] The statement that Stilicho in Claudian's work figures "almost solely as a rhetorically pregnant representation of the man and his accomplishments, one that has only the thinnest basis in reality"[6] must be verified and integrated into a broader context. This necessitates reading the rhetorical representation in terms of its specific constructive character and revealing in a differentiated way how argument and literary representation are interwoven in the text.

In the *opus Claudianeum* there is no female character who dominates the *panegyrici* analogously to the omnipresent male Stilicho. Although Stilicho's wife Serena does play a prominent role in the *Laus Serenae* and the *Epistula ad Serenam* (c. min. 30 and 31), and in the *Epithalamium dictum Honorio Augusto et Mariae* (c. 10.229–50), where she is compared with her still adolescent daughter and depicted as a beautiful woman who impresses even Venus, her function is, naturally, not to wage wars or to signify preservation of power to the outside world. Accordingly, Serena, at least if she is judged by conventional criteria and if the foremost importance in the *panegyrici* is attributed to the commander, remains a secondary figure.[7] This asymmetrical representation of the *de facto* ruling couple in Claudian's oeuvre will not be pursued further in this contribution. Instead, the question will be shifted to another aspect and to another layer, namely that of symbolism, i.e. to the *prosopopoeiae*. Personifications of countries and rivers and especially the appearance of Roma are commonly encountered in Claudian's poetry.[8] According to rhetorical tradition, Roma and various countries are

---

[4] The essential treatment on this matter is still Klinger/Knapp 2007, 19–41; in particular 32–7.

[5] Nathan 2015, 10–27 examines maleness, masculinity and the underlying strategy of the panegyrist based on the figure of Stilicho, not without emphasising that Claudian's depiction of the latter is "full of errors, distortions and omissions" (12). Nathan does not make a comparison with analogous designs of femininity in Claudian.

[6] Nathan 2015, 12.

[7] If, however, one considers Claudian's overall design of the work in appreciation of the *Carmina minora*, Serena is equally accorded first place. She then becomes the muse of the poet's 'minor poetry'. See Harich-Schwarzbauer 2009, 11–31.

[8] See for example the list of personifications of countries in *Cons. Stil.* 2 at the meeting of Hispania (230–46), Britannia (247–55), Africa (256–62) and Oenotria (262–8) on the Palatine Hill.

represented as female characters, while rivers — as is well known — are characterised as masculine.

In this paper, I will on the basis of selected examples explore how the female personifications of Roma and Africa are described, in particular, what criteria are activated for femaleness as a representation of ethnicity. The genre of panegyrics formulates rules on how countries, cities etc. must be praised.[9] Without doubt, rhetorical guidelines were known to Claudian.[10] Recent research also confirms that panegyrics generally aimed to confirm traditional gender attributions.[11] This assessment shall not be questioned here on a fundamental level. However, we will examine which aspects are defined in the context of *inuentio* as suitable examples for revealing gender attributions. As regards the macrostructure of Claudian's panegyrics as a whole, the following must be noted first: male personifications are comparatively rare. There is at least one prominent example in the appearance of the river Tiber, who, fascinated by the spectacle, rises from the waters during the adventus of the new consuls in Rome in 395.[12] With Tiber's appearance the Children Consuls, the brothers Olybrius and Probinus, are celebrated. The personified river is introduced here, as elsewhere[13] in Claudian's work, at a moment when the aim is to signal the potency of Western Roman rule. The situation is different with the *prosopopoeiae* of countries and regions of the world. Female characters repeatedly symbolise crisis and inferiority. They complain, they submit, they articulate their weakness and need for protection. For Claudian, a panegyrist who advocates for the Western Roman Empire, and to whom the *Roma aeterna* figure of thought is attributed, personifications are ideal surfaces of projection for pointing out the political tensions of the time without touching upon specific politically sensitive subjects. They make it possible, among other things, for the brothers Honorius and Arcadius to not directly confront each other as political actors.

---

Roma intervenes on behalf of those regions of the world with Jupiter on Mount Olympus (279–339).
9 See Men. Rhet., 344.15–346.25; esp. 346.6–8 (fertile/arid regions).
10 Rees 2018, 138–9 argues that Claudian with regard to the pleading Roma had in mind not only Menander Rhetor but also the *Panegyrici Latini*.
11 Gleason 2008, 55–81.
12 *Olybr. Probin.* 236–62.
13 Cf. the *prosopopoeia* of the River Eridanus (Po) in 6. *Cons. Stil.* 159–92.

## 1 Roma (*De Bello Gildonico* 17–127)

Roma, who a few years earlier (395) in the Panegyricus on Olybrius and Probinus had symbolised the strength of the West,[14] is imagined in *De bello Gildonico* (398) as an old woman.[15] The age of the Roman Empire is projected onto the female character.[16]

> exitii iam Roma timens et fessa negatis
> frugibus ad rapidi limen tendebat Olympi
> non solito uultu nec qualis iura Britannis
> diuidit aut trepidos summittit fascibus Indos.
> uox tenuis tardique gradus oculique iacentes;
> interius fugere genae; ieiuna lacertos
> exedit macies. umeris uix sustinet aegris
> squalentem clipeum; laxata casside prodit
> canitiem plenamque trahit rubiginis hastam.
> attigit ut tandem caelum genibusque Tonantis
> procubuit, tales orditur maesta querellas.[17]
>
> (*Gild.* 17–27)

Rome, fearing her end and weak, since the harvest had been refused to her, hurried to rapidly revolving Olympus; her face was not the accustomed, not the familiar one, which she showed when assigning law to the Britons or subjecting the frightened Indians to her rule. Her voice was feeble, her steps slow, her eyes downcast. Her cheeks were hollow and hunger had emaciated her arms. Scarcely she supported her unpolished shield on her week shoulders, her ill-fitting helmet showed her white hair and the spear she carried was rusty. Finally, when she reached heaven, she sank down at the Thunderer's feet and started her sad lamentations.[18]

The fear of her demise drives Roma to seek help from Jupiter. Age is here equated in a gender-specific sense with exhaustion, as Roma is no longer allowed to share

---

**14** On the personification of Roma in Claudian's work, see Roberts 2001, 533–65; on old Roma ibid. 535; Berlincourt 2015 and Berlincourt 2016, 199–225; 200–1 (with n. 1, a detailed bibliography on the idea of *Roma aeterna*, to which reference is made here for the personification of Roma).
**15** Roberts 2001, 536 assumes that the Roma of *De Bello Gildonico* should be attributed less to the panegyric than to the epic tradition.
**16** Schindler 2009, 99 stresses that the image of the 'neglected' and weakened Roma has no epic precursor.
**17** Edition: Hall 1985.
**18** All translations are mine.

in the crop yield (17–18: *fessa negatis frugibus*). On a symbolic level, this infertility means the loss of feminine power. This loss is illustrated by the quiet voice, the sluggish gait and gauntness, especially by the hollow cheeks and emaciated arms. In this text Roma also symbolises the collective memory of the great Roman past. She interprets Roman history as a crisis-ridden but successful story. In order to emphasise her complaint, she not only invokes the gods expected to be associated with Olympus, but also, as the final and therefore important instance, to intercede with Jupiter, Cybele (116–20), identified as the mother of Jupiter and symbol of femininity and fertility par excellence.[19] Cybele's empathy for Roma is striking.[20] The personified Roma is successful with the rhetoric of the *querella* until she eventually falls silent crying. Her performance is convincing, she is able to guide emotions and arouse compassion (127–33). After Africa had also intervened — more on this later — she is rejuvenated by Jupiter, and in an optimised form:

> dixit et adflauit Romam meliore iuuenta.
> continuo redit ille uigor seniique colorem
> mutauere comae. solidatam crista resurgens
> erexit galeam clipeique recanduit orbis
> et leuis excussa micuit rubigine cornus.

> (*Gild.* 208–12)

> Thus, he spoke and breathed better youth into Rome. Instantly, her former strength returned and her hair lost its colour of old age. The crest, rising up, stood straight on her helmet again, her round shield was shining again and her spear was gleaming, since all rust had gone.

Roma as a female character is given back what is considered her symbolic capital: to be a constantly rejuvenated woman, but at the same time a woman in need of male protection. Remarkably, her youth manifests itself through the change of hair colour, away from that of an old person (209: *seniique colorem*),[21] but not

---

[19] Cybele continues to play a prominent part in this poem. She is explicitly mentioned as one of the divine characters who is touched by the speech of Rome and weeps (130).
[20] Kelly 2015, 259–60 points out that in the invective against Eutropius (2.282–4) Cybele acts as a surrogate for the (according to Claudian) enemy Constantinople. What is conspicuous here, however, is Cybele's partisanship for Roma, whose supremacy, if Kelly is followed, she does not contest.
[21] Older research literature does not always do justice to this section of the text. Döpp 1980, 138, for instance, speaks of the old woman Roma, "deren schütteres Haar dem Helm keinen rechten Halt mehr bietet" (whose sparse hair no longer provides the helmet with a firm hold), then also

through a renewed yield of fruit. Female hair plays an important role in this process of change. A comparison with Stilicho's stylisation is illuminating: His white hair, radiating far and wide, is a sign of strength and endurance (Get. 459–60: *emicuit Stilichonis apex et cognita fulsit canities*). Roma's renewed vitality is primarily shown by her insignia, first of all by her crest, which integrates aspects of masculinity and virility (*crista erexit galeam*).[22] It is characteristic of this process that Roma does not become the agent of this *erigere*. Like Roma, Stilicho too is associated with a new flowering of Rome. However, this renewal is based on Stilicho's overall appearance (Stil. 3. 124: *pristina Romuleis infloruit artibus aetas*).[23] The *Bellum Gildonicum* does not provide any attributes that would ethnically define Roma in more detail. In this respect, the character is neutralised. After all, it could be argued, it represents a multi-ethnic empire.

## 2 Africa (*De Bello Gildonico* 134–200)

In the retinue of Roma, Africa in the *Bellum Gildonicum* symbolises rule threatened by a warlord. Africa, too, appears on Olympus, begging for help:

> ... cum procul insanis quatiens ululatibus axem
> et contusa genas mediis apparet in astris
> Africa: rescissae uestes et spicea passim
> serta iacent: lacero crinales uertice dentes
> et fractum pendebat ebur, talique superbas
> inrupit clamore fores.
>
> (*Gild*. 134–9)

... when suddenly from afar Africa, who had struck her face and was shaking heaven with painful howling, appeared amidst the stars. Her clothes were torn, the shattered crown of corn was laying on the ground. Her head was wounded, broken ivory teeth from her comb hang down loosely; so shouting, she broke into the lofty hall.

---

of the "erblondenden Haaren" (hair turning blonde), which would give the helmet a firm hold again (my trans.).

**22** The subtle juncture *crista erexit* could be associated with (successful) male potency, inasmuch as in *crista erexit* the idea of 'swelling' (e.g. of the comb of the cock) is also transported. No entry to *erigere* however in Adams 1990.

**23** See also Nathan 2015, 15 on the delicate interpretation of *Romanitas* in view of Stilicho's paternal Vandal descent. Stilicho's father already possessed Roman citizenship.

Africa is driven by suffering. Her appearance resembles that of one mourning a loss. At the same time, she reminds us of a woman who has been physically abused. Her robe is torn (135: *rescissae uestes*), her head wounded (136: *lacero uertice*).[24] Thus, she is prepared to take the ultimate step: rather than being conquered by Gildo, she would endure Jupiter's violence in order to be safe from the Libyan. In an extreme and ambiguous turn of phrase Claudian summarises her fate with *me rape Gildoni* (145). Besides 'snatching away' and 'plundering', *rapere* can occasionally also refer to *rape*.[25] In fact, in Claudian's *De raptu Proserpinae*, the polysemy of *rapere* is fundamentally important for understanding the mythical epic.[26]

> si mihi Gildonem nequeunt abducere fata,
> me rape Gildoni! felicior illa perustae
> pars Libyae, nimio quae se munita calore
> defendit tantique uacat secura tyranni!
> crescat zona rubens; medius flagrantis Olympi
> me quoque limes agat. melius deserta iacebo
> uomeris inpatiens. pulsis dominentur aratris
> dipsades et sitiens attollat glaeba cerastas.
> quid me temperies iuuit? quid mitior aether?
> Gildoni fecunda fui.
>
> (*Gild*. 144–53)

If fortune cannot lead away Gildo, you may rape me. More fortunate will be that part of Libya, which — when it is seared — prepares itself with too much heat and lies fallow, secure from such a tyrant! Let the red zone grow, let the midst of burning Olympus seize me. It will be better to lie fallow without suffering the plowshare. The snakes may rule, when the ploughs are driven out and the thirsting clod of earth may bring to the fore vipers. What's the use of a well-balanced climate, what's the use of a mild ether? For Gildo I was fertile.

---

**24** Following Charlet 2000, 131 *ad loc.* the assumption is that Africa has injured herself in order to express her grief. No explanation in Müller 2011, 192 on the culprits of the lamentable state of Africa, who "vergleichbar zugerichtet auftritt" (appears comparably battered), with reference to Charlet (my trans.). Müller 2011, 190–1 (with note 39) offers a research overview on the appearance of Africa (there is also further literature).
**25** Cf. Ware 2012, 155.
**26** Cf. the programmatic *inferni raptoris* in Claud., *rapt. Pros.* verse 1.

The idea of a zone of drought is not unusual in the ancient worldview and is commonly invoked both in poetry and in scientific literature.[27] Claudian's description of Africa pleading for help was probably heavily influenced by Ovid. Two scenes from Ovid's *Metamorphoses* likely had the greatest impact on his description of Africa: the torment of Terra at the hands of Phaethon,[28] and the violence suffered by the nymph Arethusa.[29] In the *Metamorphoses*, Terra laments her imminent destruction, which will be caused by Phaethon:

> ... hosne mihi fructus, hunc fertilitatis honorem
> officiique refers, quod adunci uulnera aratri
> rastrorumque fero totoque exerceor anno ...[30]

(Ovid, *Met.* 2.285–7)

> This harvest, this honour for my fertility and for my service you render me, since I bear the wounds of the crooked plough and the hoes, being tortured all over the year?

Arethusa for her part provides Ceres with the decisive clue as to the whereabouts of her daughter: Proserpina's belt, which signals that she has been raped:

> ... signa tamen manifesta dedit notamque parenti
> illo forte loco delapsam in gurgite sacro
> Persephones zonam summis ostendit in undis.
> quam simul agnouit, tamquam tunc denique raptam
> scisset, inornatos laniauit diua capillos
> et repetita suis percussit pectora palmis.

(Ovid, *Met.* 5.468–73)

> Though she gave a clear sign and showed the belt of Persephone which was well known to the mother, the belt which had slid down on the surface of the sea. As soon as she recognized it, as if she only than had learned that her daughter had been raped, the goddess tore at her hair and repeatedly beat her breast with her hands.

---

**27** Cf. e.g. Verg., *Georg.* 1.233. For *zona rubens*, Charlet 2000 cites Lucan, *Phars.* 9.852. It is evident that Lucan in particular provides important elements for the description of Africa, including the specific types of snakes.
**28** For the lament of the abused Terra in Ovid see Keith 2000, 51–2.
**29** Ill-fated loosening of the belt is also found in Ovid, *Her.* 2.116–20 (Lament of Phyllis, whose wedding carries symbolism associated with death).
**30** Edition: Tarrant 2004.

Claudian's Africa, by means of the *zona*, claims a place for herself alongside the female characters Terra and Proserpina, and holds out the prospect of her transformation. She is thus willing to become a desert in order to escape the tyrant Gildo. To be incorporated into the *zona rubens*, even to be scorched earth and to become part of the *zona* itself, seems to her almost the only remaining way out. Africa asks Jupiter for help, who (cynically speaking) is a violently desirous ruler — and one who causes destruction by fire. She pleads with him, asking the god to enlarge the drought zone of Africa in order to obstruct Gildo.[31] Africa's self-identification as a beaten woman attempting to escape one violation by accepting another, supposedly lesser one, is presented with great pathos. Africa is prepared to accept 'legitimate violence' and at the same time to give up her 'power', i.e. her productivity, which Gildo had usurped, for good. Thus, following her own imagination, she would henceforth be abandoned and left unable to conceive, that is, barren (149–50: *melius deserta iacebo/uomeris inpatiens*). In the future, snakes are to furrow the soil of Africa in place of *aratra*.

In the course of her speech, Africa dissociates herself from a part of her own by shifting individual regions, as it were, to Gildo and the Numidians. In this context, she cuts off ethnic groups which she accuses of crimes against women, brute violence, and lawlessness. These criminal ethnic groups, which she ostracises and marks as non-affiliated, include the Ethiopians, Moors, and Nasamones:

> ... nec damna pudoris
> turpia sufficiunt: Mauris clarissima quaeque
> fastidita datur. media Carthagine ductae
> barbara Sidoniae subeunt conubia matres;
> Aethiopem nobis generum Nasamona maritum
> ingerit. exterret cunabula discolor infans.
>
> (*Gild.* 188–93)
>
> Not enough, that their pride was robbed. To the Moors are given the most noble women. In the heart of Carthage Sidonian mothers are married to barbarians. An Ethiopian as son-in-law, a Berber as husband is forced upon me. The child, with its different skin, frightens the cradle.

Textual tradition fluctuates between *discolor* (Hall) and *degener* (Charlet) for verse 193. The reading *discolor* is supported by the fact that already the cradle is frightened at the sight of the new-born child. By choosing this specific attribute,

---

31 Cf. Jupiter and Semele in Ovid, *Met.* 3.305–9.

Claudian obviously wants to focus attention on an immediately visible difference.[32] Moral deviance, as would be insinuated by the reading *degener*, would hardly have become visible in the new-born child and thus would not have spread terror immediately.

Africa thus stylises herself as a weak and abused woman. She perceives herself as part of the (Western) Roman Empire and passes on a view of herself that has internalised Rome's claim to power. Splitting off 'black' Africa, she discriminates on the basis of skin colour and associates dark skin with violence, equating nomads like Berbers and Moors with black Africans (Ethiopians). Stereotypical elements traditionally associated with Africa in iconography, such as the elephant, are nevertheless included with the mention of the destruction of symbolic attributes, especially ivory. In summary, Africa defines her function as being a servant of Rome (207: ... *et soli famulabitur Africa Romae*).

## 3 Tiberinus (*Panegyricus dictus Olybrio et Probino consulibus* 209–65)

The comparison of the *prosopopoeiae* of Roma and Africa with the epiphany of the river Tiber provides a suitable contrast for illustrating Claudian's strategy of attributing gender and ethnicity. The personified Tiber appears at the adventus of the Children Consuls of the year 395, Olybrius and Probinus, and joyfully observes their arrival. He is described as *dominus* of a flock of nymphs and equipped by his wife Ilia with a magnificent woven robe. The inclusion of these attributes serves to emphasise his power as *pater familias* and his dignified age. His splendid hair of reed is indestructible, not even *fatum* can harm it. This hair will never be destroyed, never be scorched by the sun, and expresses the invincibility of youthful vigour:

> uertice luxuriat crinalis harundo,
> quam neque fas Zephyris frangi nec sole perustam
> aestiuo candore mori, sed uiuida frondet

---

**32** The authoritative hypotext is Lucan, *Phars.* 10.128, where skin colour (*discolor ... sanguis*) and age are mentioned as distinctive features (*distinxerat*) of the servants in the palace of Alexandria. Even more so, with regard to the description of Africa and its division into zones in Lucan, *Phars.* 4.666–86, *discolor* is preferable when seen in conjunction to Lucan, *Phars.* 4.678–9 (*concolor Indo Maurus*). On the range of variation of these attributes, see Snowden 1970, 4 (with n. 28).

aequaeuum complexa caput. taurina leuantur
cornua temporibus raucos sudantia riuos ...

(*Olybr. Probin.* 217–21)

His head is adorned by a magnificent crown of reed, which neither the Zephyrs may break, nor the sun, burning with its summer heat: but which sprouts vivid green around his same-aged head. The horns of a bull sprout from his temples, sweating raucous rivulets.

Tiberinus' virility manifests itself in lush hair growth and a thick beard (222–3). His shoulders protrude powerfully in all their dignity (224: *graues umeros*). His horns, hyperbolically enhanced to a never-ending spring, signify his masculinity. Tiber is characterised by his solemn speech which stakes out his domain. His reign over all rivers is characterised as an infinite golden age. Although a dense intertextual relationship between the Tiber scene and Vergil, Ovid, and Statius, among others, has been brought to light,[33] the motif of the horns sweating rivers — symbolising unceasingly procreating masculinity — is unprecedented.[34]

# 4 Conclusion

In Claudian's work as a whole, the personifications of continents, regions, and rivers, and especially of Rome, already play a prominent role. An instance of this occurs already in the early epic on the war against Gildo, complemented here by the Tiber epiphany in the panegyric on Olybrius and Probinus. These personifications are important protagonists as well as commentators on events; their descriptions as well as their speeches are gender-determined.[35] My argument was that panegyric is comparable to highlighting and thus implies that gaps in the conceptualisation of characters are at least as meaningful and relevant for interpretation as what is explicitly praised about them. Claudian points out clear and unmistakable attributions, but only the personification of Africa contains pointed attributions that allow conclusions to be drawn about ethnicity, which

---

[33] See Taegert 1988, 204–5, who primarily cites Statius, *Theb.* 9.404–15 (Ismenus); Ovid, *Met.* 1.575 (Inachus).
[34] Cf. Taegert 1988, 205.
[35] The rules formulated by Quintilian for the occasion of a female personification speaking would have been known to Claudian. The emotional quality is explicitly signalled by the usage of the term *querella*. In the case of Africa, he resorts to the implication of inarticulate wailing (of the subjugated region). On *uirilitas* in *prosopopoeia*, but focused on the performative act, Gleason 2008, 114–5.

are then problematised within a precarious power structure. There is nothing analogous for Roma. Identity markings based on religious affiliation are missing for both Roma and Africa. Poetically allusive markings of gender, however, are frequent. Femininity is associated with mental and physical weakness, with bodies marked i.e. by age. Masculinity, however, is associated with mental and physical strength, with beauty unaffected by age, as for example when white hair is associated with radiance, with potency and timelessness. Compared to Africa and her *famula*, Roma enjoys a singular status that does not allow her to become an object of physical violence. Thus, she is not threatened by dangers aimed at her body. She is able to, as it were, transcend her body, since it is (uniquely) designed for rejuvenation. This leads to the conclusion that Roma elevates herself above ethnicity and thus symbolises the 'body' of the Roman Empire. If, in light of these observations, (the semi-Vandal) Stilicho, on whom the security and strength of Rome at that time depended, is thrown into the equation, this assumption is confirmed. For then the transcendence of ethnic attribution, which serves an all-Roman imperial identity, can be explained.

# Works Cited

## Texts and Commentaries

*Claudii Claudiani Carmina* (1985), edidit J.B. Hall, Leipzig.
Claudien. *Œuvres. Tome II 1.2. Poèmes politiques (395–398)* (2000), texte établi et traduit par J.-L. Charlet, Paris.
Claudien. *Œuvres. Tome III. Poèmes politiques (399–404)* (2017), texte établi et traduit par J.-L. Charlet, Paris.
Menander Rhetor (1981), edidit with translation and commentary by D.A. Russel and N.G. Wilson, Oxford.
P. Ovidi Nasonis *Metamorphoses* (2004), *recognovit breviqve adnotatione critica instruxit* R.J. Tarrant, Oxford.
Claudius Claudianus. *Panegyricus dictus Olybrio et Probino consulibus* (1988), edidit W. Taegert, München.

## Literature

Adams, J.N. (1990), *The Latin sexual vocabulary*, Baltimore.
Berlincourt, V. (2015), "*Innuptae ritus imitata Minervae*: une comparaison chez Claudien et ses connexions flaviennes", *Dictynna* 12.

Berlincourt, V. (2016), "Lucain et le souhait de domination de la déesse Roma (Claud. *Ol. Prob.* 160–163)" in: Berlincourt, V./Galli Milić, L./ Nelis, D. (eds.), *Lucan et Claudian: Context and Intertext*, Heidelberg, 199–225.

Charlet, J.-L. (2013), "La Romanité de Claudien, poète venu d'Alexandrie", in: Schubert, P./Ducrey, P./Derron, P. (eds.) *Les Grecs héritiers des Romains. Entretiens préparés par Paul Schubert, présidés par Pierre Ducrey et édités par Pascale Derron*, Vandœuvres/Genève 27–31 Août 2012, Genève, 321–50. (= Entretiens sur l'antiquité classique, vol. LIX).

Döpp, S. (1980), *Zeitgeschichte in Dichtungen Claudians*, Wiesbaden (= Hermes Einzelschriften 43).

Gleason, M. (2008), *Making Men. Sophists and Self-Presentations in Ancient Rome*, Princeton.

Harich-Schwarzbauer, H. (2009), "Prodigiosa silex. Serielle Lektüre der Carmina minora Claudians", in: Harich-Schwarzbauer, H./Schierl, P. (eds.), *Lateinische Poesie der Spätantike. Internationale Tagung in Castelen bei Augst, 11.–13. Oktober 2007*, Basel, 11–31.

Keith, A. (2000), *Engendering Rome. Women in Roman Epic*, Cambridge.

Kelly, G. (2015), "Claudian and Constantinople", in: Grig, L./Kelly, G. (eds.), *Two Romes: Rome and Constantinople in Late Antiquity*, Oxford, 241–64.

Klinger, C./Axeli-Knapp, G. (2007), "Achsen der Ungleichheit und Achsen der Differenz. Zum Verhältnis von Klasse, Geschlecht, 'Rasse'/Ethnizität", in: Klinger, C./Axeli-Knapp, G. (eds.), Achsen der Ungleichheit und Achsen der Differenz. Zum Verhältnis von Klasse, Geschlecht, «Rasse»/Ethnizität, Frankfurt a.M., 19–41.

McCoskey, D.E. (2012), *Race. Antiquity and its Legacy*, Oxford.

Müller, G.M. (2011), *Lectiones Claudianeae. Studien zur Poetik und Funktion der politisch-zeitgeschichtlichen Dichtungen Claudians*, Heidelberg.

Mulligan, Bret (2007), "The Poet from Egypt? Reconsidering Claudian's Origin", *Philologus* 15.2, 285–310.

Nathan, G. (2015), "The Ideal Man in Late Antiquity: Claudian's Example of Flavius Stilicho", *Gender & History* 27.1, 10–27.

Rees, R. (2018), "Ghosts of Authors Past in Claudian's *De Bello Gildonico*", in: Berlincourt, V./ Galli Milic, L./ Nelis, D. (eds.), *Lucan et Claudian: Context and Intertext*, Heidelberg, 127–45.

Roberts, M. (2001), "Rome Personified, Rome Epitomized: Representations of Rome in the Poetry of the Early Fifth Century", *AJP* 122, 533–65.

Schindler, C. (2009), *Per Carmina laudes. Untersuchungen zur spätantiken Verspanegyrik von Claudian bis Coripp*, Berlin/New York.

Snowden Jr., F.M. (1970), *Blacks in Antiquity. Ethiopians in the Greco-Roman Experience*, Cambridge/Massachusetts.

Tougher, S. (2005), "Two views on the gender identity of byzantine eunuchs", in: Shaw, A./Ardener, S. (eds.), *Changing Sex and Bending Gender*, New York, 60–73.

Ware, C. (2012), *Claudian and the Roman Epic Tradition*, Cambridge.

# List of Contributors

**Federica Bessone** is Professor of Latin at the University of Turin. She is the author of *P. Ouidii Nasonis Heroidum Epistula XII. Medea Iasoni* (1997) and *La 'Tebaide' di Stazio. Epica e potere* (2011); she co-edited *The Literary Genres in the Flavian Age: Canons, Transformations, Reception* (2017) and *Lettori latini e italiani di Ovidio* (2019). She is a member of the scientific board of *Eugesta*, MD, RCCM, and the *Oxford Commentaries on Flavian Poetry*.

**Charles Delattre** is a Professor of Ancient Greek Language and Literature at the University of Lille. His research focuses on the mythographic corpus of the imperial period and, more broadly, on ancient narrative practices involving the modern notion of "mythology". He devotes himself to the annotated edition of part of the mythographic corpus and to a reflection on contemporary definitions of "myth", from a perspective of literary theory and cultural anthropology.

**Jacqueline Fabre-Serris** is Professor of Latin Literature at the University of Lille. She is co-editor of *Dictynna* and *Eugesta*. Her research focuses on Latin literature, on mythography, and on Gender studies. Monographs include *Mythe et poésie dans les* Métamorphoses *d'Ovide* (1995), *Mythologie et littérature à Rome* (1998), *Rome, l'Arcadie et la mer des origines* (2008). She is co-editor of *Women and War in Antiquity* (2015) and *Lire les mythes* (2016). She is currently writing a book on Ovid and Sulpicia.

**Andrew Feldherr** is Professor of Classics at Princeton University. He works on Latin Literature with particular interests in historiography and Augustan poetry. A main focus of his scholarship has been on how political and social forces shape conceptions of the function of literature during the late republic and early empire. His publications include *Spectacle and Society in Livy's* History (1998), *Playing Gods: The Politics of Fiction in Ovid's* Metamorphoses (2010), and *After the Past: Sallust on History and Writing History* (2021).

**Therese Fuhrer** has held Chairs of Latin at the Universities of Trier, Zurich, Freiburg, the Free University of Berlin, and since 2013 at the LMU Munich. She has published on topics ranging from Hellenistic Greek through republican and Augustan poetry and prose to Augustine. She is currently engaged in a number of research projects in the field of ancient philosophy and rhetoric, on Roman historiography, on the authorial voice, and Late Antiquity.

**Florence Gherchanoc** is Professor in Ancient Greek History at the University of Paris, and member of ANHIMA. She is a specialist of the family. Since a decade, her research is more focused on body, garments and beauty, through a historical anthropological perspective. From this approach, she studies social and political identities in the Greek cities. Her publications include *L'oikos en fête* (Paris 2012) and *Concours de beauté et beautés du corps en Grèce ancienne* (Bordeaux 2016).

**Judith P. Hallett**, Professor of Classics and Distinguished Scholar-Teacher Emerita at the University of Maryland, College Park, has published widely in the areas of Latin language and literature; women, the family and sexuality in Greco-Roman antiquity; and the study and reception of classics in the Anglophone world. A 2013 collection of essays from Routledge—*Domina Illustris*: Latin Literature, Gender and Reception, edited by Donald Lateiner, Barbara Gold and Judith Perkins—celebrates her academic career.

**Henriette Harich-Schwarzbauer**, Ordinaria of Latin Philology, University of Basel since 2002, studied Classics and French Literature at the University of Graz, at Sorbonne IV and was Erwin Schrödinger research fellow at Tübingen. She held a visiting scholarship at Paris, Sorbonne I. Her research focuses on the literature of the Early Roman Empire, Late Antiquity, Neolatin, the History of Classical Scholarship and Reception Studies.

**Alison Keith** teaches Classics and Women's Studies at the University of Toronto. She has written extensively about the intersection of gender and genre in Latin literature and Roman society, and is the author of books on Ovid (1992), Propertius (2008), Latin epic (2000, 2012), and most recently Virgil (2020). Current projects include monographs on Sulpicia and on Latin literature and Roman Epicureanism. She directs the Jackman Humanities Institute at the University of Toronto.

**Florence Klein** is Associate Professor of Latin Literature at the University of Lille. Her reseach focuses on Hellenistic and Roman poetry, literary theory and intertextuality, and gender studies. Her publications include *La représentation du couple Virgile-Ovide dans la tradition culturelle de l'Antiquité à nos jours* (with S. Clément-Tarantino, 2015) and *Faire voir. Etudes sur l'enargeia de l'Antiquité à l'époque moderne* (with R. Webb, 2021). She is co-editor of *Dictynna* and member of the editorial board of *Eugesta*.

**François Lissarrague** is Directeur d'études at the EHESS holding a chair on Anthropology and Images: the Greek experience. In 2014 he gave the Sather Lectures at Berkeley. He is the author of several books on ancient Greek imagery, among them *A city of Images* (C. Bérard ed., Princeton 1986), *The Aesthetics of Greek Banquet* (Princeton 1990), *Greek Vases : The Athenians and their Images* (Riverside 2001) and more recently *La Cité des Satyres. Une anthropologie ludique* (Paris 2013).

**Alison Sharrock** is Professor of Classics at the University of Manchester. She has published on many Latin authors, especially Plautus, Terence and Ovid, as well as on literary theory. Her most recent publications include *Metamorphic Readings: Transformation, Language, and Gender in the Interpretation of Ovid's Metamorphoses* (Cambridge, 2020, with Mats Malm and Daniel Möller), and *Maternal Conceptions in Classical Literature and Philosophy* (Toronto, 2020, with Alison Keith).

# General Index

Achaemenid
–dynasty 62
–elite 38
–empire 6, 27, 31, 37
–reliefs 33n32
Achaemenides 198
Achilles 117n10, 119, 143n19, 155n1, 163n23, 165, 183
Actaeon 200
Actium, battle of 110, 115n1, 116, 117, 118, 119, 123, 125, 126, 129, 139, 141, 145, 146, 149, 150
Adonis 207n29
adultery 69, 150, 211n37
advice 7, 51, 52, 57, 60, 63, 105, 189, 191–2n28, 241
*aemulatio* 126
Aeneas 3, 135, 136n5, 137, 138, 168, 176, 183–90, 183n15, 186n17, 187n19, 188n20, 191, 195–6n4, 198, 199n10, 248
–Ecphrasis of the shield of 117, 120, 126, 135
Aeschylus 144n22
–*Persians* 31, 33
Africa 2, 4, 95n9, 97, 192, 258n27, 260n32
personification of 13, 252–3n8, 253, 255, 256–8, 257n24, 259–62, 261n35
African(s) 3, 260
Agamemnon 165
age, old 220, 238, 254
Agesilaus 39
Agrippa 198n8
Agrippina 139
Aiaia 220
αἰδώς 166
Ainianes 224
Ajax 207n29, 239n18
Alcithoe 210, 213, 214
Alexander 120, 122, 124, 136, 137, 138, 138n10, 143n19, 144, 144n24, 146, 202n17
Alexandria 3, 10, 110, 116, 120, 122, 124, 125, 127, 140, 147, 251, 260n32

Alexandrian poetry (see also "culture")
9, 115, 116, 117, 118, 121, 122, 123, 124, 125, 127, 128, 130, 131, 132, 150
Alice in the Wonderland 229
Allecto 102
allusion (see also "intertextuality") 10, 115, 116, 118, 122, 123, 124, 127, 132, 136, 143, 145, 210, 212, 236
Alphaeus 208, 209
Amata 101–2
*amicitia* 103, 108
Aminias 49, 51, 53, 58, 60–1, 65
*amores peregrini* 10, 155, 156, 158, 162, 162n21, 163, 165–6, 167, 171
anachronism 141, 159n13, 207
Anacreon 19, 20
anacreontics 6, 17, 18–20, 25, 33n31
ἄνδρες 49, 52, 59, 61, 63, 65, 66, 248
ἀνδρεία 7, 35n41, 53n16, 58, 59, 61, 64, 235, 240, 248
Annaea 79, 88
Annius Asellus 8, 77–9, 88
*Anthologia Latina* 199n9
Antigone 247
Antoninus Liberalis 211, 244n40
Aphrodite (see also "Venus") 124, 144
Appian 94, 95, 237–8, 239
Apollo 22, 23, 125, 127–32, 129n52, 130n55, 148, 197
–defeating Pytho 130
Apollonius 158n9, 169, 213n43
appropriation 9, 115, 116, 117, 121, 123, 125, 126, 128, 131, 138
Apuleius 12, 221, 223, 223n23, 223n24, 224n25, 225, 226n31, 229n47, 230
–*Metamorphoses* 12, 219, 224, 226, 230
Arachne 203, 205n24
Arcadians 3, 5n14, 155n1
Arcadius 251, 253
Aretaphila 247
Arete 183
Arethusa 208, 209, 258
Argonauts 166
Argos 145

https://doi.org/10.1515/9783110719949-016

Argus 210
Aristomenes 223–4, 225n29, 226, 228
Aristotimos of Elis 248
Arria 240n19
Arsinoe II Philadelphus 118, 121–4, 127
Artemis 244, 245, 245n43
Artemisia of Halicarnassus (see also "Halicarnassus, queen of") 7, 49–55, 51n7, 53n16, 55n25, 55n27, 56, 57, 59, 63, 64, 65–6, 69
– and gender 58–60
– and oracular powers 55–7
Ascanius 188, 190
Asia 4, 31, 33, 41, 42, 70, 75, 93n4, 117, 155n1, 156, 156n3
– Minor 204
Asian(s) 31, 33, 33n31, 36, 39, 42, 42n62, 76, 157
– art 71
– clothing 6, 28, 31, 33
– women 33, 156
Attalus I 239
Athenian(s) 2, 6, 7, 17, 18, 20, 25, 27, 28, 28n4, 28n5, 31, 38, 38n48, 41, 42, 49, 50, 51, 53, 54, 54n21, 56, 59–65, 66, 66n62, 167, 168, 176, 183, 192, 197, 238, 239
Athens 2, 20, 51, 54n21, 56, 158, 165, 166, 175n1, 197, 200n13, 205, 237n11, 239
Atossa 29, 32
Attic
– inscriptions 60, 60n41
– tragedy 165
– vase painting 6, 17, 23
Augustus (see also "Octavian") 9, 10, 94, 109, 118, 119, 121, 122, 123, 124, 125, 125n35, 126, 127, 128, 132, 135, 136, 140n14, 147, 149, 160, 161, 168, 197, 198n8, 224n26, 230
Autoboulos 240n20, 241, 241n23, 242
avarice 75, 75n19, 77, 80, 81, 87

Babylon 11, 35, 119, 204, 205, 210, 212n40
Babylonian(s) 200, 203, 204, 206, 207, 207n27, 212n40

Bacchon 242
Bacchus (see also "Dionysus") 11, 83, 200–3, 202n17
Ballio 175, 180, 180n9, 181, 181n11, 182, 189, 190, 190–1n25
banquet 72, 89, 131, 137–8, 137n8, 140–1, 141n16, 183–4, 187, 189
barbarian(s) 2–3, 5, 7, 8, 17, 24, 27, 31, 38, 39, 40, 41, 42, 53, 99, 103, 119, 156, 157, 162, 165, 166, 168n38, 171, 186n18, 197, 198, 214, 237
Baucis and Philemon 205n24
Berenice II 116, 122, 128
*blanditiae* 98
Bocchus 182
Boeotia 227, 229, 229n45
Britannia, personification of 252n8
brothel 11, 82–3, 83n42, 85, 88, 175, 180–2, 180n9, 181n11, 192
Busiris 17, 20
Byrrhena 226n31, 227, 227n39, 228, 228n41

Cadmus 200, 202
Caecina Paetus 240n19
Caesarion 136n5, 148
Caieta 210n4
Calidorus 175, 176, 179–82, 186, 188n20, 190, 191
Callicrates of Samos 121, 124
Callimachus 115, 115n1, 116, 122, 124, 125, 126, 127, 128, 129, 130, 130n55, 131
– *Aetia* 116
– *Hecale* 205n24
– *Hymns* 118, 125, 128; to Apollo 127, 129, 132; to Delos 127–8
– *Lock of Berenice* 116, 122, 124
– *Victory of Berenice* 116, 122
Calliope 197
Calypso 183
Camma 12, 235–6, 238, 240, 242–7, 245n43
Camilla 5, 155n1, 162n21, 169–70, 170n44, 171, 199n10
Canopus 120, 124
captive 8, 10, 94, 95, 96, 97, 98, 99, 108, 116, 117, 125, 163

Carthage 95n11, 107, 137, 167, 168, 175n1, 184, 185
Carthaginian(s) 8, 11, 94, 95n9, 95n11, 97, 98, 99, 101, 101n24, 102, 106, 110, 168, 168n37, 175, 175n1, 182, 182n13, 186n18, 199n10
Cassandra 144, 146, 150, 165
Cassius Dio 94, 95, 96n14, 139n13
Cato, the Elder 4, 141n17, 180, 180n8
Catullus 116, 117, 117n10, 158, 169
Cecrops 205
Celtic 237
Ceres 74, 197, 258
Cerinthus 191
Chaldeans 222n19
chastity 70, 73, 80
Chelidon 8, 81, 81n37, 82, 83, 84, 85, 88, 89
Chiomara 246
Chloreus 162n21, 169, 199n10
Cicero 7, 8, 69, 69n6, 70, 71, 72, 73, 74, 75, 76, 77, 78, 79, 79n30, 80, 80n33, 81, 81n37, 82, 83, 83n42, 84, 84n45, 85, 86, 87, 88, 90, 144, 182, 182n25, 190–1n25
–*Actio Secunda* 69
–*Divinatio in Caecilium* 69
–*Pro Caelio* 77, 84n45
–*Verrines* 69, 69n1, 69n2, 70, 75n19, 77, 79n31, 82, 87–8
Cilicia 8, 11, 71, 75, 204, 210
Cilician(s) 131, 208, 209
Circe 183, 219, 229n47
civil war 5n14, 136, 137, 138, 141, 150, 167, 169, 220
Claudian 251, 251n3, 252, 252n5, 253, 253n10, 254n14, 255n20, 257, 258, 260, 261, 261n35
–*Bellum Gildonicum* 256
–*Epistula ad Serenam* 252
–*Epithalamium dictum Honorio Augusto et Mariae* 252
–*Laus Serenae* 252
Clea 244, 244n42, 247
Clelia 248
*Clementia* 149, 166

Cleopatra 9–10, 106–10, 109n42, 109n44, 117–9, 118n14, 120n18, 121–6, 125n31, 127n45, 135–50, 135n1, 135n2, 136n5, 143n19, 144n24, 144n25, 168, 198
–as Erinys 143–4, 144n25, 145, 146, 149
cliché(s) 12, 145, 156, 157, 163, 168, 169, 230
Clodia Metelli 229n47
Clytie 212
Colchis 119, 166, 219, 220, 221n12
comedy 243
–New 11, 79n31, 205, 209, 222n17
–Plautine 182n13, 183n14, 186
–Roman 176n3, 191–2n28
–Terentian 183n14
comparison 1, 8, 55n25, 75, 94, 122, 137n8, 143, 145, 159, 200, 204, 207, 235–41, 239n16, 241n25, 246, 252n5, 256, 260
Constantinople 251, 251n3, 255n20
Corinth 223, 224, 228
Cornelius 71, 72
Cornelius Gallus 189, 190
courage 4, 9, 12, 41, 42, 42n62, 53n16, 54, 58, 64, 66, 96, 107, 110, 122, 136, 235, 236, 245, 247, 248
courageous 58, 61, 62, 65, 235, 236, 248
cowardice 33, 61–3, 66
Crocus 210
Cupid 74, 88, 183, 184, 187, 188
Cyane 210
Cybele 13, 255, 255n19, 255n20
Cynthia 158
Cyparissus 207n29
Cyrus 34–5, 35n41, 36, 39–40, 42, 62, 212n40

Damasithymos 53
Daphneus 241n26
Darius 29, 29n11, 51, 52, 61, 63, 122
de Certeau, Michel 223
Deianira 163–4, 163n24
Deiotaros Philoromaios 247
Deiotaros Philopator 247
Delphi 22
–sack of 237

–oracle at 56, 57, 213
Demaratus 52
democracy 7, 50, 60, 61
Demodokos 211n37
Derceto 203
Dickens, Charles 229
Dido 11, 136n5, 137, 142, 158n9, 167, 168, 175–6, 175n1, 182n13, 183–92, 183n15, 185n16, 186n17, 186n18, 187n19, 188n20, 190n23, 191–2n28, 199n10
–and Anna 184, 188, 189
–and Sychaeus 184, 186–8
Diodorus Siculus 94, 95, 101n24, 182, 238, 239
Diomedes 183
Dionysos/us 23, 33n31; dionysiac 20, 25
Docimus 84, 85, 86
Dolabella 71, 75, 76, 77
domestication 11, 196, 200, 204, 207, 210, 211n37, 213, 214
*domus* and *urbs* 160, 160n16
Don Quixote 227
dress 4, 6–7, 19, 20–1, 23–4, 27, 31, 31n16, 34, 37, 87, 87n28
–female 18, 25, 165n27, 168
–foreign 28, 31, 31n16, 40, 42
–Roman 87n48

Echo 200
Egypt 3, 20, 109, 115, 116, 117, 118, 119, 120, 122, 125, 126, 127, 128, 131, 132, 138, 143, 149, 150, 168, 197
Egyptian(s) 3, 6, 9, 20, 21, 24, 109, 110, 116, 118, 119, 120, 122, 123, 124, 125, 125n31, 128, 143, 148, 195–6n4, 198, 198n8, 200, 207n27, 222n19, 251
elegy 119, 126, 131
–Roman 94, 99, 109, 155, 158, 189, 191–2n28, 205
Empona 240, 243, 245n43, 247
Ennius 144, 144n22, 144n25, 145, 146
epic 9, 126, 128, 138, 143, 146, 155, 158, 168, 175, 176, 184, 186, 187, 189, 190, 195, 200, 251, 254n15, 254n16, 257, 261
–epicized topic 131
Epicurus 191

Epicurean 189–90
ἐπιθυμία 241
Erictho 220, 222, 225
Eridanus/Po (see also "prosopopoeia") 253n13
Eros/ἔρως 12, 155, 156, 161, 162, 170, 240, 241, 241n23, 242, 242n30, 243
Ethiopian 13, 126n36, 142, 259, 260
ethnic, foreignness 220, 220n6
–location 221
ethnicity 1, 6, 7–13, 17, 18, 20, 24, 28, 50, 58, 66, 70, 87, 94, 117, 118, 119, 127, 132, 137, 149, 149n35, 175, 176, 251n1, 253, 260, 261–2
–ethnography 195, 195n4
*ethos* 236, 238, 238n14, 240, 248
Etruscans 4, 5n14, 222n19
Eumenes II of Pergamon 246n51
Euripides 169
–*Alexandros* 144n23
–*Helen* 146n27
Europe 3, 41, 156
Europeans 42, 42n62, 214
Eutropius 251, 255n20
excess (see also "luxury and eros") 10, 31, 33, 36, 40, 41, 70, 155, 161–2, 165, 203, 237
exotic, charm of 10, 155, 156, 162, 171

fear 13, 63, 84, 109, 139, 140, 149, 156, 158, 162, 163, 212, 220, 254
*femineus amor* 169–70
femininity 10, 13, 28, 59, 118, 124, 129, 170, 252n5, 255, 262
*ferox* 109–10, 110n45
ferocity 9, 107, 109–110
fertility (see also "procreation") 253n9, 255
–infertility 255
*fides* 8, 97, 98, 103, 106, 108, 108n40, 182
Floronia 212
*furor*, amorous 94, 99, 101–2

Galatians 236, 236n6, 239, 246n51, 249
Gaul 74, 93n3, 127, 236n6, 237–9, 237n8, 237n9, 237n10, 237n12

## General Index

gender (see also "identity", "stereotypes") 1, 2, 5, 6, 7, 8, 9, 10, 12, 17–8,
  20, 21, 24, 27, 28, 36, 37, 37n46, 38,
  51, 51n7, 55, 58, 59, 65, 66, 69, 69n5,
  70, 77, 77n22, 86, 87, 102n26, 110, 117,
  117n7, 117n11, 118, 119, 120, 127, 132,
  137, 149, 149n35, 150, 155, 155n1, 156,
  162, 163, 163n23, 166, 167, 169, 170,
  175, 200, 214, 220, 220n8, 235n2, 236,
  238, 239, 241, 252, 254, 260, 261, 262
–attributions 253
–bias 53
–equality 248
–gender roles 10, 149, 157, 161, 164–6,
  238, 251
–order 50
genderization 124, 128
geographic 157
geographical 5, 11, 12, 97, 137, 155, 162,
  171, 195–6, 211, 219, 220, 222, 223,
  223n24, 224n25, 230, 231, 246, 251,
  252
geography 1, 41, 55, 195, 195n2, 195n4
Gildo 13, 251, 257, 259, 261
Great King (see also "Xerxes") 7, 31,
  31n19, 50–2, 54–6, 58–9, 63–5
Greece 2, 4, 54, 58, 59, 115, 128, 155n1,
  157, 158, 166, 166n32, 219, 220
Greek(s) 2, 3, 6, 7, 27, 28, 32, 37, 39, 41,
  42, 51, 52, 53, 55, 57, 58, 59, 61, 62, 63,
  64, 65, 66, 72, 73, 155n1, 156, 182, 200,
  203, 207, 237, 238, 239

Halicarnassus 2, 50
–Queen of (see also "Artemisia") 7, 49,
  51, 53, 54, 56, 65
Hannibal 8, 87, 182
Harmonia 202
Harpalyce 210
Hasdrubal 94, 95, 95n11, 97, 99, 109
Hecate 219–20
Hector 161, 183
Hecuba 158
Helen 34, 143, 143n19, 144, 144n25, 145–
  6, 145n26, 146n27, 156, 158, 162
–and Paris 33, 157, 158
–episode in the *Aeneid* 143n20

Helios (see also "Sun") 210
Heracles / Hercules 20, 122, 163, 163n23,
  163n24, 165, 165n27
–and Omphale 10, 119, 164
Herbita 84, 85
Herbitenses 85, 87
Herennius 182
hermaphroditism 200
Hermaphroditus 213–4
Herodotus 7, 49n2, 50, 51, 51n7, 52, 53,
  54, 55, 56, 57, 58, 59, 60, 63, 65, 168
–*Histories* 49, 50n4, 51, 57, 59, 168
Hesiod 57
heterosexuality 242n30
Hilaria, festival 228–9n44
Hispania, personification of 252n8
Homer
–*Odyssey* 183
homosexuality 23
Honorius 253
Horace 9, 106, 107, 107n37, 110, 135n1,
  138, 139, 145, 149, 162
Hortensius 72
Hypata 12, 223–6, 224n28, 226n31,
  226n33, 227n36, 228–9, 228–9n44,
  230

Iarbas 189
identity
–and gender 12, 123, 155, 155n1, 162,
  167, 236, 239
–and nationality 155n1, 162, 167, 168
–and individualism 155n1, 167
–ethnic 6, 28, 88, 144n25, 155, 155n1,
  214, 219, 220, 222n19, 230
–Roman 93, 155n1, 168, 168n38
ideology 135n1
–court 122
–erotic 159
–political 28, 150, 168
Ilia 260
Ilioneus 199n10
Inachus 261n33
incest 10, 124, 139–40, 148, 149
India 195–6n4, 201, 202n16
–Indian 197, 201, 202
–Indians 195–6n4

intelligence 7, 8, 49, 51, 53, 54, 55, 57, 242n30, 244, 245
intertextuality (see also "allusion") 9, 115, 117, 118
Iolcus 221, 222n20
Iphis 199
Isis 120, 198, 198n8, 199, 227n37
Ismenodora 240, 242–3, 247
Ismenus 261n33
Italian(s) 3, 4, 5, 115, 128, 155n1, 169, 170, 199n10, 220n4

Janus 159
Jason 37n46, 166, 221
Jews 3, 222n19
Julian 236
Julius Caesar 109n44, 136n5, 137–9, 144, 144n24, 145–50, 175n1, 197
–*Gallic Commentaries* 141
Juno 185, 186n17, 187, 190n23, 191–2n28
Jupiter 13, 197, 252–3n8, 254, 255, 259, 259n31

Lacedaemonian(s) 28, 31, 40
Laevius 156–7, 157n7, 158, 169
–*Sinerocirca* 162n22
Lampsacenes 72, 73
Lampsacus 8, 70, 71, 72, 73, 74, 79, 80, 83, 89
Laodamia 157, 158
Larissa 224–5, 226n34, 228, 229
Lefebvre, Henri 223
Lemnos 166
Leontis 244, 247
Leuconoe 203n18, 211–2, 211n37, 212n40
Leucothoe 203n18, 211–2, 212n40, 213
*lex Voconia* 77–9, 78n23, 79, 79n27, 88
Livy 4, 8, 9, 93, 93n3, 93n4, 94, 94n7, 95, 95n10, 95n11, 96, 96n13, 97, 98, 98n19, 99, 100, 101, 102, 102n25, 102n26, 103, 103n28, 104, 104n30, 105, 106, 106n36, 107, 108, 109, 110, 170n44, 186n18, 212, 213
Lucan 10, 135, 135n2, 136, 136n5, 137, 137n8, 138, 138n10, 139, 139n13, 140, 141, 142, 143, 143n19, 143n20, 144, 144n25, 145, 146, 147, 148, 149, 149n35, 150, 220, 222, 225, 227, 258n27
–*Bellum Ciuile* 135, 220, 225, 227
Lucian 41
[Lucian]
–*Amores* 241
–*Onos* 223n23, 224n25
Lucius 12, 223–4, 224n25, 226, 226n31, 226n33, 227–31, 227n36, 228n41, 228n42, 228n44
Lucius of Patrai
–*Metamorphoses* 223n23
Lucretia, death of 107n37
Lucretius 176, 189–90
–*DRN* 176, 189
'Ludovisi Gaul', statuary group of 239
luxury (see also "excess") 3, 6, 10, 28, 29, 33, 33n29, 36, 37, 62, 131, 140–2, 141n16, 146, 157, 159, 160, 160n16, 161, 161n18, 168, 197
–and eros 10, 155, 157, 158, 159, 161, 162, 163
Lydia 33n31, 39, 163, 164, 165
Lydian 57, 119, 157n7
Lyncus 197

Macareus 198
magic 12, 219n1, 220, 220n8, 221, 222n19, 225, 226, 226n33, 227n37, 228, 228n42, 229, 229n46, 230, 231, 231n50
magical 99–100n21, 166, 219, 219n1, 220, 221, 222, 222n20, 224, 226, 229, 230
magician 219, 219n3, 222n18, 222n20
male fantasies 229, 231
maleness (see also "manliness", "masculinity", "virility") 19, 20, 252n5
Malleolus 8, 76, 77, 88
manliness (see also "maleness", "masculinity", "virility") 7, 58, 64–5
Marathon, battle of 38
Marc Antony 108, 109, 109n42, 117, 119, 138, 139, 140, 142, 148, 149, 150, 168, 198
marginalization 220

marriage  8, 94, 94n7, 95, 95n11, 100, 101, 102, 106, 109, 139, 166, 188, 204, 206, 214, 240n20, 241, 242n30, 243, 245
Mars  211, 211n37
Martial  161
masculinity (see also "maleness", "manliness", "virility")  7, 20, 42, 163n23, 200, 214, 252 n5, 256, 261, 262
Masinissa  8, 94, 95, 95n11, 96, 96n14, 97, 97n15, 98, 98n19, 99, 100, 101, 101n24, 102, 103, 104, 105, 105n35, 106, 107, 108, 108n39, 108n40, 109
Massalia  237
*matrona*  10, 94, 161, 249n47
Medea  37n46, 119, 156, 158, 158n9, 162, 162n21, 166, 166n32, 197, 219, 219n3, 220, 221, 221n12, 221n13, 222n20
Medic/ Median Wars (see also "Persian")  27, 239
Mediterranean
–peoples  5
–societies  5
–world  3
Memnon  183
Memphis  120
Menander  79n31, 221
–*Phasma*  209
Menander Rhetor  253n10
*meretrix* (see also "prostitutes")  10, 84, 161
Meroe  224, 228
metamorphosis  161, 195, 203, 203–4n20, 207, 207n29, 210, 211, 227, 230
Midas  197
Milan  251
Milo  226, 226n31, 227, 228, 229
Minyeides  11, 196, 200–3, 203n18, 203n19, 203n20, 204, 206, 211n37, 212
*miseratio*  144
Mithridates  247
modesty (see also *pudicitia*)  71, 77, 245
Moor  13, 251, 259, 260
Mousaios  22

Narcissus  200
narrators, male  12, 230

Nasamones  13, 259
Naucleides of Sparta  40
Nausicaa  158n9
Nero  10, 138n10, 138n11, 139, 139n13, 140, 140n14, 140n15, 147, 147n31, 148, 148n32, 149, 150
–as Alcmaeon and Orestes 148; as Niobe 148; as Oedipus 148
Nessus  221
Nicocrates  248n58
Nicolaus of Myra  208
Nicomedes IV Philopater of Bithynia  71
Nike  8, 86, 87, 88
Nile  120, 137–8, 149, 198n8, 203–4n20
Nineveh  206
Ninus  205, 206, 209
Niobe  148, 210
Nonnus  209, 209n35
Numanus Remulus  155n1
Numidian(s)  8, 94, 96, 97, 98, 98n19, 99, 99n20, 100, 101, 102, 103, 106, 108, 182, 186n18, 259

*Octavia*  140
Octavian (see also "Augustus")  115, 116, 117, 122, 127, 128, 138, 145, 224n26, 230
Odysseus (see also "Ulisses")  57, 183, 183n15
Oenotria, personification of  252n8
Olybrius  253, 254, 260, 261
Omphale (see also "Hercules")  10, 119, 163, 164
Opimia  212
Orchamus  212
oriental  2, 158
–clothing  6, 27, 28, 37, 168
–luxury  10, 29, 33, 37, 155, 157, 161, 163, 168
–peoples  10, 161
–queen (see also "Dido", "Cleopatra")  10, 168
orientalising  1, 116n4, 125, 168, 195, 195–6n4, 198, 201, 214
Orientalism  117, 117n11, 195–6n4
Orpheus  6, 17, 22–4, 22n14, 167n34
Ortiagon  246

Other  1–2, 11, 19, 27, 28n5, 42, 156, 168n37, 168n38, 195–6, 195n4, 198, 200, 200n13, 201, 202, 204, 206, 214
–otherness  1, 6, 10, 13, 17, 28, 38, 39, 120, 136, 155, 158n8, 162, 165, 205n24, 213
outsider  219n3, 221
Ovid  11, 158, 159, 161, 162, 163, 166, 169, 195n1, 195n2, 196, 198, 200, 200n13, 202n16, 203, 203n19, 204, 204n21, 206, 207, 208, 209, 209n35, 210, 211, 212, 213, 214, 221, 258, 258n28, 261
–*Ars Amatoria*  159, 211n37
–*Heroides*  158
–*Metamorphoses*  195, 196n5, 198, 200, 203, 204, 208, 221, 227, 258

Pamplile  12, 226–30, 229n47
panegyrics  13, 125, 131, 252, 253, 254n15, 261
Pan  197, 198n7
pantomime  143, 147, 148
Paris (see also "Helen and Paris")  33, 144, 144n24, 146, 155n1, 157, 158, 159, 159n12, 160, 161, 162, 168, 224n28
parallelism  117, 239n16, 240
Parthenopaeus  155n1
Parthenios of Nicaea  244n40
Parthians  126n36, 195–6n4
–Parthian Wars  167
passion, sexual (see also "amorous *furor*")  70, 73, 94, 99, 109, 167, 183, 184, 187, 187n18, 188, 189, 190
Pelias  221
Penelope  162–3, 183
Penthesilea  117n10, 119, 165
Pentheus  200–2
*perfidus hospes*  158
Persian(s)  2, 6, 7, 12, 27, 28, 28n4, 30, 31, 31n15, 31n16, 31n19, 32, 32n22, 33, 33n32, 34, 36, 36n43, 37, 37n46, 38, 38n48, 39, 42, 49, 50, 51, 51n7, 52, 53, 54, 56, 57, 58, 59, 60, 61, 62, 63, 64, 65, 65n59, 66, 122, 156, 156n3, 159n12, 167, 168, 212n40, 222n19, 239, 246, 249
– Persian Wars (see also "Medic")  157

Phaethon  258
Pharsalus  220, 225
–battle of  150
Philip, II  39, 120, 123–4
Philitas  126, 131
Philodamus  71–3, 75, 80, 88, 89
Philodemus  190
Philomela  197, 203, 210
Phoenician(s)  11, 175, 175n1, 176, 181, 182, 184, 186, 187, 190, 191, 191–2n28, 192
Phoenicium  11, 175, 175n1, 176, 176n3, 178–81, 178–9n5, 180n9, 181n11, 182, 182n13, 186, 188–92, 188n20, 191–2n28
Photios  223n23
Photis  228–30, 228n42
Phrygian(s)  159, 159n12, 162, 168, 168n38, 169, 170, 171, 245n43
Phyllis  158n9, 258n29
Pip  229
Pipa  8, 83, 84–5, 87, 88, 89
Plato
–*Phaedrus*  241n23
–*Symposium*  241n23
Plautus  11, 85, 175, 175n1, 176, 179, 180, 180n8, 180n9, 181, 181n12, 182, 182n13, 186, 187, 188, 191, 190–1n25, 192
–*Casina*  85
– *Miles Gloriosus*  209
–*Pseudolus*  11, 175, 175n1, 176, 178n4, 186, 190, 190–1n25
Plutarch  12, 24, 57, 57n35, 62, 62n49, 89n52, 138, 142–3, 229n45, 235, 235n1, 236, 238–49, 240n20, 240n22, 241n23, 242n30, 244n40, 244n42, 245n23, 246n48, 247, 248, 249
–*Erotikos*  12, 236, 240, 241, 241n43, 243, 244, 245, 245n43, 246, 247
–*Isis and Osiris*  244n42
–*Mulierum Virtutes*  12, 235, 236, 244, 245, 246, 246n48, 247, 248, 248n59
–*Parallel Lives*  236, 244
–*Praecepta Conjugalia*  241, 244n42
Polla  161
Pollius Felix  161

Polybius 39, 95n9
Polygnotos 22
Polyphemus 158
Pompey 120, 137, 149
–death of 138
Poppaea Sabina 229n47
Porter, Cole 136
Poseidon 209
Posidippus 115, 121, 122, 124
*potestas* 106
Pothinus 137
Priam 156n3, 183, 185, 199n10
Probinus 253, 254, 260, 261
Probus 115
procreation (see also "fertility") 261
*progymnasmata* (see also "rhetorical topoi") 69, 70
προθυμία 31n19, 60n41, 61–4
Propertius 10, 108, 109, 118, 118n14, 119, 120, 120n18, 121, 122, 123, 124, 125, 126, 126n36, 127, 128, 129, 129n52, 130, 131, 131n57, 143, 157, 158n8, 164, 195–6n4
Proserpina 258, 259
–rapture of 74
*prosopopoeia* 13, 252, 253, 253n13, 260, 261n35
prostitute(s) (see also "meretrix") 8, 81, 81n35, 81n37, 82, 82n41, 83, 84, 85, 86, 87, 89n50, 89n51, 89n52, 120, 182, 191
Protesilaus 156
Protogenes 241, 241n26
Prudentius 199n9
Pseudolus 175, 176, 177, 178, 179, 180, 182
–letter of 176–9, 178–9n5, 180n9, 186, 188, 190
Ptolemy, brother of Cleopatra 137, 138, 138n11, 144
Ptolemy II, Philadelphus 118, 125, 127, 128
Publius Memmius Theocles 244n41
*pudicitia* (see also "modesty") 70, 71, 72, 73
*puella* 10, 126n36, 158, 160, 161, 164, 164n25, 191

Punic 175n1, 182n13, 186n17
–Wars 8, 93, 94, 95, 95n9, 97, 109, 167, 182
*Punica fides* 182
Pyramus 11, 200, 204, 204n21, 205, 205n24, 206–10
Pythia 56, 57
Pythias 226

*querella* 255, 261n35
Quintilian 261n35

Ravenna 251
religion 4, 80, 198, 202, 203
rhetoric 10, 13, 69–74, 75n19, 76, 80, 81, 82, 83, 139, 159, 180, 182, 188, 239n16, 252, 253
–rhetorical topoi 4, 71, 73, 74–5
–of gender and ethnicity (see also "gender", "ethnicity", and "national identity") 8
Rhome 248
Risus 228, 228–9n44
*Roma aeterna* 253, 254n14
Rome 3, 4, 5n16, 8, 9, 10, 11, 13, 71, 75n18, 76, 77, 80, 81, 82, 83, 85, 86, 87, 89, 89n52, 93, 97, 97n16, 99, 100, 101n24, 103, 104, 107, 109, 109n44, 110, 115n1, 117, 118, 119, 120, 121, 122, 125, 125n31, 126, 127, 127n46, 132, 136, 137, 140, 143, 144, 146, 147, 149, 150, 155n1, 157, 159, 161, 167, 168, 168n37, 168n38, 192, 195, 196, 198, 198n8, 199, 200, 200n13, 213, 237, 239n15, 248, 251, 253, 256
–personification of 251n3, 252–6, 253n10, 254, 254n14, 254n15, 254n16, 255, 255n19, 255n20, 255n21, 260, 261, 262
Rubrius 71, 72–4, 83
Roscius 190, 190–1n25
Rufinus 251

Salamis 52, 56
–battle of 7, 49, 50, 51, 54, 55, 57, 59, 60, 63, 64, 65
Salmacis 200, 203, 213–4

Sappho 181
'scene', form of narrative 96, 98, 100
Scipio 8, 94, 95n9, 95n11, 97, 100, 100n23, 101n24, 102–5, 104n30, 104n32, 106, 107, 108, 109, 182n13
Season, personification of 210
semanticisation 223n24
Semiramis 37, 119, 203–6, 209
*semiuir* 10, 161, 162
Sempronia 229n47
Seneca 135n3, 141, 162
Serena 252, 252n7
*seruitium amoris* 163–4
sex 19, 20, 21, 229, 241n30
sexes, relationship between 1, 126, 166–7, 248
sexual 8, 11, 69, 69n6, 70, 71, 73, 74, 80, 81, 84, 85, 87, 88, 89, 94, 98, 99, 101, 103, 103n28, 104, 106, 108, 124, 125, 125n32, 175, 179, 181, 183, 186, 187, 190, 191, 204, 207, 211, 220, 227, 229
sexuality 94, 191, 238
sexualization 69n6, 120, 124
Shakespeare 200n12, 206
–*A Midsummer Night's Dream* 200
–*Merchant of Venice* 200n12
–*Romeo and Juliet* 200n12
Sicilian(s) 8, 69, 69n2, 70, 74, 75, 78, 80, 81, 82, 83, 84, 84n44, 86, 87, 88, 90
Sicily 8, 71, 73, 74, 75, 80, 81, 82, 83, 84n44, 85, 86, 87, 89, 90
Silius Italicus 195–6n4
Sinatos 12, 235, 242
Sinorix 235, 242, 245–7
slave(s) 3, 11, 24, 42, 72–3, 76, 85, 87, 99, 105, 120, 163, 165, 175, 176, 180n9, 181, 181n11, 192, 224n27
–sex 176, 180
Smilax 210
Socrates 224
sorceress 12, 219, 221, 222, 224, 225, 226n33, 228, 230, 231
Solon 31, 41
Sophonisba 8, 9, 94, 94n7, 95, 95n9, 95n11, 96, 96n14, 97, 97n15, 98, 99, 99n21, 100, 101, 101n24, 104, 104n32, 105, 105n35, 106, 107, 107n37, 108, 109, 110
Sparta 36, 39, 40, 65, 66, 158n11, 159, 159n13, 162n20
Spartan(s) 3, 31, 40, 52, 66, 143, 144n25, 157
spoliation, of cities and temples 74, 75
Statius 161, 261
–*Achilleid* 155n1
–*Thebaid* 155n1
Stella 161
stereotype (see also "gender") 1, 8, 11, 12, 29, 58, 69–70, 69n6, 139n13, 156, 170, 182, 186, 186n17, 186n18, 192, 196, 219, 220, 223, 229, 235–8
Stilicho 13, 252, 252n5, 256, 256n23, 262
strategy 65, 140, 150, 220, 235
–mimetic 137
–rhetorical 81, 82, 83
Stratonice 247
Suetonius 139n13, 148n34
Sulpicia 11, 176, 189–92, 190n23, 191n26, 191n27
Sun (see also "Helios") 210, 211, 212
Sygambri 126n36
Syphax 8, 94–7, 94n7, 95n9, 95n10, 95n11, 99–104, 101n24, 106, 107n38, 108, 108n39, 109
Syria 83
Syrian 158, 203

Tacitus 139n13, 140
tactical 49, 51, 53n16, 58, 64
Tamyris 51n7
τάξις 64
Telethusa 198
*temperantia* 8, 94, 103–4, 103n29, 104n30
Terentia 76–7, 79n30, 88, 89
Tereus 196–7
Terra 258, 258n28, 259
Tertia 8, 83, 84, 85, 86, 87, 88, 89
Thamyras 23, 24
theatricality (see also "tragedy") 10, 35, 135n1, 140, 142, 143, 148
Thebes 62, 165, 200–1, 200n13, 203
Thelyphron 225, 228

Themistocles  51, 56, 57, 61, 64–6, 66n62
–and Eurybiades  65–6
–and Mnesipilus  66n62
Theocritus  115
therapy  182, 184, 185, 191
Theseus  166
Thessalian  12, 155n1, 219, 220, 221, 222n18, 222n19, 222n20, 224n28, 225, 229, 230
–women  221, 222, 222n18
Thessaly  12, 219–29, 221n12, 222n18, 222n20, 224n26, 224n28, 225fig.13, 226n33, 226n34, 229, 229n45, 229n47, 230–1
Thisbe  11, 200, 203–4, 204n21, 205, 205n24, 206, 208, 209, 210
Thrace  36, 196, 196n6
Thracian(s)  6, 17, 22, 23–5, 28, 197, 197n6
Thucydides  36, 39, 247
Tiber  120, 248
–personification of  13, 253, 260–1
Tiberinus  261
Tissaphernes  39
topographical  220, 224, 231
tragedy (see also "theatricality")  29, 33, 137, 143–7, 145n26, 165, 166, 167, 168, 222
trauma  183, 183n15, 185
Trebelius Rufus  237n11
Triptolemus  197
Trojan(s)  3, 5, 5n14, 102, 144, 155n1, 157, 158, 159, 160, 167, 168, 168n37, 168n38, 169, 171, 183, 184, 185, 189, 198, 247, 248
–War  157, 185, 187
Troy  138, 143, 144, 159, 160, 183, 184
–fall of  144, 145, 146, 189
Turnus  102, 198

ultimatum  179, 180n9, 181, 188n20, 191
universalism  195, 249
universalising  197, 204
unreliability  99, 101, 106
Ulixes (see also "Odysseus")  162–3, 162n22

vase-painting  6, 17, 22, 23, 24
–Attic  6, 17, 23
–early classical  22
Vedius Pollio  160
Vergil  5, 11, 101, 102, 116, 118, 118n14, 120, 122, 126, 128, 135, 135n1, 137, 143n20, 144n25, 146, 149, 167, 175, 175n1, 176, 183, 183n15, 184, 185, 186, 186n17, 186n18, 187, 188, 189, 190, 190n13, 190–1n25, 191, 192
–*Aeneid*  5, 11, 102n25, 137, 138, 143n20, 145, 155n1, 167, 168, 168n37, 169, 175, 175n2, 183, 186n18, 198, 199
–*Georgics*  116
Verres  7–8, 69–90, 69n6, 78n25, 81n37
–as a Greek tyrant  70–1, 73–4, 80, 83
–as Dis  74
Venus (see also "Aphrodite")  74, 88, 183, 184, 186, 186n17, 187, 191–2n28, 211, 211n37, 252
Vestals  212–3
victory
–military  9, 100, 116, 117, 118, 119, 122, 125, 128, 131, 132, 144, 149, 170, 197, 239, 246n51
–poetic  127
Vidal-Naquet, Pierre  17
violence  8, 13, 23, 89n54, 117, 141, 165, 246, 248, 257, 258, 259, 260, 262
Violentilla  161
virility (see also "maleness", "manliness", and "masculinity")  31, 35n41, 39, 41–2, 59, 130, 201, 256, 261
virtue  3, 4, 8–9, 54, 60n41, 64, 93, 103, 104, 108n40, 110, 160, 161, 220, 235, 242, 242n30, 244, 245, 247, 248
voodoo  229

weaving  11, 197, 200, 203, 203n19, 210, 212
West, vs East  1, 117n11, 118, 118n13, 195, 196, 202n17, 207n17, 212, 251, 252
wife  8, 76, 83, 84, 86, 87, 95n9, 97, 98, 99, 101, 105, 105n35, 106, 108, 108n40, 136, 163, 165, 183, 186n87, 199, 207, 226, 227, 235, 239, 240, 240n19, 241,

243, 243n36, 244, 246, 247, 249, 252, 260
witch  12, 219, 219n2, 220n8, 221, 221n12, 222, 222n19, 223, 224, 225, 226, 227, 227n37, 228, 229, 230, 231
womaniser  161, 162
women
–provincial  70, 71, 83, 84, 86, 87, 88
–and inheritance  75–80, 89, 89n51
–in republican Rome  77, 89n52
–in Roman trials  77
wordplay  147, 147n29, 181, 208n30

xenophobia  87, 220
Xenophon  37
–*Cyropaideia*  62
[Xenophon]
*Constitution of the Athenians*  27
Xerxes (see also "Great King")  7, 29, 32–3, 49, 51–2, 55–61, 63–5, 65n59
–Mardonios and Artabanus  52, 60, 62

# Index Locorum

**Aelian**
*Historical Miscellany*
14.7                40

**Aeschylus**
*Agamemnon*
749                143–4
*Edonoi*
TGF 3, F. 61 (Radt)    33n31
TGF 3, F. 62 (Radt)    33n31
*Persians*
135                32n22
181–5              29
465–71             32
532–47             32n22
541                32n22
658–64             29
834–36             32
845–50             32
1025–6             31n19
1030               33
1060               33

**Anacreon**
158                157n7

**Apollonius Rhodius**
*Argonautica*
3.795              162n21

**Appian**
*Excerpta de uirtutibus et uitiis*
Fr. 7.11           237–8
*Punic Wars*
10                 95n10
10.27              100n23, 101n24
10.28              105n35

**Apuleius**
*Metamorphoses*
1.2.1              226n33
1.5–19             223–4
1.5.4              224
1.7                224
1.17               224
1.20–8             224
2.1.1              226
2.1.2              226–7
2.1.3              227
2.6.1              228n41
2.31.2             228
2.31.3             228n43
3.24               224
3.28               224

**Aristophanes**
*Scholia ad Aristophanum Nubes*
749                221n13
794                221n9

**Aristotle**
*Politics*
1.1260a.13–4       50

**Athenaeus**
12.550c–f          40

**Aulus Gellius**
*Noctes Atticae*
13.15.11–4         180n8

**Byron, George Gordon, 6ᵗʰ Baron Byron**
*The Isles of Greece*
19–23              49

**Callimachus**
*Aetia*
Fr. 1 Pf, 27–8     125
Fr. 110 Pf, 57–8   124n28
*Hymns*
2.35–8             130
2.36–8             129
2.100–2            130

**Catullus**
64.137–8           166
66.39–40           117

https://doi.org/10.1515/9783110719949-017

# 280 — Index Locorum

| | | | |
|---|---|---|---|
| 66.51–2 | 117 | 2.3.34.78 | 84–5 |
| 66.57–8 | 124 | 2.3.34.79 | 85, 85–6 |
| | | 2.3.35.82 | 86 |
| **Cicero** | | 2.3.36.83 | 86 |
| *Pro Caelio* | | 2.3.68.159–60 | 80 |
| 46 | 190n25 | 2.4.48.107 | 74 |
| *Verrines* | | 2.4.50.111 | 74–5 |
| 1.4.12 | 75 | 2.4.52.116 | 74 |
| 1.5.14 | 70 | 2.4.55.123 | 82 |
| 2.1.3.9 | 70, 74 | 2.4.71 | 81n37 |
| 2.1.12.33 | 70 | 2.5.10.27 | 83 |
| 2.1.24.62 | 70–1 | 2.5.11.28 | 83 |
| 2.1.24.63 | 71–2 | 2.5.12.29–30 | 86 |
| 2.1.25.64 | 71 | 2.5.12.30 | 86–7 |
| 2.1.26.65 | 72 | 2.5.13.31 | 87 |
| 2.1.26.66 | 72 | 2.5.13.34 | 83 |
| 2.1.26.67 | 72 | 2.5.15.38 | 82–3 |
| 2.1.27.68 | 73 | 2.5.16.40 | 87 |
| 2.1.31.78 | 73 | | |
| 2.1.32.81 | 72 | **Claudian** | |
| 2.1.32.82 | 73 | *Bellum Gildonicum* | |
| 2.1.34.86 | 70 | 17–8 | 255 |
| 2.1.36.90 | 76 | 17–27 | 254 |
| 2.1.36.91 | 76 | 134–9 | 256 |
| 2.1.36.92 | 76 | 135 | 257 |
| 2.1.37.93 | 76 | 136 | 257 |
| 2.1.37.94 | 76–7 | 144–53 | 257 |
| 2.1.39.101 | 81 | 145 | 257 |
| 2.1.40.104 | 81–2 | 149–50 | 259 |
| 2.1.41.104 | 77 | 188–93 | 259 |
| 2.1.41.105 | 78 | 207 | 260 |
| 2.1.41.106 | 78, 82 | 208–12 | 255 |
| 2.1.42.107 | 78 | 209 | 255 |
| 2.1.42.109 | 78 | 210–1 | 256 |
| 2.1.43.110 | 78 | *De Bello Gothico* | |
| 2.1.43.111 | 79 | 459–60 | 256 |
| 2.1.44.112 | 79 | *De Consulatu Stilichonis* | |
| 2.1.44.113 | 79 | 3.124 | 256 |
| 2.1.46.118 | 75 | *De Raptu Proserpinae* | |
| 2.1.50.137 | 88 | 1 | 257n26 |
| 2.1.52.137 | 78n25 | *Olybr. Probin* | |
| 2.2.9.24 | 82 | 217–21 | 260–1 |
| 2.2.47.116 | 81n37, 88 | 224 | 261 |
| 2.3.3.6 | 80 | | |
| 2.3.12.30 | 82 | | |
| 2.3.33.76–7 | 83 | | |
| 2.3.33.77 | 84 | | |

## Ctesias
*Persica*
FGrHist 688 F1bn 184–9    37
FGrHist 688 F8d(3)–(6)    35n41

## Diodorus Siculus
| | |
|---|---|
| 2.6.6 | 37 |
| 5.32.2 | 238 |
| 11.44.5 | 36n43 |
| 27.7 | 95n10, 105n35 |
| 27.10 | 99–100n21, 101n24 |

## Euripides
*Bacchae*
| | |
|---|---|
| 4 | 33n31 |
| 53–4 | 33n31 |
| 235–6 | 33n31 |
| 353 | 33n31 |

*Cyclops*
| | |
|---|---|
| 182–6 | 34n33, 159n12 |

*Iphigenia at Aulis*
| | |
|---|---|
| 73–4 | 34n33 |

*Medea*
| | |
|---|---|
| 263–6 | 166 |
| 410–31 | 167 |
| 439–41 | 166 |
| 534–44 | 167n34 |

*Trojan Women*
| | |
|---|---|
| 987–97 | 158n11 |
| 991–3 | 34 |

## Heracleides of Pontus
*apud Athenaeus* 12.512c    38

## Herodotus
| | |
|---|---|
| 1.4 | 156n3 |
| 1.53 | 57 |
| 1.135 | 31 |
| 1.198 | 207n27 |
| 4.98.3 | 63 |
| 5.78 | 59, 60–1, 64 |
| 6.58 | 31 |
| 7.61.1 | 30–1 |
| 7.62.1 | 30–1 |
| 7.99 | 54–5 |
| 8.62 | 66 |
| 8.68 | 52, 63, 65 |
| 8.68–9 | 52 |
| 8.84 | 61 |
| 8.86 | 31n19 |
| 8.86.1 | 63–4 |
| 8.87 | 53, 65 |
| 8.87–8 | 49 |
| 8.88 | 54 |
| 8.144 | 27 |
| 9.60 | 61 |
| 9.67 | 62 |
| 9.122 | 42 |

## Hesiod
*Theogony*
| | |
|---|---|
| 32–8 | 57 |

## Hippocrates
*Airs, Waters, Places*
| | |
|---|---|
| 12.1–17 | 41 |
| 12.2 | 42 |
| 16.1 | 42n62 |

*Diseases of Women*
| | |
|---|---|
| 1.13 | 39n54 |

## Homer
*Iliad*
| | |
|---|---|
| 3.39 | 161 |

## Horace
*Carmina*
| | |
|---|---|
| 1.11 | 212n40 |
| 1.15.13–4 | 161–2 |
| 1.15.19–20 | 162 |
| 1.27.21–2 | 221n9 |
| 1.37.25 | 135, 138 |
| 1.37.31 | 145 |
| 3.3.18–21 | 162n20 |
| 3.3.25–6 | 162n20 |

*Epistles*
| | |
|---|---|
| 2.1.156 | 117n10 |

*Odes*
| | |
|---|---|
| 1.37.25–32 | 106–7 |

## Isocrates
*To Philip*
| | |
|---|---|
| 5.90 | 39–40 |

**Julian**
*Epistles*
8            237
9            237
*Misopogon*
7            236

**Laevius**
*Protesilaudamia*
Fr. 18 Courtney [= 18 Morel, Traglia, Büchner = 21 Blänsdorf]    156–7

**Livy**
22.57           212–3
25.36.16        104n30
29.23.4         99
29.23.6         99
29.23.7         99
30.7.8          99
30.12.11        94, 96
30.12.12        96
30.12.13        96–7
30.12.15        97
30.12.16        97
30.12.17        98
30.12.18        98
30.12.19        100
30.13.1         100
30.13.2         100
30.13.8         100
30.13.9–10      100
30.13.12        101
30.13.14        101
30.14.1         101
30.14.3         102
30.14.4         103
30.14.5         103, 104n30
30.14.6–8       103
30.14.10        104
30.14.11        104
30.15.1         104–5
30.15.3         105
30.15.4         105
30.15.5         105
30.15.6         105–6
30.15.7         106
30.15.8         106
30.15.12        107
30.15.14        108
38.56.11        104n30
38.58.6         104n30

**Lucan**
4.678–9         260n32
10.19           138
10.21           146
10.53–4         138
10.58           144
10.59           143
10.60           150
10.61           143, 145
10.63           144
10.66           145
10.68           136
10.82–3         144
10.91–2         149
10.92–3         147
10.105          145
10.107          141
10.110          141
10.114–9        142
10.127          141
10.128          260n32
10.130–1        141
10.137          142
10.142          142
10.301–2        138

**Lucian**
*Anacharsis*
25              41
*Dialogues of the Gods*
22(18).1        33n31

**[Lucian]**
*Asinus*
1               223n23
4               226n33

**Lucretius**
1.926–7         125n33
4.1193          190

**Manilius**

| | |
|---|---|
| 50 | 125n33 |

**Martial**
*Liber de Spectaculis*

| | |
|---|---|
| 2.4 | 160n16 |

**Nonnus**
*Dionysiaca*

| | |
|---|---|
| 6.347–55 | 209 |
| 12.84–9 | 210 |

**Ovid**
*Amores*

| | |
|---|---|
| 1.8.103–4 | 191n28 |

*Ars Amatoria*

| | |
|---|---|
| 2.8 | 162n21 |
| 3.107–8 | 160 |
| 3.437–8 | 161 |

*Fasti*

| | |
|---|---|
| 1.233–6 | 159 |
| 6.639–48 | 160n16 |
| 6.641 | 160 |

*Heroides*

| | |
|---|---|
| 1.75–6 | 162–3 |
| 1.77–8 | 163 |
| 2.116–20 | 258n29 |
| 9.47–54 | 163 |
| 9.55–63 | 164–5 |
| 9.65–6 | 164–5 |
| 9.69–72 | 164–5 |
| 9.100–4 | 164–5 |
| 9.105–6 | 165 |
| 9.115–8 | 164–5 |
| 12.111 | 162n21 |
| 16.33–4 | 159n13 |
| 16.177–96 | 159n13 |
| 16.179–80 | 159 |
| 16.188 | 159 |
| 16.195–6 | 160 |
| 17.191–2 | 158n9 |

*Medicamina*

| | |
|---|---|
| 23–4 | 160 |

*Metamorphoses*

| | |
|---|---|
| 1.583 | 199n11 |
| 2.285–7 | 258 |
| 3.531–7 | 201 |
| 4.13–6 | 201 |
| 4.20–1 | 201–2 |
| 4.31–6 | 202 |
| 4.55–8 | 204–5 |
| 4.65–70 | 205–6 |
| 4.73–5 | 206 |
| 4.85 | 206 |
| 4.99–101 | 206 |
| 4.121–4 | 207 |
| 4.125 | 207 |
| 4.125–7 | 208 |
| 4.164–5 | 208 |
| 4.165 | 207 |
| 4.189 | 211 |
| 4.208–11 | 212n40 |
| 4.209–13 | 211 |
| 4.218–21 | 212 |
| 4.605–6 | 202 |
| 5.468–73 | 258 |
| 5.657 | 197 |
| 6.423 | 197 |
| 6.458–60 | 196 |
| 6.576 | 197 |
| 7.39 | 162n21 |
| 7.48–61 | 166n34 |
| 9.686–94 | 198 |
| 12.612–3 | 155n1 |
| 15.829–31 | 197 |

**Philochorus of Athens**

| | |
|---|---|
| FGrH 328 F7 | 33n31 |

**Plautus**
*Amphitruo*

| | |
|---|---|
| 1043–4 | 221n9 |

*Pseudolus*

| | |
|---|---|
| 3–78 | 177–9 |
| 13 | 179 |
| 21 | 179 |
| 38–9 | 181 |
| 44 | 186 |
| 64 | 180 |
| 65 | 180 |
| 68 | 180 |
| 70 | 180 |
| 71–3 | 179 |
| 73 | 188n20 |

| | | | |
|---|---|---|---|
| 74 | 179 | **Posidippus** | |
| 225–9 | 181 | 36 AB | 122–3 |
| | | 39 AB | 121–2 |
| **Pliny the Elder** | | | |
| *Naturalis Historia* | | **Propertius** | |
| 30.7 | 222n17 | 1.2.1–6 | 157–8 |
| | | 2.10.8 | 126, 126n36 |
| **Pliny the Younger** | | 2.20.18 | 98 |
| *Epistles* | | 2.20.39 | 143 |
| 3.16.6 | 240n19 | 2.34.61–2 | 126n40 |
| | | 3.1.1–2 | 126, 126n37 |
| **Plutarch** | | 3.3.13–14 | 128 |
| *Amatorius* | | 3.11.16 | 117n10 |
| 750D | 241 | 3.11.17–20 | 164n25 |
| 750E | 241 | 3.11.29–50 | 119–20 |
| 755E | 242 | 3.11.30 | 120, 120n18, 125n32 |
| 768B | 243 | 3.11. 30–2 | 121 |
| 768C | 245–6n44 | 3.11.31 | 109 |
| 768D | 245 | 3.11.39 | 120, 124 |
| 769F | 242 | 3.11.40 | 124n27 |
| 770C | 243 | 3.11.49 | 120n18, 121 |
| 771E | 242–3 | 3.11.49–50 | 125n31 |
| *Life of Artaxerxes* | | 3.11.51 | 125n31 |
| 24.11 | 62 | 3.11.55 | 125n31 |
| *Life of Sulla* | | 3.11.67–9 | 109 |
| 2.4 | 89n52 | 3.11.71–2 | 121 |
| *The Malice of Herodotus* | | 4.6.3–4 | 126 |
| 38.869–70 | 57 | 4.6.3–6; 9–10 | 131 |
| *Marcellus* | | 4.6.21–4 | 126–7 |
| 3.3.7 | 237n10 | 4.6.22 | 123 |
| *Mulierum Virtutes* | | 4.6.27–9 | 127–8 |
| 242E | 247 | 4.6.31–6 | 129–30 |
| 242F | 244, 247 | 4.6.57 | 127 |
| 243C | 248 | 4.6.69 | 126n36 |
| 250F | 248 | 4.6.71 | 131n57 |
| 252D | 248 | 4.9.47–50 | 164n25 |
| 255E | 247 | | |
| 258A | 245, 245nn45–6 | **Quintilian** | |
| 258B | 245 | *Institutio Oratoria* | |
| 258C | 245, 246n47 | 11.3.162 | 73n13 |
| **Polybius** | | **Sallust** | |
| 14.1.4 | 95n9 | *Bellum Catilinae* | |
| 14.17.6 | 95n9 | 12.3 | 160n16 |
| | | **Sappho** | |
| | | 98.10–1 V. | 157n7 |

## Seneca the Younger
*Epigrams*
69.3             135n3
*Epistles*
90.43            160n16
*Medea*
114–5            162n20
*Naturales Quaestiones*
7.31.2           160–1

## Sosiphanes
TrGF I 92, Fr. 1    222n18

## Strabo
4.1.5            237
11.13.9          37n46
11.13.10         37n46

## Sulpicia
8                191n27
10               191n27
10.15–6          191
11.6–7           190
12               191n27
12.8             190

## Thales
DK 11A1 [ = Laks Most 5 P17b = Diogenes Laertius 1.33]    17

## Thucydides
1.6.4–5          39
1.6.6            38n47
1.130            36

## Valerius Maximus
3.8.6            77n22

## Vergil
*Aeneid*
1.344            186–7
1.450–2          185
1.459–62         185
1.488            185
1.539            199n10
1.712–4          187
1.717            188
1.722            188
1.748–56         183
1.749            187
2.1–13           184
2.504            199n10
2.573            143
4.12–4           184
4.22             188
4.30             188
4.74–9           184–5
4.117–18         187
4.307–8          188
4.314–8          188
4.328–9          136n5
4.369–70         188–9
4.529–32         187
4.535            188n20
6.450            187
6.456            187
6.474            187
7.10–24          220n4
7.321            168
7.345            102
7.377            102
7.392            102
7.805–7          170
8.685–8          199
8.696            147n29
8.696–700        199
8.697            135
11.777           199n10
11.655–8         5
11.772           171
11.772–7         171
11.778–82        169
*Georgics*
2.490            189
3.19–20          115n2, 128

## Xenophon
*Agesilaus*
1.28             39
*Anabasis*
1.8.28–9         31
*Cynogetica*
4.1              238n13

*Cyropedia*
| | |
|---|---|
| 1.6.13 | 62 |
| 8.1.36–8 | 35 |
| 8.1.40–3 | 34 |
| 8.3.5 | 35 |
| 8.3.13 | 35 |
| 8.3.13–4 | 35 |
| 8.8.8–27 | 36–7 |

**[Xenophon]**
*Constitution of the Athenians*
| | |
|---|---|
| 2.8 | 27 |

**Zonaras**
| | |
|---|---|
| 9.11 | 95n11 |
| 9.13 | 95n11, 99–100n21, 100n23, 105n35 |

www.ingramcontent.com/pod-product-compliance
Lightning Source LLC
Chambersburg PA
CBHW070936180426
43192CB00039B/2224